SIMPLY DELICIOUS

CLB 3070

Printed and bound in Singapore by Tien Wah Press

ISBN 0 86283 915 7

Recipes Compiled by Denise Jarrett-Macauley, Maureen McCall, Judith Ferguson, Beverley Piper, Carolyn Garner, Lalita Ahmed and Helen Walsh
Photography by Peter Barry
Designed by Philip Clucas

SIMPLY DELICIOUS

The Complete Guide to Successful Entertaining

COLOUR LIBRARY BOOKS

CONTENTS

Section 1

Soups and Starters

Section 2

FISH AND SEAFOOD

Section 3

HOME FARE

Section 4

SALADS AND VEGETABLES

Section 5

MEALS WITH FLAIR

Section 6

Cakes and Desserts

Section 1

SOUPS AND STARTERS

Hot and Sour Seafood Soup

PREPARATION TIME: 20 minutes
COOKING TIME: 20 minutes
SERVES: 4 people

3 dried Chinese mushrooms, soaked in hot water for 20 minutes
1 cake fresh bean curd, diced
115g (4oz) prawns or shrimps, shelled and de-veined
600ml (1 pint) fish stock
60g (2oz) white fish fillet
15ml (1 tbsp) oyster sauce
15ml (1 tbsp) light soy sauce
15ml (1 tbsp) lemon juice
½ tsp lemon rind, cut into slivers
15ml (1 tbsp) vegetable oil
1 red chilli, seeds removed, and finely sliced
1 green chilli, seeds removed, and finely sliced
2 spring onions, sliced
Salt
Pepper
1 tsp sesame oil

Garnish
Fresh coriander, if desired

Soak mushrooms in hot water and set aside. Heat vegetable oil, and add prawns, chillies, lemon rind and spring onions. Add stock, oyster sauce and light soy sauce and bring to the boil. Reduce heat and simmer for 5 minutes. Season to taste. Remove hard stalks from mushrooms and slice caps finely. Dice white fish fillets and add them with bean curd and Chinese mushrooms to the soup, cooking for a further 5 minutes. Stir in lemon juice and sesame oil. Adjust seasoning, and serve sprinkled with fresh coriander leaves if desired.

Egg and Lemon Soup

PREPARATION TIME: 15 minutes
COOKING TIME: 15 minutes
SERVES: 4 people

750ml (1¼ pints) chicken stock
30g (1oz) small noodles/soup pasta
2 small eggs, separated
1 lemon
Salt
White pepper
Sugar, if desired

Garnish
Slivers of pared lemon rind

Bring stock to the boil and add the noodles. Cook for 10 minutes or until noodles are tender, stirring occasionally. Meanwhile, juice lemon, and beat the egg whites until stiff. Add the yolks and beat until light and creamy. Add lemon juice gradually, beating all the time. Add a cup of the soup to the egg mixture and whisk. Pour back into the soup, whisking continuously. Adjust seasoning to taste. Garnish with pared lemon rind. Serve immediately.

This page: Hot and Sour Seafood Soup.

Facing page: Egg and Lemon Soup (top) and Celery and Apple Soup (bottom).

French Onion Soup

PREPARATION TIME: 15 minutes

COOKING TIME: 1 hour

SERVES: 4 people

450g (1lb) onions, peeled and sliced thinly
60g (2oz) butter or margarine
45g (1½oz) flour
1 litre (2 pints) boiling water
2 beef stock cubes
1 small French loaf
30g (1oz) Parmesan or Gruyère cheese, grated
Salt
Pepper

Melt butter in a thick saucepan. Add onions and cook gently over moderate heat until golden brown – about 15 minutes – being careful not to burn them. Stir occasionally. Meanwhile, dissolve stock cubes in boiling water and put aside to cool. Stir flour into onions and cook for 2 minutes. Add stock gradually, stirring continuously. Simmer for 30 minutes. Add salt and pepper to taste. Pre-heat oven or grill. Slice bread thickly and place in bottom of ovenproof serving dish. Pour over soup. Sprinkle the bread with cheese and place under the grill or in a hot oven until browned. Serve very hot.

Tomato Soup

PREPARATION TIME: 15 minutes

COOKING TIME: 45 minutes

SERVES: 4 people

450g (1lb) ripe tomatoes
1 carrot
1 onion
600ml (1 pint) water
1 chicken stock cube
30g (1oz) butter or margarine
30g (1oz) flour
Pinch of grated nutmeg
1 tsp basil
Salt
Pepper

Garnish
Chopped parsley

Peel and finely dice onion and carrot. Cut tomatoes into quarters and squeeze out pips into a sieve.

This page: Goulash Soup (top) and Curried Chicken Soup (bottom).

Facing page: Tomato Soup (top) and French Onion Soup (bottom).

Strain pips and retain the juice. Melt butter in a pan. Fry the onion and carrot gently until the onion is transparent. Draw off heat and stir in the flour, nutmeg and basil. Add tomatoes, juice and water, return to heat and stir until boiling. Add crumbled chicken stock cube and salt and pepper to taste. Cover and simmer for 30 minutes. Push the soup through a sieve and return to pan. Adjust seasoning and reheat. Garnish with chopped parsley.

Bumper Soup

PREPARATION TIME: 30 minutes
COOKING TIME: 1 hour 45 minutes
SERVES: 4 people

1 litre (2 pints) good beef stock
450g (1lb) spinach, stalks removed, and shredded
2 onions, peeled and diced
2 carrots, scraped and diced
2 potatoes, peeled and diced
3 sticks celery, sliced
1 tbsp chopped parsley
2 tbsps tomato purée
½ cup lentils
Salt
Pepper

Heat stock in pan. When hot, add vegetables, parsley, tomato purée and seasoning. Bring to boil and simmer for 1 hour. Add lentils and simmer for a further 30 minutes stirring occasionally. Adjust seasoning if necessary. Serve hot.

Red Pepper Soup

PREPARATION TIME: 15 minutes
COOKING TIME: 45 minutes
SERVES: 4 people

1 medium onion, peeled and finely chopped
3 tomatoes
3 red peppers
30g (1oz) butter or margarine
1 litre (2 pints) chicken stock
Salt
Pepper

Garnish
Chopped parsley and sliced red pepper

Remove core and seeds from peppers. Slice a pepper for garnish and set aside. Chop remaining peppers and tomatoes into small pieces. Melt butter in a large saucepan and add onion, tomatoes and peppers and fry gently for 5 minutes, stirring continuously. Pour on chicken stock, add salt and pepper and bring to the boil. Simmer for 30 minutes. Push the soup through a sieve to remove skin and any pips. Adjust seasoning. Add a pinch of sugar if desired. Serve hot or cold, sprinkled with parsley and garnished with a slice of red pepper.

Curried Chicken Soup

PREPARATION TIME: 10 minutes
COOKING TIME: 20 minutes
SERVES: 4 people

30g (1oz) butter or margarine
2 tsps curry powder
1 tbsp flour
1 chicken stock cube
1 litre (2 pints) water
½ tsp paprika
2 tbsps tomato chutney
60g (2oz) cooked chicken, chopped
30g (1oz) rice
Yolk of 1 egg
60ml (4 tbsps) single cream
Salt
Pepper

Garnish
Chopped parsley or coriander

Melt butter in pan. Stir in curry powder and flour. Cook gently for 2 minutes. Draw off heat. Gradually stir in stock cube disolved in water. Add paprika and bring to the boil to thicken. Add chutney, chicken, and rice and simmer for 12-15 minutes. Mix egg yolk with cream and gradually add to soup off the heat. Do not re-boil. Season to taste. Serve hot, garnished with chopped parsley or coriander.

Goulash Soup

PREPARATION TIME: 20 minutes
COOKING TIME:
2 hours 45 minutes
SERVES: 4 people

750g (1½ lbs) skirt or chuck steak, cut into 2.5cm (1") cubes
4 medium onions, peeled and chopped roughly or quartered
1 green pepper, cored, seeds removed, and chopped
4 tomatoes, skinned and quartered
4 tbsps tomato purée
600ml (1 pint) good beef stock
1 tbsp paprika
30g (1oz) butter or margarine
15ml (1 tbsp) oil
450g (1lb) potatoes, peeled and cut into bite-size pieces
15g (½oz) flour
Salt
Pepper

Heat oil in pan. When hot, add steak in batches so as not to overcrowd, and sauté over a high heat until well browned all over. Remove and set aside. Add butter, onion and green pepper, and fry until onion is lightly browned. Stir in flour. Remove from heat. Add stock, return to heat and bring to the boil, stirring continuously. Add tomato, tomato purée, paprika and salt and pepper to taste. Reduce heat, return meat, cover and simmer for 2 hours, stirring occasionally and adding more stock or water if necessary. Add potatoes and cook gently for a further 20 minutes, or until potatoes are cooked through.

Celery and Apple Soup

PREPARATION TIME: 15 minutes
COOKING TIME: 45 minutes
SERVES: 4 people

1 onion, peeled and chopped
3 sticks celery, chopped
3 cooking apples, peeled and sliced
30g (1oz) butter or margarine
1 chicken stock cube
1 litre (2 pints) water
1 bay leaf
1 tbsp cornflour
Salt
Pepper

Garnish
Finely sliced celery

Melt butter in pan. Add onion and fry for 5 minutes, then add apple and a third of the celery, and fry a further 5 minutes. Heat water. Add to crumbled stock cube and pour onto onion/apple mixture. Add salt, pepper and bay leaf. Bring to the boil and simmer for ½ hour. Push through a sieve and then return to the pan. Blend cornflour with a little water, and stir into the soup. Bring soup to the boil, and cook for 2-3 minutes, stirring continuously. Cook remaining celery in water until tender. Add to soup. Garnish with finely sliced celery. Serve immediately.

Minestrone

PREPARATION TIME: 30 minutes
COOKING TIME: 1 hour 15 minutes
SERVES: 4 people

1 carrot, cut into strips
1 leek, sliced
1 turnip, cut into strips
3 tomatoes, skinned and diced
1 stick celery, chopped
4 rashers streaky bacon, blanched and diced
¼ small cabbage, sliced
3 cloves garlic, crushed
1 onion, peeled and sliced
30g (1oz) butter or margarine
1 litre (2 pints) good, fat-free chicken stock
60g (2oz) short-cut or elbow macaroni
Salt
Pepper

Red Pepper Soup (right) and Bumper Soup (bottom).

Accompaniment
Freshly grated Parmesan cheese, if desired

Melt butter in pan, and add garlic, onion, leek and celery. Cover and cook over a gentle heat for 15 minutes without coloring. Add carrot and turnip, stock, and salt and pepper to taste. Bring to the boil, cover and simmer for 30 minutes. Add cabbage and simmer a further 5 minutes. Add tomato and macaroni, and simmer gently, uncovered, for 15 minutes. Meanwhile, broil bacon until crisp. Serve on top of soup with a side serving of Parmesan cheese if desired.

Cream of Cauliflower Soup

PREPARATION TIME: 10 minutes

COOKING TIME: 45 minutes

SERVES: 4 people

1 cauliflower
4 tbsps butter or margarine
1½ tbsps flour
2½ cups chicken stock
1 onion, peeled and chopped
2 medium egg yolks
⅔ cup heavy cream
Cheese, grated
Nutmeg
Salt
Pepper

Garnish
Snipped chives

Trim and break cauliflower into flowerets. Cook in gently boiling salted water for 5 minutes. Drain and set aside. Melt butter in pan and stir in the flour. Cook for 1-2 minutes, stirring. Remove from heat and stir in chicken stock. Add onion, and return to heat. Bring to

This page: Cream of Cauliflower Soup (top) and Lettuce Soup (bottom).

Facing page: Minestrone.

boil, stirring continuously, and simmer for 20 minutes. Allow to cool. Add cauliflower and blend. Push through a sieve. Return to pan, and re-heat. Lightly beat together egg yolks, cream and grated cheese. Stir in some soup, and then put all of the mixture back into the pan. Cook gently until thickened, but do not let it boil. Season with salt and pepper and grated nutmeg. Garnish with snipped chives.

Watercress Soup

PREPARATION TIME: 15 minutes
COOKING TIME: 45 minutes
SERVES: 4 people

4 bunches watercress, washed and trimmed
1 leek, cleaned and sliced thinly
225g (8oz) potatoes, peeled and sliced thinly
60g (2oz) butter or margarine
600ml (1 pint) chicken stock
Pinch grated nutmeg
45ml (3 tbsps) cream
Salt
Pepper

Garnish
Watercress

Heat butter and slowly soften leek. Add potatoes, stock and seasoning. Bring to the boil and simmer 15 minutes. Add watercress and simmer a further 10 minutes. Blend soup and push through a sieve. Adjust seasoning and add cream. Re-heat or chill as required. Garnish with watercress.

Carrot and Orange Soup

PREPARATION TIME: 15 minutes
COOKING TIME: 40 minutes
SERVES: 4 people

1 onion, peeled and chopped finely
2 carrots, grated
1 strip lemon rind
1 orange
600ml (1 pint) water
1 chicken stock cube
60g (2oz) butter or margarine
30g (1oz) flour
15ml (1 tbsp) cream, if desired
Sugar, salt and pepper to taste
Pared orange rind, cut into fine shreds

Garnish
Carrot flowers

Melt half the butter in pan. Add onion, carrots and lemon rind. Cover and cook until onion is transparent. Push through a sieve and set aside. Pare and shred rind of orange. Squeeze orange. Blanch orange rind in boiling water. Drain and save. Melt remaining butter in the pan and stir in flour. Remove from heat and add water. Return to heat and bring to the boil, stirring continuously. Add crumbled stock cube, orange juice and vegetables. Simmer for 5 minutes, blend and return to pan. Add salt, pepper and sugar to taste. Add cream and orange rind, and stir. Serve garnished with carrot flowers. To make carrot flowers, slice strips out lengthways to produce flower shape when cut across in rounds.

Pumpkin Soup

PREPARATION TIME: 10 minutes
COOKING TIME: 1 hour
SERVES: 4 people

450g (1lb) pumpkin, peeled, seeds removed and diced
30g (1oz) butter or margarine
1 onion, peeled and chopped
1 litre (2 pints) beef stock
30ml (2 tbsps) cream
Pinch of turmeric
Salt
Pepper

Garnish
Croûtons

Melt butter in pan. Add onion and cook over gentle heat until lightly coloured. Add stock and pumpkin. Add salt and pepper and turmeric and bring to the boil. Reduce heat. Cover and simmer for 30 minutes. Purée and push through a sieve. Return to pan and bring to boil. Remove from heat, stir in cream, and serve garnished with croûtons. Serve immediately.

This page: Watercress Soup (top) and Pumpkin Soup (bottom).

Facing page: Pea and Ham Soup (top) and Carrot and Orange Soup (bottom).

To Make Croûtons
Take one slice of bread and cut into 1cm (¼″) cubes. Fry in hot oil until browned well all over. Remove with a slotted spoon and drain on absorbent paper. Sprinkle with salt. Add to soup at last minute otherwise they will go soggy.

Mussel Soup

PREPARATION TIME: 15 minutes

COOKING TIME: 20 minutes

SERVES: 4 people

2 litres (4 pints) live mussels, scrubbed clean
2 onions, peeled and chopped
2 cloves garlic, crushed
2 tbsps chopped parsley
60g (2oz) butter or margarine
300ml (½ pint) dry white wine
30ml (2 tbsps) lemon juice
Salt
Pepper

Garnish
Chopped parsley

Place mussels, butter, garlic, onions, wine, parsley and a pinch of freshly ground black pepper in a pan, and cover. Place over a high heat and cook for a few minutes. Shake the pan to move the mussels and distribute the heat well. When mussels have all opened, transfer to serving dish and keep warm. Discard any that remain closed. Strain juices and return to pan. Reduce liquid by half over a high heat. Adjust seasoning. Whisk in lemon juice and pour hot soup over mussels. Serve immediately sprinkled with chopped parsley.

Cream of Spinach Soup (left), Vegetable Soup (below) and Mussel Soup (facing page).

Cream of Spinach Soup

PREPARATION TIME: 10 minutes
COOKING TIME: 30 minutes
SERVES: 4 people

325g (11oz) packet frozen chopped spinach
1 onion, peeled and chopped
30g (1oz) butter or margarine
30g (1oz) flour
900ml (1½ pints) milk
150ml (¼ pint) cream
Pinch of ground nutmeg
Salt
Pepper

Garnish
Cream

Allow spinach to thaw. Drain off excess liquid. Heat butter in pan and fry chopped onion until transparent. Stir in flour and gradually add milk, stirring all the time until thickened. Season with salt and pepper and nutmeg. Stir in spinach and cook for 10 minutes. Stir in all but 15ml (1 tbsp) of cream. Re-heat carefully, do not re-boil. Garnish with remaining cream and serve.

Pea and Ham Soup

PREPARATION TIME: 1 hour
COOKING TIME: 1 hour
SERVES: 4 people

115g (4oz) dried split peas
115g (4oz) tinned shoulder or leg ham, diced
30g (1oz) butter or margarine
1 onion, peeled and chopped
600ml (1 pint) chicken stock
2 tbsps chopped mint
1 stick celery, diced
Salt
Pepper

Garnish
Sprig of mint

Cover peas with boiling water, and leave to soak for 30 minutes. Drain and repeat process, and leave for a further 30 minutes. Melt butter in a pan. Add onion and celery and fry gently for 5 minutes or until transparent. Add drained peas, stock, 1 tbsp mint, and salt and pepper, and simmer gently for 45 minutes. Sieve the soup or blend until smooth. Return to pan. Add ham, and remaining mint, and cook for a further 5 minutes. Adjust seasoning. Serve immediately, garnished with a sprig of mint if desired.

Lobster Bisque

PREPARATION TIME: 20 minutes
COOKING TIME: 1 hour
SERVES: 4 people

1 cooked lobster
1 onion, peeled and diced
1 stick celery, cut into 2.5cm (1") slices
1 carrot, diced
1 litre (2 pints) fish stock or water
1 bay leaf
6 peppercorns
Parsley stalks
Salt
Pepper
30g (1oz) butter or margarine
30g (1oz) flour
5ml (1 tsp) lemon juice
30ml (2 tbsps) cream
45ml (3 tbsps) white wine
2 tsps tomato purée

Garnish
Soured cream and chopped parsley

Remove meat from body, tail and claws of lobster. Put lobster shell, stock or water, onion, carrot, celery, herbs and seasoning into a pan. Bring to boil and simmer for 45 minutes. Allow to cool. Strain and reserve stock. Meanwhile, cut lobster meat into bite-size pieces. Melt butter in pan, stir in flour, and cook for 1 minute. Remove from heat and stir in reserved stock gradually. Return to heat. Bring to the boil, and simmer for 5 minutes, stirring continuously. Remove from heat and add lemon juice, tomato purée, wine and cream, and whisk in well. Adjust seasoning. Add lobster meat and garnish with soured cream and chopped parsley if desired. Serve immediately.

Lettuce Soup

PREPARATION TIME: 10 minutes
COOKING TIME: 30 minutes
SERVES: 4 people

175g (6oz) lettuce leaves
1 small onion, peeled and diced
30g (1oz) butter or margarine
300ml (½ pint) chicken stock
150ml (¼ pint) milk
60ml (4 tbsps) single cream
½ tsp grated nutmeg
Salt
Pepper

Blanch lettuce leaves in boiling water for 30 seconds. Rinse under cold water and drain well. Chop roughly. Fry the onion in the butter for 5 minutes, or until it is soft. Add lettuce and stock, and bring to the boil. Simmer gently for 10 minutes. Season with nutmeg and salt and pepper. Blend the soup. Add milk and re-heat. Stir in cream and re-heat gently, being careful not to boil the soup. Serve immediately.

Sweetcorn and Bacon Soup

PREPARATION TIME: 10 minutes
COOKING TIME: 20 minutes
SERVES: 4 people

1 onion, peeled and chopped
30g (1oz) butter or margarine
2 tbsps flour
150ml (¼ pint) water
300ml (½ pint) milk
300g (10oz) can sweetcorn
4 rashers bacon, rind removed
Salt
Pepper

Garnish
Chopped chives

Heat butter in pan. Add onion, and fry until transparent. Stir in flour, remove from heat and add water and milk gradually. Return to heat, stirring until thickened. Add undrained sweetcorn to pan, and season to taste. Bring to the boil, and simmer for 10 minutes. Meanwhile, pre-heat grill. Cut rashers in half lengthways and form into rolls. Grill and serve in soup. Garnish with chopped chives.

Vegetable Soup

PREPARATION TIME: 20 minutes
COOKING TIME: 50 minutes
SERVES: 4 people

2 medium onions, peeled and finely chopped
1 carrot, finely diced
½ small turnip, finely diced
900ml (1½ pints) beef stock
30g (1oz) butter or margarine
1 leek, cut into small rings
1 tbsp tomato purée
2 tbsps chopped parsley
Salt
Pepper

Garnish
Chopped parsley

Melt butter in a saucepan and add onions. Cook gently over a low heat for 5 minutes or until transparent. Add carrot and turnip, stock, seasoning and parsley. Bring to the boil and simmer gently for 15 minutes. Add leek, and tomato purée and simmer for a further 20 minutes. Garnish with chopped parsley. Serve hot.

Mushroom Soup

PREPARATION TIME: 10 minutes
COOKING TIME: 45 minutes
SERVES: 4 people

225g (8oz) flat or cup mushrooms
1 small onion
45g (1½oz) butter or margarine
45g (1½oz) flour
600ml (1 pint) water
1 chicken stock cube
15ml (1 tbsp) lemon juice
200ml (⅓ pint) milk
1 tbsp chopped parsley
1 tbsp chopped chives
Salt
Pepper

Garnish
Chopped parsley

Melt butter in a pan. Peel and chop onion and fry gently until transparent. Wash, trim and finely slice mushrooms. Add to pan and cook for 5 minutes, stirring often. Stir in flour and cook for 1 minute. Draw off heat and gradually add water. Return to heat and bring to boil, stirring continuously. Add crumbled chicken stock cube and stir until soup has thickened. Add lemon juice and milk. Cover and simmer for 15 minutes. Add chives and parsley and season with salt and pepper. Garnish with chopped parsley.

Facing page: Mushroom Soup (top) and Sweetcorn and Bacon Soup (bottom).

Fish Soup

PREPARATION TIME: 15 minutes

COOKING TIME: 40 minutes

SERVES: 4 people

1kg (2lbs) of sea-bass, whiting, monkfish and/or John Dory, skin and bones removed, and cut into bite-size pieces
2 onions, peeled and chopped
3 cloves garlic, crushed
2 tomatoes, skinned and chopped
15ml (1 tbsp) oil
Sprig of fresh thyme
1 bay leaf
2 pieces thinly pared orange rind
150ml (¼ pint) dry white wine
Salt
Pepper

Garnish
Chopped parsley

Make a court bouillon with the heads and trimmings of fish, one-third of the onion and 1 litre (2 pints) of water. Simmer 15 minutes, then strain. Put oil in a heavy pan and heat gently. Add garlic and remaining onion. Cover and fry gently for 5 minutes without colouring. Add fish, tomatoes, herbs, orange rind, wine, salt and pepper and court bouillon. Bring to boil and simmer for 10 minutes. Remove bay leaf, thyme and orange rind. Serve hot, sprinkled with parsley.

This page: Fish Soup (top) and Lobster Bisque (bottom).

Facing page: Avocado Cream Soup (top) and Tomato and Cucumber Soup (bottom).

Cold Soups

Tomato and Cucumber Soup

PREPARATION TIME:
20 minutes, plus chilling time

SERVES: 4 people

6 tomatoes, skinned
2 large cucumbers, peeled and cut into pieces, reserving 5cm (2") at end for garnish
45ml (3 tbsps) lemon juice
150ml (¼ pint) soured cream
1 onion, peeled and grated
1 tsp tomato purée
Salt
Pepper

Garnish
Cucumber slices

Chop tomatoes. Remove pips. Strain juice, and discard pips. Put tomato flesh and juice, cucumber, onion, tomato purée and lemon juice into a blender. Blend at high speed for a few minutes until smooth. Stir in soured cream, and salt and pepper to taste. Serve chilled, garnished with cucumber slices.

Prawn and Cucumber Soup

PREPARATION TIME:
20 minutes, plus chilling time

SERVES: 4 people

450g (1lb) prawns, cooked, shelled and de-veined
200g (7oz) cream cheese
1 small cucumber
½ tsp dry mustard
Salt
White pepper
150ml (¼ pint) single cream
300ml (½ pint) milk

Garnish
Finely sliced cucumber
Dill

Finely chop prawns. Peel and slice cucumber. Place prawns, cucumber, mustard, white pepper and a pinch of salt in a bowl. Beat cream cheese until soft and creamy, and gradually add cream and milk. Add cucumber and prawn mixture, and blend thoroughly. Cover and chill. If

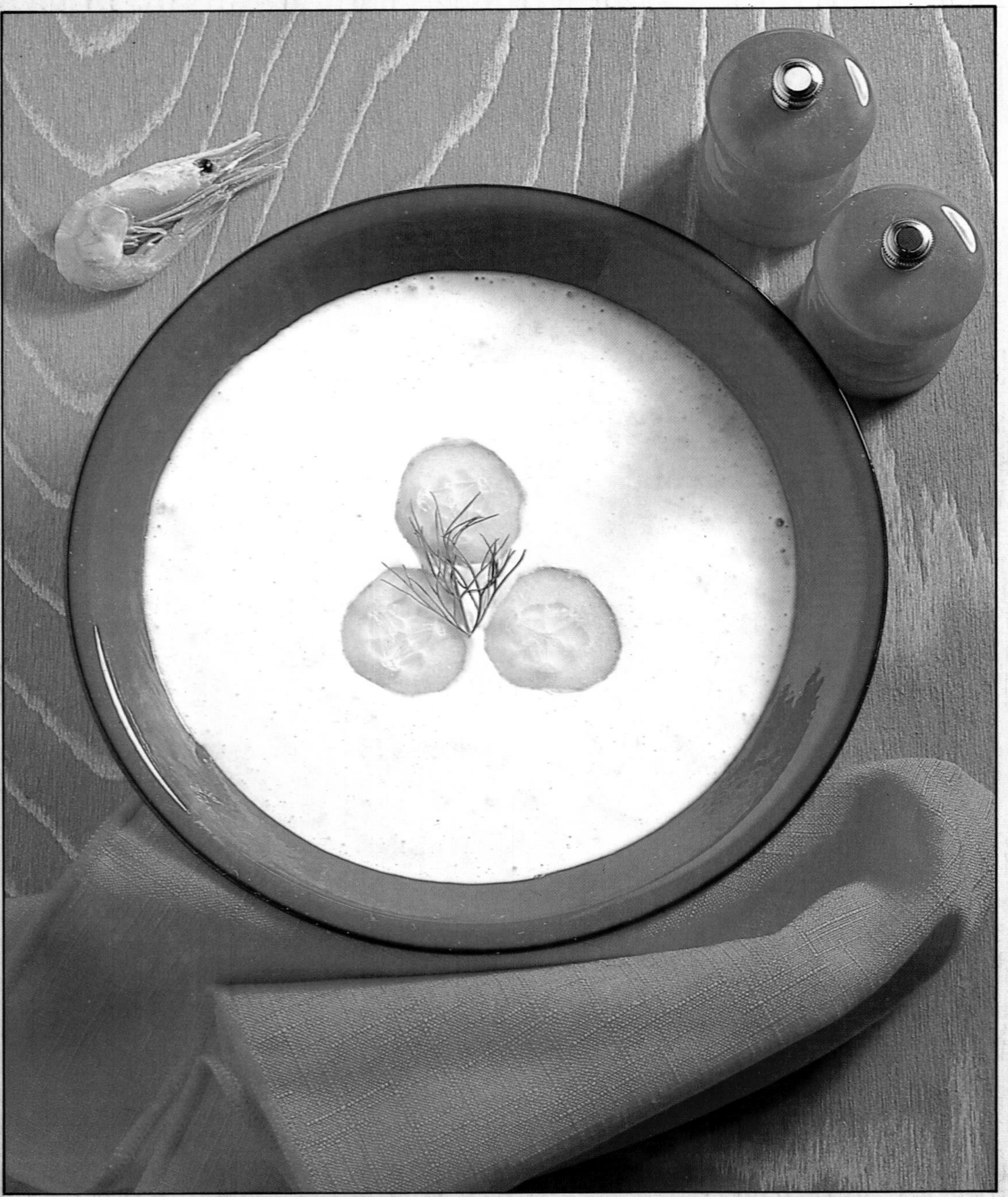

necessary, thin soup further with milk. Garnish with sliced cucumber and dill.

Blackberry and Apple Soup

PREPARATION TIME:
5 minutes, plus chilling time

COOKING TIME: 30 minutes

SERVES: 4 people

450g (1lb) blackberries, fresh, or frozen and thawed
2 apples, skinned, cored and sliced
60g (2oz) granulated sugar
600ml (1 pint) water
Crushed ice

Place apples and water in a pan and bring to the boil. Simmer covered for 15 minutes until apples are softened. Add sugar and blackberries, and simmer a further 15 minutes. Purée and push through a sieve. Chill. Serve with crushed ice.

Rhubarb Soup

PREPARATION TIME:
15 minutes, plus chilling time

COOKING TIME: 20 minutes

SERVES: 4 people

450g (1lb) rhubarb, trimmed and cut into 2.5cm (1") lengths
2 tbsps redcurrant jelly
60g (2oz) granulated sugar
300ml (½ pint) orange juice
300ml (½ pint) water

Garnish
Slivered, pared rind of orange

Place rhubarb, redcurrant jelly, sugar and water in pan. Cover and heat gently for 10 minutes. Add orange juice and bring to the boil. Simmer uncovered for 5 minutes. Remove from heat, and allow to cool. Purée or push through a sieve, and chill. Serve garnished with slivered orange rind and crushed ice if desired.

Avocado Cream Soup

PREPARATION TIME:
10 minutes, plus chilling time

SERVES: 4 people

300ml (½ pint) good, fat-free chicken stock
2 ripe avocados
15ml (1 tbsp) lemon juice
150ml (¼ pint) milk
150ml (¼ pint) single cream
Salt and white pepper

Garnish
Snipped chives, if desired

Peel avocados, remove seeds, chop and put in blender with cream, lemon juice and milk, and blend until smooth. Put avocado mixture and chicken stock in a bowl, and stir until combined. Push through a sieve. Season with salt and white pepper. Chill in refrigerator. Garnish with chives, if desired.

Raspberry Soup

PREPARATION TIME:
5 minutes, plus chilling time

COOKING TIME: 20 minutes

SERVES: 4 people

225g (8oz) raspberries, fresh, or frozen and thawed
30ml (2 tbsps) lemon juice
45ml (3 tbsps) sweet sherry
30g (1oz) granulated sugar
300ml (½ pint) single cream
300ml (½ pint) water
Crushed ice

Put sugar, raspberries, lemon juice, sherry and water in a pan, and heat gently for 10 minutes. Bring to the boil and simmer for 5 minutes. Remove from heat and push through a sieve, and allow to cool. Stir in cream. Chill. Serve with crushed ice.

Blackberry and Apple Soup (left), Rhubarb Soup (centre), Raspberry Soup (bottom) and Prawn and Cucumber Soup (facing page).

Vichyssoise (Leek and Potato Soup)

PREPARATION TIME:
15 minutes, plus chilling time

COOKING TIME: 30 minutes

SERVES: 4 people

3 large leeks
2 medium potatoes, peeled and sliced thinly
1 small onion, peeled and sliced
30g (1oz) butter or margarine
600ml (1 pint) boiling water
½ chicken stock cube
150ml (¼ pint) single cream
Salt
White pepper

Garnish
Parsley or chives

Wash and trim leeks, discarding roots and any green part. Slice thinly. Melt butter in pan and add leek and onion. Cover, and allow to sweat gently over low heat for about 10 minutes. Dissolve ½ chicken stock cube in boiling water. Add potatoes to leek and pour over the stock. Season to taste. Cover and cook for a further 15 minutes, or until potatoes are soft. Push through a fine sieve. Cool. Stir in cream. Adjust seasoning. Chill well for at least 2 hours. Serve garnished with parsley or snipped chives.

Gazpacho

PREPARATION TIME:
20 minutes, plus chilling time

SERVES: 4 people

450g (1lb) ripe tomatoes, skinned and roughly chopped
1 onion, peeled and diced
1 green pepper, cored, seeds removed, and diced
Half a cucumber
2 tbsps stale white breadcrumbs
2 cloves garlic, crushed
30ml (2 tbsps) red wine vinegar
1 large can tomato juice
Salt
Pepper

Accompaniments
Diced cucumber, onion, tomato and green pepper

Soak breadcrumbs in vinegar. Reserve tomato flesh, and half the onion and half the green pepper for garnish. Blend remaining onion and remaining green pepper with tomato juice, breadcrumbs, vinegar, and garlic, and season to taste. Push through a sieve. Chill well. Meanwhile, skin and chop cucumber. Serve with crushed ice and small bowls of cucumber, onion, tomato and green pepper.

Beetroot Soup

PREPARATION TIME:
10 minutes, plus chilling time

COOKING TIME: 1 hour 15 minutes

SERVES: 4 people

450g (1lb) raw beetroot
1 shallot, peeled and quartered
2 tbsps sugar
15ml (1 tbsp) lemon juice
Bouquet garni
1 litre (2 pints) water
1 chicken stock cube
Salt
Pepper

Bring water to boil. Peel and dice beetroot. Add to water with crumbled stock cube, shallot, bouquet garni, sugar, lemon juice and salt and pepper. Bring to the boil. Reduce heat, and simmer, uncovered, for about an hour. Blend and push through sieve and leave to cool. When cool, put into refrigerator to chill.

Beetroot Soup (left) and Vichyssoise (Leek and Potato Soup) (bottom).

Dips and Pâtés

Tzatziki (Cucumber and Yogurt Salad)

PREPARATION TIME: 15 minutes
SERVES: 4 people

1 cucumber, peeled
1 clove garlic, crushed
1 medium-sized carton plain yogurt
10ml (2 tsps) lemon juice
1 tsp chopped mint
Salt

Garnish
Cucumber slices
Sprig of mint

Grate the cucumber and drain off any excess liquid. Mix cucumber with garlic and yogurt. Stir in lemon juice and mint, and add salt to taste. Garnish with a few cucumber slices and a sprig of mint.

Taramasalata (Cod Roe Salad)

PREPARATION TIME: 30 minutes
SERVES: 4 people

225g (8oz) smoked cod roe
½ onion, peeled and grated
2 cloves garlic, crushed
115g (4oz) white bread, crusts removed
60ml (4 tbsps) milk
90ml (6 tbsps) olive oil
30ml (2 tbsps) lemon juice
Pepper

Garnish
Lemon
Parsley

Crumble bread into a bowl, and add milk. Leave to soak. Scoop the cod roe out of its skin and break it down with a wooden spoon. Squeeze bread dry in a sieve. Add onion, garlic and bread to cod roe,

This page: Taramasalata (Cod Roe Salad) (top) and Tzatziki (Cucumber and Yogurt Salad) (bottom).

Facing page: Gazpacho

and mix well. Very gradually add oil and lemon juice, alternating between the two. Beat until smooth and creamy. Add pepper to taste, and salt if necessary. Garnish with lemon and parsley, and serve with Melba toast (see recipe for Guacamole) or sliced French loaf, and unsalted butter.

Crudités with Anchovy Dip, Oxford Dip, and Tomato and Chilli Dip

Crudités
Half a cauliflower, broken into florets
Half a cucumber, cut into batons
115g (4oz) button mushrooms, cleaned
3 carrots, scraped and cut into sticks
8 small radishes, cleaned
1 red pepper, cored, seeds removed, and cut into strips
8 spring onions, trimmed
2 courgettes, cut into strips

Anchovy Dip
45g (1½ oz) can anchovy fillets, drained and mashed
2 cloves garlic, crushed
30g (1oz) butter or margarine
150ml (¼ pint) double cream, lightly whipped
1 tsp marjoram or oregano
1 tsp chopped fresh parsley
Pinch sugar or salt, to taste

Melt butter in pan, add garlic, and cook for 1 minute. Add anchovies, herbs and sugar or salt to taste. Cook for 10 minutes, stirring continuously. Set aside. When cool, fold in whipped cream. Chill.

Oxford Dip
Pared rind of 1 lemon
5ml (1 tsp) lemon juice
1 tsp English mustard
½ tsp grated root ginger
2 tbsps redcurrant jelly
60ml (4 tbsps) red wine
1 tsp arrowroot

Blanch rind in boiling water for 30 seconds. Remove and shred finely. Put all ingredients except wine and arrowroot into a pan, and bring to the boil, stirring continuously. When mixed, stir in wine and simmer, uncovered, for 15 minutes. Slake arrowroot in 15ml (1 tbsp) of water and add to pan. Simmer a further 3 minutes, stirring continuously. Chill.

Tomato and Chilli Dip
400g (14oz) can plum tomatoes, drained, reserving juice, and pips removed
1 red chilli, seeds removed, sliced finely
1 clove garlic
1 onion, peeled and chopped finely
15ml (1 tbsp) lemon juice or white wine vinegar
1 tbsp chopped fresh parsley
15g (½ oz) butter or margarine
Salt
Pepper

Melt butter in pan. Add garlic and fry until browned. Discard garlic. Add onion and cook gently till softened. Add chilli and cook a further 3 minutes. Add tomatoes, lemon juice or vinegar, reserved tomato juice and salt and pepper and simmer gently for 10 minutes. Remove from heat and set aside to cool. Push through a sieve, stir in parsley, and chill.

Pâté aux Herbes

PREPARATION TIME: 20 minutes
COOKING TIME: 1 hour
OVEN TEMPERATURE: 170°C; 350°F; Gas Mark 2
SERVES: 4 people

450g (1lb) pork, finely minced
325g (11oz) packet frozen spinach
225g (8oz) rashers of streaky bacon, rind removed
1 onion, peeled and chopped
2 cloves garlic, crushed
2 tbsps finely chopped fresh basil
2 tbsps chopped parsley
Freshly grated nutmeg
Freshly ground black pepper
½ tsp sage
1 can leg or shoulder ham
1 egg, lightly beaten
Pinch of cayenne pepper
150ml (¼ pint) double cream
Salt

Cook spinach in boiling salted water for 5 minutes. Drain and press between two plates to remove excess water. Chop finely and mix with pork. Combine onion, garlic, herbs and spices, cayenne pepper, cream, and salt and pepper. Cut ham into strips. Line bottom and sides of ovenproof tureen with rashers of streaky bacon. Mix pork and spinach into cream mixture. Add egg and stir thoroughly. Press one-third mixture into tureen. Add half the ham strips. Repeat until all ham and mixture is used up. Cook in a slow oven for 45 minutes. Remove from oven, cool, and serve sliced.

Guacamole

PREPARATION TIME: 15 minutes
COOKING TIME: 5 minutes
SERVES: 4 people

2 ripe avocados
15ml (1 tbsp) lemon juice
1 clove garlic, crushed
1 red chilli, seeds removed, sliced finely
1 shallot, very finely chopped, or grated
¼ tsp ground chilli powder
Pinch of paprika
Salt

Garnish
Lemon slices and parsley
Serve with melba toast if desired

Blanch chilli and shallot in boiling water for 2 minutes. Drain and set aside. Peel the avocados. Pierce the skin with the point of a sharp knife and run down from top to bottom of the pear in quarters. Pull skin back off fruit and remove stone from centre and any dark bits of flesh. Mash the flesh to a purée and mix in lemon juice. Stir in garlic and shallot. Add chilli, chilli powder, paprika and salt, a bit at a time, to desired taste. Garnish with lemon and parsley. Serve with Melba toast if desired.

Melba Toast
Pre-heat grill. Put slices of bread in toaster and toast until golden brown. Remove crusts and cut horizontally through toast whilst still hot. Cut into triangles and toast untoasted side under the grill until golden brown. Keep inside a clean tea-towel until ready to serve.

Crudités (right) with Anchovy Dip (bottom), Oxford Dip (far right) and Tomato and Chilli Dip (below).

Tomato, Carrot and Spinach Slice

PREPARATION TIME: 30 minutes, plus chilling time

SERVES: 4 people

6 tomatoes, skinned, with pips removed
450g (1lb) spinach, cooked
Pinch of nutmeg
3 carrots, finely grated
150ml (¼ pint) double cream, whipped
11g (⅓ oz) gelatine
60ml (4 tbsps) water
Salt
Pepper

Grease and line a loaf tin with greaseproof paper. Blend tomato in a food processor until smooth. Add salt and pepper to taste. Set aside. Put water in a small bowl. Sprinkle over gelatine and leave 15 minutes to soak. Place bowl in a saucepan of hot water, so that water is part way up side of bowl. Heat gently until gelatine has dissolved. Meanwhile, chop spinach, squeeze out excess liquid and stir in half the cream. Add nutmeg, and salt and pepper to taste. Set aside. Stir one-third of gelatine into tomato mixture, and return bowl of gelatine to saucepan. Fill tomato into loaf tin. Level out, and put into freezer compartment. Leave 10 minutes. Meanwhile, stir carrot and remaining cream together. Stir half of remaining gelatine into carrot mixture, and pour over tomato mixture. Return tin to freezer for 10 minutes. Stir remaining gelatine into spinach mixture, and pour onto carrot layer. Smooth out and put into freezer for a further 10 minutes. Remove from freezer and chill in refrigerator overnight.

This page: Tomato, Carrot and Spinach Slice.

Facing page: Salmon, Watercress and Tomato Slice (top) and Pâté aux Herbes (bottom).

Salmon, Watercress and Tomato Slice

PREPARATION TIME: 30 minutes

SERVES: 4 people

6 tomatoes, skinned, and pips removed
Half a bunch of watercress
225g (8oz) can red or pink salmon
150ml (¼ pint) double cream, whipped
11g (⅓ oz) gelatine
60ml (4 tbsps) water
Salt
Pepper

Garnish
Watercress

Grease and line a loaf tin with greaseproof paper. Drain, and place salmon and one-third of the cream into a food processor, and process until smooth. Add salt and pepper to taste. Set aside. Put water in a small bowl, and sprinkle over gelatine. Leave 15 minutes to soak. Place bowl in a sauepan of hot water so that water is partway up side of bowl. Heat gently until gelatine has dissolved. Meanwhile, chop watercress, squeeze out excess liquid, and stir in half the remaining cream. Add salt and pepper to taste. Set aside. Place tomatoes and remaining cream in food processor, and process. Stir one-third of gelatine into tomato mixture and return bowl of gelatine to saucepan. Fill tomato into loaf tin. Level out, and put into freezer compartment for 10 minutes. Stir half the remaining gelatine into watercress mixture and pour over tomato mixture. Return tin to freezer for 10 minutes. Stir remaining gelatine into salmon mixture and pour onto watercress layer. Smooth out and put into freezer for 10 minutes. Remove from freezer and chill in refrigerator overnight. Garnish with watercress.

Salmon Pâté

PREPARATION TIME: 15 minutes

SERVES: 4 people

225g (8oz) can red or pink salmon, drained
115g (4oz) curd cheese
30g (1oz) butter
Pinch of ground mace or ground nutmeg
Few drops of lemon juice
¼ tsp tabasco sauce
30ml (2 tbsps) double cream
Salt
Pepper

Garnish
Gherkins (slice each gherkin horizontally 4 or 5 times, and splay into a fan)

Remove any bones from salmon. Work into a paste with the back of a spoon. Cream the butter and cheese until smooth. Add salmon, lemon juice, seasonings and cream, and mix well. Put into a large dish or individual ramekins. Garnish dish with a gherkin fan.

Chicken Liver Pâté

PREPARATION TIME: 15 minutes

COOKING TIME: 15 minutes

SERVES: 4 people

225g (8oz) chicken livers, trimmed
1 onion, peeled and diced finely
30g (1oz) butter for frying
60g (2oz) butter, creamed
1 clove garlic, crushed
15ml (1 tbsp) brandy
5ml (1 tsp) Worcestershire sauce
Salt
Pepper

Garnish
Dill

Heat butter in frying pan. Add garlic, onions, salt, and freshly ground black pepper, and fry gently until onions have softened. Increase heat, and sauté chicken livers in hot butter for about 2 minutes on each side, until just cooked through. Add Worcestershire sauce and stir. Blend contents of frying pan and push through a wire sieve with the back of a spoon into a bowl. Beat in creamed butter, brandy, and adjust seasoning. Place in one large dish or individual ramekin dishes. If not being eaten straight away, seal surface with clarified butter and refrigerate. Garnish with dill.

Smoked Mackerel Pâté

PREPARATION TIME:
30 minutes, plus chilling time

SERVES: 4 people

225g (8oz) smoked mackerel fillets, skinned and bones removed
60g (2oz) butter
Juice of half an orange
1 tsp tomato purée
5ml (1 tsp) white wine vinegar
Black pepper, freshly ground
Salt, if desired

Garnish
1 can pimentos

Aspic
300ml (½ pint) clear, strained chicken stock
2 tsps powdered gelatine
30ml (2 tbsps) dry sherry
30ml (2 tbsps) cold water
or
1 packet commercial aspic, used as directed

Cream butter. Place butter, smoked mackerel, orange juice, tomato purée, vinegar and black pepper in a blender. Blend until smooth. Add salt if necessary. Place in one dish or individual dishes. Cut pimentos into strips. Sprinkle gelatine over a small bowl with 15-30ml (1-2 tbsps) of cold water in it and leave to soak for 15 minutes. Place bowl in a saucepan of simmering water, and leave until gelatine has dissolved. Heat stock in pan. Add gelatine. Allow to cool, and stir in sherry. Make a lattice of pimento on top of mackerel pâté. Carefully pour over aspic to just cover pimento. Chill in refrigerator.

Smoked Mackerel Pâté (right) and Salmon Pâté (bottom).

Vegetables and Fruit Starters

Stuffed Radicchio

PREPARATION TIME: 10 minutes
COOKING TIME: 5 minutes
SERVES: 4 people

1 radicchio (8 good whole leaves; the rest finely chopped)
60g (2oz) rice, cooked
1 tbsp chopped parsley
200g (7oz) can tuna fish, drained
2 tbsps capers
5ml (1 tsp) lemon juice
30ml (2 tbsps) double cream, whipped
30ml (2 tbsps) vermouth or dry sherry
Salt
Pepper

Garnish
Lemon slices
Parsley

Flake tuna fish and mix with rice, chopped radicchio, parsley, lemon juice, capers, double cream and wine and salt and pepper to taste. Divide mixture evenly between 4 whole radicchio leaves and place remaining 4 on top. Serve garnished with lemon slices and parsley.

Asparagus with Hollandaise Sauce

PREPARATION TIME: 10 minutes
COOKING TIME: 30 minutes
SERVES: 4 people

20-32 asparagus spears
Nut of butter
Salt

Hollandaise Sauce
3 egg yolks
5ml (1 tsp) lemon juice if desired
175g (6oz) unsalted butter, diced
15ml (1 tbsp) wine vinegar
Salt
White pepper

Wash and trim asparagus stalks, removing woody ends where necessary. Place in a large, shallow pan or large saucepan of boiling salted water. Add nut of butter and allow to simmer gently until tender – about 10-15 minutes. If size of spears varies greatly, add thicker ones first so that they will all be ready together. Drain. Meanwhile, half-fill bottom half of double saucepan with boiling water. Place egg yolks and wine vinegar in top half of double saucepan. Whisk together until well mixed. Place over bottom of saucpan and heat gently, keeping water hot, but not boiling. Stir until yolks are smooth. Whisk in small pieces of butter, a few at a time, until all butter has been absorbed. Whisk sauce until thick and creamy. Season with salt and white pepper to taste and add lemon juice if desired. Serve asparagus spears with warm Hollandaise sauce.

This page: Stuffed Raddichio (top) and Asparagus with Hollandaise Sauce (bottom).

Facing page: Guacamole (top) and Chicken Liver Pâté (bottom).

Tomato and Pepper Frostie

PREPARATION TIME:
15 minutes, plus freezing time

SERVES: 4 people

115ml (4 fl oz) can tomato juice
Juice of 1 lemon
6 ice cubes
5ml (1 tsp) Worcestershire sauce
½ small green pepper
½ small red pepper

Garnish
4 tomato flowers

Crush ice. Put tomato juice, lemon juice, ice and Worcestershire sauce in blender. Blend together. Put into ice-trays and place in freezer for ½ hour or until half-frozen. Meanwhile, remove core and seeds from peppers and dice finely. Remove tomato ice from freezer and transfer to a bowl, breaking up with the back of a fork. Mix in peppers. Re-freeze for a further 2 hours, stirring occasionally. For a garnish, make tomato flowers. Peel tomatoes (drop into boiling water; count to ten slowly; then rinse in cold water; remove skins). Starting at one end, with a sharp knife slice a continuous strip around the tomato. Form into a rose shape. Serve on top of tomato and pepper frostie.

Pepper Appetiser (left), Aubergine Appetiser (bottom) and Tomato and Pepper Frostie (facing page).

Onion-Egg-Tomato Bake

PREPARATION TIME: 15 minutes

COOKING TIME: 20 minutes

OVEN TEMPERATURE:
200°C, 400°F, Gas Mark 6

SERVES: 4 people

4 eggs, hard boiled
2 medium onions, peeled and sliced
60g (2oz) butter or margarine
30g (1oz) flour
150ml (¼ pint) milk
2 tomatoes, skinned and sliced thinly
1 tbsp breadcrumbs
1 tbsp freshly grated Parmesan cheese
Salt
Pepper

Garnish
Parsley

Melt butter in pan. Add onions and fry over gentle heat until softened but not coloured. Remove with a slotted spoon and set aside. Stir in flour and cook for 1 minute. Remove from heat and gradually stir in milk. Beat well and return to heat. Cook for 3 minutes, stirring continuously. Add onions and plenty of seasoning to counteract the sweetness of the onions. Cut eggs in half. Remove yolks, sieve and set aside. Rinse and slice egg whites. Place in the bottom of an ovenproof dish. Cover with onion mixture, then with a layer of sliced tomatoes. Mix together egg yolk, breadcrumbs and Parmesan cheese. Sprinkle over top and place in a hot oven until golden on top. Garnish with parsley.

Pepper Appetiser

PREPARATION TIME: 15 minutes

COOKING TIME: 1 hour 15 minutes

SERVES: 4 people

1 green pepper
1 red pepper
2 tomatoes
2 onions
60ml (4 tbsps) white vinegar
30ml (2 tbsps) oil
Salt

Remove core and seeds from peppers and slice lengthways. Peel and slice onions and tomatoes. Heat oil in a large suacepan. Add vegetables and salt to taste and simmer, covered, for 1 hour, stirring occasionally. Remove lid and add vinegar, and simmer for a further 15 minutes. Allow to cool, and chill in refrigerator.

Aubergine Appetiser

PREPARATION TIME: 15 minutes

COOKING TIME: 20 minutes

SERVES: 4 people

1 large aubergine
2 ripe tomatoes, peeled, seeds removed, and chopped
2 cloves garlic, crushed
60ml (4 tbsps) oil
1 tbsp tomato purée
60ml (4 tbsps) water
Salt
Pepper

Cut aubergine lengthwise into strips 1cm x 6cm (¼" x 2½"). Heat oil in pan until hot. Add aubergine and cook for 5 minutes or until cooked. Remove from pan with slotted spoon. Add extra oil as necessary and heat. Fry garlic for 30 seconds. Add tomatoes, tomato purée, salt and pepper, and water and cook for 10 minutes or until sauce is thick. Add aubergine and stir together. Adjust seasoning and cook for a further 5 minutes. Serve hot or cold.

Avocado Lemon Ring

PREPARATION TIME:
10 minutes, plus setting time

SERVES: 4 people

2 avocado pears
1 pkt lemon jelly
150ml (¼ pint) hot water
1 lemon
10ml (2 tsps) Worcestershire sauce
150ml (¼ pint) double cream
Salt

Garnish
Slices of lemon
Watercress

Dissolve the jelly in hot water and leave to cool. Grate finely the rind of the lemon, and squeeze and strain the juice. Peel the avocado pears and remove the pips. Mash well with a fork. Pour on the cooled jelly and whisk or blend. Add lemon juice, rind, Worcestershire sauce, a pinch of salt and cream, and mix well. Pour into dampened ring mould and leave to set. Turn out to serve and garnish with slices of lemon and watercress in centre.

Grilled Grapefruit

PREPARATION TIME: 45 minutes

COOKING TIME: 10 minutes

SERVES: 4 people

2 grapefruit
60g (2oz) brown sugar
30ml (2 tbsps) Grand Marnier or Cointreau liqueur
1 tbsp clear honey

Garnish
Fresh or maraschino cherries
Fresh mint leaf

Cut grapefruit in half around equators. With a grapefruit knife or sharp knife, cut around edge between flesh of fruit and pith. Then cut down between each segment, removing skin from flesh. Take core between finger and thumb and pull out, removing with skin. Remove any pips. Pour excess juice into bowl. Sprinkle each grapefruit half with sugar and pour over liqueur. Leave to stand for 30 minutes. Meanwhile, mix together honey and grapefruit juice. Pre-heat grill. Pour over honey/grapefruit juice mixture and grill until just browning on top. Trim away any burnt skin and garnish with a cherry and mint leaf.

Broccoli Timbales

PREPARATION TIME: 10 minutes

COOKING TIME: 30 minutes

OVEN TEMPERATURE:
190°C, 375°F, Gas Mark 5

SERVES: 4 people

4 broccoli florets
30g (1oz) butter or margarine
30g (1oz) plain flour
300ml (½ pint) milk
1 tsp ground nutmeg
2 eggs, beaten
Salt
Pepper

Blanch broccoli in boiling salted water for 3 minutes. Drain and refresh under cold water. Drain and set aside. Melt butter in pan. Stir in flour and nutmeg and cook for 1 minute. Remove from heat and stir in milk gradually. Return to heat and bring to the boil, stirring continuously. Cook for 3 minutes. Add salt and white pepper to taste and beat well. Set aside to cool. Butter 4 ramekin dishes. Place a floret of broccoli in each dish with stem pointing upwards. Beat eggs into cooled white sauce, and pour into each ramekin dish. Place ramekins in a shallow baking tin. Pour boiling water into tin to a depth of 2.5cm (1"). Bake in a pre-heated oven for 15 minutes, or until just setting. Remove from oven and turn out onto individual plates. Serve immediately.

Onion-Egg-Tomato Bake (right) and Broccoli Timbales (bottom).

Fanned Avocado Salad with Prawn and Tomato Dressing

PREPARATION TIME: 20 minutes

SERVES: 4 people

2 ripe avocados
Juice of ½ lemon or 1 lime
225g (8oz) prawns or shrimps, shelled and de-veined
3 tbsps mayonnaise
1 tbsp tomato purée
15ml (1 tbsp) single cream
Salt
Pepper

Garnish
Lemon or lime rings
Lettuce leaves

Mix together mayonnaise, tomato purée, cream and salt and pepper to taste. Mix prawns with 2 tbsps mayonnaise mixture and set aside. Cut avocados in half. Remove pips and peel back and remove skin. Slice down through flesh 5 or 6 times. Keep thin end intact. Place on lettuce leaves on serving dishes and press down so that avocado fans out. Sprinkle over lemon or lime juice to prevent flesh browning. Place prawns at side of dish, around avocado. Garnish with lemon or lime rings.

Stuffed Mushrooms

PREPARATION TIME: 15 minutes

COOKING TIME: 20 minutes

OVEN TEMPERATURE:
200°C, 400°F, Gas Mark 6

SERVES: 4 people

4 large or 8 medium flat or cap mushrooms, stalks discarded
15ml (1 tbsp) olive oil
2 medium onions, peeled and chopped finely
225g (8oz) spinach, trimmed, cooked and chopped finely
2 tbsps fresh white breadcrumbs
60g (2oz) butter or margarine
4 cloves garlic, crushed
1 egg, beaten
½ tsp nutmeg
Salt
Pepper

Garnish
1 tbsp chopped parsley

Heat butter in pan. Add garlic, onion and nutmeg and fry gently until onion has softened. Remove from pan and set aside to cool. Meanwhile, heat oil in pan and sauté mushrooms on both sides until lightly browned. Place underside-up in a shallow oven-proof dish. Mix together onion mixture, spinach, breadcrumbs, and salt and freshly ground black pepper to taste. Stir in beaten egg. Cover each mushroom cap with the mixture, shaping neatly. Cover with aluminium foil and bake in a hot oven for 10 minutes. Serve immediately, garnished with chopped parsley.

This page: Grilled Grapefruit (top) and Avocado Lemon Ring (bottom).
Facing page: Stuffed Mushrooms (top) and Fanned Avocado Salad with Prawn and Tomato Dressing (bottom).

Melon Balls in Mulled Wine

PREPARATION TIME: 1 hour

COOKING TIME: 10 minutes

SERVES: 4 people

1 melon
½ bottle red wine
2 cinnamon sticks
4 cloves
3 blades mace
Juice and pared rind of 1 orange
1 tsp freshly grated nutmeg
60g (2oz) granulated sugar

Put wine, orange juice and rind, spices and sugar into a pan and heat gently. Do not allow to boil. When hot, remove from heat and leave to infuse for an hour. Strain. Meanwhile, cut melon in half and scrape out pips. Then make melon balls with a melon-ball scoop, or cut into chunks. Place in individual serving dishes and pour over mulled wine.

Orange, Grapefruit and Mint Salad

PREPARATION TIME:
20 minutes, plus chilling time

SERVES: 4 people

2 grapefruit
3 oranges
1 tbsp granulated sugar
4 sprigs of mint

Garnish
Mint sprig

Cut the peel and pith off the grapefruit and oranges. Cut carefully inside the skin of each segment to remove each section of flesh. When skin only is left, squeeze to extract juices over a pan. Repeat with all fruit. Add sugar to pan and set over a gentle heat until sugar dissolves. Cool. Meanwhile, arrange orange and grapefruit segments alternating in dish. Chop mint finely and add to fruit syrup. Carefully spoon syrup over fruit. Chill. Garnish with a sprig of mint.

Orange, Grapefruit and Mint Salad (right) and Melon Balls in Mulled Wine (inset below).

Traditional Soups and Snacks

Nettle Soup

PREPARATION TIME: 15 minutes
COOKING TIME: 30 minutes
SERVES: 6-8 people

It has been established that nettle soup was part of the diet of the monks in Ireland as far back as the 6th century. It would often have been made with milk alone, or even milk and water, and you can vary the proportions of stock and milk used in this recipe.

1½ pints (900ml) stock
½ pint (300ml) milk
1 pint (600ml) nettles
1oz (30g) oatmeal
2oz (60g) butter

Wear gloves when you are collecting the nettles and only choose the young, bright green leaves. Remove any stalks and chop up the leaves. These days a food processor will do the job in a fraction of the time it takes to chop them by hand. Melt the butter in a large saucepan. Add the oatmeal and cook until the mixture is a golden brown. Remove the pan from the heat and add the stock. Bring it to the boil and add the milk. When it is boiling again, add the chopped nettles and cook for another few minutes. You may need more seasoning, depending how much seasoning there is in the stock.

Potato Soup

PREPARATION TIME: 20 minutes
COOKING TIME: 1 hour 15 minutes
SERVES: 8-10 persons

Potato soup can be made with milk and water but its flavour is much improved if you use stock instead of the water. Boil down a chicken carcass with an onion, a carrot and some herbs. Strain off the stock and let it get cold. Remove any fat from the top and you will have a lovely, thick jelly which will keep for a week in the refrigerator or can be kept in the freezer for longer. The same can be done with all meat bones.

2lb (900g) potatoes
2 onions
1 small carrot
Bayleaf, parsley and thyme
Salt and pepper
2 pints (1.2l) stock
1 pint (600ml) milk
2oz (60g) butter

Peel and slice the potatoes, onions and carrot. Melt butter in a large

This page: Potato Soup (top) and Country Broth (bottom). Facing page: Nettle Soup (top) and Smoked Salmon Bisque (bottom).

saucepan and sweat onions in it until soft but not brown. Add potatoes and carrot. Stir in the stock and milk. Tie the bayleaf, thyme and parsley together and add with pepper and salt to taste. Simmer gently for about an hour then either liquidise or put through a sieve or vegetable mill. Add some cream or top of milk before serving and sprinkle with chopped chives.

Smoked Salmon Bisque

PREPARATION TIME: 30 minutes
COOKING TIME: 1 hour
SERVES: 6-8 persons

A side of smoked salmon is a rare gift these days, the price being what it is. If you should be the lucky recipient of one, be sure to save the skin and trimmings as they will make a delicious soup.

Skin and trimmings of a side of smoked salmon
1 onion, stuck with cloves
Bayleaf
1 tsp (5ml) salt
Few peppercorns
1 carrot
1-2 stick of celery
2oz (60g) butter
2oz (60g) flour
1 tblsp (15ml) tomato purée
1 glass white wine
Cream and parsley to decorate

Put the skin and trimmings in a saucepan with the onion, stuck with 5-6 cloves, and the carrot and celery cut in chunks. Cover with cold water, add the bayleaf, salt and peppercorns. Cover the pan and simmer for about 30 minutes. Remove the bayleaf. Take out the onion, remove the cloves and return the onion to the pan. With a slotted spoon, take out the fish skin and scrape off any remaining flesh, which should also be returned to the pan. Strain half the liquid into a bowl.
In another large pan melt the butter, stir in the flour and make a roux. Stir in the tomato purée and gradually add the strained stock, stirring all the time until it thickens. Add a glass of white wine, or a glass of sherry will do very well! Put the rest of the stock, containing the fish and vegetables, in the liquidiser and run it for half a minute. Add this to the soup. Test for seasoning. You can either stir in cream to the soup before serving or put a spoon of cream on top of each bowl of soup with a little chopped parsley sprinkled on top.

Sausage Pie

PREPARATION TIME: 15 minutes
COOKING TIME: 45 minutes
SERVES: 6 persons

This can be eaten hot or cold and is excellent for picnics.

¾lb (350g) frozen puff pastry
1lb (450g) lean sausage meat
1 small onion, minced
1 cup breadcrumbs
Level tsp (5ml) dried sage
Salt and pepper
7oz (200g) tin tomatoes
1 egg
1 tblsp (15ml) milk

Cut defrosted pastry in two. Roll each half out into a 10 inch (25.5cm) square and put it in the refrigerator while you mix the filling. Mix the onions and breadcrumbs, herbs and salt and pepper together and mix in with the sausage meat. Add the tomatoes and mix well. Break in the egg and stir that in well. Line a greased 10 inch (25.5cm) pie plate with one layer of the pastry. Spread the sausage mixture over it to within 1 inch (2.5cm) of the edge. Moisten the edge with milk and place the other piece of pastry on top. Trim the edges and crimp them together all around. Cut a cross in the centre on top and use the pastry trimmings to make a leaf pattern in the centre. Brush the top with milk and bake in a pre-heated oven, 200°C, 400°F, Gas Mark 6, for 45 minutes.

Country Broth

PREPARATION TIME: 20 minutes
COOKING TIME: 1 hour
SERVES: 8-10 persons

Homemade soups make a nourishing addition to a family meal and this one is almost a meal in itself. It is really made from what is available rather than from set ingredients. I always boil down chicken carcases and meat bones, strain off the stock and keep it in the refrigerator. If I happen to have more than I need for the week I keep some in the freezer. Then, at the end of the week, I collect all the remaining vegetables and salad stuffs and use them to make this lovely soup. If you have a lot of leftover vegetables and the soup is very thick, it can be diluted with milk as you use it, or with the vegetable stock from the main course. Typical ingredients might be as follows:

1 onion
1 carrot
1 potato
¼ cucumber
½ green pepper
2 tomatoes
Some lettuce leaves
2 sticks celery
1 handful macaroni
1 handful pearl barley
1 handful lentils
Some chopped fresh herbs or
1 tsp (5ml) dried herbs
2 tblsp (30ml) oil and 1 tblsp (15ml) butter
3 pints (1.8l) stock or stock made with stock cubes
Glass of sherry
2-3 tblsp (30-45ml) cream or top of milk

Prepare all the vegetables and salad stuffs and chop them roughly. Sweat them in the oil and butter, or in butter only, if you prefer. Add the pearl barley, macaroni and lentils then stir in the stock. Add the herbs and seasoning. Bring to the boil and simmer for half an hour. Test for seasoning. If you like it chunky, mash it down with a potato masher overwise put it through the coarse shredder of a vegetable mill or in the liquidiser. Return it to the pan, add the sherry and the cream or, if necessary, dilute with milk first. Bring back to simmering point and serve.

Stuffed Vine Leaves (right) and Sausage Pie (below).

Stuffed Vine Leaves

PREPARATION TIME: 30 minutes
COOKING TIME: 30 minutes
SERVES: 8 persons

I have always been intrigued by the fact that so many Irish country houses have vines growing in their conservatories or even against a south-facing wall. Although they seem to flourish in the mild climate, there is not enough sun to make the grapes suitable for wine making, or certainly not on a large scale. However, vine owners might like to try this recipe for stuffed vine leaves. The tangy flavour of the leaf goes well with the filling.

24 vine leaves
2-3 tblsp (30-45ml) oil
8oz (225g) cooked rice
4oz (115g) cold lamb, minced
2-3 scallions, finely chopped
1 tblsp (15ml) finely chopped walnuts
½ tsp (2.5ml) marjoram
Salt and pepper
½ pint (300ml) stock

Fry the scallions in the oil then add the lamb, rice, herbs and walnuts. Season with salt and pepper. Have ready a pan of boiling water and a bowl of iced water. Hold the vine leaves by their stalks and dip each one into the boiling water for about 10 seconds then plunge it into the iced water. Lay the leaves, underside up, on a board and put a tsp (5ml) of the filling on each. Roll each one up into a sausage shape, tucking in the edges, and gently squeeze into shape in the palm of your hand. Pack the little parcels into a large pan in one layer. Pour the stock over them and cover with a plate to keep them in position. Simmer them for half an hour. Serve them with wedges of lemon.

Crubeens

PREPARATION TIME: 5 minutes
COOKING TIME: 3 hours

These could be called the 'traditional Irish take-away', and are served in the pubs on a Saturday night to help mop up the alcohol! They may be eaten hot or cold. Taken straight from the pot they are eaten with brown soda bread and Guinness. If they are allowed to cool in the pot the meat will be firmer but they will be coated with a thick jelly. Either way, they are eaten in the fingers and much mopping up is required afterwards. Some Irish restaurants now include them on the menu, but usually they are de-boned and rolled in well-seasoned egg and breadcrumbs, before being grilled. It is much less of a challenge to eat them when they are prepared in this way.

To cook Crubeens you need one pig's trotter per person and they say there is more meat on the hind ones. Put them in a pan with an onion, a carrot, salt, a few peppercorns, a bayleaf, some thyme and parsley. Cover with cold water, bring to the boil and simmer for three hours.

Drisheen

PREPARATION TIME: 40 minutes
COOKING TIME: 45 minutes
SERVES: 8 persons

Drisheen is a white pudding which is only found in County Cork. It is made from sheep's blood mixed with salt (which keeps it liquid), cream, oatmeal or breadcrumbs and seasoned with mace and tansy. It can be bought ready-made in Cork and in Dublin in the shape of thick sausages, as shown in the photograph, but the home made sort was usually made in a wide, shallow pan and steamed or baked in the oven in a bain marie

We used to love it for breakfast when we were children but I'm sure we would not have even tasted it if we had been told how it was made. Just in case you can find some sheep's blood and are not too squeamish here is the recipe.

2 pints sheep's blood
1 dsp (10ml) of salt
1 pint (600ml) creamy milk
Pinch tansy or thyme
2 cupfuls breadcrumbs

Strain the blood into a mixing bowl, add all the other ingredients and mix well. Allow to stand for half an hour then pour mixture into a greased ovenproof dish, cover with foil and place in a roasting tin with water to come halfway up the sides of the dish. Cook in the oven at 180°C, 350°F, Gas Mark 4 for 45 minutes or until set.

Savoury Pancakes

PREPARATION TIME: 1 hour 30 minutes
COOKING TIME: 45 minutes
SERVES: 6 persons

This is a very useful way of using up leftover cooked mince or cold meat. In fact, it is a good idea to cook more than you need on some previous occasion and freeze some of it. If you are using cooked beef or lamb, put it through the mincer or in a food processor with a small onion and bind it with gravy or stock, thickened with a little cornflour.

8oz (225g) cooked mince
1 cup cooked rice
1 level tsp (5ml) curry powder

Pancakes
4oz (115g) plain flour
1 level tsp (5ml) salt
1 egg
½ pint (300ml) milk
Cooking oil

Sauce
1½oz (45g) butter
1½oz (45g) flour
Salt and pepper
1 pint (600ml) milk
3oz (85g) grated cheese

Sift flour and salt into a mixing bowl, break in the egg and add the milk gradually, beating out any lumps and beating the batter with a whisk for several minutes. This can be done in an electric blender all at once in just one minute. The batter should be allowed to stand for at least an hour before making the pancakes. Grease a heavy, cast-iron frying pan with a tsp (5ml) of cooking oil and heat it until it is very hot. Put in 2 tblsp (30ml) batter mixture and quickly tilt the pan around until the batter covers the bottom. While it is cooking, loosen the edges with a spatula, ready to turn the pancake as soon as the bottom is done. Turn onto a plate. Add another tsp (5ml) of oil to the pan and repeat the process

Drisheen (top) and Crubeens (bottom).

until all the batter is used up. Should make 10 or 12 thin pancakes.
Heat up the mince in a saucepan, stir in the curry powder and cook gently for a minute or two. Mix in the cooked rice. Grease an oblong ovenproof dish. Put a tablespoonful of filling into each pancake, roll them up and place them in one layer in the dish.

Sauce
Melt the butter in a saucepan, add the flour and make a roux. Very gradually add the milk, stirring all the time. When it comes to the boil continue cooking for a further minute then remove from heat and stir in grated cheese. Season with salt and pepper. Pour the sauce over the pancakes and bake in the oven, 190°C, 375°F, Gas Mark 5, for 45 minutes until just brown on top.

Creamed Mushrooms on Toast

PREPARATION TIME: 5 minutes
COOKING TIME: 20 minutes
SERVES: 4-6 persons

Cultivated mushrooms, so plentiful in the shops these days, bear no relation to the field mushrooms we used to gather in the fields in Ireland in the late summer. They were supposed to be gathered before breakfast, though, since there was no one else around who would be likely to take them, I could never understand why they wouldn't be there later in the day. However, my father would drag us out to search for them early in the morning, and it was worth it to savour the delicate flavour when they were cooked for breakfast.

8oz (225g) freshly gathered field mushrooms, or use the large, flat cultivated mushrooms
1 pint (600ml) milk
2oz (60g) butter
2oz (60g) flour
Salt and pepper

Wipe mushrooms with damp paper towelling. Slice and place in a saucepan with the milk. Bring slowly to the boil and simmer gently for ten minutes. Meanwhile, melt butter in another pan, add flour and stir. Cook over very low heat for about a minute. Strain the milk in which the mushrooms were cooked into a jug and gradually add it to the roux, stirring all the time. When the sauce has thickened add the mushrooms, season with salt and pepper and serve on buttered toast. Serves 4-6 persons.

Irish Rarebit

PREPARATION TIME: 5 minutes
COOKING TIME: 20 minutes
SERVES: 4 persons

1oz (30g) butter or margarine
1oz (30g) plain flour
1 tsp (5ml) French mustard
1 tsp (5ml) honey
4 fl oz (100ml) milk
4 fl oz (100ml) Guinness
4oz (115g) Cheddar cheese, grated
Salt and pepper

Melt the butter in a heavy saucepan and stir in flour to make a roux. Cook on a low heat for a further minute without allowing it to brown. Remove pan from heat and gradually beat the milk into the roux. Return to heat and stir until the mixture thickens. Stir in mustard and honey and finally the Guinness. Cook this mixture fairly rapidly for 2-3 minutes then add grated cheese and stir over very low heat only until all the cheese has melted. Spread thickly on four slices of toast and brown under the grill.

Stuffed Marrow

PREPARATION TIME: 15 minutes
COOKING TIME: 1 hour 15 minutes
SERVES: 4-6 persons

1 large marrow
6-8oz (175-225g) cooked lamb

This page: Creamed Mushrooms on Toast (top) and Irish Rarebit (bottom). Facing page: Savoury Pancakes (top) and Stuffed Marrow (bottom).

1 cup of gravy or stock made with stock cube
1 onion
1 carrot
3 large tomatoes or 7oz (200g) can of tomatoes, drained
½ tsp (2.5ml) oregano plus chopped mixed garden herbs if available
1-2 cups of cooked rice, according to the size of the marrow
2oz (60g) grated cheese

Put the lamb, onion and carrot through the mincer or chop in food processor. Mix in a bowl with the gravy or stock. Put tomatoes in boiling water and leave to stand for a few minutes then remove skins, chop and add to mixture. If using tinned tomatoes, drain off liquid, chop up tomatoes and add to mixture. Add rice and herbs and season with salt and pepper to taste. Scrub marrow well. Cut in half lengthwise, remove seeds and fill both halves with stuffing. Place side by side in a greased meat tin with about half an inch of water in it. Cover tin with foil and bake at 200°C, 400°F, Gas Mark 6 for one hour. Remove from oven, take off foil, sprinkle grated cheese over marrow and return to oven for a further ten minutes.

Bacon and Egg Pie

PREPARATION TIME: 15 minutes
COOKING TIME: 40-45 minutes
SERVES: 6 persons

During the summer months, most Irish families take off for the coast whenever the opportunity arises. There are miles of golden strands where it is easy to find a secluded spot well out of earshot of other peoples transistors. Inland, too, there are many beauty spots in the midst of mountain and lakeland scenery. I remember at Glendalough, in the Wicklow Mountains, some years ago, when one person brought a bacon and egg pie and it was very popular. It is such an easy dish to transport and very little trouble to make, which is especially important if you are on holiday. In fact, you can use frozen pastry and you should be able to find a shop which sells frozen food even in the most remote villages in Ireland.

12oz (350g) plain flour
1 level tsp (5ml) salt
3oz (85g) margarine
3oz (85g) lard
3-4 tblsp (45-60ml) cold water
6 rashers streaky bacon
6 eggs

Sift flour and salt into a bowl. Cut up fats and rub into the flour. Gradually add the water, mixing it in with a knife until the mixture forms a ball and leaves the bowl clean. Lightly shape on a floured board and cut in two. Grease a 10-inch (25cm) tart plate, roll out half the pastry and line the plate with this. Place the rashers like the spokes of a wheel and break an egg into each space. Roll out the other half of the pastry and carefully cover the filling with this. Crimp the edges all round, lightly mark segments with a knife so that each person gets a rasher and egg, and brush the top with milk. Place in a pre-heated oven 200°C, 400°F, Gas Mark 6 for 40-45 minutes. The pie can be wrapped in layers of newspaper to keep it hot during a journey, or may be served cold with a salad.

Huntsman's Sandwich

PREPARATION TIME: 10 minutes
COOKING TIME: 6-8 minutes
SERVES: 2 persons

2 ½ inch (1.5cm) thick fillet steaks
1 medium onion
2 tblsp (30ml) vegetable oil
1 tblsp (15ml) butter
French mustard
Salt and pepper
2 round, crusty rolls

Peel onion and slice it finely. Heat oil and butter in a heavy frying pan. When sizzling hot put steaks in pan, turn immediately to seal and cook for 1-2 minutes on either side, according to how you like them done. Season with the salt and pepper. Slice rolls through the middle, spread French mustard on the bottom half and put steaks on top of that. Add onion to the pan juices and cook until softened. Divide this between two steaks, cover with the top halves of the rolls. Eat hot or cold. Serves 2 persons (or one very hungry huntsman).

Potatoes

The potato was first introduced to Ireland by Sir Walter Raleigh in the sixteenth century. He lived in Youghal, County Cork and the house he lived in still stands today. Potatoes flourished so well that it wasn't long before they became the staple diet in Ireland because they were so cheap to grow and the majority of the population was extremely poor. It was the failure of the potato crop which was the main cause of the famine in Ireland. The potatoes I can remember as a child were best served bursting out of their jackets – we used to be asked if we liked them laughing or smiling – and eaten with a

Huntsman's Sandwich (right) and Bacon and Egg Pie (below).

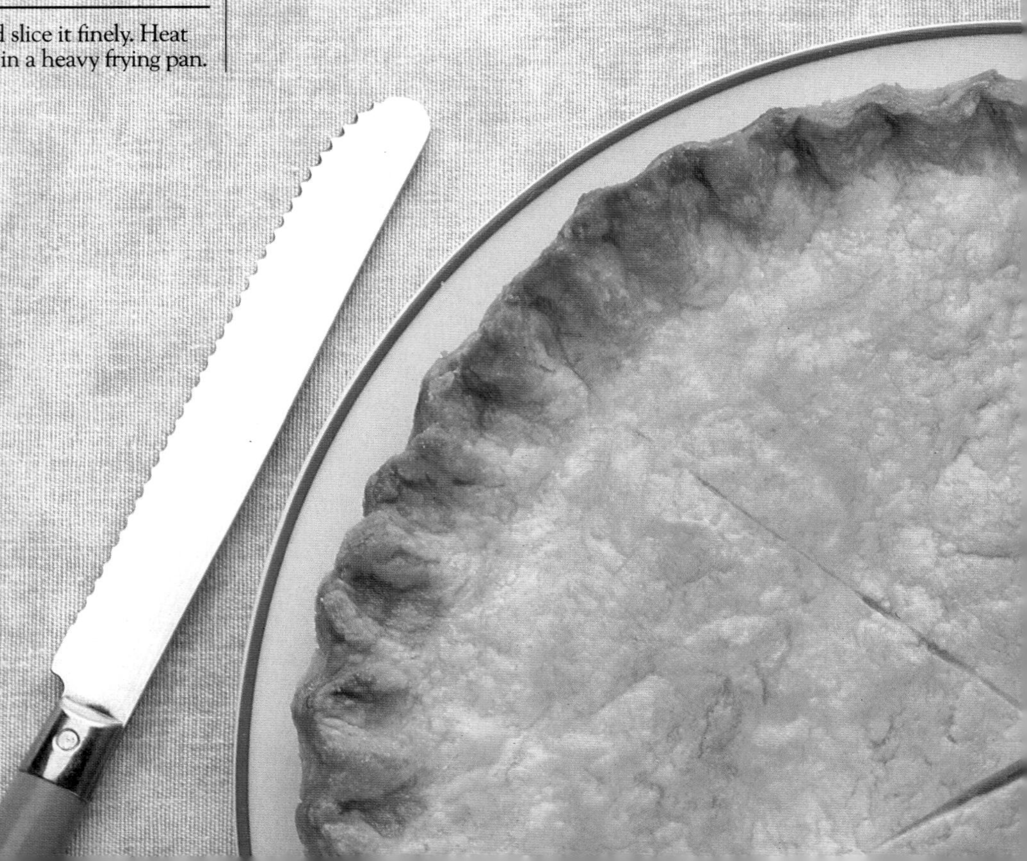

This page: Boxty Pancakes (top right), Flummery (centre left) and Oaten Farls (bottom). Facing page: Colcannon (top) and Potato Cakes (bottom).

generous amount of homemade, salty, country butter. I suppose one reason for the marvellous flavour was the fact that they would be dug up from the garden the same day they were eaten, but there does not seem to be anything to compare with them in the shops today.

In the north they have many traditional potato recipes. A friend who grew up in Belfast tells me that when she was a child meat was a luxury which, in many households, was served only at weekends, and dishes such as colcannon and champ were the main dish for the main meal of the day.

Colcannon

PREPARATION TIME: 10 minutes

COOKING TIME: 20 minutes

SERVES: 4 persons

Colcannon is another traditional potato dish and it is always associated with Hallowe'en. It is a mixture of cabbage or kale and mashed potato which sometimes has leeks or spring onions mixed in with them as in Champ.

Being a dish to serve at Hallowe'en, with all its accompanying folklore, the tradition is to hide a ring for a bride, a bachelor's button, a sixpence for wealth and the thimble for a spinster in the colcannon. When cold, it is very good fried in bacon fat and browned on both sides.

1lb (450g) cooked mashed potato
½lb (225g) cooked cabbage
2oz (60g) butter
2 fl oz (50ml) creamy milk
4oz (115g) finely chopped onion, leek or scallion

Gently fry onion in melted butter until soft. Add creamy milk and the well-mashed potatoes and stir until heated through. Chop cabbage finely and beat into the mixture over a low heat until all the mixture is pale green and fluffy. It is an excellent accompaniment for boiled bacon.

Boxty Pancakes

PREPARATION TIME: 20 minutes

COOKING TIME: 15 minutes

SERVES: 6 persons

These are made with a mixture of cooked and raw potatoes, combined with flour and bound with potato starch and fat. Milk or buttermilk is added to make the mixture into a dropping consistency and the pancakes are cooked on a griddle

8oz (225g) mashed potatoes
8oz (225g) raw potatoes
8oz (225g) flour
1 level tsp (5ml) bicarbonate of soda
1 level tsp (5ml) salt
Pepper
2oz (60g) butter, margarine or bacon fat
Milk

Peel and grate the raw potatoes. Wrap them tightly in a cloth and

squeeze over a bowl to extract as much of the starch liquid as possible. Mash the grated raw potato into the cooked mashed potato. Pour the liquid off the bowl of potato starch and scrape the starch into the potato mixture. Sift the salt and bicarbonate of soda with the flour and mix this in and then add the melted fat. Add as much milk as necessary to make the mixture into a batter of dropping consistency and cook in spoonfuls on a greased griddle or heavy pan, turning until crispy and golden on both sides.

Potato Apple

PREPARATION TIME: 25 minutes
COOKING TIME: 12-15 minutes
SERVES: 6-8 persons

I have been told of two versions of Potato Apple. One is made by sandwiching sliced apple between two rounds of potato cake and cooking it on both sides on a

greased griddle or pan. When it is cooked through and the apple is soft, the lid is lifted and sugar, or sugar mixed with cinnamon, is sprinkled over the apple. Then the lid is replaced and the apple cake cut into wedges for serving.
But, as many of these traditional recipes were concocted to use up leftover ingredients for economy's sake, another method involves the use of cooked apple.
The potato mixture was rolled out into circles, the size of a large saucer. Cooked apple was put on one half and the other half folded over and the edges sealed. Then it was cooked in the same way as in the previous recipe.

Potato Cakes

PREPARATION TIME: 20 minutes
COOKING TIME: 8-12 minutes
SERVES: 8 persons

These are a great favourite in the north of Ireland. They are eaten with lots of butter and go well with sausages and bacon and eggs.

1¼lb (550g) mashed potato
4oz (115g) flour
½ tsp (2.5ml) salt
½ tsp (2.5ml) baking powder
1oz (30g) butter
Bacon fat or dripping

Sift flour, salt and baking powder. Rub in the butter. Mix in the potatoes and knead into a ball. Cut this in two and roll half out on a floured board or work surface into a circle ¼ inch (5mm) thick. Divide into four farls or segments. Cook them for 2-3 minutes each side, on a very hot pan or griddle greased with bacon fat or dripping. Repeat the process with the other half.

Champ

PREPARATION TIME: 15 minutes
COOKING TIME: 45 minutes
SERVES: 4 persons

Champ is a traditional Irish dish more commonly found in northern counties. It is made of potatoes mixed with scallions or spring onions. Each portion is served in a mound with an indentation on top with a pat of butter in it and the potato is dipped into the melted butter.

1½lbs (675g) cooked potatoes
4oz (115g) scallions (spring onions)
4 fl oz (100ml) milk
Salt and pepper
4 large pats butter

Peel the potatoes and boil them in salted water. Drain them well and allow to dry out completely. Meanwhile, trim and wash the scallions. Slice them finely, including the green part, and put them in a saucepan with the milk to simmer gently until soft. Drain the scallions, reserving the milk, and beat them into the potato, gradually adding the hot milk until you have a nice fluffy mixture. Season well with salt and pepper and divide between four bowls, shaping each serving into a mound with a dent in the top into which you put the butter. It is eaten by dipping the potato into the melted butter.

Oaten Farls

PREPARATION TIME: 20 minutes
COOKING TIME: 8-12 minutes
SERVES: 8 persons

In the north of Ireland, the nearer one gets to the coast of Scotland, the more the Scottish influence is noticed in the food, and many recipes in this part of Ireland contain oatmeal. Here is one for potato cakes mixed with oatmeal.

Make the potato cakes as in that recipe but before rolling out, knead a handful of oatmeal into each half. Sprinkle the board with more oatmeal and roll out the potato mixture, turning it over so that both sides are well coated with oatmeal. Divide into farls and cook in a little fat on a heavy frying pan or griddle.

Flummery

PREPARATION TIME: 24 hours
COOKING TIME: 30 minutes
SERVES: 4-6 persons

Oatmeal was sometimes used to make gruel – the thinnest imaginable mixture of oatmeal and water, or milk and water. There was just about enough nourishment in it to keep people alive during the famine. The lucky ones – that is! Flummery is a more substantial version of this, and it was given to children and to invalids.

1 pint (600ml) oatmeal
1 quart (1.2l) water
½ tsp (2.5ml) salt

Soak the oatmeal in the water for at least 24 hours. Strain through muslin, and boil the liquid for 20-30 minutes, stirring all the time. Add salt and serve with milk or cream.

Champ (above left) and Potato Apple (left).

Elegant Pasta Starters

Chick-Pea Soup

PREPARATION TIME: Chick-peas soaked overnight plus 5 minutes

COOKING TIME: 1 hour 20 minutes

140g (5oz) dried chick-peas
115g (4oz) soup pasta
2 cloves garlic
45ml (3 tbsps) olive oil
1 tsp basil
400g (12oz) can plum tomatoes, chopped
1 litre (1½ pints) water
1 chicken stock cube
2 tbsps Parmesan cheese, grated
Salt and pepper

Soak chick-peas overnight in enough water to cover by 25mm (1 inch). Discard water in which the chick-peas have soaked. Place the chick-peas in a large, heavy pan, and cover with 25mm (1 inch) of water. Bring to the boil and simmer, covered, for about 1 hour until chick-peas are tender, ensuring that they do not boil dry. Heat olive oil in a heavy pan, and sauté garlic cloves. When browned, remove and discard garlic cloves. Add tomatoes and their juice, water and basil, and cook together for 20 minutes. Add drained chick-peas, crumbled stock cube, and salt and pepper to taste. Stir well; simmer a further 10 minutes. Bring back to boil. Add pasta, and cook, stirring frequently, for 10 minutes. Mix in half of the Parmesan cheese. Adjust seasoning, and serve immediately, with remaining Parmesan cheese sprinkled on top. Serves 4.
Note: Soup may be puréed before pasta is added, if desired.

Tagliatelle with Egg and Caviar

PREPARATION TIME: 5 minutes

COOKING TIME: 15 minutes

225g (8oz) red tagliatelle
30g (1oz) red caviar or lumpfish roe
4 small eggs, hard boiled
60g (2oz) butter or margarine
Black pepper

Put eggs into boiling water and cook for 12 minutes. Rinse under cold water, to stop further cooking. Remove shells, cut in half, and scoop out yolks with a teaspoon. Push yolks through a sieve. Wash egg-whites, and cut into strips. Set aside. Cook tagliatelle in plenty of boiling salted water until *al dente*. Rinse in hot water, and drain well. Heat butter in pan, add freshly-ground black pepper and tagliatelle. Add egg whites, and toss well. Sprinkle caviar over, and top with egg-yolk. Serve immediately. Serves 4 as a starter.

Minestra

PREPARATION TIME: 15 minutes

COOKING TIME: 45 minutes

115g (4oz) short-cut/elbow macaroni
30ml (2 tbsps) olive oil
1 onion
1 carrot
1 stick celery
1½ litres (3 pints) water
225g (8oz) fresh spinach
2 tomatoes
1 tsp rosemary
2 tbsps chopped parsley
2 cloves garlic, crushed
60g (2oz) Parmesan cheese, grated
Salt and pepper

Cut onion, carrot and celery into thick matchstick strips. Heat oil in a large, heavy pan, and fry vegetable strips until just browning, stirring occasionally. Pour on water, add salt and pepper, and let simmer for 20 minutes. Meanwhile, wash and cut spinach leaves into shreds, add to soup and cook for 10 minutes. Scald and skin tomatoes, and chop roughly, removing seeds. Add tomatoes, macaroni, garlic, parsley and rosemary to the soup, and simmer a further 10 minutes. Adjust seasoning. Serve with grated Parmesan cheese if desired.

Meatball Soup

PREPARATION TIME: 10 minutes

COOKING TIME: 1 hour 40 minutes

OVEN: 180°C, 350°F, Gas Mark 3

225g (8oz) minced beef
60g (2oz) breadcrumbs
1 egg, beaten
450g (1lb) beef bones
1 stick celery
1 carrot
1 onion
15ml (1 tbsp) oil
400g (14oz) can plum tomatoes
175g (6oz) soup pasta
1 tbsp chopped parsley
Salt and pepper

Place bones, peeled carrot, onion and celery in a large saucepan and cover with cold water. Bring to the boil: cover and simmer for one hour at least. Meanwhile, mix together lightly beaten egg with minced beef, breadcrumbs and plenty of seasoning. Roll a teaspoon amount into small balls and place on a roasting tin with the oil. Bake in a preheated oven for 45 minutes, turning occasionally. Strain stock into a saucepan. Push tomatoes and their juice through sieve, and add to stock. Bring to the boil, and simmer for 15 minutes. Add pasta and cook for 10 minutes, stirring frequently. Add meatballs, adjust seasoning, and stir in chopped parsley. Serve hot.

This page: Tagliatelle with Egg and Caviar.

Facing page: Minestra (top), Meatball Soup (centre right) and Chick-Pea Soup (bottom).

Tomato Soup

PREPARATION TIME: 15 minutes
COOKING TIME: 45 minutes

115g (4oz) short-cut/elbow macaroni
30g (1oz) butter or margarine
1 small onion, peeled and chopped
1 small green pepper, cored, seeds removed, and chopped
15g (½oz) flour
1 litre (2 pints) brown stock, or water plus 2 beef stock cubes
450g (1lb) tomatoes, chopped
2 tbsps tomato purée
1 tbsp grated horseradish
Salt and pepper

Garnish:
2 tbsps soured cream,
1 tbsp chopped parsley

Heat the butter in a pan. Cover and cook the onion and green pepper for 5 minutes. Add the flour and stir. Add stock, tomatoes and tomato purée. Simmer for 15 minutes. Purée soup and pass through a sieve. Return to pan, and season with salt and pepper to taste. Add macaroni 10 minutes before serving. Simmer and stir occasionally. Add horseradish before serving. Garnish with soured cream and parsley. Serve immediately.

Tagliatelle with Smoked Salmon and Caviar

PREPARATION TIME: 5 minutes
COOKING TIME: 15 minutes

225g (8oz) green tagliatelle
90g (3oz) smoked salmon, cut into strips
Juice of half a lemon
30g (1oz) red caviar or lumpfish roe
30g (1oz) butter or margarine
2 tbsps double cream
Black pepper

Garnish:
Lemon slices

Cook tagliatelle in lots of boiling salted water for 10 minutes, or until tender but still firm. Rinse under hot water, and drain well. Heat butter in pan, and add lemon juice and freshly-ground black pepper. Return tagliatelle to pan, and add smoked salmon. Toss together. Serve topped with double cream and a sprinkling of red caviar. Garnish with lemon slices. Serve immediately. Serves 4 as a starter.

Shell Pasta with Taramasalata

PREPARATION TIME: 15 minutes
COOKING TIME: 15 minutes

225g (8oz) shell pasta
225g (8oz) taramasalata
30ml (2 tbsps) lemon juice
10 black olives, pips removed, and chopped
1 tbsp black caviar or lumpfish roe

To Make Taramasalata:
225g (8oz) smoked cod roe
Half onion, grated
225g (8oz) white bread, crusts removed
60ml (4 tbsps) milk
90ml (6 tbsps) olive oil
30ml (2 tsps) lemon juice
Black pepper

Crumble bread into a bowl and add milk. Set aside to soak. Scoop the cod roe out of its skin, and break it down with a wooden spoon. Squeeze the bread dry in a sieve. Add onion and bread to cod roe, and mix well. Add oil and lemon juice very gradually, alternating between the two. Beat until smooth and creamy. Add pepper to taste, and salt if necessary. Cook pasta shells in lots of boiling salted water for 10 minutes or until *al dente*. Rinse in hot water, and drain well. Sprinkle over lemon juice; toss together with taramasalata, and garnish with caviar and black olives. Serve immediately. Serves 4 as a starter.

Bean Soup

PREPARATION TIME: 15 minutes
COOKING TIME: 1 hour 45 minutes

430g (15oz) can kidney beans
60g (2oz) bacon, rind removed, and chopped
1 stick celery, chopped
1 small onion, peeled and chopped
1 clove garlic, crushed
90g (3oz) can plum tomatoes, chopped and seeds removed
1 litre (2 pints) water
1 chicken stock cube
1 tbsp chopped parsley
1 tsp basil
115g (4oz) wholemeal ring pasta
Salt and pepper

Place kidney beans, bacon, celery, onion, garlic, parsley, basil, tomatoes and water in a large pan. Bring to the boil and add stock cube and salt and pepper to taste. Cover and cook over a low heat for about 1½ hours. Raise heat and add pasta, stirring well. Stir frequently until pasta is cooked but still firm – about 10 minutes. Serve immediately.

Tagliatelle with Smoked Salmon and Caviar (top left), Shell Pasta with Taramasalata (left). Top picture: Bean Soup (top) and Tomato Soup (bottom).

Meat and Egg Starters

Cold Roast Beef and Horseradish Cream

PREPARATION TIME: 20 minutes

SERVES: 4 people

8 slices medium-rare roast beef
150ml (¼ pint) double cream
1 tbsp fresh grated horseradish
5ml (1 tsp) lemon juice
1 tsp sugar
Pinch of salt and pepper

Garnish
Lettuce
Spring onion flowers (trim and slice lengthways, keep one end intact, and leave in cold water in refrigerator until curling)
Cucumber

Whip cream and salt together until stiff. Add horseradish, sugar and lemon juice. Check seasoning, and add more salt and pepper if desired. Place one-eighth of each mixture at end of each slice of beef. Roll up in a cornet shape and serve on a bed of lettuce. Garnish with spring onion flowers and sliced cucumber.

Stuffed Eggs

PREPARATION TIME: 20 minutes

COOKING TIME: 15 minutes

SERVES: 4 people

6 medium eggs
15ml (1 tbsp) vinegar
1 small can of pink salmon
Paprika
30g (1oz) peas
30g (1oz) mushrooms
225g (8oz) cream cheese
Salt
Pepper

Garnish
Stuffed olive
Red pepper or tomato
Black olive

This page: Stuffed Eggs.

Facing page: Chicken Tongue Rolls (top) and Cold Roast Beef and Horseradish Cream (bottom).

Put eggs into a saucepan of gently boiling water with 15ml (1 tbsp) of vinegar and boil gently for 12 minutes. Rinse immediately in cold water. Remove shells carefully and keep eggs in cold water until ready to use. Cut boiled eggs in half and carefully remove yolks. Rinse whites. Push yolks through a sieve and put aside for fillings. Soften cream cheese by beating. Drain and flake salmon. Mix carefully with one-third of cream cheese. Add a pinch of paprika and salt and pepper to taste. Pipe or spoon filling into 4 egg whites. Garnish with half a stuffed olive.
Wash and trim mushrooms. Chop very finely and add to one-third of cream cheese. Add salt or pepper to taste. Pipe or spoon filling into 4 egg whites. Garnish with red pepper or tomato.
Cook peas until tender. Push through a sieve. Add yolk of eggs and one-third of cream cheese. Pipe or spoon filling into remaining 4 egg whites and garnish with a slice of black olive.

Chicken Tongue Rolls

PREPARATION TIME: 15 minutes

COOKING TIME: 20 minutes

SERVES: 4 people

4 chicken legs
1 small can of tongue, sliced, or 4 slices of tongue
2 tbsps grated Parmesan cheese
1 tbsp grated Gruyère or Cheddar cheese
1 tbsp chopped parsley
15ml (1 tbsp) oil
Salt
Pepper

Garnish
Parsley
Tomato

Remove bone carefully from chicken leg, keeping meat in one piece. Flatten out, and divide the tongue equally between each piece. Mix together grated cheeses, parsley and salt and pepper to taste. Place a tbsp of the mixture on each piece of chicken. Roll up chicken and tie each with string, 2 or 3 times. Heat oil in pan and fry chicken rolls gently for about 20 minutes, turning occasionally to cook evenly. Remove from heat and allow to cool. Cut off string and remove gently. Slice into rounds and serve garnished with parsley and tomato.

Egg Flower

PREPARATION TIME: 20 minutes

COOKING TIME: 15 minutes

SERVES: 4 people

6 eggs
15ml (1 tbsp) vinegar
3 tbsps mayonnaise
15ml (1 tbsp) single cream
5ml (1 tsp) lemon juice (or to taste)
Salt
White pepper

Garnish
Watercress
Pinch of paprika

Fill a saucepan with water and 15ml (1 tbsp) of vinegar and bring to the boil. Reduce heat and simmer. Gently add eggs and cook for 12 minutes. Rinse under cold water to stop cooking. Crack and peel off shells and set eggs aside in a bowl of cold water. Mix together mayonnaise, cream, lemon juice and salt and white pepper to taste. Cut 4 eggs in half. Place yolk-side down in a circle on a serving dish. Cut remaining eggs in half and separate yolks from whites. Rinse whites and cut into shreds. Push yolks through a sieve and set aside. Pour mayonnaise over eggs on serving dish. Sprinkle egg white around outside. Sprinkle yolk on top towards the centre. Sprinkle with paprika. Finally garnish with a bunch of watercress in the centre.

Eggs baked in Tarragon Cream

PREPARATION TIME: 5 minutes

COOKING TIME: 8 minutes

OVEN TEMPERATURE:
180°C, 350°F, Gas Mark 4

SERVES: 4 people

4 large eggs
Nut of butter
60ml (4 tbsps) cream
1 tbsp chopped tarragon
Salt
Pepper

Butter individual oven-proof ramekin dishes. Break an egg into each dish. Add chopped tarragon, and salt and pepper to cream and mix well. Add 15ml (1 tbsp) of cream mixture to each ramekin. Place ramekins on a baking sheet in a pre-heated oven until set, about 6-8 minutes. Serve hot.

Eggs baked in Tarragon Cream (left) and Egg Flower (below).

Fish Terrines and Pâtés

Smoked Trout Pâté

PREPARATION TIME: 20 minutes

SERVES: 4 people

4 lemons
2 fillets or 1 whole smoked trout
85g (3oz) butter
225 (8oz) cream cheese
Lemon juice
Tabasco
Ground nutmeg
Salt
Pepper

Garnish
Fresh bay leaves

Cut lemons in half and trim the ends so the shells sit upright. Scoop out the lemon flesh completely. Remove skin and bones from trout. Put fish into a food processor with the butter, cream cheese, seasoning, lemon juice, nutmeg and Tabasco. Work until smooth. Put the pâté into a piping bag fitted with a rose nozzle and pipe into the lemon shells. Garnish each with a bay leaf. Serve with hot toast.

Pâté of Salmon and Scallops

PREPARATION TIME: 30 minutes

COOKING TIME: 1 hour

OVEN TEMPERATURE: 180°C, 350°F, Gas Mark 4

SERVES: 4 people

340g (12oz) salmon
450g (1lb) haddock
5 scallops with roe attached
240ml (8oz) double cream
3 eggs
1 tbsp chopped parsley
1 tbsp chopped fresh tarragon
1 tbsp lemon juice
1 tbsp dry white wine
175g (6oz) unsalted butter
Salt
Pepper
Pinch Cayenne pepper

Separate eggs and set aside yolks. Remove skin and bone from haddock and salmon. Put salmon into a food processor bowl with half the egg whites and half the double cream. Season and process until smooth. Put into separate bowl, and repeat the process with the haddock. Lightly butter a 1kg (2lb) loaf tin. Put half of haddock mixture into the bottom of the tin and smooth out. Cover with half of the salmon mixture. Clean scallops and separate roe from white part. Cut white part in half through the middle. Chop roe roughly and put it down the centre of the salmon mixture. Place the rounds of white scallops on either side of the roe. Put another layer of salmon mixture over, and then the

This page: Pâté of Salmon and Scallops (top) and Smoked Mackerel Mousse (bottom). Facing page: Smoked Trout Pâté (top) and Crabmeat Mousse (bottom).

remaining haddock mixture on top and smooth out. Cover well with double thickness of buttered foil. Put into a roasting tin and fill it halfway up with hand-hot water. Bake pâté in oven for about 1 hour. Meanwhile, prepare a quick Bernaise sauce. Put reserved egg yolks into a food processor bowl or liquidiser. Chop herbs roughly and add to egg yolks along with Cayenne pepper, pinch of salt, lemon juice and white wine. Process until mixed thoroughly and the herbs are chopped. Melt butter and, when foaming, turn on machine and pour the melted butter through feed tube very gradually. This will cook the egg yolks and the sauce will thicken. Keep warm in a double boiler. When pâté has finished cooking, allow to cool slightly in the tin. Gently turn fish pâté out and cut into 2cm (1") thick slices. Arrange on serving plates and pour over some of the Bernaise sauce. Serve the rest of the sauce separately.

Smoked Salmon Mousse

PREPARATION TIME: 20 minutes

COOKING TIME: 5 minutes

SERVES: 4 people

340g (12oz) smoked salmon
600ml (1 pint) prepared mayonnaise
15g (½oz) powdered gelatine
Lemon juice
60g (2oz) double cream
15g (½oz) flour
15g (½oz) butter
180g (6 fl oz) milk
1 egg white
1 small cucumber
1 jar red caviar
1 bunch watercress
1 small head iceberg lettuce
Salt and pepper

Lightly oil ramekin dishes or small individual moulds. Mix lemon juice with enough water to make 3 tbsps, and dissolve gelatine in the liquid. Warm gelatine through gently to melt. Prepare sauce by melting butter and, when foaming, adding flour. Stir together well and blend in the milk gradually. Put back on the heat and bring to the boil to thicken. Allow to cool slightly. Chop the smoked salmon roughly and put into a food processor bowl with half the prepared mayonnaise. Add seasonings and prepared sauce. Process until smooth and, with machine still running, pour in the melted gelatine. Pour in cream and process briefly. Set mixture over ice or in a cool place until thickening. When thickened, whisk egg white until stiff but not dry, and fold into salmon mousse mixture. Put mixture into individual moulds and chill until firm. Meanwhile, prepare green mayonnaise. Pick over the watercress leaves, wash them well, remove thick stalks and the root ends. Chop roughly and put into food processor bowl. Add remaining prepared mayonnaise, seasonings and lemon juice to taste, and process until well blended and a good green colour. Spread mayonnaise onto individual serving plates. When mousse is chilled and set, turn out on top of green mayonnaise. Garnish the plate with shredded lettuce. Garnish the top of each mousse with a thin slice of cucumber and a little red caviar.

Crabmeat Mousse

PREPARATION TIME: 30 minutes

SERVES: 4 people

450g (1lb) crabmeat, cooked and flaked
60g (2oz) prepared mayonnaise
300ml (½ pint) double cream
60ml (2 fl oz) sherry
2 egg whites
2 tsps Dijon mustard
1 small bunch chives
15g (½oz) commercial aspic powder
Juice of 1 lime or lemon
1 ripe avocado
15g (½oz) powdered gelatine
Salt and pepper

Dissolve gelatine in some of the lemon or lime juice. Warm gently to dissolve, and mix with mayonnaise, mustard, and salt and pepper to taste. Lightly whip the cream and fold into mayonnaise mixture along with crabmeat. Put over ice or in a cool place until thickened, then whisk the egg whites until stiff but not dry, and fold into mixture. Quickly pour into a glass bowl or soufflé dish, smooth the top and chill until set. Meanwhile, bring 240ml (8 fl oz) water to boil. Stir in sherry, add 15g (½oz) commercial aspic powder and stir until dissolved. Allow to cool slightly. Chop chives and add to aspic. When mousse mixture is set, chill aspic until it begins to thicken slightly. Pour about 0.5cm (¼") of the aspic over the top of the set mousse, and return to refrigerator to set the aspic. Cut avocado in half lengthways and remove stone. Peel carefully and cut each half into thin slices. Brush with lemon juice and arrange slices on top of set aspic. Spoon over some of the aspic to set the avocado slices, and chill. When avocado is set, pour remaining aspic over to fill to the top of dish, and chill until set.

Smoked Mackerel Mousse

PREPARATION TIME: 20 minutes

SERVES: 4 people

6 small or 3 large smoked mackerel fillets
180ml (6oz) double cream
150ml (¼ pint) prepared mayonnaise
1 tbsp brandy
1 tbsp grated horseradish
½ clove garlic
1 shallot, finely chopped
15g (½oz) powdered gelatine
Salt
Pepper
Lemon juice
Vegetable oil

Garnish
Sliced cucumbers
Sliced lemon
Chives

Skin mackerel fillets and remove any bones. Mix lemon juice with water to make 3 tbsps. Dissolve gelatine in this liquid, and heat gently to melt gelatine. Put fillets into food processor with brandy, mayonnaise, salt, pepper, garlic, and finely chopped shallot. Work until smooth, then, with the machine running, pour the liquid gelatine through feed tube to blend. Put mixture over ice or in a cool place until it begins to thicken. Lightly whip cream and fold into thickened mousse mixture. Lightly oil a mould with vegetable oil. Pour in the mousse mixture. Smooth down and tap to remove any air bubbles. Chill overnight, or until set. Turn out onto a serving plate and surround with a garnish of thinly sliced cucumbers, and thinly sliced lemons. Chives may be used to decorate the mould if desired.

Tricolour Terrine

PREPARATION TIME: 25 minutes

COOKING TIME: 15 minutes

SERVES: 4 people

115g (4oz) smoked haddock
115g (4oz) fresh haddock
1 double kipper fillet
150ml (¼ pint) prepared mayonnaise
25g (¾oz) flour
25g (¾oz) butter
300ml (½ pint) milk
1 tbsp chopped parsley
3 tbsps double cream
15g (½oz) gelatine
1 egg white
Juice of 1 lemon
150ml (¼ pint) sour cream
1 tbsp grated horseradish
1 bunch dill, reserving 4 small sprigs
Iceberg lettuce
Watercress

Poach smoked haddock in water and half the milk to cover for 10 minutes. Skin and remove any bones. Cook fresh haddock separately, using fresh water and the remaining milk. Skin kipper fillet. Mash the fish well, or work in a food processor, keeping each fish separate. Prepare the sauce by melting the butter, adding flour off the heat. Stir in the cooking liquid from the fish and put the sauce back onto the heat. Stir until boiling, then season well. Soak gelatine in 1 tbsp lemon juice plus enough water to make 3 tbsps. Melt over gentle heat until dissolved. Whip cream lightly until it just holds its shape. Put haddock, smoked haddock and kipper in separate bowls. Divide sauce, gelatine and mayonnaise equally

Smoked Salmon Mousse (right) and Tricolour Terrine (bottom).

between each bowl. Mix together well and fold in the double cream, similarly divided. Lightly oil a 450g (1lb) loaf tin. Set the mixtures in a cool place until thickening and, when starting to thicken, whip the egg white. Divide that equally into the fish mixtures. Put smoked haddock mixture into the bottom of a 450g (1lb) loaf tin and smooth out. Spoon the fresh haddock over the smoked haddock mixture and spread out on top. Spoon kipper mixture on top of that, and level out. Chill in the refrigerator until well set. Mix sour cream, horseradish, chopped dill, chopped parsley, and lemon together for the sauce, and season well. When the tureen is set, turn out of the tin and slice into 1.5cm (¾″) thick slices. Place on a serving plate with a garnish of lettuce, watercress and reserved dill, and a spoonful of the horseradish sauce. Serve the rest of the horseradish sauce separately.

Crêpes and Pastries

Chicken Vol-au-Vents

PREPARATION TIME: 30 minutes
COOKING TIME: 30 minutes
OVEN TEMPERATURE: 210°C, 425°F, Gas Mark 7
SERVES: 4 people

225g (8oz) frozen puff pastry, thawed
1 egg, beaten

Filling
60g (2oz) butter or margarine
45g (1½oz) flour
300ml (½ pint) milk
Salt
Pepper
4 chicken breasts, cooked and shredded
1 tbsp chopped parsley
6 peppercorns
2 parsley stalks
Slice of onion
Half a bay leaf

On a lightly floured board roll out pastry to about 1cm (¼″) thick. Using a 7.5cm (3″) fluted pastry-cutter, cut out pastry. With a 5cm (2″) fluted pastry-cutter mark centre of each, being careful not to cut right through. Brush with beaten egg, being careful not to get any down sides or in groove made by 5cm (2″) cutter, as this will prevent rising. Place on a dampened baking tray and chill in refrigerator for 15 minutes. Make pattern on outer edge with back of knife if desired. Bake in a hot oven until golden brown. Remove from oven and gently prise off centre cap. Remove any soft pastry from inside. Return to oven for 1 minute to dry out. To help prevent pastry from toppling over, 4 cocktail sticks may be placed at equal intervals around outside circle and removed after cooking. Heat milk with peppercorns, parsley stalks, onion and ½ bay leaf until just simmering. Remove from heat, cover and leave to cool for 7 minutes. Strain. Melt butter in pan; stir in flour and cook for 1 minute. Remove from heat and gradually stir in infused milk. Return to heat, bring to the boil and cook for 3 minutes, stirring continuously. Add salt and pepper to taste. Stir in shredded chicken and parsley. Fill vol-au-vent cases with hot chicken filling. Place lids on top at an angle. Serve hot.

Prawn Vol-au-Vents

PREPARATION TIME: 30 minutes
COOKING TIME: 30 minutes
OVEN TEMPERATURE: 210°C, 425°F, Gas Mark 7
SERVES: 4 people

225g (8oz) frozen puff pastry, thawed
1 egg, beaten

Filling
60g (2oz) butter or margarine
45g (1½oz) flour
300ml (½ pint) chicken stock
Salt
Pepper
225g (8oz) prawns or shrimps, shelled and de-veined
15ml (1 tbsp) tarragon vinegar or lemon juice
1 tsp tomato purée
Pinch of sugar

On a lightly floured board, roll out pastry to about 1cm (¼″) thick. Using a 7.5cm (3″) fluted pastry-cutter, cut out pastry. With a 5cm (2″) fluted pastry-cutter mark the centre of each, being careful not to cut right through. Brush with beaten egg, being careful not to get any down sides or in groove made

Roquefort Tartlets (top) and Cheese Puffs (bottom).

Facing page: Chicken Vol-au-Vents (top) and Prawn Vol-au-Vents (bottom).

by 5cm (2″) cutter, as this will prevent rising. Place on a dampened baking tray and chill in refrigerator for 15 minutes. Make pattern on outer circle with back of knife if desired. Bake in a hot oven until golden brown. Remove from oven and gently prise off centre cap. Remove any soft pastry from inside and return to oven for 1 minute to dry out. To help prevent pastry from toppling over, 4 cocktail sticks may be placed at equal intervals around outside circle, and removed after cooking. Melt butter in pan. Stir in flour and cook for 1 minute. Remove from heat and gradually stir in chicken stock. Return to heat, bring to the boil, and cook for 3 minutes, stirring continuously. Stir in prawns, tomato purée, tarragon vinegar or lemon juice, sugar and salt and pepper to taste. Simmer for a further 3 minutes. Fill vol-au-vents with hot prawn filling. Place lids on top at an angle. Serve hot.

Mushroom Vol-au-Vents

PREPARATION TIME: 30 minutes

COOKING TIME: 20 minutes

OVEN TEMPERATURE: 210°C, 425°F, Gas Mark 7

SERVES: 4 people

225g (8oz) frozen puff pastry, thawed
1 egg, beaten

Filling
60g (2oz) butter or margarine
45g (1½oz) flour
300ml (½ pint) chicken stock
Salt
Pepper
225g (8oz) cup or flat mushrooms
1 onion, peeled and chopped finely
30ml (2 tbsps) cream
1 tsp chopped parsley

Garnish
Chopped parsley

On a lightly floured board roll out pastry to about 1cm (¼″) thick. Using a 7.5cm (3″) fluted pastry-cutter, cut out pastry. With a 5cm (2″) fluted pastry-cutter mark centre of each, being careful not to cut right through. Brush with beaten egg, being careful not to get any down sides or in groove made by 5cm (2″) cutter, as this will prevent rising. Place on a dampened baking tray and chill in refrigerator for 15 minutes. Make pattern on outer circle with back of knife if desired. Bake in a hot oven until golden brown. Remove from oven and gently prise off centre cap. Remove any soft pastry from inside, and return to oven for 1 minute to dry out. To help prevent pastry from toppling over, 4 cocktail sticks may be placed at equal intervals around outside circle and removed after cooking. Wash mushrooms. Chop half of them very finely, the remainder roughly. Melt butter in pan. Add roughly-chopped mushrooms and cook for 3 minutes. Remove with slotted spoon and set aside. Add onion to pan and, after a minute, finely chopped mushrooms. Cook for 4 minutes. Stir in flour and cook for 1 minute. Remove from heat and gradually stir in chicken stock. Return to heat, bring to the boil and cook for 3 minutes, stirring continuously. Add cream, rough-chopped mushrooms, parsley and salt and pepper and simmer for 1 minute. Fill vol-au-vents with hot mushroom filling. Sprinkle with parsley and place lids on top at an angle. Serve hot.

Quiche Lorraine

PREPARATION TIME: 30 minutes

COOKING TIME: 45 minutes

OVEN TEMPERATURE: 190°C, 375°F, Gas Mark 5

SERVES: 6 people

Pastry
175g (6oz) plain flour
Pinch of salt
90g (3oz) butter or margarine
30g (1oz) lard
Cold water

Filling
15g (½oz) butter or margarine
2 eggs, beaten
30g (1oz) Gruyère or Cheddar cheese, grated
150ml (¼ pint) single cream
10 spring onions, cut into 5cm (2″) slices
½ tsp dried mustard
60g (2oz) streaky bacon, diced
Salt
Pepper

Sift flour and salt into a bowl. Cut cold fat into small pieces and drop into flour. With 2 round-ended knives cut fat into flour. When well cut in, use fingers to rub in completely. Mix to a firm but pliable dough with cold water. Knead on a lightly floured board until smooth. Chill for 15 minutes in the refrigerator. Roll out on a lightly floured board and line a 24cm (9½″) flan ring. Melt butter in frying pan and add bacon and spring onions, and fry gently until turning a light golden-brown colour. Place in a bowl. Add beaten eggs, cheese, cream, mustard and salt and pepper to taste, and stir well. Pour into prepared pastry case. Bake in oven for 20-25 minutes until golden brown. Serve hot or cold.

Cheese Puffs

PREPARATION TIME: 20 minutes

COOKING TIME: 20 minutes

OVEN TEMPERATURES:
190°C, 375°F, Gas Mark 5
200°C, 400°F, Gas Mark 6

SERVES: 4 people

Pastry
115g (4oz) plain flour
Pinch of salt
90g (3oz) butter or margarine
225ml (8 fl oz) water
3 medium eggs, lightly beaten

Filling
75g (2½ oz) Gruyère cheese, grated
75g (2½ oz) Emmenthal cheese, grated
1 egg, beaten
10ml (2 tsps) kirsch
1 egg yolk, beaten, for glaze

Pre-set oven to 190°C or equivalent. Sift flour and salt onto a sheet of greaseproof paper. Place butter and water in pan over gentle heat. When butter has melted, bring to boil and straightaway add all flour. Beat well until mixture is smooth. Leave to cool. Add eggs gradually to mixture, beating well. Using a teaspoon or a piping bag with a plain nozzle, shape mixture into balls about the size of golf balls onto a lightly greased baking tray. Place in oven and increase heat to 200°C or equivalent. Bake for 10 minutes until firm on outside. Remove from oven and make a hole in bottom or side. Mix together cheese, egg and kirsch. Pipe in cheese mixture and brush tops with egg-yolk. Return to oven for 5 minutes. Serve immediately.

Roquefort Tartlets

PREPARATION TIME: 30 minutes

COOKING TIME: 20 minutes

OVEN TEMPERATURE:
190°C, 375°F, Gas Mark 5

SERVES: 4 people

Pastry
175g (6oz) plain flour
Pinch of salt
90g (3oz) butter or margarine
30g (1oz) lard
Cold water

Filling
115g (4oz) Roquefort cheese
115g (4oz) cream cheese
30ml (2 tbsps) single cream
2 eggs, lightly beaten

Sift salt and flour into a bowl. Cut cold fat into small pieces and drop into flour. With 2 round-ended knives cut fat into flour. When well cut in, use fingers to rub in completely. Mix to a firm but pliable dough with cold water. Knead on a lightly floured board until smooth. Chill for 15 minutes in the refrigerator. Meanwhile, gently melt together Roquefort cheese and cream cheese in a pan, stirring continuously. When melted, set aside to cool. Mix together cream and beaten eggs, and add to cheese mixture, stirring well. Roll out dough on a lightly floured board. Using a 7.5cm (3″) fluted pastry-cutter, cut out rounds of pastry. Line a patty tin. Prick bottom of pastry cases with a fork. Spoon mixture into individual pastry cases and bake in the oven for about 15 minutes until golden brown.

Chicken and Ham Crêpes

PREPARATION TIME: 5 minutes

COOKING TIME: 30 minutes

OVEN TEMPERATURE: 200°C, 400°F, Gas Mark 6

SERVES: 4-6 people

Crêpe Batter
115g (4oz) plain flour
Pinch of salt
2 medium eggs
300ml (½ pint) milk
15ml (1 tbsp) olive oil or vegetable oil
Oil to grease pan

Filling
2 chicken breasts, cooked and shredded
2 slices ham, shredded
1 tsp French mustard
2 tbsps grated Cheddar or Gruyère cheese
60g (2oz) butter or margarine
45g (1½oz) flour
300ml (½ pint) milk
Salt
Pepper

Garnish
Parsley

Sift flour and salt into a bowl. Make a well in the centre and drop in eggs. Start to mix in eggs gradually, taking in flour around edges. When becoming stiff, add a little milk until all flour has been incorporated. Beat to a smooth batter, then add remaining milk. Stir in oil. Cover bowl, and leave in a cool place for 30 minutes. Heat small frying pan, or 19cm (7″) crêpe pan. Wipe over with oil. When hot, add enough batter mixture to cover base of pan when rolled. Pour off any excess batter. When brown on underside, loosen and turn over with a palette-knife, and brown on other side. Pile on a plate and cover with a clean tea-towel until needed. Melt butter in pan. Stir in flour and cook for 1 minute. Remove from heat and gradually stir in milk. Return to heat, bring to the boil, and cook for 3 minutes, stirring continuously. Add cheese, chicken, ham and French mustard, and salt and pepper and stir until heated through. Do not re-boil. Divide the mixture evenly between the pancakes and roll up or fold into triangles. Place in a baking dish and cover with aluminium foil. Heat in a hot oven for 10 minutes. Garnish with parsley. Serve immediately.

Mushroom Vol-au-Vents (left) and Quiche Lorraine (bottom).

Seafood Crêpes

PREPARATION TIME: 45 minutes

COOKING TIME: 20 minutes

OVEN TEMPERATURE: 200°C, 400°F, Gas Mark 6

SERVES: 4-6 people

Crêpe Batter

115g (4oz) plain flour
Pinch of salt
2 medium eggs
300ml (½ pint) milk
15ml (1 tbsp) olive oil or vegetable oil
Oil to grease pan

Filling

115g (4oz) prawns or shrimps, peeled and de-veined
2 scallops, cleaned and sliced
115g (4oz) white fish fillets
Squeeze of lemon juice
15ml (1 tbsp) lemon juice
8 spring onions, sliced

60g (2oz) butter or margarine
45g (1½oz) flour
300ml (½ pint) milk
Salt
Pepper

Sift flour and salt into a bowl. Make a well in the centre and drop in eggs. Start to mix in eggs gradually, taking in flour around edges. When becoming stiff, add a little milk until all flour has been incorporated. Beat to a smooth batter, then add remaining milk. Stir in oil. Cover bowl and leave in a cool place for 30 minutes. Heat small frying pan or 19cm (7″) crêpe pan. Wipe over with oil. When hot, add enough batter mixture to cover base of pan when rolled. Pour off any excess batter. When brown on underside, loosen and turn over with a palette-knife and brown on other side. Pile on a plate and cover with a clean tea-towel until needed. Poach scallops and fish in water with a squeeze of lemon juice for 4 minutes or until cooked through. Melt butter in pan. Add spring onions and cook for 3 minutes. Remove with slotted spoon and set aside. Stir in the flour and cook for 1 minute. Remove from heat and gradually stir in milk. Return to heat, bring to the boil, and cook for 3 minutes, stirring continuously. Add spring onions, seafood and lemon juice, and salt and pepper and stir well until heated through. Do not re-boil. Divide the mixture evenly between the pancakes and roll up or fold into triangles. Place in a baking dish and cover with aluminium foil. Heat in a hot oven for 10 minutes. Serve immediately.

This page: Egg and Fish Flan.

Facing page: Chicken and Ham Crêpes (top) and Seafood Crêpes (bottom).

Egg and Fish Flan

PREPARATION TIME: 30 minutes
COOKING TIME: 45 minutes
OVEN TEMPERATURE: 190°C, 375°F, Gas Mark 5
SERVES: 6 people

Pastry
175g (6oz) plain flour
Pinch of salt
90g (3oz) butter or margarine
30g (1oz) lard
Cold water

Filling
2 eggs, beaten
225g (8oz) white fish fillets
45g (1½oz) can anchovy fillets, drained
10 black olives, halved and pips removed
30ml (2 tbsps) single cream
15ml (1 tbsp) lemon juice
1 bay leaf
6 peppercorns
Parsley stalks
Slice of onion
300ml (½ pint) cold water
1 onion peeled and chopped
60g (2oz) butter
45g (1½oz) flour
Salt
Pepper

Poach fish in 300ml (½ pint) water, with lemon juice, peppercorns, bay leaf, slice of onion and parsley stalks, for 10 minutes or until just cooked. Remove from poaching liquid. Strain, reserving liquid, and cool. Melt butter in pan. Add onion and fry gently until softened. Stir in flour and cook for 1 minute. Draw off heat and gradually stir in reserved liquid, stirring continuously. Add salt and pepper to taste. Return to heat and cook for 3 minutes. Set aside to cool. Sift salt and flour into a bowl. Cut cold fat into small pieces and drop into flour. With 2 round-ended knives, cut fat into flour. When well cut in, use fingers to rub in completely. Mix to a firm but pliable dough with cold water. Knead on a lightly floured board until smooth. Chill for 15 minutes in the refrigerator. Roll out on a lightly floured board and line a 24cm (9½") flan ring. Flake fish and place in bottom of prepared pastry case. Stir cream into lightly beaten egg. Add mixture to sauce gradually, and pour over fish. Arrange anchovy fillets in a lattice over top, with a piece of olive in the centre of each diamond. Bake in oven for 20-25 minutes until golden brown. Serve hot or cold.

Section 2

FISH AND SEAFOOD

Fish Soups and Starters

Chilled Prawn, Avocado and Cucumber Soup

PREPARATION TIME: 15 minutes
COOKING TIME: 15 minutes
SERVES: 4 people

225g (8oz) unpeeled prawns
1 large ripe avocado
1 small cucumber
1 small bunch dill
Juice of half a lemon
300ml (½ pint) chicken stock
600ml (1 pint) plain yogurt
Salt and pepper

Peel all prawns, reserving shells. Add shells to chicken stock and bring to boil. Allow to simmer for about 15 minutes. Cool and strain. Peel avocado and cut it into pieces. Cut 8 thin slices from the cucumber and peel the rest. Remove seeds and chop the cucumber roughly. Put avocado and cucumber into a food processor or liquidiser and process until smooth. Add a squeeze of lemon juice, and strain on the cold chicken stock. Reserve a sprig of dill for garnish, and add the rest to the mixture in the processor and blend again. Add about 450ml (¾ pint) of yogurt to the processor and blend until smooth. Add salt and pepper. Stir in peeled prawns by hand, reserving a few as garnish. Chill soup well. Serve in individual bowls, garnished with a spoonful of yogurt, a sprig of dill, and thinly sliced rounds of cucumber.

Matelote

PREPARATION TIME: 20 minutes
COOKING TIME: 20 minutes
SERVES: 4 people

450g (1lb) brill or lemon sole
450g (1lb) monkfish
1 small wing of skate
1 litre (2 pints) mussels
225g (8oz) unpeeled prawns
3 onions
85g (3oz) butter
450ml (¾ pint) dry cider or white wine
30g (1oz) flour
2 tbsps chopped parsley
Salt
Freshly ground black pepper
Lemon juice

Fillet and skin brill or lemon sole. Cut fillets into large pieces. Cut monkfish similarly. Chop wing of skate into 4 large pieces. Peel prawns and set aside. Scrub mussels well, discarding any with broken shells. Chop onion finely and soften in half the butter. Add mussels and about 3-4 tbsps water. Cover the pan and shake over a high heat until all mussels have opened, discarding any that have not. Strain liquid into a bowl, allow mussels to cool, then shell them. Put cooking liquid back into pan. Add wine or cider, and the pieces of fish so that they are barely covered by the liquid. Simmer gently for about 8 minutes or until fish is just cooked. Mix flour with

This page: Chilled Prawn, Avocado and Cucumber Soup (top) and Matelote (bottom).

Facing page: Devilled Stuffed Crab (top) and Soufflés St Jacques (bottom).

remaining butter to a paste. Remove cooked fish from liquid and put into a serving dish to keep warm. Bring liquid back to boil. Add flour and butter paste, a little

at a time, whisking it in and allowing liquid to boil after each addition, until liquid is thickened. Add parsley, shelled prawns, shelled mussels, a little lemon juice, and seasoning. Heat for a few minutes to warm shellfish through. Pour over fish in serving dish and sprinkle with more chopped parsley if desired.

Devilled Stuffed Crab

PREPARATION TIME: 10-15 minutes

COOKING TIME: 20 minutes

OVEN TEMPERATURE: 190°C, 375°F, Gas Mark 5

SERVES: 4 people

2 cooked crabs
30g (1oz) shelled pistachio nuts
2 hard-boiled eggs
15g (½oz) flour
15g (½oz) butter
300ml (½ pint) milk
1 green pepper
1 medium onion
2 tbsps chilli sauce or hamburger relish
2 tsps white wine vinegar
2 tsps chopped gherkins
1 tsp Dijon mustard
½ tsp Worcestershire sauce
Tabasco
60g (2oz) butter or margarine
4 tbsps brown breadcrumbs
Chopped parsley
Salt
Pepper

Garnish
Lemon wedges
Watercress

Ask your fishmonger to dress the crabs. If you wish to do it yourself, twist off all the legs, separate body from shell, and remove lungs and stomach. Cut body into 3 or 4 pieces with a sharp knife and pick out all the meat. Scrape brown meat from inside shell; crack large claws and remove meat, adding add all this meat to the body meat. Crab shells may be washed and used to bake in. Prepare cream sauce. Melt 15g (½oz) butter in a small saucepan. When foaming, take it off the heat and stir in flour, then the milk, gradually. Mix well. Return to heat and bring to boil, allowing it to thicken. Set aside to cool slightly. Chop egg roughly, and green pepper and onion into small dice. Break up crabmeat roughly. Chop pistachio nuts, and add all other ingredients to the white sauce. Lightly butter the clean shell or individual baking dishes. Fill with crabmeat mixture and top with brown crumbs. Melt 60g (2oz) butter and sprinkle over top of crumbs. Bake for 15 minutes, and brown under grill if necessary. Sprinkle with chopped parsley and garnish with watercress and lemon wedges.

Soufflés St Jacques

PREPARATION TIME: 20 minutes

COOKING TIME: 20 minutes

OVEN TEMPERATURE: 225°C, 450°F, Gas Mark 8

SERVES: 4 people

8 large or 16 small scallops, with roe attached
300ml (½ pint) milk
45g (1½oz) butter
45g (1½oz) flour
45g (1½oz) grated Cheddar cheese
4 eggs
Salt
Pepper
¼ tsp Dijon mustard

Tomato Sauce
350g (14oz) tinned tomatoes
1 small onion, finely chopped
Bay leaf
Pinch of thyme
Sugar
Half a clove of garlic, crushed
1 tbsp Worcestershire sauce
Salt
Pepper

First prepare tomato sauce. Combine onion with rest of the ingredients in a small, heavy saucepan. Bring to the boil, then lower heat, leaving to simmer, half-covered, for 20 minutes. Strain the sauce and set aside. Poach scallops in milk for about 5 minutes. Remove from milk and set aside. Melt butter in a small saucepan, and when foaming remove from heat, and stir in flour. Add milk in which scallops were poached. Bring to the boil, stirring constantly until thickened. Add salt and pepper, then stir in the grated cheese. Leave to cool slightly. Separate eggs, beat the yolks and add them to cheese sauce. Butter 4 deep scallop shells or porcelain baking dishes. Slice scallops through the middle, horizontally. Reserve 1 whole roe per serving. Place scallops in bottom of the shells. Beat egg whites until stiff but not dry, and fold into cheese mixture. Divide soufflé mixture between the scallop shells, and place them on a baking tray. Bake in a hot oven for about 10 minutes or until well risen. Meanwhile, re-heat tomato sauce and spoon some of it, when scallops are ready, into each dish. Serve remaining tomato sauce separately. Garnish each serving with the reserved whole roe.

Garlic Fried Scallops

PREPARATION TIME: 10 minutes

COOKING TIME: 6-8 minutes

SERVES: 4 people

16 scallops
1 large clove garlic, peeled and chopped finely
60-85g (2-3oz) butter
3 tbsps chopped parsley
2 lemons
Seasoned flour

Rinse scallops and remove black veins. If scallops are large, cut in half horizontally. Squeeze the juice from 1 lemon. Sprinkle scallops lightly with seasoned flour. Heat butter in a frying pan and add chopped garlic and scallops. Fry until pale golden brown. Pour over lemon juice, and cook to reduce the amount of liquid. Toss in the chopped parsley. Pile scallops into individual scallop shells or porcelain baking dishes. Keep warm, and garnish with lemon wedges before serving.

Scampi and Avocado Cocktail

PREPARATION TIME: 20 minutes

SERVES: 4 people

225g (8oz) cooked scampi
2 oranges
2 large, ripe avocados
1 small red onion or 2 spring onions
60g (2oz) double or whipping cream
2 tbsps tomato ketchup
2 tbsps mayonnaise
2 tsps lemon juice
12 (approx) black olives, stoned and sliced
2 tsps brandy
Pinch of Cayenne pepper
Pinch sugar
Salt
Freshly ground pepper
Lettuce

Peel oranges over a bowl to reserve juice. Peel cooked scampi and set aside. To prepare dressing, whip cream until thick, and mix with tomato ketchup, mayonnaise, lemon juice, Cayenne, sugar, salt and pepper, brandy and some of the reserved orange juice to let down to the proper consistency – the dressing should be slightly thick. Chop onion finely. Cut avocados in half lengthways and take out stones. Peel them carefully and cut each half into 4-6 long slices. Shred lettuce and put onto serving dishes. Arrange avocado slices in a fan shape on top of the lettuce. Brush each slice lightly with orange juice to keep green. Arrange an orange segment in between each slice. Pile scampi up at the top of the avocado fan and coat with some of the dressing. Garnish with olives and sprinkle over chopped onion.

Quenelles au Beurre Blanc

PREPARATION TIME: 25 minutes

COOKING TIME: 20 minutes

SERVES: 4 people

450g (1lb) pike or other white fish
115g (4oz) white breadcrumbs
4 tbsps milk
85g (3oz) butter
2 eggs
Salt
Pepper
Nutmeg
Cayenne pepper

Beurre Blanc Sauce
115g (4oz) unsalted butter
1 small onion, peeled and chopped finely
1 tbsp white wine vinegar
2 tbsps lemon juice
3 tbsps dry white wine
1 tsp snipped chives
Salt

Vegetable Garnish
1 medium courgette, topped and tailed
1 leek, trimmed, with some green attached
1 carrot, peeled
1 stick celery, washed and trimmed

First prepare quenelle mixture. Skin and bone fish and cut into small pieces. Place in a food processor bowl. Soak the breadcrumbs in milk; drain away most of the liquid, and put into the food processor with the fish. Melt butter and pour into the fish mixture with the machine running. Work mixture to a smooth purée. Add eggs, continuing to mix until smooth. Add seasoning, cayenne pepper and nutmeg. Chill mixture in refrigerator for at least 1 hour, or overnight.
To cook quenelles, fill a saute pan with salted water. Bring to the boil. Reduce heat until water is just

Garlic Fried Scallops (right) and Scampi and Avocado Cocktail (below).

simmering. With two spoons, shape quenelles into little ovals. Poach them in water for about 6 minutes, turning them over about half way through. Remove them with a slotted spoon. Drain and put them in a dish to keep warm in the oven, covered. To prepare beurre blanc sauce, put chopped onion into a small saucepan with the vinegar and wine. Bring to boil and allow to reduce by half. Remove pan from heat, and allow to cool a little. Cut butter into small pieces and add to onion mixture, a little at a time, whisking well to a creamy sauce. After 2-3 pieces have been added, place pan back over low heat and continue whisking until all butter has been added. Season the sauce, add lemon juice, strain, add the snipped chives and serve hot over quenelles.

To prepare garnish, cut all vegetables into 4 cm (2″) lengths, then cut those into thin strips. Bring water in a large saucepan to the boil, with a pinch of salt. Cook carrots for about 5 minutes. Then add celery strips and cook for another 5 minutes. Add courgette and leek, and cook for 3 minutes more. Drain vegetables well, add them to the sauce and pour over the quenelles to serve.

This page: Cucumbers and Prawns (top) and Quenelles au Beurre Blanc (bottom). Facing page: Marinated Smoked Fish (top) and Mussels in Lemon Cream (bottom).

Cucumbers and Prawns

PREPARATION TIME: 20 minutes

SERVES: 4 people

1 large or 2 small cucumbers
225g (8oz) unpeeled prawns
75ml (2½ fl oz) double cream
75ml (2½ fl oz) plain yogurt
½ tsp French mustard
Juice of 1 lemon
1 tbsp chopped parsley
Pinch caster sugar
Large bunch of chervil, chopped, but reserving some whole for garnish
1 head of red chicory
1 head of cos lettuce
Salt and pepper

Peel cucumber and slice in half lengthways. Scoop out seeds and cut each half into thin slices. Sprinkle slices with salt and leave to drain for about 1 hour. Peel prawns, reserving 4 unpeeled for garnish. Whip cream lightly and fold together with yogurt, mustard, 1 tsp of the lemon juice, parsley and chervil. Add seasoning and sugar, and mix the dressing together with the prawns. Wash salt from cucumber, and dry slices well. Divide lettuce and chicory between 4 serving plates and toss cucumber together with the prawns. Peel shells from the tails of the reserved prawns, and set aside. Pile cucumber and prawn mixture onto lettuce leaves and garnish with reserved prawns and whole sprigs of chervil.

Mussels in Lemon Cream

PREPARATION TIME: 10 minutes

COOKING TIME: 10 minutes

SERVES: 4 people

1 litre (2 pints) mussels
Grated rind and juice of 2 lemons
1 shallot, finely chopped
300ml (½ pint) double cream
2 tbsps chopped parsley
Flour or oatmeal
30g (1oz) butter

Scrub mussels well, discarding any with broken shells. Put into a bowl with clean, cold water, and add a handful of flour or oatmeal. Leave for ½ hour, then drain mussels under clean water. Put the butter and finely chopped shallot into a large pan and cook until shallot is soft, but not coloured. Add lemon juice, then mussels. Cover and cook quickly, shaking the pan until mussel shells open. Discard any that do not open. Remove mussels and keep them warm. Strain the liquid and return it to the rinsed-out pan. Add the cream and bring to the boil. Allow to boil for 5 minutes to thicken slightly. Pour over the mussels, and sprinkle grated lemon rind and chopped parsley over.

Marinated Smoked Fish

PREPARATION TIME: 10 minutes, plus 1 hour to marinate

SERVES: 4 people

1 double kipper fillet
115g (4oz) smoked salmon
1 large fillet of smoked mackerel
1 large smoked trout on the bone
120ml (4 fl oz) vegetable oil
Juice of 1 large lemon
1 tbsp white wine vinegar
1 red onion, sliced
Lettuce
Parsley
Salt and pepper

Remove skin from kipper and mackerel, and cut each into 8 pieces. Fillet and skin the trout, and cut each fillet into 4 pieces. Shred the smoked salmon. Put fish into a large, shallow dish. Scatter onion slices on top of the fish. Mix oil, lemon juice and vinegar together. Add salt and pepper, and pour over fish. Leave to marinate for at least 1 hour. Serve on a bed of lettuce with some of the onions from the marinade, and chopped parsley.

Solianka

PREPARATION TIME: 10 minutes

COOKING TIME: 1 hour 10 minutes

SERVES: 4 people

1kg (2lbs) fish bones
675g (1½lbs) salmon or salmon trout
300ml (½ pint) tinned tomatoes
1 litre (2 pints) water
1 onion, roughly chopped
1 stick celery, roughly chopped
1 carrot, roughly chopped
1 small bunch spring onions
4 gherkins
2 tbsps capers
1 tbsp chopped black olives
1 bay leaf
Salt and pepper
150ml (¼ pint) sour cream

Garnish
1 small jar Danish caviar

Cook fishbones in water with the carrot, celery and onion. Add bay leaf, and simmer for about 1 hour. Drain off stock and reserve. Add tomatoes to stock. Chop spring onions, gherkins, olives and capers. Cut salmon into 2cm (1") cubes, add to stock, season and cover. Simmer for 10-12 minutes or until salmon is cooked. Put soup into warm serving dishes and top with sour cream and Danish caviar.

Oyster Bisque

PREPARATION TIME: 10 minutes

COOKING TIME: 27 minutes

SERVES: 4 people

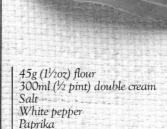

300ml (1 pint) oysters, cleaned and shelled
150ml (¼ pint) dry white wine
Water to make up to 600ml (1 pint) of liquid
30g (1oz) butter
45g (1½oz) flour
300ml (½ pint) double cream
Salt
White pepper
Paprika
Squeeze of lemon juice

Chop oysters roughly, reserving 4 for garnish. Put chopped oysters and their liquid into a medium saucepan with the water and wine. Bring to boil and allow to simmer for 15 minutes. Liquidise and measure the amount of liquid. Reduce, or add water, to make 1 pint. Melt 30g (1oz) butter in a saucepan and when foaming, remove from heat and add flour. Cook flour and butter together for about 1 minute until very pale brown. Add oyster liquid gradually. Stir well, bring back to boil and simmer gently for about 10 minutes. Season with salt, a pinch of paprika and a good pinch of white pepper. Add double cream, return to heat and allow to boil for 1-2 minutes. Add lemon juice, if desired. Cook reserved oysters quickly in a remaining butter. Put soup into warm serving dishes. Top each with 1 oyster and a sprinkling of paprika.

Mussels alla Genovese

PREPARATION TIME: 15 minutes

COOKING TIME: 5-8 minutes

SERVES: 4 people

1 litre (2 pints) mussels
Lemon juice
1 shallot, finely chopped
1 handful fresh basil leaves
1 small bunch parsley
30g (1oz) walnuts halves
1 clove garlic
2 tbsps freshly grated Parmesan cheese
3-6 tbsps olive oil
30g (1oz) butter
Salt and pepper
Flour or oatmeal

Garnish
Fresh bay leaves or basil leaves

Solianka (above), Oyster Bisque (right) and Mussels alla Genovese.

Scrub the mussels well and discard any with broken shells. Put mussels into a bowl of clean water with a handful of flour or oatmeal. Leave for ½ hour, then rinse under clear water. Chop shallot finely and put into a large saucepan with lemon juice. Cook until shallot softens. Add mussels and a pinch of salt and pepper. Cover the pan and cook the mussels quickly, shaking the pan. When mussel shells have opened, take mussels out of the pan, set aside and keep warm. Strain the cooking liquid for possible use later. To prepare Genovese sauce, wash the basil leaves and parsley, peel the garlic clove and chop roughly, and chop the walnuts roughly. Put the herbs, garlic, nuts, 1 tbsp grated cheese and salt and pepper into a food processor and work to chop roughly. Add butter and work again. Turn machine on and add oil gradually through the feed tube. If the sauce is still too thick, add the reserved liquid from cooking the mussels. Remove top shells from mussels and discard. Arrange mussels evenly in 4 shallow dishes, spoon some of the sauce into each, and sprinkle the top lightly with remaining Parmesan cheese. Garnish with bay or basil leaves and serve.

Grilled Oysters

PREPARATION TIME: 10 minutes

COOKING TIME: 2-3 minutes

SERVES: 4 people

2 doz oysters
60g (2oz) butter
300ml (½ pint) double cream
1 small jar red caviar
Salt
Pepper
Tabasco

Garnish
Watercress

Open oysters and leave them in their half-shells (or ask the fishmonger to do it). Put a drop of Tabasco on each oyster, season, then a dessertspoon of double cream. Melt butter and sprinkle it over oysters. Put them under a hot grill for 2-3 minutes. When cooked, top each one with 1 tsp red caviar, and serve hot with bouquets of watercress as garnish.

French Beans, Hazelnuts and Scampi

PREPARATION TIME: 15 minutes

COOKING TIME: 19-21 minutes

OVEN TEMPERATURE: 180°C, 350°F, Gas Mark 4

SERVES: 4 people

450g (1lb) French beans, topped and tailed
330g (12oz) cooked scampi
30g (1oz) whole hazelnuts, shelled
1 red pepper, stem and seeds removed, and sliced thinly
6 tbsps olive oil
3 tbsps white wine vinegar
1 tsp Dijon mustard
1 tbsp chopped parsley
1 small head iceberg lettuce, shredded
Salt
Pepper

Toast hazelnuts in moderate oven for about 15 minutes or until golden brown. Allow to cool. Chop roughly. Bring salted water to the boil in a saucepan, and cook beans in it for about 4-6 minutes – they should remain crisp. Drain, refresh under cold water, drain again and dry. Cook pepper slices in boiling water for about 1 minute. Drain and refresh under cold water, and allow to dry. Whisk oil, vinegar, Dijon mustard and seasonings together. Peel scampi, and mix together with beans, pepper, hazelnuts and dressing. Arrange lettuce on individual serving dishes, and pile remaining ingredients on top. Sprinkle parsley over the top to serve.

This page: Devilled Whitebait (top) and French Beans, Hazelnuts and Scampi (bottom).
Facing page: Grilled Oysters (top) and Crab and Citrus (bottom).

Smoked Salmon Stuffed Cucumbers

PREPARATION TIME: 15 minutes

SERVES: 4 people

115g (4oz) smoked salmon
170g (6oz) curd cheese
1 large cucumber
1 head iceberg lettuce
1 bunch chives
1 bunch dill
150ml (¼ pint) plain yogurt
2 tbsps whipping cream
Squeeze of lemon juice
Salt
Pepper

Garnish
1 tsp red salmon caviar

Peel cucumber and trim off the ends. Cut in half lengthways and scoop out the seeds. Sprinkle the surface with salt and leave on draining paper for 1 hour. Meanwhile, prepare the filling. Work the smoked salmon and the curd cheese in a food processor until smooth. Snip the chives and stir in by hand. Prepare the dressing by mixing the yogurt, whipping cream and finely chopped dill together with salt, pepper and lemon juice to taste. Rinse and dry the cucumber very well. Using a piping bag fitted with a 1.5cm (½") plain nozzle, fill the bag with the smoked salmon mixture and pipe the filling into the hollow left in the cucumber. Put the other half on top, press together firmly, and wrap tightly in clingfilm. Chill in the refrigerator for 1 hour. Separate the lettuce leaves, wash and dry well, and place on individual serving dishes. Unwrap the cucumber and slice into 0.5cm (¼") slices. Place on top of lettuce. Spoon over some of the dressing and top with caviar. Serve the rest of the dressing separately.

Devilled Whitebait

PREPARATION TIME: 10 minutes

COOKING TIME: 5-6 minutes

SERVES: 4 people

450g (1lb) whitebait
Flour
Salt
Pepper
¼ tsp Cayenne pepper
¼ tsp dry mustard powder
1 large pinch ground ginger
Paprika
Oil for deep frying

Garnish
Lemon wedges
Parsley

Pick over, but do not wash, whitebait. Mix flour with salt, pepper, Cayenne, ginger and mustard, and roll whitebait in mixture until lightly coated. Heat oil in deep-fat fryer to 180°C, 350°F. Put small amount of floured whitebait into frying basket, lower into the fat, and fry for 2-3 minutes. Drain on crumpled draining paper. Sprinkle lightly with salt, and continue until all whitebait are fried. Re-heat fat, and add all whitebait. Fry for 1-2 minutes until crisp. Turn out onto hot serving dish. Sprinkle with salt and paprika. Serve at once with lemon wedges and bouquets of parsley.

Crab and Citrus

PREPARATION TIME: 20 minutes

SERVES: 4 people

225g (8oz) crabmeat, or 1 large crab
2 oranges
2 lemons
2 limes
1 pink grapefruit
1 small iceberg lettuce
150ml (¼ pint) plain yogurt
6 tbsps double cream
1 tbsp chilli sauce
½ tbsp brandy
Pinch of Cayenne pepper
Salt
2 tbsps salad oil

Separate body from shell of whole crab, and remove and discard lungs and stomach sac. Chop body into 3 or 4 pieces with a very sharp knife and pick out the meat. Scrape brown meat from inside shell and add to body meat. Break off large claws and remove meat from legs; then crack the claws and remove claw meat. Mix all meat together and reserve legs for garnish. (If using tinned or frozen crabmeat, pick over the meat to remove any bits of shell or cartilage.) Mix together yogurt, chilli sauce, cream, brandy, Cayenne pepper and a pinch of salt, and toss with the crabmeat. Take a thin strip of peel from each of the citrus fruits, scraping off the bitter white pith. Cut each strip of peel into thin slivers. Put into boiling water and allow to boil for about 1 minute. Drain, refresh under cold water, and set aside. Peel each of the citrus fruits and cut into segments; do all this over a bowl to reserve juices. Add 2 tbsps salad oil to the juice in the bowl, and toss with citrus segments. Shred iceberg lettuce and arrange on plates. Put the crabmeat in its dressing on top of lettuce. Arrange citrus segments over and around crabmeat and sprinkle citrus peel over the top.

Lobster à la Creme

PREPARATION TIME: 10 minutes

COOKING TIME: 5 minutes

SERVES: 4 people

1 cold, boiled lobster
300ml (½ pint) double cream
85g (3oz) butter
75ml (2½ fl oz) dry sherry or Madeira
Squeeze of lemon juice
Ground nutmeg
3 tbsps dry breadcrumbs
1 small bunch of tarragon, chopped
Salt and pepper

Cut lobster in half lengthways with a sharp knife. Remove meat from tail. Crack claws and remove meat. Remove as much meat as possible from all the legs. Chop all meat roughly. Melt 60g (2oz) of the butter in a sauté pan and sauté the lobster with the seasonings, lemon juice, nutmeg and tarragon. Flame the sherry or Madeira and pour over the lobster in the sauté pan. Shake the pan until flames die out. Pour over double cream and bring to the boil. Allow to boil for 5 minutes until cream begins to thicken. Spoon into individual serving dishes. Melt remaining butter in a small frying pan and brown the dry breadcrumbs. When golden brown and crisp, sprinkle over the top of lobster.

Prawn and Watercress Bisque

PREPARATION TIME: 20 minutes

COOKING TIME: 25 minutes

SERVES: 4 people

600ml (1 pint) plain yogurt
225g (8oz) potatoes
½ clove garlic
2 bunches watercress
30g (1oz) butter
225g (8oz) cod or other white fish
16 (approx) unpeeled prawns
Milk
Salt
White pepper

Shell all the prawns, and reserve shells. Place cod in a pan with enough water to cover. Bring to boil, reduce heat and allow to simmer for about 5 minutes. Remove fish from pan and peel the skin away. Reserve the liquid. Return cod skin to pan with the shells from the prawns. Cook for a few minutes and leave to cool. Meanwhile, peel and cook potatoes until tender, and mash with a little milk and the butter. Pick over watercress, discarding any yellow leaves and root ends. Reserve small sprigs of leaves for garnish and chop the rest roughly. Reserve 4 tbsps yogurt per serving for garnish. Put remaining yogurt, potatoes, salt, pepper, garlic and watercress into the bowl of a food processor. Add skinned cod and strain in fish liquid, discarding skin and prawn shells. Work until to the consistency of thick cream, using as much milk as necessary. When soup is smooth and desired consistency is reached, put into a clean saucepan and warm gently – do not allow to boil. Put into warm soup bowls or tureen to serve. Garnish with a spoonful of yogurt, peeled prawns and watercress leaves.

Chinese Crabmeat Soup

PREPARATION TIME: 10 minutes

COOKING TIME: 10 minutes

SERVES: 4 people

115g (4oz) crabmeat
Small piece fresh ginger
2 tbsps light soy sauce
900ml (1½ pints) light chicken stock
4 spring onions
1 piece of to-fu or soy bean curd, well drained
2 tsps cornflour
1 tsp sesame seed oil
1 tbsp dry sherry
Salt
Pepper

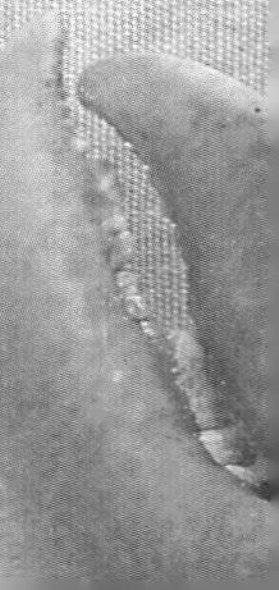

Smoked Salmon Stuffed Cucumbers (below) and Lobster á la Creme (bottom).

Heat oil in medium-sized saucepan, and fry crabmeat for about a minute. Peel and grate ginger, and add it to pan with sherry, salt and pepper and soy sauce. Stir together and add stock, reserving about 2 tbsps to mix with the cornflour. Bring soup to boil. Add a little of the boiling liquid to the cornflour mixture, then add to the soup. Stir until slightly thickened. Slice spring onions on a slant and add to soup. Slice bean curd into 1cm (½″) cubes, add to the soup, and heat through with the sesame seed oil. Serve.

Soupe de Poisson Provençal

PREPARATION TIME: 20 minutes

COOKING TIME: 30-40 minutes

SERVES: 4 people

Soup

1.5kg (3lbs) white fish
225g (8oz) prawns or scampi
1 large onion
2 leeks
1 pint tinned tomatoes
2 cloves garlic
1 bay leaf
1 sprig thyme
1 small piece fennel or 2 parsley stalks
2 pinches saffron
Strip of orange rind
150ml (¼ pint) white wine
30g (1oz) butter
30g (1oz) flour
150ml (¼ pint) olive oil
1.5 litres (3 pints) water
Salt
Pepper
Tomato purée
Single cream

Sauce Rouille

60g (2oz) chopped red pepper or tinned pimento
1 small chilli pepper
3-4 tbsps fresh breadcrumbs
3 cloves garlic
1 egg yolk
150ml (¼ pint) olive oil
Salt
Pepper

Accompaniment

Grated Parmesan cheese
Croûtons

First prepare soup. Chop onion. Clean and chop leeks, and cook them slowly, with the onion, in the olive oil until tender, but not browned. Mash garlic cloves and add to leeks and onion, along with the tinned tomatoes. Bring to the boil and cook for 5 minutes. Meanwhile, skin and bone fish, shell scampi or prawns, and tie the bay leaf, thyme, fennel and orange peel together with a small piece of string. Put the water, wine, the bundle of herbs, the saffron, salt and pepper, fish and shellfish into the pan and cook, uncovered, on a moderate heat for 30-40 minutes. Meanwhile, prepare Sauce Rouille. Cut chilli pepper in half and rinse out seeds. Use half or all, depending on desired hotness. Chop chilli pepper together with sweet red pepper. Peel and chop garlic. Soak breadcrumbs in water and press them dry. Put peppers, breadcrumbs, garlic and egg yolk into a liquidiser with a pinch of salt and pepper and blend to a smooth paste, or work together with mortar and pestle. Gradually add oil in a thin, steady stream. The consistency should be that of mayonnaise. Set aside. When soup is cooked, remove the bundle of herbs. Put contents of soup pan into the food processor and work to a smooth purée. Strain if necessary, correct seasoning, and add some tomato purée for colour, if necessary. Return to saucepan. Mix butter and flour into a paste. Add about 1 tsp of the paste to the soup, whisking it in well, and bring the soup up to the boil. Add more paste as necessary to bring the soup to the consistency of thick cream. Stir in the single cream. Serve soup with the rouille, cheese and croûtons.

This page: Soupe de Poisson Provençal.
Facing page: Chinese Crabmeat Soup (top) and Prawn and Watercress Bisque (bottom).

Cold Dishes and Salads

Salad Niçoise

PREPARATION TIME: 20 minutes
COOKING TIME: 15-20 minutes
SERVES: 4 people

1 tin skipjack tuna
115g (4oz) prawns
1 tin anchovy fillets
4 ripe tomatoes
4 hard-boiled eggs
1 red pepper
85g (3oz) black olives, stoned
115g (4oz) French beans
2 large potatoes, or 6 small new potatoes
2 tbsps white wine vinegar
6 tbsps olive oil
3 tbsps chopped mixed herbs
1 tbsp French mustard
Salt and pepper

Peel and cook potatoes (skins may be left on new potatoes if desired) until tender. If using large old potatoes, cut into 1cm (½″) dice (new potatoes may be sliced into 0.5cm (¼″) rounds. Top and tail beans, put into boiling salted water for about 3-4 minutes or until just barely cooked. Drain and rinse under cold water, then leave to drain dry. Cut the olives in half, lengthways. Cut anchovy fillets in half, lengthways, then through the middle. Cut tomatoes into quarters (or eighths, if large) and remove the cores. Mix the vinegar and oil together for the vinaigrette dressing, and add seasoning, chopped herbs, and a little French mustard if desired. Drain oil from tuna fish. Cut red pepper into thin shreds. Mix together all the ingredients, including the prawns, and toss in the dressing. Quarter the eggs and toss into the other ingredients very carefully – do not break up the eggs. Pile onto dishes and serve.

Spanish Rice and Sole Salad

PREPARATION TIME: 20 minutes
COOKING TIME: 8-10 minutes
OVEN TEMPERATURE: 180°C, 350°F, Gas Mark 4
SERVES: 4 people

2 large lemon soles, filleted
4-6 peppercorns
Slice of onion
Lemon juice
5 tbsps olive oil
175g (6oz) long-grain rice
1 red pepper
1 shallot, finely chopped
1 small aubergine
1 green pepper
2 bunches watercress
300ml (½ pint) prepared mayonnaise
1 clove garlic
1 level tsp tomato purée
1 level tsp paprika
1 tbsp chopped mixed herbs
Salt and pepper

Put sole fillets into a baking dish. Add onion, a squeeze of lemon

This page: Marinated Herring in Sour Cream with Beetroot Salad.
Facing page: Salad Niçoise (top) and Spanish Rice and Sole Salad (bottom).

juice, peppercorns and enough water to cover. Sprinkle with salt, cover with buttered foil, and bake in a moderate oven for about 8-10 minutes. Allow fish to cool in the liquid, then cut into 2cm (1″) pieces. Cook rice in boiling salted water for 12 minutes. Drain under hot water, then cold, and leave to drain completely dry. Chop green and red peppers into 0.5cm (¼″) dice. Cut aubergine in half lengthways, score each half, sprinkle with salt, and leave to sit for about ½ hour. Wash aubergine well, then dry it. Cut it into 1cm (½″) cubes and fry very quickly in 2 tbsps olive oil. Add salt and pepper, and toss with the cooked rice, and red and green pepper. Add a pinch of chopped herbs. Make a vinaigrette dressing with 1 tbsp lemon juice, 3 tbsps olive oil and shallot. Toss with the rice. Crush clove of garlic and work it together with the mayonnaise, tomato purée and paprika. Add salt, pepper and the rest of the chopped herbs. Thin with a little milk or hot water. Adjust seasoning. Arrange rice salad on one side of serving dish, and put sole fillets on the other. Spoon mayonnaise dressing over fillets. Divide the two sides with bunches of watercress.

Mussels à la Grecque (top left) and Fin and Feather (left).

Mussels à la Grecque

PREPARATION TIME: 15 minutes

COOKING TIME: 15 minutes

SERVES: 4 people

2 pints mussels
1 onion, chopped
120ml (4 fl oz) white wine
675g (1½lb) tomatoes (or the equivalent in tinned tomatoes)
1 clove garlic
Lemon juice
Salt and pepper
Pinch Cayenne pepper
1 chopped shallot
1 tsp fennel seed
1 tsp coriander seeds
1 tsp crushed oregano
1 bay leaf
1 tbsp chopped fresh basil leaves
2 tbsps olive oil

Garnish
Chopped parsley
Black olives

Scrub mussels well, discarding any with broken shells. Put into a pan with chopped onion, white wine, squeeze of lemon juice, salt and pepper. Cover and cook quickly until mussels open, discarding any that do not. Remove mussels from shells and leave to cool. Heat olive oil in a saucepan and add crushed garlic and shallot. Cook until just lightly brown. Blend in the tomatoes, herbs, fennel and coriander seeds. Add seasoning and cooking liquid from the mussels and bring to the boil. Allow the sauce to boil rapidly until well reduced. Leave sauce to cool, then mix with mussels. Serve garnished with chopped parsley and black olives. Serve with green salad and French bread.

Fin and Feather

PREPARATION TIME: 20 minutes

COOKING TIME: 15-20 minutes

OVEN TEMPERATURE: 180°C, 350°F, Gas Mark 4

SERVES: 4 people

4 chicken supremes (boned chicken breasts)
85g (3oz) fresh salmon, or tinned red salmon
White wine
4 anchovy fillets
115ml (¼ pint) olive oil
2 egg yolks
Salt and pepper
1½ tbsps lemon juice
1 tbsp chopped parsley

Garnish
4 small gherkins
1 tbsp capers
Curly endive

Ask the butcher to prepare the chicken breasts for you. Put them on a sheet of foil and sprinkle over salt, pepper and a little white wine. Seal foil well. Put into a roasting tin and bake in the oven for about 15 minutes, or until cooked through. Open foil packet and allow to cool. Reserve juices from the chicken. Poach the fresh salmon (or drain tinned salmon) and remove bones. Put the salmon and anchovies into a food processor bowl or liquidiser and work until broken up. Work in the egg yolks, and salt and pepper. With the machine running, add the oil gradually. Add lemon juice to taste and adjust seasoning. Stir in the cooking liquid from the chicken to give the sauce the consistency of thin cream: if it is too thick add a few drops of milk or water. Put cold chicken breasts onto a plate and coat with all the sauce. Before serving, garnish the dish with capers and gherkins. Serve with the green salad or a cold rice salad.

Marinated Herring in Sour Cream with Beetroot Salad

PREPARATION TIME: 20 minutes

COOKING TIME: 30 minutes

SERVES: 4 people

4 fresh herrings

Marinade
300ml (½ pint) dry white wine
4 tbsps white wine vinegar
1 tsp sugar
1 shallot
1 bay leaf
6 black peppercorns
2 sprigs thyme
1 whole clove

Dressing
300ml (½ pint) sour cream or yogurt
½ tsp dry mustard
Salt and pepper

Salad
1tbsp chopped fennel or dillweed
4 spring onions
8 even-sized cooked beetroots
60g (2oz) chopped walnuts
2 tbsps red wine vinegar
6 tbsps vegetable oil
Sugar
Salt
Pepper

Fillet the herring, removing heads and tails. Pick out as many of the bones as possible and separate the two fillets of each herring. Put all ingredients for the marinade into a saucepan, bring to the boil and cook for 20 minutes. Pour marinade over herring in a shallow sauté pan. Bring back to the boil and simmer, covered, for about 10 minutes. Leave fish to cool in marinade, then lift out and remove skin. Put herring into a shallow serving dish. Mix sour cream with 2 tbsps of strained marinade, and add mustard, salt and black pepper. Mix until smooth, and pour over fillets. Scatter over the chopped dill and half of the chopped spring onions. Peel and slice beetroot into rounds about 0.5cm (¼") thick, and marinate in the oil, vinegar and sugar. Sprinkle with chopped walnuts and the remaining spring onions, and arrange around the marinated herring fillets.

Seafood and Shell Salad

PREPARATION TIME: 20 minutes

COOKING TIME: 25 minutes

SERVES: 4 people

450g (1lb) halibut
225g (8oz) prawns
6 giant prawns
¼ pint mussels
1 red pepper
2 tbsps chopped tarragon, or a good pinch of dried tarragon
2 tbsps chopped parsley
4 spring onions
Handful of black olives, pitted
225g (8oz) pasta shells, cooked
100g (4oz) sorrel or fresh spinach
1 bunch watercress
15g (½oz) butter
15g (½oz) flour
300ml (½ pint) single cream, or milk
150ml (¼ pint) double cream
Salt and pepper

Put halibut into a saucepan and just cover with cold water. Bring to the boil and poach gently till the fish is cooked. Remove pan from heat and allow fish to cool in the liquid. When cool, drain fish, remove all skin and bone, and break flesh into large flakes. Set aside. Scrub mussels. Cook them in their shells with 4 tbsps water or lemon juice. Cover the pan and cook them over the heat quickly until the shells open. Discard any mussels that do not open. Take mussels out of shells and set aside. Shell all the prawns. Cook pasta shells until just tender. Rinse under hot, then cold water, and leave to

drain dry. Chop red pepper into small cubes, chop the olives and slice the spring onions. Mix pasta with peppers, olives, tarragon, parsley and salt and pepper. Arrange in a large serving dish or small individual dishes, and pile mixed fish and seafood on top. Chill. Cook sorrel or spinach briefly in boiling water. Drain and refresh under cold water. Squeeze dry and chop to a fine purée. Pick over watercress leaves, removing discoloured leaves and chopping off thick ends of stalks with the root hairs. Chop watercress very finely or work in a food processor. Melt butter in a small saucepan over a low heat. Stir in flour and cook over the heat for 2 minutes, stirring all the time. Pour on the milk or cream and stir until well blended. Simmer for about 3 minutes. Allow sauce to cool slightly, then blend with purée'd sorrel and watercress. Add chopped parsley and tarragon, salt

This page: Prawns in Melons (top) and Red Mullet Niçoise (bottom).
Facing page: Seafood and Shell Salad (top) and Seviche (bottom).

and pepper. Cover top of sauce with a sheet of buttered greaseproof paper to prevent a skin from forming, and allow to cool completely. Whip the double cream lightly and fold into the sauce. Pour some of the sauce over the fish, shellfish and pasta. Serve rest of the sauce separately. Garnish with a whole giant prawn if desired.

Red Mullet Niçoise

PREPARATION TIME: 15 minutes
COOKING TIME: 15 minutes
SERVES: 4 people

4 red mullet
2 tbsps olive oil
Lemon juice
Small tin anchovy fillets
85g (3oz) pitted black olives
2 hard-boiled eggs
1 green pepper
1 chopped shallot
1 clove garlic, crushed
115g (4oz) button mushrooms
450g (llb) ripe tomatoes
Salt
Pepper
Seasoned flour

Vinaigrette Dressing
2 tbsps red wine vinegar
6 tbsps olive oil
¼ tsp French mustard
Handful of chopped mixed herbs (eg basil, oregano, thyme)

Scale and clean fish, trimming fins but leaving head and tail on (your fishmonger will do this for you if you wish). Cut tomatoes into quarters and remove cores. Cut eggs into quarters. Cut olives in half, lengthways. If mushrooms are small, leave whole; if not, quarter them. Cut green pepper into thin slices, and cut anchovies in half, lengthways. Prepare vinaigrette dressing and add chopped herbs, garlic and shallot. Put in the mushrooms and leave to marinate in the refrigerator for about 1 hour. Meanwhile, toss fish in seasoned flour to coat lightly. Heat 2 tbsps olive oil in a frying pan and fry fish on both sides until cooked through – about 2-3 minutes per side. When cooking the second side, sprinkle over some lemon juice. Season lightly, and leave to go cold. When ready to serve, add tomatoes, green peppers, eggs and olive to the mushrooms in their marinade, and toss. Pile the salad into a serving dish and arrange the cold, cooked red mullet on top. Garnish the mullet with anchovy fillet strips.

Seviche

PREPARATION TIME: 20 minutes
SERVES: 4 people

450g (1lb) codfish
150ml (¼ pint) lemon or lime juice
1 tbsp chopped shallot
1 green chilli
1 green pepper
2 tomatoes
1 tbsp chopped parsley
1 tbsp chopped fresh coriander
2 tbsps vegetable oil
1 small head iceberg lettuce
4 spring onions
Salt
Pepper

Skin cod and remove any bones. Wash and pat dry, then cut across grain into slices approximately 1cm (½") thick and 6cm (2½") long. Put into a bowl and pour over lime or lemon juice. Put in shallot. Slice chilli and remove the seeds, then chop finely and add it to the fish. Add seasoning and put into the refrigerator for 24 hours, well covered. Stir occasionally. When ready to serve, chop spring onions and herbs. Slice pepper into short, thin strips. Plunge tomatoes into boiling water for about 4 seconds, then into cold water, and peel. Cut tomatoes in half, squeeze out the seeds, and slice into fine strips. Drain off lemon or lime juice from fish, and stir in oil. Add herbs, peppers and tomatoes, and toss. Spoon onto lettuce leaves in a serving dish and sprikle over spring onions.

Prawns in Melons

PREPARATION TIME: 25 minutes
SERVES: 4 people

2 small melons
225g (8oz) peeled prawns
Juice of half a lemon
1 small cucumber
4 medium tomatoes
85g (3oz) toasted flaked almonds
1 orange
4 tbsps light vegetable oil
3 tbsps double cream
Salt
Pepper
2 tbsps chopped mint, reserving 4 sprigs for garnish
Pinch of sugar
1 tsp chopped lemon thyme (optional)

Cut melons in half through the middle and scoop out flesh with a melon-baller or spoon, leaving a 0.5cm (¼") border of fruit on the inside of each shell. Cut a thin slice off the bottom of each shell so that they stand upright. Cut the melon flesh into 1cm (½") cubes or leave in balls. Peel cucumber, cut in half lengthways, then into 1cm (½") cubes. Peel and squeeze seeds from tomatoes and cut tomatoes into strips. Peel and segment orange. Mix lemon juice, oil and double cream together for the dressing. Add chopped mint, and thyme (if desired), a pinch of sugar, and salt and pepper to taste. Toss fruit and vegetables together with the prawns. Pile ingredients evenly into each melon shell. Chill well and garnish with a small sprig of mint leaves and the almonds.

Lobster and Smoked Chicken Salad

PREPARATION TIME: 25 minutes
SERVES: 4 people

Salad
1 small smoked chicken
1 large cooked lobster
4 sticks celery
4 spring onions
115g (4oz) mangetout, topped and tailed
85g (3oz) browned cashew nuts
1 head Chinese leaves
1 head curly endive

Dressing
300ml (½ pint) prepared mayonnaise
2 tbsps soy sauce
1 tsp honey
Sesame seed oil
½ tsp ground ginger
1 tbsp dry sherry, if desired

Garnish
1 red pepper, thinly sliced
2 tbsps chopped parsley

Twist off the claws and legs of lobster. Cut body in half, take out tail meat and set aside. Crack claws and remove meat. Remove as much meat as possible from all the legs. Cut breast meat from the smoked chicken into thin, even slices. Shred the rest of the chicken meat. Mix the shredded chicken and the meat from the lobster claws and legs together. Cut lobster tail meat lengthways into 3-4 thin slices (depending on size of tail). Set sliced lobster tail and sliced chicken breast aside. Mix celery, cashew nuts and spring onions together with the shredded lobster and chicken. Mix the dressing ingredients together – the mayonnaise, soy sauce, sesame oil and honey – and add some black pepper and salt if necessary. Add ground ginger and sherry, if desired. Mix dressing with shredded lobster and chicken. Slice red pepper into thin strips. Slice Chinese leaves into thin shreds. Tear curly endive leaves into bite-sized pieces. Pile the greens and mangetout onto a large serving dish. Mound the shredded chicken and lobster salad in the middle. Arrange sliced chicken breast and lobster tail neatly over the top. Garnish with sliced red pepper and chopped parsley. Serve any remaining dressing separately.

Salade aux Fruits de Mer

PREPARATION TIME: 20 minutes
COOKING TIME: 10 minutes
SERVES: 4 people

Salad
8 scallops with roe attached
115g (4oz) scampi, cooked and shelled
115g (4oz) prawns, peeled
300ml (½ pint) mussels
115g (6oz) monkfish
Lemon juice
1 head cos lettuce
2 heads Belgian endive

Dressing
115g (4oz) curd cheese
150ml (¼ pint) yogurt
Juice of 1 lemon
3 tbsps milk
1 tbsp Dijon mustard
1 tbsp chopped tarragon
1 tbsp chopped chives
1 tbsp chopped parsley
Salt and pepper

Poach scallops and monkfish in lemon juice and enough water to cover, for about 5 minutes and

leave to cool in the liquid. Scrub mussels well and put into a covered saucepan with 4 tbsps water. Shake pan over heat for about 5 minutes, or until the shells open. Discard mussels whose shells remain closed. Remove mussels from shells and set aside. When scallops and monkfish are cool cut scallops in half, horizontally, and cut monkfish into 2.5cm (1″) pieces. Mix all fish and shellfish together. Remove core from Belgian endive; separate leaves and wash and dry well. Wash cos lettuce, remove core and shred finely. To make dressing, blend cheese and milk in a liquidiser or with an electric mixer. Add lemon juice, salt and pepper to taste, and mustard, and stir in the chopped herbs. Arrange leaves of Belgian endive onto serving plates. Pile shredded lettuce on top, leaving points of endive leaves showing. Toss shellfish in half the dressing and pile on top of lettuce. Put another spoonful of dressing on top of each serving and serve any remaining dressing separately.

Salade aux Fruits de Mer (above) and Lobster and Smoked Chicken Salad (left).

Smoked Salmon Rolls with Prawn Filling

PREPARATION TIME: 15 minutes

SERVES: 4 persons

8 slices of smoked salmon, about 1oz (30g) each
8oz (225g) frozen prawns
2 tblsp (30ml) mayonnaise
1 tblsp (15ml) whipped cream
2 tsp (10ml) tomato purée
Squeeze lemon juice

Defrost prawns and drain, or use fresh, shelled prawns instead. Mix mayonnaise and cream, tomato purée and lemon juice in a bowl and fold in prawns. Divide the mixture between the 8 slices of smoked salmon, placing it on top in a wedge shape and rolling the salmon around it in a cone shape. Allow two for each person. Garnish with lemon wedges and sliced cucumber and tomato. Serve with thinly sliced soda bread and butter. Serves 4 persons.

Poached Salmon Garni

PREPARATION TIME: 2-3 hours

COOKING TIME: 20-30 minutes

SERVES: 8-10 persons

A whole salmon, beautifully dressed, looks splendid at a buffet supper or a dinner party but it is tricky to serve and, if people are helping themselves, it looks rather mangled after the guests have attacked it. Also, you need to be the proud posessor of a fish-kettle in which to cook it and, of course, the preparation of salmon cooked in this way takes a lot of time and care. Here is a simple way to cook and serve fresh salmon.

1 fresh salmon, approx 2½lb (1kg)
1 large lettuce
1 cucumber
5-6 hard boiled eggs
3-4 firm tomatoes
2 lemons

Have the fishmonger clean the fish and remove the head. Cut the fish in two, near the gills. Place each piece on a well buttered piece of foil and make a parcel, folding the join several times and folding in the ends. Place the two pieces in a saucepan large enough to hold them side by side, cover them with cold water, add a tblsp (15ml) of vinegar and bring slowly to the boil. Gently turn the parcels over in the water. Turn off the heat, put on the lid, and leave to cool. Before the fish is completely cold put the parcels on a large plate, unwrap them and carefully skin the fish and remove the bones. Divide each section into serving-size pieces along the grain of the fish. Select large lettuce leaves, one for each portion of fish, and lay them in two

This page: Salmon Flan (top) and Poached Salmon Garni (bottom).
Facing page: Dublin Bay Prawn Cocktail (top) and Smoked Salmon Rolls with Prawn Filling (bottom).

rows, the length of a large serving platter, with a piece of salmon on each. Place quarters of hard-boiled egg and lemon slices between them and, down the centre of the dish, arrange two rows of alternating cucumber and tomato slices overlapping. Decorate the dish with parsley and serve mayonnaise separately and, of course, home-made brown soda bread.

Dublin Bay Prawn Cocktail

PREPARATION TIME: 15 minutes

SERVES: 4 persons

Dublin Bay Prawns are very large and rather expensive, so for prawn cocktail it is better to use ordinary prawns and garnish the cocktail with king prawns.

½lb (225g) cooked, shelled prawns (frozen prawns will do)
4 king prawns
5-6 lettuce leaves
4 lemon wedges
A little chopped parsley

Cocktail sauce
4 heaped tblsp (80ml) mayonnaise
2 level tblsp (30ml) tomato purée
1 tsp (5ml) Worcestershire sauce
2 tsp (10ml) lemon juice
1 dsp (20ml) medium sherry
2 tblsp (30ml) whipped cream

To make the sauce, add the purée, Worcestershire sauce, lemon juice and sherry to the mayonnaise and mix well, then fold in the whipped cream. Shred the lettuce finely and divide between four glass goblets. If using frozen prawns, drain them well and place equal amounts on top of the lettuce. Just before serving, coat the prawns with the cocktail sauce and sprinkle a pinch of the chopped parsley on top of each. Garnish with a king prawn and a lemon wedge on each glass. Serve with buttered brown soda bread.

Curried Prawn Salad

PREPARATION TIME: 15 minutes

SERVES: 4 persons

Not so many years ago, in the West of Ireland, you could buy a lobster for a few shillings if you knew the right person, and on the quaysides where the fishing boats landed their catch, fish cost only a few pence, while crabs and prawns were almost given away. It is a different story today, since fishing has become a major industry in Ireland, and almost all the shellfish is flown out to France almost as soon as it has left the water, or is ordered by the big hotels in Ireland. When I was staying at a Dublin Hotel recently, lobster was on the menu at £21 a portion. If you should be fortunate enough to buy fresh prawns, they need only butter and a little lemon juice to enhance their delicate flavour after they have been cooked in lightly salted water which has only just been allowed to come to the boil. However, frozen prawns are easily available everywhere in Ireland and here is an easy supper dish to serve with brown soda bread and butter.

8oz (225g) frozen prawns
¾ cup cooked rice
4 heaped tblsp (80ml) mayonnaise
A squeeze of lemon juice
2 tsp (10ml) of tomato purée
1 tsp (5ml) curry powder

Thoroughly defrost the prawns. Drain them well. Mix tomato purée, lemon juice and curry powder into the mayonnaise. Fold in rice and prawns. Divide in two and serve on large lettuce leaves. Garnish with sliced, hard boiled egg, cucumber and tomato. This would be sufficient for a first course for four people.

Salmon Flan

PREPARATION TIME: 10 minutes

COOKING TIME: 40-45 minutes

SERVES: 4-6 persons

This would make an excellent luncheon or supper dish for four people. Serve it either with a tossed salad and brown bread and butter or with baked potatoes and petit pois.

¼lb (115g) frozen puff pastry
6oz (175g) cooked fresh salmon or 7½oz (210g) tin of salmon
¼ pint (150ml) milk
Level dessertspoonful cornflour
Salt and pepper
1 egg

Thaw pastry. Roll out into a square large enough to line a greased 8 inch (20cm) quiche dish or flan tin. Trim pastry and crimp edges. Mix cornflour with a tblsp (15ml) of the milk, bring the rest to the boil, pour onto the cornflour mix, stir well and return to the pan. Bring back to the boil and cook for 1 minute, stirring all the time. Season well with salt and pepper. If using tinned salmon drain the liquid

Smoked Mackerel Pate (above right) and Curried Prawn Salad (right).

from the tin into the sauce. If using fresh salmon add a knob of butter. Remove the pan from the heat and break in the egg, beating it in thoroughly. Flake up the salmon, removing any bones and skin, fold it into the sauce and turn into the pastry case. Cook in the oven, 190°C, 375°F, Gas Mark 5, for 35-40 minutes.

Smoked Mackerel Pate

PREPARATION TIME: 10 minutes

SERVES: 4 persons

8oz (225g) skinned, smoked mackerel fillets
3oz (85g) softened butter
Juice of 1 lemon
Black pepper

This takes only seconds to make in a food processor or electric blender, but if you don't have access to either of these you can mash up the mackerel in a bowl and thoroughly mix in melted butter and lemon juice. Season with freshly ground black pepper and either divide between small individual ramekins or arrange it attractively in a serving dish, garnished with lemon slices and parsley. Serve with brown toast or brown soda bread.

Baked Stuffed Mackerel

PREPARATION TIME: 15 minutes

COOKING TIME: 30 minutes

SERVES: 4 persons

Mackerel should be eaten the day it is caught so this is a recipe for people living near the sea. It is also very useful for people on self-catering holidays at the seaside because it is so easy to prepare.

4 mackerel which have been cleaned and washed thoroughly
2oz (60g) butter
1 small onion, finely chopped
1 tblsp (5ml) oatmeal
1 heaped tsp (7ml) fresh chopped lemon thyme
1 heaped tsp (7ml) fresh chopped parsley or
½ tsp (2.5ml) of each, dried
2oz (60g) breadcrumbs
Salt and pepper
2-3 tblsp (30-45ml) hot water

Fry the chopped onion in the butter to soften. Add oatmeal, breadcrumbs, herbs and seasoning. Mix well. Bind with the hot water. Fill the cavities of the fish with the stuffing and wrap each one separately in well-buttered foil. Place in a roasting tin or on a baking sheet and put in a pre-heated oven at 190°C, 375°F, Gas Mark 5, for half an hour.

Scallops au Gratin

PREPARATION TIME: 10 minutes

COOKING TIME: 15 minutes

SERVES: 4 people

4 scallops
2-3 tblsp (30-45ml) finely chopped shallots (a small onion will do)
2 tblsp (30ml) oil
2oz (60g) butter
A wineglass of white wine
2 egg yolks
4 tblsp (60ml) grated Cheddar cheese
4 tblsp (60ml) white breadcrumbs
4-5 pieces of Kerrygold frozen cream or 2 tblsp (30ml) double cream

The fishmonger will prepare the scallops, removing the inedible bits and leaving you with what seems like a small amount of fish, but one each should be quite enough for a first course. Be sure to ask for the deeper section of the scallop shell to serve them in.

Heat the oil and butter in a heavy frying pan. Add the shallots and cook gently until they soften. Slice the white parts of the scallops. Increase the heat, stir in the white wine and then the sliced scallops and cook fairly briskly for 2-3 minutes. Slice the coral of the scallops and add to the pan, cooking the mixture for a further minute. Kerrygold frozen cream is a great asset here because by adding it straight from the freezer it reduces the heat of the mixture quickly, enabling you to add the lightly beaten egg yolks. Stir gently over a low heat until the mixture thickens, adding a sprinkling of salt and pepper. Divide between four scallop shells, making sure each one has its fair share of the coral. Place a tblsp (15ml) of grated cheese and a tblsp (15ml) of breadcrumbs on each and place under the heated grill until just beginning to brown on top. Serve immediately with brown bread.

Mackerel Rolls

PREPARATION TIME: 20 minutes

SERVES: 4 persons

The seas around Ireland are teeming with mackerel, the only problem about them is that, once out of the water, they don't stay fresh for very long. If you should be offered some freshly caught mackerel and you don't want to eat them that day, don't turn them down. Take them home and poach then in a little very lightly salted water, preferably with a dash of cider or white wine added. This will only take ten minutes. Cool them, put them in the refrigerator and next day you can have a delicious lunch or picnic of mackerel rolls.

4 long, crusty rolls or one French loaf
12oz (350g) skinned and filleted cooked mackerel
Small carton plain yogurt
Few chopped walnuts
1 medium eating apple
Thyme
Mint

Split rolls or loaf lengthways. Scoop out some of the centre. Chop up breadcrumbs on the breadboard with two knives. Put the breadcrumbs in a bowl and mix in finely chopped herbs and some freshly ground black pepper. Peel, core and quarter the apple; chop it up finely and fold it into the yogurt with the chopped walnuts. Flake up the mackerel, mix with the seasoned crumbs and bind with the yogurt mixture. Fill the scooped out rolls with the mixture and either serve as open sandwiches or put tops on and wrap in foil or clingfilm if using for a picnic. Fill French loaf in similar manner and cut into sections.

Grilled Trout with Almonds

PREPARATION TIME: 10 minutes

COOKING TIME: 15 minutes

SERVES: 4 persons

4 fresh trout
1 lemon
2oz (60g) butter
1oz (30g) flaked almonds

Clean the trout. Place a lemon wedge in the cavity of each. Line the grill tray with buttered foil and carefully lay the fish on it. Smear a little butter on each. Preheat the grill and cook the trout under it for 5 minutes. Turn them very carefully, put a little more butter on top and grill for another five minutes. Keep the fish warm on plates while you toss the almonds in the butter in the grill pan and brown them under the grill. Sprinkle them over the fish. Serve with a garnish of lemon slices and parsley. Eat with brown bread and butter.

Seafood Pancakes

PREPARATION TIME: Pancakes 1 hour 15 minutes. Filling 15 minutes

COOKING TIME: 45 minutes

SERVES: 6 persons

These are especially nice when made with sole and two or three scallops, but you can use 1½lb (675g) of any white fish, filleted. Ask the fishmonger for the bones and trimmings for the fish stock. The pancake recipe is the same as the one for Savoury Pancakes.

12 thin pancakes
1½lb (675g) fish
4oz (115g) prawns (cooked)
4oz (115g) mushrooms
1 tblsp (15ml) butter
1 tblsp (15ml) lemon juice in 2 fl oz (50ml) water
1 medium onion
Bayleaf
6 peppercorns
1 tsp (5ml) salt
3oz (85g) butter
3oz (85g) flour
Glass white wine
1 pint (600ml) fish stock
Grated nutmeg
¼ pint (150ml) whipped cream

Put washed fish trimmings in a saucepan with the bayleaf, peppercorns, salt and 1 pint (600ml) water. Bring to the boil and simmer for half an hour. Strain. Cut the sole, or other fish, diagonally into 1 inch (2.5cm) strips and poach in the fish stock for two minutes. Remove the fish from the stock with a slotted spoon and set aside. Melt the tblsp (15ml) of butter in a pan, add the mushrooms sliced, the lemon juice and 2 fl oz (50ml) water, bring to the boil, reduce heat and cook for 1 minute. Remove mushrooms with a slotted spoon.
Melt 3oz (85g) butter in a saucepan, stir in the flour and cook over a low heat for a minute or two. Add the white wine and bring to the boil. Remove the pan from the heat and slowly add the fish and mushroom stocks, stirring all the time. Return to the heat and simmer for 2 minutes. Season with salt and pepper and a little grated nutmeg. Remove from heat and stir in the whipped cream. Use half the sauce to mix in with the fish, prawns and mushrooms. Divide this mixture between the 12 pancakes, rolling each one up and placing them, side by side, in a large, shallow, greased ovenproof dish. Pour over the rest of the sauce and heat through in the oven, 180°C, 350°F, Gas Mark 4, for about half an hour or until the top begins to brown. Allow 2 pancakes per person for a main course, or one each as a first course.

Facing page: Baked Stuffed Mackerel (top) and Grilled Trout with Almonds (bottom).

This page: Scallops au Gratin (top right) and Sole Surprise (bottom left).
Facing page: Mackerel Rolls (top) and Seafood Pancakes (bottom).

Sole Surprise

PREPARATION TIME: 30 minutes

COOKING TIME: 30 minutes

SERVES: 4 persons

This consists of little puff pastry 'boxes' filled with spinach, with the fillets of sole laid on top and coated with a cheese sauce. It makes an interesting luncheon for four people.

4 small or 2 large fillets of sole
8oz (225g) frozen puff pastry
8oz (225g) frozen spinach
2oz (60g) butter

Sauce
1oz (30g) butter
1oz (30g) flour
½ pint (300ml) milk
Pinch fennel
Salt and pepper
2oz (60g) grated cheese

Roll out the defrosted pastry into a rectangle 5x8 inches (13x20cm). Cut it down the centre in both directions to make four rectangles 2½x4 inches (6.5x10cm). Carry out the following procedure with each one. Fold over, short sides together. Cut out the centre with a sharp knife, leaving ½ inch (1.5cm) all round. Roll out the centre piece on a floured board until it is the same size as the ½ inch (1.5cm) 'frame'. Brush the edges with milk and put the 'frame' on the base. Brush the top with milk and put them on a greased baking sheet. Bake them in the oven, 220°C, 425°F Gas Mark 7, for 10-15 minutes.
Meanwhile, put the spinach in a pan with ¼ inch (5mm) water and a little salt. Cover and cook for 4-5 minutes. Drain and beat in half the butter. Skin the fillets and, if necessary, cut them in two. Use the rest of the butter to coat two plates and put the fillets on one and cover them with the other. Cook them over a pan of boiling water for twenty minutes.
For the sauce, melt 1oz (30g) butter with the flour to make a roux. Gradually stir in the milk. Bring to the boil. Reduce heat and add fennel and salt and pepper; cook for another minute or two. Remove from the heat and stir in the grated cheese.
Divide the spinach between the four boxes. Lay the sole on top and coat with the cheese sauce.

Seafood with Pasta

This page: Vermicelli Pescatore.

Facing page: Spaghetti Marinara (top) and Pasta Shells with Seafood (bottom).

Spaghetti Marinara

PREPARATION TIME: 10 minutes

COOKING TIME: 20 minutes

300g (10oz) spaghetti
450g (1lb) prawns, shelled and de-veined
225g (8oz) scallops, cleaned and sliced
45g (1½oz) can anchovy fillets
400g (14oz) can plum tomatoes, seeded and chopped
75ml (5 tbsps) dry white wine
75ml (5 tbsps) water
1 bay leaf
4 peppercorns
30ml (2 tbsps) olive oil
1 tsp basil
2 cloves garlic, crushed
1 tbsp tomato purée
1 tbsp chopped parsley
Salt and pepper

Drain anchovies and cut into small pieces. Place water, wine, bay leaf and peppercorns in a pan. Heat to a slow boil. Add scallops and cook for 2 minutes. Remove and drain. Heat the oil, add garlic and basil, and cook for 30 seconds. Add tomatoes, anchovies and tomato purée. Stir until combined. Cook for 10 minutes. Meanwhile, cook the spaghetti in a large pan of boiling salted water for 10 minutes, or until tender but still firm. Drain. Add seafood to sauce, and cook a further 1 minute. Add parsley and stir through. Season with salt and pepper to taste. Toss gently. Pour sauce over spaghetti and serve immediately, sprinkled with parsley.

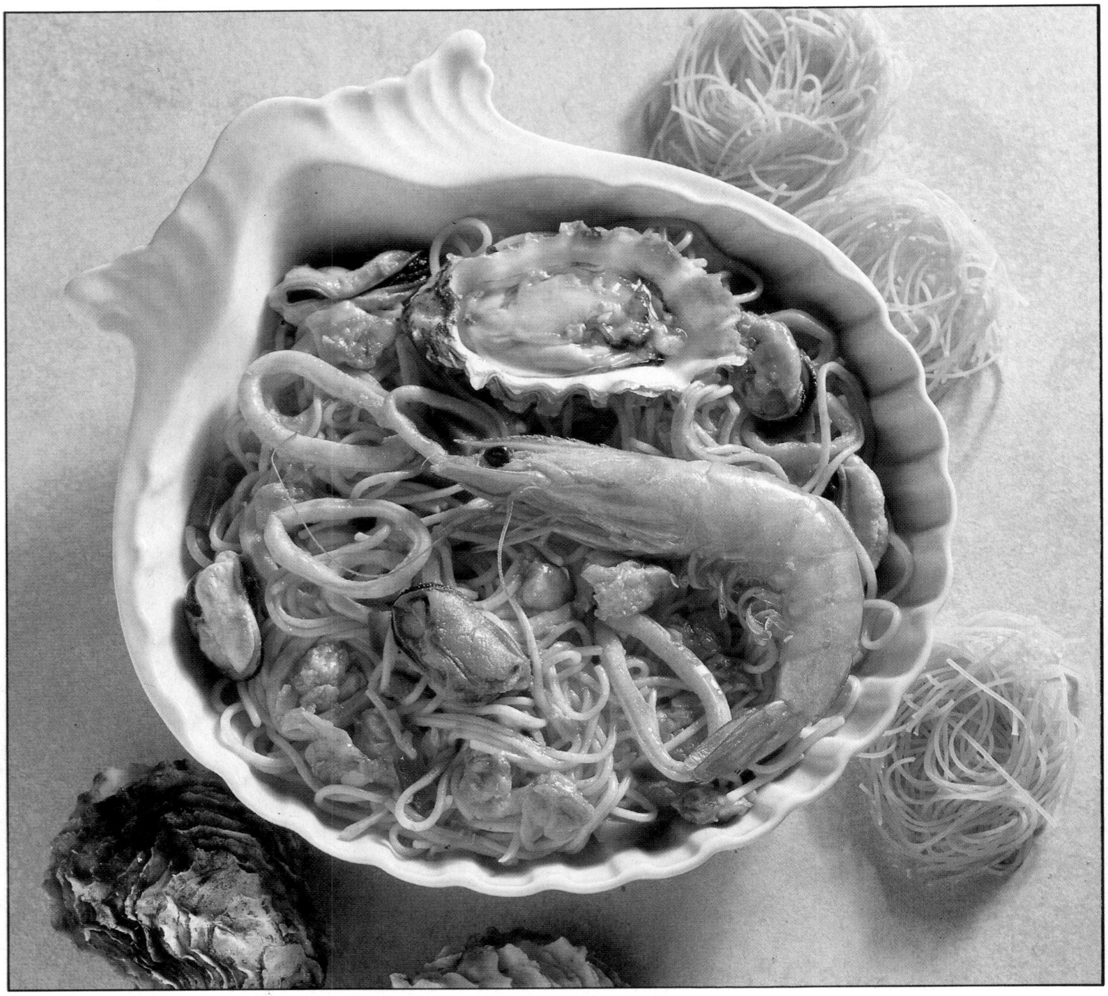

Pasta Shells with Seafood

PREPARATION TIME: 5 minutes

COOKING TIME: 15 minutes

300g (10oz) pasta shells
450g (1lb) prawns, shelled and de-veined
115g (4oz) scallops, cleaned and sliced
60g (2oz) butter or margarine
2 cloves garlic, crushed
75ml (5 tbsps) dry white wine
300ml (½ pint) single cream
30ml (2 tbsps) water
1 tbsp cornflour
1 tbsp lemon juice
1 tbsp chopped parsley
Salt and pepper

Melt butter in a pan. Add garlic, and cook for 1 minute. Add wine and cream, and bring back to boil, and cook 2 minutes. Slake cornflour with the water, and pour into sauce. Stir until boiling. Add lemon juice and salt and pepper to taste. Meanwhile, cook the pasta in plenty of boiling salted water, until tender – about 10 minutes. Drain, shaking to remove excess water. Add prawns and scallops to sauce and cook 3 minutes. Pour over pasta shells, toss, and garnish with parsley.

Vermicelli Pescatore

PREPARATION TIME: 15 minutes

COOKING TIME: 40 minutes

115g (4oz) mussels
115g (4oz) cockles
225g (8oz) cod fish fillets
115g (4oz) squid, cleaned
4 large prawns
4 fresh oysters
300g (10oz) vermicelli
250ml (8 fl oz) dry white wine
60ml (4 tbsps) olive oil
2 400g (14oz) cans plum tomatoes
Half a green pepper, diced

Prepare seafood. If using fresh mussels, clean closed mussels, removing beard, and cook in boiling water for 3 minutes until they open. (Discard any that remain closed). Cool and remove from shells, keeping a few in shells for garnish if desired. Skin and bone fillets, and cut fish into 1.5cm (½ inch) pieces. Clean squid and cut into rings. Force tomatoes and their juice through a sieve, and set aside. Heat 30ml (2 tbsps) oil in a pan, and add the squid. Fry gently until golden brown, then add wine, tomato purée, green pepper, and salt and pepper to taste. Simmer for 20 minutes then add fish. Simmer for a further 10 minutes, stirring occasionally. Add cockles and mussels and, when mixture reboils, adjust seasoning. Meanwhile, cook spaghetti in lots of boiling salted water for 10 minutes, or until tender but still firm. Drain well. Add seafood, and toss. Garnish with prawns and fresh oysters.

Pasta and Smoked Salmon

PREPARATION TIME: 10 minutes

COOKING TIME: 18 minutes

SERVES: 4 people

85g (3oz) plain tagliatelle
85g (3oz) wholemeal tagliatelle
85g (3oz) spinach tagliatelle
225g (8oz) smoked salmon
60g (2oz) button mushrooms
1 egg
150ml (¼ pint) double cream
1 tbsp chopped parsley
1 tsp chopped fresh basil
2 spring onions, finely chopped
1 tbsp butter
1 jar red salmon caviar
Salt and pepper

Cook the pasta in boiling salted water until just tender. Drain under hot water and keep it warm. Slice and cook the mushrooms, with the onion, in the butter. Slice the smoked salmon into thin strips and set aside. Beat together the egg and double cream with the chopped herbs, salt and pepper. Add these to the onion and mushrooms, and heat through, stirring constantly. Do not allow mixture to boil. Toss with the pasta and the salmon. Top with red salmon caviar to serve.

Sole au Vin Rouge

PREPARATION TIME: 15 minutes

COOKING TIME: 25 minutes

OVEN TEMPERATURE: 160°C, 325°F, Gas Mark 3

SERVES: 4 people

2 lemon or Dover sole
150ml (5 fl oz) red wine
75ml (2½ fl oz) water
3-4 peppercorns
1 bay leaf
1 slice onion
15g (½ oz) butter
15g (½ oz) flour
150ml (5 fl oz) single cream
1 small bunch black grapes
Salt
Pepper

Fillet and skin the fish. Wash fillets and dry well, and fold the ends under to make small parcels. Put into an ovenproof dish and pour over the wine and water. Put in the onion slice, peppercorns and bay leaf. Add a pinch of salt, and cover with foil. Put into a pre-set oven and poach for about 10 minutes. Meanwhile, wash and pip the grapes, but leave whole unless very large, in which case halve them. Remove fish from baking dish, cover and keep fillets warm. Heat butter in a small saucepan. When foaming, add flour and cook for

This page: Sole au Vin Rouge (top) and Trout en Papillote (bottom).
Facing page: Pasta and Smoked Salmon (top) and Fritto Misto Mare (bottom).

about 2-3 minutes, until flour is lightly brown. Strain on the cooking liquid from the fish and stir until the sauce comes to the boil. Allow to continue boiling for about 2 minutes. Add cream and re-boil. Season to taste. Arrange fillets in a serving dish. Put the pipped grapes into the sauce to heat them through, reserving a few to garnish. Coat the fish with the sauce to serve.

Spiced Salmon Steaks

PREPARATION TIME: 15 minutes

COOKING TIME: 12-15 minutes

SERVES: 4 people

4 salmon steaks, 2cm (1") thick
225g (8oz) light brown sugar
1 tsp ground all-spice
1 tsp dry mustard powder
1 tsp grated fresh ginger
1 cucumber
1 bunch spring onions
2 tsps chopped fresh dill or 1 tsp dry dill weed
1 tbsp chopped parsley
Salt
Pepper
Lemon juice
30g (1oz) butter

Mix the sugar and spices together and rub into the surface of both sides of the salmon steaks. Set in a refrigerator for about 1 hour. Peel the cucumber and cut into quarters lengthways, then remove seeds and cut each quarter into 2cm (1") strips. Trim roots of spring onions; trim down the green part but leave some green attached. Put these and the cucumber into a saucepan with the butter, lemon juice, salt, pepper, parsley and dill, and cook over a gentle heat for about 10-15 minutes, or until tender. Place salmon steaks under a moderate grill, and grill for about 5-6 minutes on each side. Serve with the cucumber and spring onion accompaniment.

Fritto Misto Mare

PREPARATION TIME: 10 minutes

COOKING TIME: 5-6 minutes

SERVES: 4 people

115g (4oz) scallops with roe attached
225g (8oz) uncooked scampi
450g (1lb) whitebait, smelts or sprats, or whitefish such as sole or cod
300ml (½ pint) shelled mussels
Vegetable oil for deep frying
Salt

Batter

300ml (½ pint) water
2 tbsps olive oil
115g (4oz) plain flour
1 tsp ground nutmeg
1 tsp ground oregano
Pinch salt
1 egg white

Garnish

Parsley sprigs
1 lemon

First make the batter so that it can rest for ½ hour while fish is being prepared. Blend oil with water, and gradually stir it into flour sifted with a pinch of salt. Beat batter until quite smooth, and add the nutmeg and oregano. Just before using, fold in stiffly-beaten egg white. If using smelts or sprats, cut heads off the fish; if using whitefish, cut into chunks about 2cm (1") thick. Shell scampi if necessary. If the scallops are large, cut them in half. Heat oil to 190°C, 375°F. Dip fish and shellfish, one at a time, into batter, allowing surplus batter to drip off. Then put them into the frying basket and into the hot oil. Fry for 5-6 minutes, or until crisp and golden. Drain on crumpled absorbent paper. Sprinkle lightly with salt. Put fish on a heated dish. Garnish with parsley sprigs and lemon wedges. If desired, a tartare sauce may be served.

Trout en Papillote

PREPARATION TIME: 15 minutes

COOKING TIME: 10-15 minutes

OVEN TEMPERATURE: 180°C, 350°F, Gas Mark 4

SERVES: 4 people

4 small trout, about 225g (8oz) each
2-3 shallots
Sprigs of rosemary
Lemon juice
115g (4oz) butter
115g (4oz) flaked almonds
Salt
Pepper

Garnish

Slices of lemon

Clean fish well, trim the fins, wash and dry, then season insides. Place a sprig of rosemary inside each, reserving 1 tbsp of leaves for use later. Chop the shallots. Melt the butter. Cut 4 large rounds of foil or greaseproof paper, brush them with melted butter and place the fish on them. Cut 2-3 slashes on the side of each fish to help them cook quickly. Scatter over the chopped shallots, salt, pepper and some lemon juice, and pour over some of the melted butter. Fold the paper or foil over the fish and seal well. Place fish on a baking sheet and bake for about 10-15 minutes. Meanwhile, brown the almonds in the remaining melted butter and add salt, pepper and a good squeeze of lemon juice. Just before serving, add the reserved rosemary leaves to the hot butter and almonds. Pour over the fish when the parcels are opened, and garnish with lemon slices.

Paella

PREPARATION TIME: 20 minutes

COOKING TIME: 30 minutes

SERVES: 4 people

450g (1lb) Mediterranean prawns or scampi
600ml (1 pint) mussels in their shells
225g (8oz) prawns in their shells
115g (4oz) chorizo (Spanish sausage), sliced
150ml (¼ pint) dry white wine
225g (8oz) rice
1 small onion
1 clove garlic, crushed
4 tbsps olive oil
Lemon juice
Saffron
4 tomatoes
2 green peppers
Small bunch spring onions, chopped
Salt and pepper

Wash all the prawns and scrub mussels well, discarding any with broken shells. Cook mussels in the wine over a high heat until the shells open. Discard any that do not open. Strain the liquid for use in cooking the rice. Leave mussels in their shells. Peel half the washed prawns. Chop the onion finely, heat the oil in a shallow, heatproof dish, and cook the onion and garlic until they become a pale brown. Add the chorizo and cook for 1-2 minutes, then add rice and cook till it looks clear. Add the shellfish liquid, lemon juice, a pinch of saffron and enough water to cover the rice. Cook for 20 minutes on a moderate heat. Remove cores from tomatoes and chop roughly. Slice the peppers and add to the rice during the last 5 minutes of cooking. Add the tomatoes and peeled prawns to heat through, then add all the remaining shellfish. Adjust seasoning and sprinkle the chopped spring onion over to serve.

Paella (left) and Spiced Salmon Steaks (below).

Scampi and Ham Brochettes

PREPARATION TIME: 20 minutes

COOKING TIME: 25 minutes

SERVES: 4 people

16 large raw scampi
225g (8oz) smoked gammon or bacon, cut in a thick slice
1 small fresh pineapple
1 green pepper
Oil for basting

Sauce
200ml (7½oz) tinned tomatoes
1 tbsp Worcestershire sauce
1 tbsp cider vinegar
1-2 tbsps soft brown sugar
1 clove garlic, crushed
½ tsp dry mustard powder
1 bay leaf

Garnish
225g (8oz) mangetout
225g (8oz) hot, cooked rice, tossed in butter and black pepper
60g (2oz) toasted flaked almonds
30g (1oz) butter
Salt and pepper

Cut rind and most of the fat from the gammon. Cut the gammon into 2cm (1″) cubes and put into a saucepan of cold water. Bring to the boil and allow to boil for about 2-3 minutes. Strain and rinse under clear water. Peel scampi. Halve green pepper, remove the seeds, and cut into 2cm (1″) pieces. Peel and quarter the pineapple, remove the core, and cut each quarter into 2cm (1″) chunks. Thread a piece of scampi, of pepper, of gammon, and of pineapple onto each of 4 skewers, continuing until all the ingredients are used. Prepare sauce by putting tomatoes and remaining sauce ingredients into a saucepan and bringing to the boil. Turn down the heat and allow to simmer for about 10-15 minutes, then set aside. Bring a large saucepan of salted water to the boil. Top, tail and wash the mangetout and put them in the boiling water to cook for about 1-2 minutes. Drain and refresh them under cold water. Heat the grill to moderate. Brush brochettes with oil and grill for about 3-5 minutes on each side, basting occasionally with the sauce. Heat some butter in a saucepan and toss the mangetout over the heat with salt and pepper, and heat through. Serve brochettes on their skewers on a bed of cooked rice with almonds, garnished with the lemon wedges and mangetout. Re-heat remaining sauce to serve with brochettes.

Prawn Creole with Saffron Rice Ring

PREPARATION TIME: 15 minutes

COOKING TIME: 30 minutes

SERVES: 4 people

450g (1lb) shelled prawns
1 green pepper
1 red pepper
115g (4oz) button mushrooms
1 medium onion
2 sticks celery
400ml (14oz) tin tomatoes
60g (2oz) butter
1 tsp sugar
1 bay leaf
½ tsp Tabasco
Pinch nutmeg
½ tsp chopped thyme
2 tbsps chopped parsley
225g (8oz) long-grain rice
1 shallot, finely chopped
Good pinch saffron, or 1 pkt saffron powder
Salt
Pepper

This page: Prawn Creole with Saffron Rice Ring.
Facing page: Tuna and Fennel (top) and Scampi and Ham Brochettes (bottom).

Rinse the rice, put into a large saucepan of boiling salted water and cook for about 12 minutes. Measure 3 tsps of the boiling water and soak the saffron in it. Melt half the butter and cook the shallot. Butter a 600ml (1 pint) ring mould well, and set aside. Drain rice when cooked, and mix with cooked shallot, seasoning, 1 tbsp chopped parsley and saffron liquid. Stir well and ensure rice is evenly coloured with the saffron. Put this mixture into the ring mould, pressing down well, and leave to keep warm. Melt the remaining butter, chop the onion and celery finely, slice peppers into fine shreds, and slice the mushrooms. Cook the onion in the butter until just lightly coloured, then add peppers and mushrooms and cook gently for several minutes. Add celery and tomatoes and bring to the boil. Reduce heat and add the bay leaf, remaining parsley, thyme, Tabasco, sugar and seasoning. Allow to simmer for about 12 minutes, then add prawns and heat through. Carefully unmould the rice ring onto a serving plate and pour the prawn creole into the centre.

Herring and Apples

PREPARATION TIME: 15-20 minutes

COOKING TIME: 50 minutes

OVEN TEMPERATURES: 180°C, 350°F, Gas Mark 4, rising to 200°C, 400°F, Gas Mark 6

SERVES: 4 people

4 herrings
1 onion
2 large dessert apples
Dry breadcrumbs
4 large potatoes, peeled and sliced
150ml (¼ pint) dry cider
1 tsp caster sugar
60g (2oz) butter
Salt
Pepper
1 tbsp chopped parsley

Cut heads and tails from herrings, split and bone them, but do not cut into separate fillets. Wash and dry them well. Peel, quarter, core and slice 1 apple. Slice the onion thinly. Butter a shallow baking dish well. Layer the potatoes, apple and onion, seasoning between each layer with salt and pepper, and neatly arranging the final layer of potato slices. Pour the cider over the potatoes, cover the dish with foil and bake for about 40 minutes. Then take the dish from the oven and place herrings on top. Cook, uncovered, for 10 minutes, then sprinkle herrings lightly with breadcrumbs and dot with some of the butter. Increase heat and bake until herrings brown – about 5-10 minutes. Meanwhile, core remaining apple and slice into rounds, leaving peel on. Melt remaining butter in a saucepan and fry the apples in the butter. Sprinkle them lightly with caster sugar and continue to fry until a good brown. When herrings have browned, garnish with the apple slices and chopped parsley. Serve in the baking dish.

Tuna and Fennel

PREPARATION TIME: 15 minutes

COOKING TIME: 6-8 minutes

SERVES: 4 people

4 tuna steaks, cut 2cm (1") thick
4 tbsps olive oil
4 tbsps white wine
Crushed black pepper
1 clove garlic
Salt
1 head Florentine fennel

Peel garlic and cut into thin slivers. Stick these into the tuna steaks with a sharp knife. Mix oil, wine and pepper and pour over steaks in a shallow dish. Leave to marinate in a refrigerator for 1 hour. Heat grill to high and grill fish for 3-4 minutes per side, basting frequently with the marinade. Reserve the green, feathery tops of the fennel. Cut the head in half and slice into 0.5cm (¼") pieces. Put into boiling salted water and cook for 5 minutes. Season and keep warm. Garnish the tuna steaks with reserved fennel top and serve with the cooked, sliced fennel.

Buttered Perch

PREPARATION TIME: 10 minutes

COOKING TIME: 12-15 minutes

SERVES: 4 people

1kg (2lbs) perch (or sole or other whitefish) fillets
115g (4oz) butter
3 tbsps oil
Seasoned flour
2 eggs, beaten
Fine corn meal
Lemon juice
Salt

Garnish
Lemon wedges
Parsley sprigs

Skin, wash and dry the fillets well, cut each lengthways into 4 strips and toss in seasoned flour. Beat the eggs, adding a pinch of salt, then coat the fish before tossing it in the corn meal. Shake off the excess. Heat oil in a large frying pan and add 1 tbsp butter. Shallow-fry the fish briskly for about 5-6 minutes, frying in 2 or 3 batches. Drain on absorbent paper and keep warm. Melt remaining butter and add lemon juice. Pour over the fish and serve with lemon wedges and sprigs of parsley.

Hazelnut Brill

PREPARATION TIME: 15 minutes

COOKING TIME: 10 minutes

SERVES: 4 people

2 large brill, filleted (lemon sole or plaice may be used)
2 eggs, lightly beaten, with a pinch of salt
60g (2oz) dry breadcrumbs
115g (4oz) ground browned hazelnuts
2 tbsps oil
60g (2oz) butter
Salt
Pepper
Flour

Garnish
1 large bunch watercress
60g (2oz) hazelnuts, crushed
Lemon wedges

Buttered Perch (left) and Herring and Apples (below).

Fillet the fish and coat lightly in flour. Dip fillets into the beaten eggs, then into a mixture of the crumbs and nuts. Sauté the fillets quickly in oil until browned on both sides. Add salt and pepper to taste. Remove fillets from pan and keep warm. Wipe out the pan and melt the butter in it. Add crushed hazelnuts to the butter and fry them until they are a nice golden brown. Serve the fillets with these hazelnuts on top, garnished with lemon wedges and a bunch of watercress.

Stuffed Salmon Trout

PREPARATION TIME: 10-15 minutes

COOKING TIME: 40-60 minutes

OVEN TEMPERATURE: 180°C, 350°F, Gas Mark 4

SERVES: 4 people

1 fresh whole salmon trout weighing 1-1.25kg (2-2½lbs)
1 head Florentine fennel
1kg (2lbs) fresh spinach
60g (2oz) walnuts
1 shallot, chopped
115g (4oz) fresh white breadcrumbs
1 tbsp chopped parsley
1 tbsp chopped thyme
60g (2oz) butter, melted
Juice of 2 lemons
Grated nutmeg
Salt
Pepper

Garnish
Lemon slices

Ask the fishmonger to bone the salmon for stuffing. The head and tail should be left on. Sprinkle the inside with some of the butter and all but 2 tbsps of the lemon juice. Place fish in the centre of a large, lightly buttered square of foil, and set aside. Prepare the stuffing. Cut the head of fennel in half (or, if large, into quarters), then into 0.5cm (¼") slices, and put in a pan of boiling water to cook for 2-3 minutes. Meanwhile, wash the spinach leaves well, and tear off any coarse stalks. Put into a large pan, sprinkled with salt. Cover and cook for about 3 minutes, then

drain and chop finely. Chop the shallot finely and soften in 1 tbsp of the remaining melted butter. Add to the spinach with the fennel slices, chopped walnuts, parsley, thyme, nutmeg, salt and pepper, 1 tbsp of the lemon juice, and the breadcrumbs. Fill the salmon with the stuffing, leaving a border of stuffing showing. Seal the foil over the top of the fish to enclose it, but do not wrap too tightly. Place in a roasting tin and bake for 40-60 minutes, depending on weight. To serve, unwrap and transfer to a large serving dish. Remove skin from one side, turn over carefully and remove skin from the other. Serve with remaining melted butter sharpened with remaining lemon juice, and garnish with sliced lemon.

Hazelnut Brill (left), Salmon with Cucumber Cream (below) and Stuffed Salmon Trout (facing page).

Coulibiac

PREPARATION TIME: 30 minutes
COOKING TIME: 35-40 minutes
OVEN TEMPERATURE: 200°C, 400°F, Gas Mark 7
SERVES: 4 people

Pastry
450g (1lb) plain flour
185g (6oz) butter or margarine
Salt
150ml (5 fl oz) iced water
1 egg, beaten

Filling
450g (1lb) fresh salmon
4 small leeks
60g (2oz) rice
2 hard-boiled eggs
115g (4oz) butter or margarine
225g (8oz) button mushrooms
2 tbsps chopped parsley
1 tbsp chopped thyme
Salt
Pepper

Sauce
300ml (½ pint) sour cream
¼ tsp grated horseradish
1 small bunch chives
Salt and pepper

Skin, trim and bone the salmon, and cut into 4 equal-sized pieces. Cook rice in boiling salted water until tender, then drain and rinse under hot water and set aside to cool. Slice mushrooms and clean leeks well, trimming their root ends. Cut leeks into lengths equal to those of the salmon, put them into a saucepan of cold water and bring to the boil. Cook until almost completely tender, drain and allow to cool. Cook mushrooms for a few minutes in the butter. Add rice, parsley, thyme and seasoning. Boil the eggs for about 10 minutes or until hard cooked, and leave to sit in cold water.

To prepare the pastry, cut the butter into 1cm (½") cubes. Sieve flour with a pinch of salt into a bowl and add cubed butter until it is well coated. Mix in the iced water, a little at a time, until the mixture just holds together. (The full quantity of water may not be needed). Chill mixture for about 10 minutes in the refrigerator. Turn the dough out onto a well-floured surface and shape it into a rough square. Using a well-floured rolling pin, roll out to a rectangle 3 times as long as it is wide. Fold the bottom third of the dough up to the middle and the top third over it. Give the dough a half-turn, then roll out and fold again in the same way. Repeat the process once more, chilling the dough in between operations if the pastry gets too soft. Chill before using.

Roll out the pastry to a square about 0.5cm (¼") thick and cut into 4 even-sized pieces approximately 12cm (6") square. Save the trimmings. Brush each square with water and put a layer of the rice and mushroom mixture onto each. Place the cut pieces of leek on top of the rice, then put on another layer of rice. Cut the hard-boiled eggs in half and put one half on the rice layer. Add another layer of rice and, finally, the salmon piece. Fold the pastry over the salmon like a parcel and seal the edges well. Turn the parcels over and put onto a lightly-greased baking sheet. Brush each parcel with lightly beaten egg and cut the pastry trimmings into shapes to decorate the top. Brush these decorations with egg. Make a small hole in the centre of each parcel.

Bake until pastry is brown and has had time to cook – about 30 minutes. Meanwhile, prepare a sour cream sauce. Chop the chives and mix with the sour cream, horseradish and seasoning. Keep the sauce at room temperature, but just before serving heat it over a gentle heat. Do not allow to boil. Serve the sauce with the coulibiac and garnish with watercress if desired.

This page: Coulibiac (top) and Grilled Cod Steaks (bottom). Facing page: Sea Bass with Vegetables.

Grilled Cod Steaks

PREPARATION TIME: 10 minutes
COOKING TIME: 9 minutes
SERVES: 4 people

4 cod steaks, each about 2cm (1") thick
60g (2oz) butter
Dry breadcrumbs
Pepper

Flavoured Butters
115g (4oz) unsalted butter
1 tbsp chopped parsley and 1 tbsp chopped thyme,
or 1 clove crushed garlic,
or 2 tsps anchovy essence or paste, or 2 tsps tomato purée and 1 tbsp chopped chives and a few drops of Tabasco
Salt and pepper

Garnish
4 ripe tomatoes

Melt the 60g (2oz) butter. Heat grill to moderate. Brush both sides of the cod steaks with some of the melted butter. Wash tomatoes, dry them well and cut them in half. Grill with the cod steaks for about 3 minutes. Turn the steaks, brush with more melted butter, and season with pepper. Dust with dry breadcrumbs. Grill for a further 6 minutes, basting well with the butter. To serve, top each steak with a slice of one of the flavoured butters and the grilled tomato halves.
To prepare flavoured butters, cream the unsalted butter until soft. Beat in either the herbs, or garlic, or anchovy essence, or tomato purée, chives and Tabasco. Add seasoning to taste and a squeeze of lemon juice if desired. When well mixed, pile onto a sheet of clingfilm or greaseproof paper and twist ends to shape the butter into a cylinder. Chill in the refrigerator until firm. The butter may also be frozen.

Grilled Red Mullet with Garlic Sauce

PREPARATION TIME: 15 minutes
COOKING TIME: 8-10 minutes
SERVES: 4 people

4 medium-sized red mullet
Olive oil
Lemon juice
Pepper

Garlic Sauce
2 egg yolks
½ tsp mustard powder
300ml (½ pint) olive oil
2 tbsps lemon juice
1 or 2 cloves crushed garlic
Salt
White pepper

Garnish
Lemon wedges
Watercress

Put egg yolks, mustard, garlic, salt and pepper into a food processor or liquidiser (an electric mixer can also be used). Beat ingredients together until yolks thicken slightly. Begin adding oil in a thin, steady stream while beating yolks. Be sure to use all the oil. When sauce has thickened, adjust seasoning, add lemon and set aside. Scale and clean the fish well, leaving heads and tails on. Cut 2-3 slashes on both sides of each fish, brush with oil, and sprinkle with pepper and some lemon juice. Put under a moderate grill for 4-5 minutes each side. Serve with lemon wedges and the garlic sauce. Garnish with watercress if desired.

Turbot in Lettuce Leaves

PREPARATION TIME: 15 minutes
COOKING TIME: 18 minutes
OVEN TEMPERATURE: 180°C, 350°F, Gas Mark 4
SERVES: 4 people

1kg (2lbs) turbot fillets
1 large cos lettuce
1 chopped shallot
150ml (¼ pint) dry Italian vermouth
150ml (¼ pint) double cream
60g (2oz) butter
30g (1oz) flour
1 tbsp chopped chervil or parsley
Salt and pepper
Lemon juice

Skin and wash the turbot fillets well. Trim into even-sized pieces. Trim and separate the lettuce leaves. Keep them whole and put the largest, best-looking ones into boiling water for less than 1 minute. Remove them with a draining spoon, refresh in cold water and leave to drain. Cut remaining lettuce into thin strips and put into boiling water. Drain almost immediately and refresh them. Season the fillets and place on the whole lettuce leaves, hiding the fish trimmings underneath. Wrap the leaves securely round the fillets. Butter a large ovenproof dish and put in the wrapped fillets, folded side down. Pour over the wine. Sprinkle over the chopped shallot and poach for about 10-12 minutes. When cooked, take fillets out of the baking dish, leave them in their lettuce leaves and keep warm. Melt remaining butter in a saucepan and, when foaming, stir in the flour. Cook for 2-3 minutes or until flour is pale brown. Strain in the cooking liquid from the fish, stir well and bring to the boil. When sauce thickens, add cream and re-boil. Add the blanched lettuce shreds, adjust seasoning and add lemon juice if necessary. Stir in the chopped chervil or parsley just before serving and pour the sauce into the serving dish. Set the fish parcels on top of the sauce to serve.

Sea Bass with Vegetables

PREPARATION TIME: 30 minutes
COOKING TIME: 40-60 minutes
OVEN TEMPERATURE: 180°C, 150°F, Gas Mark 4
SERVES: 4 people

1 sea bass, weighing 1-1.25kg (2-2½lbs)
225g (8oz) broccoli or French beans
450g (1lb) new potatoes
4 courgettes
4 very small turnips
1 small bunch spring onions
2 carrots
60g (2oz) butter
30g (1oz) flour
300ml (½ pint) milk
1 small bunch fresh thyme
3 lemons
Paprika
Chopped parsley
Salt and pepper

Clean the bass, trim the fins, but leave the head and tail on. Put seasoning and thyme inside the fish. Put the fish in the centre of a large square of buttered foil. Add the juice of 1 lemon, wrap fish loosely, and bake for 40-60 minutes, depending on weight. Cut broccoli into small florets (or top and tail beans, but leave whole). Scrub potatoes and turnips but do not peel. Top and tail the courgettes and cut into 6cm (2″) strips. Trim roots and tops from the spring onions, leaving on some of the green. Peel carrots, and cut to same size as courgettes. Keeping the vegetables in separate piles, steam potatoes and turnips for 15-20 minutes, the carrots, broccoli or beans for 6 minutes, and the courgettes and spring onions for 3 minutes. Arrange on a serving dish and keep warm.
Remove fish from wrapping and place in the middle of the vegetables, keep them warm while preparing the sauce. Melt the butter and cook the flour in it for 1-2 minutes until pale brown. Stir in the milk and allow sauce to boil for 1-2 minutes until thick. Strain in the cooking liquid from the fish. Peel and segment remaining lemons, working over a bowl to collect any juice. Chop the thyme and add to sauce along with lemon segments and juice. Sprinkle paprika on the potatoes, and chopped parsley on the carrots. Coat the fish with the lemon sauce and serve.

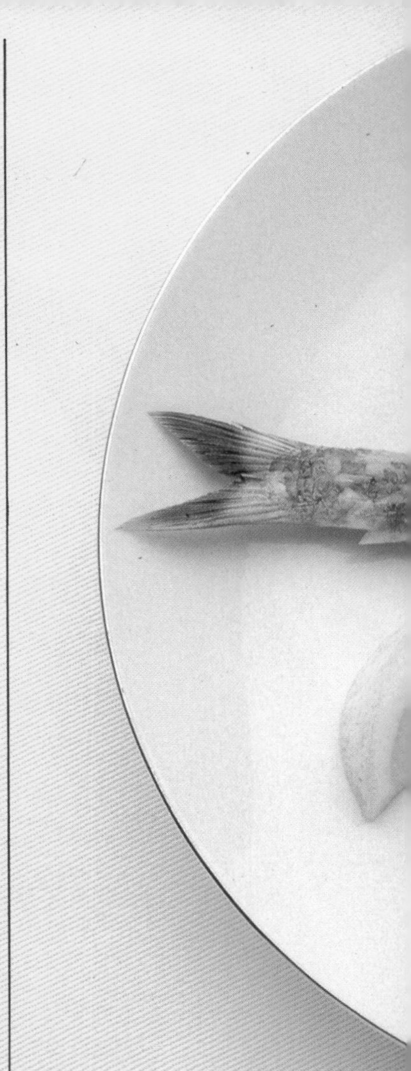

Salmon with Cucumber Cream

PREPARATION TIME: 15 minutes
COOKING TIME: 20 minutes
OVEN TEMPERATURE: 180°C, 350°F, Gas Mark 4
SERVES: 4 people

4 salmon cutlets (tail pieces)
30g (1oz) butter
1 small cucumber
30ml (1 fl oz) light stock
150ml (¼ pint) milk
30g (1oz) flour
Salt
Pepper
Lemon juice
Pinch sugar
Nutmeg
60ml (2oz) double cream

Grate cucumber. Melt the butter in a saucepan, add half the cucumber and cook slowly for about 10 minutes. Add flour and stir to blend. Stir in the stock and milk, bring to boil, then allow to cook slowly until cucumber has softened. Put the contents of the pan into a liquidiser or food processor and purée with the lemon juice, sugar, nutmeg, salt and pepper until smooth. Stir in remaining cucumber. Pour the cream over the top of the hot sauce and set aside in a saucepan while cooking the fish. Skin the cutlets and put into a baking dish with water and seasoning. Poach for 10 minutes, then remove from oven and keep warm. Re-heat cucumber sauce, stir in the cream and allow to boil for 1 minute. Spoon some of the sauce onto serving plates and put the salmon cutlets on top. Coat with more of the sauce.

Grilled Red Mullet with Garlic Sauce (left) and Turbot in Lettuce Leaves (below).

Lobster Newburg

PREPARATION TIME: 10 minutes
COOKING TIME: 12 minutes
SERVES: 4 people

1 large cooked lobster
300ml (½ pint) double cream
2 egg yolks
30g (1oz) butter
60ml (2 fl oz) dry sherry
Salt
Pepper
¼ tsp paprika
Cayenne pepper
1 tsp tomato purée

Heat the butter in a medium saucepan, add paprika and cook for 1 minute. Cut lobster in half. Take off tail and claws, remove the meat from these sections. Remove as much meat from the rest of the lobster as possible, add it to the pan along with tail and claw meat. Put in the sherry and cook for 1 minute. Remove the tail and claw meat and set aside for garnish. Mix egg yolks and cream together, and put in the pan with the lobster. Add the paprika, Cayenne, tomato purée and seasoning, and cook over a very low heat until the mixture begins to thicken. Serve with buttered rice, tossed with parsley. Garnish with the tail and claw meat.

Grilled Swordfish Steaks with Grapefruit

PREPARATION TIME: 10 minutes
COOKING TIME: 10 minutes
SERVES: 4 people

4 swordfish steaks, 2.5cm (1") thick
60g (2oz) melted butter (or 2 tbsps oil)
2 grapefruit
1 tbsp caster sugar
Coarsely ground pepper

Melt butter, and brush fish steaks on both sides. Heat grill to moderate. Season steaks with coarsely ground pepper. Grill on one side for about 5 minutes, turn, brush again with butter, then grill for about 3 minutes. Slice one grapefruit thinly, and peel and segment the other. Sprinkle the slices with caster sugar and brown under the grill. Put the segments on top of the fish and heat through for 1 minute. Overlap the grilled grapefruit slices on serving plates and put the fish on top.

Scampi Florentine

PREPARATION TIME: 15 minutes
COOKING TIME: 15-20 minutes
SERVES: 4 people

450g (1lb) cooked scampi
1kg (2lbs) fresh spinach
225g (8oz) button mushrooms
2 tomatoes, seeds removed
1 shallot
60g (2oz) butter
15g (½oz) flour
300ml (½ pint) milk
60g (2oz) grated Cheddar cheese
½ tsp Dijon mustard
Salt
Pepper
Nutmeg

Rinse spinach well, removing any thick stalks, and put it into a saucepan with a good pinch of salt. Cover and cook for about 3-5 minutes. In a small saucepan, heat half of the butter. Chop the shallot finely and cook it in the butter until soft. Wipe and slice the mushrooms and cook with the shallots. Drain the spinach well and chop finely. Mix the shallots, mushrooms and tomatoes with the spinach, add seasoning and a pinch of nutmeg, and put into an ovenproof dish. Melt half the remaining butter in a saucepan and

This page: Scampi Florentine (top) and Grilled Swordfish Steaks with Grapefruit (bottom).
Facing page: Lobster Newburg (top) and Skate with Capers, Olives and Shallots (bottom).

add the flour. Gradually stir in the milk, return the sauce to the heat and bring to the boil. Season with salt and pepper, and add mustard. Grate the cheese and add half to the sauce. Shell scampi if necessary. Heat remaining butter and quickly toss scampi in it over heat. Put scampi on top of the spinach and cover with sauce. Sprinkle remaining cheese over, and brown quickly under a hot grill. Serve immediately.

Skate with Capers, Olives and Shallots

PREPARATION TIME: 10 minutes

COOKING TIME: 15 minutes

OVEN TEMPERATURE: 180°C, 350°F, Gas Mark 4

SERVES: 4 people

4 wings of skate
2 tbsps capers
2 shallots, chopped
30g (1oz) stoned black olives, sliced
115g (4oz) butter
1 tbsp chopped mixed herbs
300ml (½ pint) white wine and water mixed
1 bay leaf
4 peppercorns
Salt
Lemon juice

Put the skate into a baking dish with the wine, water, bay leaf, salt and peppercorns. Cover and poach in the oven for 10 minutes. Drain well, removing any skin, and keep warm. Melt the butter and cook the shallots quickly, to brown both. Add capers and olives to heat through. Add herbs and lemon juice. Pour over the skate and serve immediately.

Monkfish Piperade

PREPARATION TIME: 20 minutes

COOKING TIME: 30 minutes

OVEN TEMPERATURE: 180°C, 350°F, Gas Mark 4

SERVES: 4 people

675g (1½lbs) monkfish fillets
2 onions
1 yellow pepper
1 red pepper
1 green pepper
1-2 cloves garlic
200ml (7½oz) tinned tomatoes
Salt
Pepper
2-3 tbsps olive oil
1 small French loaf
Oil for deep frying

Slice onions thinly and soften in 1 tbsp olive oil in a saucepan. Slice all the peppers in half, remove seeds, and cut into 1cm (½″) strips. Crush garlic and add to onions when tender, then cook gently for another 5 minutes. Add tomatoes and seasoning and let sauce simmer until liquid has reduced by about half. If the fish fillets are large, cut them in half again lengthways. Heat remaining oil in a saucepan and cook the fish until it is lightly brown. Transfer fish to an ovenproof dish, and when the piperade is ready, spoon it over the top of the fillets, and heat through in the oven for about 10-15 minutes. Meanwhile, slice the French loaf on the slant into 1cm (½″) slices. Fry in enough oil to barely cover until golden brown, then drain on absorbent paper. Put the monkfish piperade into a serving dish and surround with the bread.

Halibut and Crab Hollandaise

PREPARATION TIME: 15 minutes

COOKING TIME: 20 minutes

OVEN TEMPERATURE: 160°C, 325°F, Gas Mark 3

SERVES: 4 people

4 large fillets of halibut
75ml (2½ fl oz) white wine
1 bay leaf
Slice of onion
225g (8oz) crabmeat
2 tbsps double cream
15g (½oz) butter
15g (½oz) flour
2 egg yolks
115g (4oz) butter, melted
1 tbsp lemon juice
Salt and pepper
Cayenne pepper
Paprika

Poach the fish with the bay leaf, onion slice, wine and just enough water to cover. Cover the baking dish and cook for about 10 minutes in the oven. Put egg yolks, lemon juice, Cayenne and paprika into a liquidiser or food processor. Turn on the machine, and gradually pour the melted butter through the feed tube. When the sauce has thickened, set it aside. Remove fish from baking dish, cover and keep warm. Put the unmelted butter in a saucepan and add the flour, stirring well. Strain on the cooking liquid from the fish, stir well and bring to the boil. Add cream and bring back to the boil for 2-3 minutes. Adjust the seasoning of the sauce, mix it with the crab meat, and put into the bottom of an ovenproof dish that can also be used for serving. Put the fish on top of the crab meat and coat over with the Hollandaise sauce. Quickly brown the sauce under a high grill before serving.

Danish Plaice and Prawns

PREPARATION TIME: 15 minutes

COOKING TIME: 10-15 minutes

SERVES: 4 people

2 large plaice
225g (8oz) prawns
Seasoned flour
85g (3oz) butter
2 tbsps oil
Salt
Pepper
Lemon juice

Garnish
Lemon wedges

Peel the tails, shells and legs from 4 whole prawns and set aside. Fillet and skin the plaice, rinse and dry well, and coat lightly in seasoned flour. Heat the oil in a large frying pan, then drop in 30g (1oz) of the butter. Lay in the fish fillets and cook quickly to brown both sides. Transfer them to a serving dish and keep warm. Briefly cook the remaining peeled prawns in the butter remaining in the pan and scatter them over the cooked fillets. Wipe out the pan, put in the remaining butter, and cook to a good nut brown colour. Add a squeeze of lemon juice. Adjust seasoning, then pour over the plaice and prawns. Garnish with the whole prawns and lemon wedges.

Rock Salmon in Paprika Sauce

PREPARATION TIME: 20 minutes

COOKING TIME: 16 minutes

OVEN TEMPERATURE: 180°C, 350°F, Gas Mark 4

SERVES: 4 people

450g (1lb) rock salmon fillets
Lemon juice
Bay leaf
Slice of onion
6 peppercorns
30g (1oz) butter
30g (1oz) flour
60g (2oz) button mushrooms
1 small red pepper
300ml (½ pint) milk
2 tsps sweet paprika pepper
1 clove garlic, crushed
1 chopped shallot
1 tbsp chopped parsley
1 tsp chopped thyme
1 tsp tomato purée
225g (8oz) freshly cooked pasta
2 tbsps sour cream or yogurt
Salt
Pepper

Cut the fillets into 2.5cm (1″) chunks. Put into an ovenproof dish with water to cover, lemon juice,

bay leaf, onion slice and peppercorns. Cover and poach for about 10 minutes. Slice mushrooms finely. Slice the red pepper in half, core and seed it, then slice into thin shreds. Melt the butter in a saucepan, add mushrooms and shallot and cook for about 1 minute. Add garlic, red peppers, and sweet paprika pepper and allow to cook for about 2-3 minutes. Add the flour. Stir in well, and pour on the milk and the poaching liquid from the fish. Bring the sauce to the boil and allow to cook for 2-3 minutes and add thyme, parsley and tomato purée. Add salt and pepper to taste. Arrange the freshly cooked pasta in a serving dish and place the chunks of rock salmon on top of the pasta. Coat over with paprika sauce and spoon over the yogurt or sour cream to serve.

Danish Plaice and Prawns (left) and Monkfish Piperade (below).

Mackerel with Herb-Mustard Butter

PREPARATION TIME: 15 minutes

COOKING TIME: 12-20 minutes

SERVES: 4 people

4 mackerel
6 tbsps whole grain mustard
1 tbsp chopped parsley
1 tbsp snipped chives
1 tbsp chopped lemon thyme
1 tbsp chopped fresh basil
115g (4oz) butter
Salt
Pepper
Lemon juice

Garnish
1 bunch watercress

Wash and trim the mackerel, leaving heads and tails on. Cut 3 slashes on each side and spread 1 tbsp mustard over each fish. Sprinkle with freshly ground pepper. Melt the butter and sprinkle about 1 tsp over each fish. Grill them for 6-10 minutes on each side, depending on their size. Mix remaining butter and mustard with the herbs, seasoning and lemon juice. When fish are cooked put them into a serving dish and pour over the herb-mustard butter. Garnish with the watercress.

Sardine and Tomato Gratinée

PREPARATION TIME: 20-25 minutes

COOKING TIME: 15 minutes

OVEN TEMPERATURE: 225°C, 425°F, Gas Mark 8

SERVES: 4 people

1kg (2lbs) large, fresh sardines
3 tbsps olive oil
150ml (¼ pint) dry white wine
225g (8oz) tomatoes
4 anchovy fillets (optional)
60g (2oz) dry breadcrumbs
60g (2oz) grated Parmesan cheese
2 tbsps chopped fresh herbs
2 leeks, cleaned and sliced
Salt and pepper

Scale and clean the sardines. Heat oil in a large frying pan, add the sardines and brown well on both sides. Remove from the pan and set aside. Add leeks and cook slowly in the oil from the sardines. When they are soft, pour in the wine and boil to reduce by about two-thirds. Add tomatoes, salt pepper and herbs, and continue to simmer for 1 minute. Pour into an ovenproof dish and put the sardines on top. Sprinkle with the cheese and breadcrumbs. Bake for about 5 minutes. If desired, cut anchovy fillets lengthways into thinner strips and lay them on top of the gratinée before serving.

This page: Halibut and Crab Hollandaise (top) and Sardine and Tomato Gratinée (bottom). Facing page: Rock Salmon in Paprika Sauce (top) and Mackerel with Herb-Mustard Butter.

Fish Snacks and Savouries

Strawberry Prawns

PREPARATION TIME: 10 minutes

COOKING TIME: 3 minutes

SERVES: 4 people

285g (10oz) prawns, shelled and minced
1 small tin water chestnuts, peeled and minced
60g (2oz) ham, minced
1 tsp white wine
¼ tsp minced spring onion
¼ tsp grated fresh ginger
1½ tbsps cornflour
1 egg white
Sesame seeds
Pinch of salt
Oil for deep frying
4 tbsps hoisin sauce
1 tsp white or rice wine vinegar
1 tsp honey
2 tbsps water
1 tsp sesame oil

Mix prawns and water chestnuts with wine, spring onion, ginger, egg white and a pinch of salt. Chill mixture for 30 minutes before using. Form mixture into strawberry-sized balls. Cover each ball with the finely minced ham. Fry in deep oil for about 3 minutes at 190°C, 375°F. Drain, roll in sesame seeds to coat, and place on a plate. Mix hoisin sauce, honey, vinegar, water and sesame oil together, and serve with the prawn balls. Garnish prawn balls with parsley.

Fisherman's Pie

PREPARATION TIME: 20 minutes

COOKING TIME: 45 minutes

OVEN TEMPERATURE: 190°C, 375°F, Gas Mark 5

SERVES: 4 people

450g (1lb) cod fillet
450g (1lb) smoked cod fillet
150ml (¼ pint) cockles
115g (4oz) peeled prawns
300ml (½ pint) milk
150ml (¼ pint) water
1 bay leaf
30g (1oz) butter
30g (1oz) plain flour
1 heaped tbsp chopped parsley
Squeeze of lemon juice
Salt
Freshly ground pepper

Topping
675g (1½ lbs) potatoes
1-2 tbsps milk
30g (1oz) butter
Salt
Pepper

Skin fish and cut into pieces. Keep fresh cod and smoked cod separate. Put each into a separate saucepan with the milk, water, and half a bay leaf in each. Bring to the boil; lower heat, and simmer, covered, for about 10 minutes. Meanwhile, peel potatoes and cut them into even-sized chunks. Add them to a pan of cold, salted water, bring up to the boil and cook for about 20 minutes, or until tender. Drain, return to the hot saucepan and shake over heat until they are dry. Mash them, and beat in hot milk and half the butter. Season with salt and pepper and set aside. Take cooked fish from the milk and break it up, removing any bones. Strain cooking liquid from both saucepan – there should be 300ml (½ pint) in all. Melt butter in a saucepan over a low heat. Stir in the flour, and cook gently for 1 minute. Gradually stir in the reserved fish liquid. Bring to boil. Stir well and simmer for 2-3

This page: Kedgeree. Facing page: Strawberry Prawns (top) and Crab Toasts (bottom).

minutes. Take off the heat. Fold in the fish and parsley, and add lemon juice, a seasoning of salt and pepper, cockles and prawns. Butter a 900ml (1½ pint) ovenproof dish and put the fish mixture in it. Fill a piping bag, fitted with a rosette nozzle, with the mashed potato mixture and pipe in a lattice over the surface of the fish. Pipe a border round its edge. Dot over the remaining butter in pieces, and put into the oven for about 20 minutes and brown under a grill, with grated cheese sprinkled on top if desired.

Crab Ramekins

PREPARATION TIME: 10 minutes

COOKING TIME: 15 minutes

OVEN TEMPERATURE: 220°C, 425°F, Gas Mark 7

SERVES: 4 people

85g (3oz) Cheddar or Double Gloucester cheese
85g (3oz) Parmesan cheese
85g (3oz) fresh white breadcrumbs
300ml (½ pint) single cream
115g (4oz) crabmeat
3 eggs
1 tsp Worcestershire sauce
Cayenne pepper
Ground mace
Dry mustard
Salt and pepper

Separate the eggs and grate the cheese. Mix the breadcrumbs with the cream and grated cheese. Add the Worcestershire sauce, a pinch of mace, Cayenne, dry mustard and seasoning. Beat in the egg yolks. Whip the whites until stiff but not dry and fold into the cheese mixture along with the crabmeat. Pour into a large, buttered, ovenproof dish or smaller ramekin dishes. Bake until risen.

Smoked Haddock Lyonnaise

PREPARATION TIME: 15 minutes

COOKING TIME: 20 minutes

SERVES: 4 people

3 medium onions
15g (½oz) unsalted butter
2 tbsps oil
3 medium-sized potatoes
450g (1lb) smoked haddock or smoked cod
Freshly ground pepper
2 tbsps white wine vinegar
Chopped parsley

Heat oil in a large frying pan and, when hot, drop in butter. Cut smoked fish into chunks and sauté. Remove from the pan and set aside. Slice onions and cook them slowly in the butter until they turn golden brown. Slice the potatoes and cook in boiling salted water until slightly softened. Add them just as onions are turning colour, then sauté the mixture to brown lightly. Add the smoked fish, sauté for a few minutes, and adjust seasoning. Pile onto a serving platter. Add vinegar to the pan, bring rapidly to boil, add chopped parsley, and pour over potatoes and haddock.

Crab and Spinach Roulade

PREPARATION TIME: 15 minutes

COOKING TIME: 18 minutes

OVEN TEMPERATURE: 200°C, 400°F, Gas Mark 6

SERVES: 4 people

Roulade
450g (1lb) spinach, washed
15g (½oz) butter
4 eggs, separated
Parmesan cheese, grated
Salt
Pepper

Filling
115g (4oz) crabmeat
115g (4oz) mushrooms, thinly sliced
15g (½oz) butter
15g (½oz) flour
150ml (¼ pint) milk
Nutmeg
2-3 tbsps cream
Paprika
Cayenne pepper
Lemon juice

Cook the spinach in boiling salted water for about 5 minutes. Drain, rinse under cold water, and press well to remove excess liquid. Put the spinach into a food processor with the butter and egg yolks and process to a smooth purée. Whisk egg whites until they are stiff but not dry and fold into the spinach mixture. Line a 30cm x 20cm (12" x 8") Swiss roll tin with Bakewell paper. Spread in the spinach mixture very quickly and dust well with Parmesan cheese. Bake in the top half of the oven for about 10 minutes or until mixture has risen and is firm to the touch. Meanwhile, prepare filling. Sauté sliced mushrooms in butter. Remove from heat, and add flour, paprika, Cayenne, lemon juice and seasoning to taste. Pour on the milk and bring to the boil, then simmer to a creamy consistency. Draw pan from heat and stir in nutmeg and cream (a dash of Tabasco and 1 tbsp dry sherry can also be used if desired). Once the pan is again off the heat, stir in the crabmeat. When the roulade is cooked, quickly turn it out onto a sheet of greaseproof paper, cheese side down, and peel off the paper in which it was cooked. Spread it with the filling, roll up as for a Swiss roll, starting at the short end, and serve sprinkled with more Parmesan cheese if desired.

Crab Toasts

PREPARATION TIME: 10 minutes

COOKING TIME: 4 minutes per piece

SERVES: 4 people

8 slices white bread
225g (8oz) crabmeat
3 tbsps minced water chestnuts
1 egg white
½ tsp white wine
½ tsp mustard powder
½ tsp salt
½ tsp minced spring onion
¼ tsp grated ginger
1½ tsps cornflour
1 tbsp minced parsley
Oil for deep frying

Remove crusts from the bread, and slice diagonally across each piece to form 2 triangles. Mix crabmeat and chestnuts together. Add egg white, wine, salt, spring onion, ginger and cornflour. Heap the mixture generously onto each triangle of bread. Sprinkle with parsley, pressing down firmly so that the mixture will not float off during frying. Heat oil to 180°C, 350°F. Put a piece of the prepared bread, crabmeat side down, onto a slotted spoon, place it in the oil and gently remove spoon. Fry the pieces, a few at a time, until the bread side becomes a golden brown. Turn each piece over and fry again. Drain on absorbent paper and keep warm in the oven until all the pieces are finished.

Crab Ramekins (above right) and Smoked Haddock Lyonnaise (right) and Fisherman's Pie (inset above).

Oysters and Apples

PREPARATION TIME: 10 minutes
COOKING TIME: 2-3 minutes
SERVES: 4 people

105g (3½oz) tin smoked oysters
1 large dessert apple, unpeeled
4-5 strips streaky bacon
30g (1oz) Cheddar cheese

Core and quarter the apple, and cut the quarters into 8-10 slices. Divide the cheese into 8-10 small pieces. Put 1 piece on each slice of apple and an oyster on top of the cheese. Trim the rind from the bacon, remove any bones, and cut each strip in half. Wrap the bacon around the oysters and apples. Secure with a cocktail stick and grill until the bacon is crisp, turning once.

Prawn Pastry Puffs

PREPARATION TIME: 15 minutes
COOKING TIME: 25-30 minutes
OVEN TEMPERATURE: 200°C, 400°F, Gas Mark 6
SERVES: 4 people

Choux Pastry
100g (3½oz) plain flour
85g (3oz) butter
225ml (7½ fl oz) water
3 eggs
Salt

Filling
300ml (½ pint) milk
45g (1½ oz) butter
45g (1½ oz) flour
30ml (1 fl oz) white wine
175g (6oz) prawns
2 hard-boiled eggs, quartered
Nutmeg
1 bay leaf
1 tsp chopped dill
Salt
Pepper

Prepare the pastry. Sift flour with a pinch of salt. Place butter and water in a pan over a gentle heat. When butter is melted, bring water to the boil. Take off the heat and immediately tip in all the flour. Beat until the mixture is smooth and leaves the sides of the pan. Leave to cool. Whisk the eggs lightly and add by degrees to the mixture, beating thoroughly between each addition. (This part of the recipe may be done with an electric mixer or in a food processor). When finished, the paste should be smooth and shiny and hold its shape when dropped from a spoon. Lightly grease a baking sheet and sprinkle it lightly with water. Place the pastry mixture by heaped teaspoonfuls onto the sheet. If desired, the puffs can be made slightly larger by using a dessertspoon. Bake until the puffs are firm to the touch and a good golden brown. For the sauce, melt the butter over a gentle heat and blend in the flour. Stir in the milk gradually and add the bay leaf. Add the wine and bring the mixture to the boil, stirring constantly. Remove the bay leaf, add the prawns, dill and eggs, and adjust the seasoning. Cut the pastry puffs almost in half through the middle and fill with the prawn and egg mixture. Serve hot or cold.

This page: Crab and Spinach Roulade (top) and Prawn Risotto (bottom).
Facing page: Prawn Pastry Puffs (top) and Oysters and Apples (bottom).

Pizza Marinara

PREPARATION TIME: 15 minutes

COOKING TIME: 25-30 minutes

OVEN TEMPERATURE: 220°C, 425°F, Gas Mark 7

SERVES: 4 people

145g (5oz) plain flour, sifted
1 tsp baking powder
½ tsp salt
90ml (3 fl oz) milk
2 tbsp salad oil
115g (4oz) tinned tomatoes
1 tsp tomato purée
1 clove crushed garlic
½ tsp oregano
½ tsp basil
Fennel seeds
Salt
Pepper
30g (1oz) prawns
4 anchovy fillets
30g (1oz) cockles
6-8 mussels
1 tsp capers
2-3 black olives
115g (4oz) sliced mozzarella cheese

Sift flour, baking powder and salt into a bowl and add milk and oil. Stir vigorously until mixture leaves the sides of the bowl. Press it into a ball and knead it in the bowl for about 2 minutes until smooth. Cover, and leave it to sit while preparing sauce. Put tomatoes, purée, herbs, seasoning and garlic together in a small saucepan. Bring to the boil and reduce to thicken. Leave to cool. Roll out the pizza into a 24cm (12″) circle. Spread the sauce evenly, leaving a 1cm (½″) border around the edge. Scatter over the shell fish, anchovy fillets, olives and capers. Slice cheese thinly and place it on top of the fish. Bake in a pre-set oven until cheese browns lightly and the crust is crisp.

Anchovy Pâté with Crudités

PREPARATION TIME: 15 minutes

SERVES: 4 people

225g (8oz) tin anchovy fillets in olive oil
70ml (2 fl oz) olive oil
60g (2oz) curd cheese
115g (4oz) pitted black olives
60g (2oz) capers
1 tbsp Dijon mustard
1 tsp ground pepper

Put all ingredients into the bowl of a liquidiser or food processor and run the machine until well mixed. The mixture may have to be worked in 2 batches. Serve with French bread or toast, and raw vegetables of all kinds – tomatoes, mushrooms, celery, radishes, French beans, cauliflower, carrots, cucumber, peppers, spring onions, or quarters of hard boiled eggs.

Goujons

PREPARATION TIME: 20-30 minutes

COOKING TIME: 2-3 minutes

SERVES: 4 people

2 lemon soles
Seasoned flour
1 egg
1 dsp olive oil
Dry breadcrumbs
Oil for deep frying
Pinch of salt

Tartare Sauce
2 tbsps mayonnaise
1 tbsp double cream
2 tsps chopped parsley
2 tsps chopped gherkins
2 tsps chopped capers
1 tsp chopped onion

This page: Anchovy Pâté with Crudités.
Facing page: Goujons (top) and Pizza Marinara (bottom).

Curry Sauce
2 tbsps mayonnaise
1 tbsp double cream
1 tsp curry paste
1½ tsps mango chutney

Tomato Herb Sauce
2 tbsps mayonnaise
1 tbsp double cream
1 tsp chopped parsley
1 tsp chopped tarragon
1 tsp chopped chives
1 tsp tomato purée
Squeeze of lemon

Fillet the soles and skin the fillets. Rinse fillets in cold water and pat dry. Cut each fillet on the diagonal into pieces about 1cm (½″) thick and 5-8cm (2½-3″) long. Coat thoroughly with seasoned flour, shaking off any excess. Beat eggs lightly and mix in the olive oil. Dip fish pieces into the mixture and roll them in the breadcrumbs. Put fish aside in a cool place: do not coat the fish too soon before cooking. Mix ingredients for the various sauces together and set aside. Heat oil in a deep fryer to about 190°C, 375°F. Put fish in the frying basket and lower into the hot oil. Fry for 2-3 minutes until crisp and golden brown. Fry in small batches. Drain fish on crumpled, absorbent paper sprinkled lightly with salt, and then pile the fish into a hot serving dish. Garnish with wedges of lemon and sprigs of parsley, if desired, and serve the sauces separately for dipping the fish.

Prawn Risotto

PREPARATION TIME: 15 minutes
COOKING TIME: 25 minutes
SERVES: 4 people

450g (1lb) unpeeled prawns
4 tomatoes
3 cloves garlic
1 large onion
3 tbsps olive oil
2 tbsps chopped parsley
1 glass white wine
175g (6oz) round Italian or rissotto rice
1 tsp tomato purée
2 tbsps grated Parmesan cheese
Salt
Freshly ground pepper

Skin, seed and chop tomatoes, and peel and chop garlic and onion. Peel prawns, leaving 4 unpeeled for garnish. Cook wine and prawn shells together and leave to cool. Heat olive oil in a fairly wide pan or sauté pan. Soften onion in the oil without browning. Add garlic and parsley. Fry gently for a minute. Add rice and strain on the wine. Add tomato purée and more water to just barely cover rice. Season with salt and pepper, stirring the rice, adding more water as it becomes absorbed. The rice will take about 20 minutes to cook. When it is cooked, toss in the peeled prawns and cheese to heat through. Pile risotto into a serving dish and top with unpeeled prawns. Sprinkle over some chopped parsley.

Sardine Savouries

PREPARATION TIME: 10-20 minutes
COOKING TIME: 20 minutes
OVEN TEMPERATURE: 190°C, 375°F, Gas Mark 5
SERVES: 4 people

225g (8oz) shortcrust or puff pastry
60g (2oz) fresh Parmesan or Cheddar cheese
115g (4oz) (approx) sardines
Cayenne pepper
Chopped chives or spring onion
1 egg, beaten
Salt
Pepper

Prepare the pastry, or use ready-made. Roll it out and cut into 8 pieces large enough to fold up around the sardines. Remove bones from the sardines and put the fillets on top of one half of the pastry rectangles. Sprinkle over the grated cheese, Cayenne pepper, seasoning, and chives or onion, and fold the other half of the pastry over to cover the sardines. Seal the edges well and cut two slits in the top. Brush with the beaten egg and bake until golden brown and risen. Serve hot or cold.

Omelette of Cockles and Mussels

PREPARATION TIME: 5 minutes
COOKING TIME: 7-10 minutes
SERVES: 4 people

300ml (½ pint) shelled cockles
300ml (½ pint) shelled mussels, packed in brine
6-8 eggs
45g (1½oz) butter
Drop of anchovy essence
Cayenne pepper
Salt
Pepper
Finely chopped parsley and chives

Poach mussels in boiling salted water for about 2 minutes. Add a bay leaf if desired. Rinse cockles under cold water. Separate eggs and beat yolks with anchovy essence, Cayenne pepper and seasoning. Whisk whites until stiff but not dry and fold into yolks. Heat the butter in a large omelette pan and when foaming, pour in the egg mixture. Allow eggs to set on the bottom. Score the omelette down the middle. Add cockles and mussels and fold in two. Heat through for 2 minutes to cook the inside of the omelette and to warm the shellfish. Serve immediately, sprinkled with finely chopped parsley and chives. (This dish can be adapted to make individual omelettes).

Kedgeree

PREPARATION TIME: 15 minutes
COOKING TIME: 20 minutes
SERVES: 4 people

340g (12oz) smoked haddock
115g (4oz) mushrooms
115g (4oz) peeled prawns
Juice of half a lemon
175g (6oz) rice
1 small onion
600ml (1 pint) milk
30g (1oz) flour
60g (2oz) butter
½ tsp curry powder
4 hard-boiled eggs
Fresh parsley
150ml (¼ pint) single cream
Salt
Pepper

Cook rice for about 12 minutes. Drain under hot water to remove starch and leave to dry. Melt butter in a large pan. Slice the onion and fry until golden brown. Add mushrooms and fry for a few seconds before adding the flour. Add curry powder and cook for a minute or two. Gradually work in the cold milk until all is incorporated. Simmer for 5 minutes, stirring constantly, until thick. Skin smoked haddock, cut into small pieces, add to the sauce and continue to cook. Once cooked, add the lemon juice, prawns and salt and pepper to taste. Stir in the rice. If sauce seems too thick, add single cream. Mound kedgeree into a heated serving dish. Sprinkle on chopped parsley and garnish with slices or quarters of egg.

Omelette of Cockles and Mussels (left) and Sardine Savouries (below).

Section 3

HOME FARE

Family Recipes

Cod in White Sauce

675g (1½lb) cod fillet
Salt and pepper
150ml (¼ pint) milk
30ml (2 tblsp) lemon juice
25g (1oz) butter

White Sauce
25g (1oz) margarine
25g (1oz) flour
Milk
Salt and pepper
Pinch of paprika

Wash and skin the fish and cut into four pieces. Place the fish in an ovenproof dish and season well. Pour the milk and lemon juice over the fish and dot with some of the butter. Cover the dish and cook for 20 minutes at 200°C, 400°F, Gas Mark 6. Melt the margarine and remaining butter in a pan, stir in the flour and cook for 1 minute. Drain the liquid from the fish and add enough milk to make up to 300ml (½ pint). Stir the liquid slowly into the roux, bring to the boil and cook for 1 minute, stirring continuously. Add seasoning and paprika. Serve with new potatoes and broccoli.
Serves four.

Beef Surprise

1 onion, peeled and chopped
40g (1½oz) fat
25g (1oz) flour
300ml (½ pint) brown stock
Pinch of mixed herbs
450g (1lb) minced beef
Salt and pepper

Cook the onion in the fat until transparent. Add the flour and cook for 5 minutes. Add the stock, bring to the boil and cook until the sauce thickens. Add the herbs, minced beef and seasoning. Stir continuously, cook until the meat is browned. Lower the heat and simmer gently for 1 hour, stirring frequently. Arrange on a hot dish. Garnish with tomatoes and creamed potatoes, and serve.
Serves four.

Chicken Pie

Pastry
225g (8oz) flour
Pinch of salt
50g (2oz) margarine
50g (2oz) lard
Beaten egg and milk mixed together to glaze top of pie

Chicken Sauce
150ml (¼ pint) milk
15g (½oz) margarine
15g (½oz) plain flour
Salt and pepper
225g (8oz) cooked chicken, chopped
45ml (3 tblsp) white wine (optional)

First make the sauce by placing the milk, margarine and flour in a small pan. Bring to the boil, whisking continuously. Simmer for 2 minutes until the sauce thickens. Add seasoning, stir in the chopped chicken and add the wine, if desired. Sift the flour and salt into a bowl and rub in the margarine and lard until it looks like breadcrumbs. Add enough water to form a dough. Use half the dough to line a large, flat plate. Add the chicken mixture then cover with the remaining pastry, sealing the edges. Cut slits in the top. Brush the top of the pie with the beaten egg and milk mixture. Cook in the oven for 25 minutes at 200°C, 400°F, Gas Mark 6 until golden brown. Serve with creamed potatoes and carrots.
Serves four.

Spaghetti Bolognese

25g (1oz) butter
15ml (1 tblsp) olive oil
50g (2oz) mushrooms, chopped
1 onion, peeled and chopped
1 carrot, peeled and chopped
225g (8oz) minced beef
100g (4oz) tomato purée
300ml (½ pint) brown stock
225g (8oz) spaghetti
Parmesan cheese, to serve

Heat the butter and oil in a pan and fry the mushrooms, onions and carrot. Stir in the meat, cook for a few minutes then add the tomato purée and stock and simmer gently. Cook for one hour, until the mixture thickens, stirring occasionally. Meanwhile, place the spaghetti in boiling, salted water and cook for 15 minutes. Drain. Serve together with the bolognese sauce and sprinkle with Parmesan cheese.
Serves four.

Beef Bake

675g (1½lb) stewing steak
25g (1oz) flour
Salt and pepper
25g (1oz) lard
2 onions, peeled and chopped
600ml (1 pint) brown stock
15ml (1 tblsp) tomato purée
45ml (3 tblsp) red wine (optional)
2 carrots, peeled and sliced
10ml (2 tsp) dried mixed herbs

Topping
50g (2oz) white breadcrumbs
50g (2oz) butter
225g (8oz) self-raising flour
5ml (1 tsp) salt
Pepper
5ml (1 tsp) garlic salt
5ml (1 tsp) Parmesan cheese
45ml (3 tblsp) oil
150ml (¼ pint) milk

Cut the meat into cubes and toss in seasoned flour. Melt the lard in a pan and fry the onions. Add the meat and fry for 5 minutes or until the meat is brown. Remove from the heat and blend in the stock, tomato purée and red wine. Add the carrots and herbs. Return to the heat and bring to the boil. Turn the mixture into an ovenproof dish, cover and cook in the oven for 2 hours at 170°C, 325°F, Gas Mark 3. Fry the breadcrumbs in the butter until golden brown, then lift out on to a plate. Sieve together the flour, salt, pepper, garlic salt and Parmesan cheese, add the oil and milk and gradually mix to a dough. Drop large spoonfuls of the dough into the fried breadcrumbs and roll into balls. Arrange on top of the meat mixture. Return the casserole uncovered to the oven and cook for a further hour, or until the top is golden brown. Serve with peas and new potatoes.
Serves four.

Sweet and Sour Pork Chops with Rice

4 large pork chops

Sauce
400g (14oz) can of tomatoes
1 large green pepper, cored, seeded and chopped
30ml (2 tblsp) cornflour
45ml (3 tblsp) wine vinegar
30ml (2 tblsp) brown sugar
30ml (2 tblsp) soy sauce
Salt and pepper

To make the sauce place the tomatoes and 150ml (¼ pint) of their juice in a saucepan and break down with a fork. Add the green pepper, bring to the boil and simmer for 10 minutes. Blend the cornflour and vinegar together to form a paste. Add the paste to the tomato mixture. Add the remaining sauce ingredients and cook for 15 minutes. Meanwhile, cook the pork chops under a moderately hot grill. Place the chops on a flat, flameproof serving dish and pour over the sauce. Place under a hot grill for 2-3 minutes to heat through.
Serves four.

Pork Chops with Brussels Sprouts and Sweet Corn (far left, top), Beef Surprise (far left, bottom) and Cod in White Sauce (left).

Pork Chops with Brussels Sprouts and Sweet Corn

75g (3oz) butter
1 large onion, peeled and chopped
450g (1lb) Brussels sprouts
100g (4oz) frozen sweet corn
4 pork chops (large)
5ml (1 tsp) salt
5ml (1 tsp) cayenne pepper
5ml (1 tsp) chopped parsley

Melt 25g (1oz) of butter in a saucepan. Add the chopped onion and fry lightly. Cook the Brussels sprouts in boiling, salted water for about 8 minutes until cooked but still firm. Also cook the sweet corn. Drain both vegetables. Melt 25g (1oz) of the butter and add the drained Brussels sprouts and sweet corn and cook very gently, shaking the pan frequently. Melt the remaining butter. Sprinkle the pork chops with the salt and the cayenne pepper and fry them in the butter over a medium heat for about 5-10 minutes on each side. Remove the chops to a serving dish. Add 2 tablespoons of water to the juices in the pan and bring to the boil, stirring continuously. Arrange the vegetables round the chops and pour over the sauce. Sprinkle with the chopped parsley and serve.
Serves four.

Facing page: Spaghetti Bolognese (top), Chicken Pie (centre left) and Shepherd's Pie (bottom).

Chicken Casserole

25g (1oz) lard
100g (4oz) mushrooms, sliced
4 chicken joints
75g (3oz) flour
2 large carrots, peeled and sliced
1 potato, peeled and sliced
300ml (½ pint) chicken stock
300ml (½ pint) white wine
Salt and pepper
75g (3oz) peas

Melt half the lard, fry the mushrooms, then place them in an ovenproof dish. Coat the chicken in the flour and fry in the remaining lard until golden brown. Transfer to the ovenproof dish and add the sliced carrots and potato. Put the leftover flour in a pan, add the stock and wine, stirring all the time. Add the seasoning, bring to the boil and pour over the chicken and vegetables. Cover and cook in the oven for 1 hour 35 minutes at 180°C, 350°F, Gas Mark 4. Add the peas 10 minutes before the end of the cooking time. Serve with new potatoes.
Serves four.

Shepherd's Pie

25g (1oz) fat
1 onion, peeled and chopped
50g (2oz) mushrooms, chopped
2 tomatoes, skinned and chopped
350g (12oz) cooked beef or lamb, minced
Pinch of mixed herbs
Salt and pepper
300ml (½ pint) brown stock
450g (1lb) mashed potato
50g (2oz) butter

Heat the fat and fry the onion for 3 minutes. Add the mushrooms and fry for another minute. Add the tomatoes and the meat and cook for 3 minutes. Stir in the herbs and seasoning and finally add the stock. Put the mixture into a pie dish and cover with the mashed potato. Dot small pieces of butter over the mashed potato. Cook in the oven for 30-40 minutes at 200°C, 400°F, Gas Mark 6 until the top is crisp and brown. Serve with peas and leeks.
Serves four.

This page: Beef Bake (top left), Chicken Casserole (top right) and Sweet and Sour Pork Chops with Rice (bottom).

This page: Wine Coated Ham (top), Black Pudding with Apple (centre right), Gammon Rounds with Onion Sauce (bottom left).

Facing page: Steak and Kidney Pudding (top left), Crunchy Lamb Pie (top right), Meat Loaf (centre left) and Toad in the Hole (bottom right).

Toad in the Hole

225g (8oz) sausages (pork or beef)
15g (½oz) lard
100g (4oz) plain flour
2.5ml (½ level tsp) salt
Pinch of garlic salt
1 egg
300ml (½ pint) milk

Put the sausages into a large, shallow tin or dish. Add the lard and place in the oven at 220°C, 450°F, Gas Mark 7. Sieve the flour, salt and garlic salt into a bowl. Add the egg and a little milk and beat until smooth. Add the rest of the milk a little at a time, beating well, to make a batter. Pour the batter into the tin. Cook for 30-45 minutes. Serve with mixed vegetables and duchesse potatoes.
Serves three.

Meat Loaf

2 slices of bread
450g (1lb) prime minced beef
1 onion, peeled and chopped
5ml (1 tsp) Worcestershire sauce
Salt and pepper
1 egg, beaten

Grate the bread or place in a blender to produce crumbs. Mix the mince, onion, Worcestershire sauce, salt and pepper and breadcrumbs. Add the egg and bind the mixture together. Put the mixture into a greased loaf tin and cover with greaseproof paper. Cook in the oven for 50-60 minutes at 200°C, 390°F, Gas Mark 6. When the meat loaf is cooked the juices should run clear when a skewer is inserted. Turn the loaf out onto a flat serving dish. Garnish with cooked vegetables such as carrots, runner beans, peas and Brussels sprouts.
Serves four.

Black Pudding with Apple

450g (1lb) potatoes, peeled
3 large cooking apples
45ml (3 tblsp) oil
25g (1oz) butter
450g (1lb) black pudding, sliced
5ml (1 tsp) chopped parsley

Boil and mash the potatoes and keep them warm. Peel and core the apples and cut each one into 8 segments. Heat half the oil and all the butter in a pan. Add the apple, cover and cook for 5 minutes on a low heat. Drain and keep warm. In another pan heat the remaining oil and add the sliced black pudding. Fry on both sides until it is slightly crisp and heated through. Remove and drain. Place the mashed potato in the centre of a heated serving dish and surround it with alternate portions of black pudding and apple. Sprinkle the potato with the chopped parsley. Serve with a green vegetable and fresh tomatoes.
Serves four.

Wine Coated Ham

1kg (2lb) ham
Salt and pepper
225g (8oz) carrots, peeled and cut into sticks
225g (8oz) turnips, peeled and cut into sticks
225g (8oz) green beans
225g (8oz) frozen peas
15ml (1 tblsp) soft brown sugar
150ml (¼ pint) red wine
50g (2oz) butter

Cover the ham with cold water and soak for 4 hours, changing the water frequently. Place the ham in a large pan, cover with cold water and simmer for 40 minutes. Bring a large pan of salted water to the boil, add the vegetables and cook for about 10 minutes. When the vegetables are cooked drain them, rinse with cold water and drain them again. Lift the ham from the pan. Peel off the rind and place the ham in an ovenproof dish. Sprinkle the ham with sugar and place in the oven for 5 minutes at 190°C, 375°F, Gas Mark 5. Pour the wine over and return to the oven for 5 minutes, basting frequently. Melt the butter in a pan and add the drained vegetables, salt and pepper. Heat through, stirring continuously. Place the ham on a large serving dish with the vegetables and serve with the sauce from the cooking. Serve with new potatoes if required.
Serves four.

Gammon Rounds in Onion Sauce

4 gammon rounds
3 onions, peeled and sliced
50g (2oz) butter or margarine
50g (2oz) flour
Salt and pepper
600ml (1 pint) milk

Grill the gammon rounds until tender. Boil the onions until soft, then drain. Melt the butter or margarine, remove from the heat and stir in the flour. Return to the heat and cook gently for a few minutes. Remove the pan from the heat and gradually stir in the milk. Bring to the boil and cook, stirring with a wooden spoon, until smooth. Season well. If any small lumps have formed whisk thoroughly. Stir in the boiled onions and serve with the gammon. Serve with potatoes in their jackets, and runner beans.
Serves four.

Crunchy Lamb Pie

25g (1oz) margarine
1 onion, peeled and chopped
½ packet parsley sauce mix
150ml (¼ pint) milk
1 tblsp thin cream or top of the milk
175g (6oz) cold, cooked lamb, minced
½ packet instant potato
25g (1oz) Lancashire or Cheddar cheese, grated

Heat the margarine and fry the onion until soft. Make the parsley sauce as directed on the packet, using the milk, and stir in the cream, or top of the milk and the onion. Add the lamb to the sauce. Mix well and turn into a greased pie dish. Make the instant potato as directed on the packet and spread over the meat mixture. Sprinkle the cheese over the potato. Cook in the oven for 30 minutes at 200-220°C, 400-425°F, Gas Mark 6-7. Serve with a green vegetable or baked onions.
Serves two.

Farmhouse Meat and Game

Pheasant Braised in Red Wine

PREPARATION TIME: 15 minutes

COOKING TIME: 1 hour 15 minutes

SERVES: 4 persons

1 fairly large pheasant
2 tblsp (30ml) oil
1 tblsp (15ml) butter
1 heaped tblsp (20ml) flour
1 onion
2 eating apples
Rind and juice of one orange
¼ pint (150ml) red wine
¼ pint (150ml) stock or water
Salt and pepper
Bayleaf, sprig of parsley and thyme, tied together
1 heaped tsp (7ml) brown sugar

Melt oil and butter in a heavy pan. Put in pheasant, turning it to brown all over. Remove pheasant and place it in a casserole with the apples, quartered and cored but not peeled. Chop the onion and add it to the fat in the pan. Allow it to soften without browning. Stir in the flour then gradually add the stock and the wine and bring to the boil, stirring all the time. Add the grated orange rind and the orange juice and sugar. Season with pepper and pour the sauce over the pheasant. Add the herbs, cover the casserole and place in a preheated oven, 180°C, 350°F, Gas Mark 4, for one hour.

Limerick Ham

PREPARATION TIME: 12 hours

Limerick ham was smoked using a special recipe in which juniper berries were added to the fire to produce the distinctive flavour. It has been famous all over the world since the 18th century.
Smoked hams should be allowed to soak in cold water for at least twelve hours, then rinsed and covered with cold water to which a clove studded onion, a few peppercorns and a tblsp (15ml) of honey or brown sugar have been added. Bring slowly to the boil, skim, then simmer for 20 minutes to the pound (450g) and 20 minutes over. The ham is cooked when the thick skin peels back easily. Remove the ham from the water and peel off the skin. If it is to be served hot, coat the ham with browned breadcrumbs and put it in a roasting pan in the oven, 180°C, 350°F, Gas Mark 4, for 40 minutes. If it is to be eaten cold it should be replaced in the pot after the skin has been removed and allowed to cool in the liquor in

This page: Cold Chicken in Tarragon Sauce (top) and Beef Braised in Guinness.
Facing page: Limerick Ham (top) and Pheasant Braised in Red Wine (bottom).

which it was cooked. It can be glazed by heating up equal quantities of brown sugar, vinegar and apricot jam and pouring this over the ham.

Beef Braised in Guinness

PREPARATION TIME: 15 minutes
COOKING TIME: 1 hour 45 minutes
SERVES: 4 persons

1½lb (675g) leg of beef
2 medium onions
½lb (225g) carrots
2 heaped tblsp (40ml) flour
½ tsp (2.5ml) basil
Salt and pepper
1 tsp (5ml) honey
¼ pint (150ml) Guinness
¼ pint (150ml) stock or water
2-3 tblsp (30-45ml) cooking oil

The leg of beef should be about 1 inch (2.5cm) thick and cut into about twelve pieces. If you use braising steak, such as silverside or topside, it will only need about an hour.
Peel the onions and chop them fairly small. Peel the carrots and slice them into pieces about the size of your little finger. Put the flour on a plate and mix in a tsp (5ml) of salt and a good sprinkling of pepper. Heat the oil in the pan, add the onions and cook until soft. Transfer them with a slotted spoon to a large, shallow, greased, ovenproof dish. Dip the pieces of meat in the seasoned flour and brown them in the fat in the pan. Remove these as they are cooked and place in the dish on top of the onions, in a single layer. Arrange the carrots around them. If necessary, add a little more oil to the pan and stir in the remainder of the seasoned flour. Cook for a minute or two, stirring all the time, then add the basil and pour on the Guinness. Allow to boil for a minute or two then add the honey and the stock. Bring back to the boil and pour over the meat. Cover the dish either with a lid or with foil and cook in the oven at 170°C, 325°F, Gas Mark 4 for 1½ hours. This dish tastes even better if you cook it the day before and heat it up again in the oven for about 45 minutes. If the gravy looks as though it needs to be a little thicker, mix a tsp (5ml) of arrowroot with 2 tblsp (30ml) of cold water and stir into the gravy 15 minutes before the cooking time is up.

Braised Liver and Bacon in Tomatoes and Red Wine

PREPARATION TIME: 15 minutes
COOKING TIME: 30 minutes
SERVES: 4 persons

8 slices of lambs' liver
4 rashers of streaky bacon
14oz (400g) tin of chopped tomatoes
1 large onion
3 tblsp (45ml) oil
3 heaped tblsp (60ml) plain flour seasoned with salt and pepper
1 wineglass of red wine
1 heaped tsp (7ml) honey
½ tsp (2.5ml) dried basil
8oz (225g) pasta shells or macaroni

Peel and slice the onion. Heat oil in a frying pan and fry the onion until soft. Transfer onion with a slotted spoon to an ovenproof dish large enough to take all the liver in one layer. Toss liver in seasoned flour, brown lightly in remaining oil in frying pan and lay on top of onions. Mix remainder of seasoned flour with pan juices and mix to a paste over low heat. Add red wine and bring to the boil. Remove two tblsp (30ml) of the chopped tomatoes and reserve, add the rest to the pan with the honey and basil. Bring mixture to the boil, stirring well. Pour around the liver in the dish. Slice rashers in half and place on top of liver. Put dish in a preheated oven at 190°C, 375°F, Gas Mark 5 for about 20 minutes.
Cook pasta shells or macaroni in boiling, salted water, following instructions on packet. Drain. Heat remaining tomatoes in a saucepan with a pinch of basil. Toss pasta in it and transfer to a serving dish to accompany the liver and bacon. Serves 4 persons.

Stuffed Breast of Lamb

PREPARATION TIME: 15 minutes
COOKING TIME: 1 hour 30 minutes
SERVES: 4 persons

Half breast of lamb
4oz (115g) white breadcrumbs
2oz (60g) chopped suet
1 medium onion
½ level tsp (2.5ml) marjoram
½ level tsp (2.5ml) thyme
Grated rind of half a lemon
1 egg
Salt and pepper
1 tblsp (15ml) flour

It is quite easy to remove the bones from the breast of lamb with a sharp knife. Put the bones in a saucepan with half the onion and some salt and pepper. Cover them with water, bring to the boil, skim, cover and simmer for half an hour. Mix the breadcrumbs, suet, herbs, lemon rind, a little salt and pepper and the other half of the onion, minced, and bind them with the egg. Add 2-3 tblsp (30-45ml) of the bone stock and spread the stuffing on the breast of lamb. Roll up, starting at the wide end. Tie up firmly with string and place in a greased roasting tin. Bake in the oven, 200°C, 400°F, Gas Mark 6, for 1 hour.
Transfer the meat to a serving dish and keep hot while you make the gravy. Drain off any excess fat from the roasting tin, retaining about two tblsp (30ml). Stir in the flour and heat over the ring until mixture browns. Stir in about half a pint (300ml) of the bone stock. Bring to the boil, stirring all the time. Boil for a few minutes then strain into a gravy boat and serve with the stuffed lamb. Serve with new potatoes and courgettes.

Cold Chicken in Tarragon Sauce

PREPARATION TIME: 45 minutes
COOKING TIME: 1 hour 20 minutes
SERVES: 6-8 persons

Although I use a fresh or frozen roasting chicken for this dish, I find the flesh is much more moist and goes further if the chicken is poached or steamed. It is very suitable for a summer lunch or supper party as it can be prepared well in advance and served with new potatoes and a tossed salad or with rice mixed with vegetables.

3½lb (1½kg) chicken
1 bayleaf
1 onion
1 carrot
1 stick celery
Tarragon
Salt and pepper

Sauce
2oz (60g) butter
2oz (60g) flour
Glass white wine or cider
½ pint (300ml) of the strained stock
3 heaped tblsp (60ml) whipped cream
3 heaped tblsp (60ml) mayonnaise
1 tsp (5ml) chopped tarragon
2 tsp (10ml) chopped parsley
Juice of ½ lemon

Generously sprinkle the inside of the chicken with salt, pepper and tarragon. Into a saucepan, just large enough to take the chicken snugly, put the onion, carrot and celery, all quartered, and the giblets and feet from the chicken. Place the chicken on top and pour the stock over it. Cover the pan tightly, bring to the boil then reduce heat and simmer for 1 hour. Remove the pan from the heat and carefully turn the chicken breast-side down in the

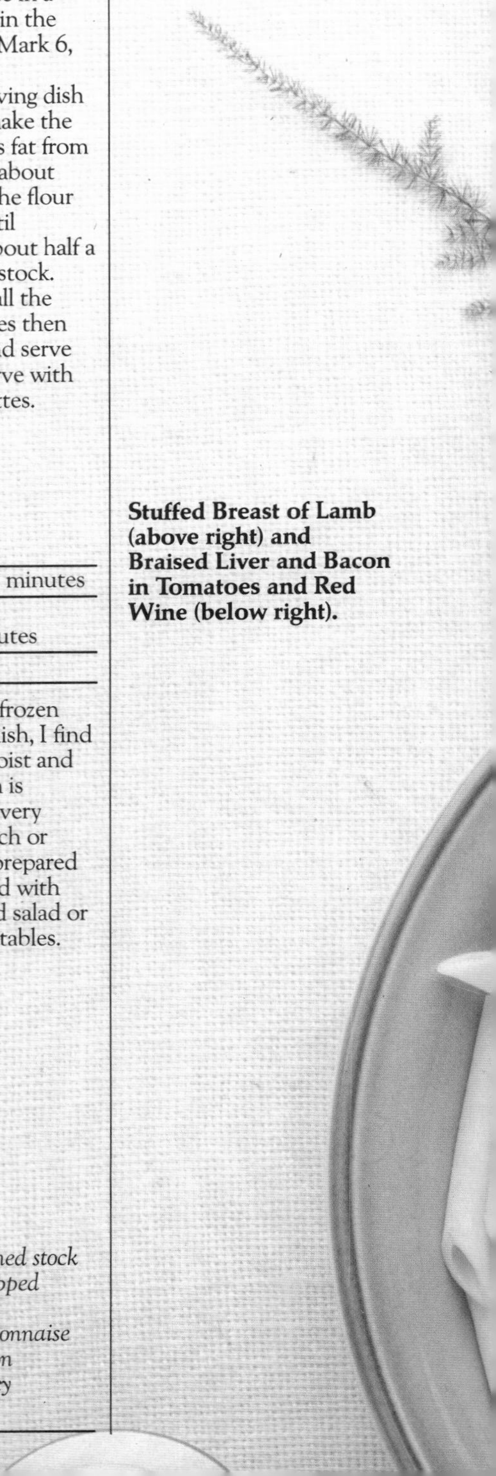

Stuffed Breast of Lamb (above right) and Braised Liver and Bacon in Tomatoes and Red Wine (below right).

stock, taking care not to break the skin. Cover again and allow to cool. This can be done the day before. Skin the chicken and remove all the flesh from the bones, slicing the meat from the legs into longish slivers and dividing the white parts up into similar sized pieces.
Melt the butter in a heavy saucepan. Stir in the flour and cook for a minute or two. Add the white wine, then gradually stir in the ½ pint (300ml) of stock. Add the tarragon, parsley and lemon juice, bring the sauce to the boil and cook for a further 2 minutes, stirring all the time. Remove from the heat and allow to cool slightly before folding in the whipped cream and finally the mayonnaise. Toss the chicken pieces in about ¾ of the sauce and pile them into a large, shallow serving dish. Coat with the remainder of the sauce and garnish with a little chopped parsley, parsley sprigs and lemon slices before serving.

Irish Stew

PREPARATION TIME: 30 minutes
COOKING TIME: 2 hours-2 hours 30 minutes
SERVES: 4 persons

Either boned mutton, cut up and with most of the fat removed, or best end of neck chops, trimmed but on the bone, can be used. The most important points to remember are not to use too much liquid in the cooking and to cook the stew very slowly so that it doesn't dry out. A little more water may be added during the cooking, if necessary.

2lb (900g) boned mutton or 3lb (1.35kg) best end of neck chops
2lb (900g) potatoes
2 large onions
1 tblsp (15ml) fresh, chopped thyme and parsley or 1 tsp (5ml) dried thyme
Salt and pepper
¾ pint (450ml) water

Trim the meat, leaving a little of the fat on. Peel and slice the potatoes and onions. Into a large saucepan – or casserole, if it is to be cooked in the oven – place layers of potato, meat and onion, seasoned with salt and pepper and herbs, starting and finishing with a layer of potatoes. Pour on the water and cover tightly. Either simmer on a very low heat on the top of the stove for 2-2½ hours or cook in a slow oven, 120°C, 250°F, Gas Mark 1 for the same length of time. The pot or casserole should be shaken occasionally to prevent the potatoes from sticking and you should check that the liquid has not dried out. The finished stew should not be too runny and the potatoes should thicken it sufficiently.

Boiled Bacon and Cabbage

PREPARATION TIME: 2-3 hours
COOKING TIME: 1 hour 45 minutes
SERVES: 6-8 persons

Piece of collar or hock about 3lb (1.350kg) in weight
1½-2lb (675-900g) green cabbage
½ medium onion or one small onion cut in two

Parsley Sauce
½ pint (300ml) milk
½ pint (300ml) stock
½ cup chopped parsley
2oz (60g) butter or margarine
1½oz (45g) flour

Soak the bacon for several hours or cover it with cold water, bring to the boil, discard water and cover meat with more boiling water. Bring it back to the boil, skim and simmer for 20 minutes to the pound (450g) and 20 minutes over.
Meanwhile, cut the cabbage in two and cut out a V in the stalk end of both halves to remove the fibrous end of the stalk. Cut the two halves down through the V and put the quarters in salted water to clean them. Put them into a large saucepan with the cut onion (this miraculously seems to prevent the usual smell of cooked cabbage permeating the house). When the bacon is cooked add 3-4 ladles of the stock to the cabbage, cover tightly and cook for about 20 minutes. Meanwhile, skin the bacon, cut a lattice pattern in the fat, coat it with brown sugar and stud it with cloves. Brown it in a hot oven while the cabbage is cooking. Drain the cabbage and remove the onion.
Measure out ½ pint (300ml) of the stock in which the cabbage was cooked to use for the parsley sauce. Melt butter or margarine in a saucepan, stir in the flour and make a roux. Cook without browning for a minute or two. Gradually add the stock and then the milk. Bring to the boil and stir for a few minutes. Add the chopped parsley. Test to see if it needs more seasoning – probably a little pepper. Serve with the bacon and cabbage and potatoes boiled in their jackets. Some people cook the cabbage in the pot with the ham, but I prefer to save some of the pure ham stock for other dishes.

Marinated Pork Chops

PREPARATION TIME: 3-4 hours
COOKING TIME: 1 hour
SERVES: 4 persons

4 pork chops
¾ pint (450ml) cider
½ tsp (2.5ml) sage
½ tsp (2.5ml) thyme
1 onion finely chopped
2oz (60g) plain flour, seasoned with salt and pepper
2 tblsp (30ml) oil
1 tblsp (15ml) butter
1 or 2 apples, peeled, cored and sliced
1 tsp (5ml) honey
1 tsp (5ml) French mustard
¼ pint (150ml) stock

Put the chops into a shallow ovenproof dish just large enough to hold them. Chop the onion, add it with the herbs to the cider and pour over the chops. Leave for several hours, turning the chops occasionally. Heat oil and butter in a frying pan. Drain chops then dip them in the seasoned flour, lightly coating both sides. Seal them in the frying pan, browning them slightly. Strain the marinade liquid into a bowl, wash and grease the dish, place sliced apple on the bottom and chops on top. Add strained onion from the marinade to the fat in the frying pan; cook until soft and stir in remainder of the seasoned flour. Allow it to brown, stirring all the time, then gradually add liquid from the marinade and

Boiled Bacon and Cabbage (top) and Irish Stew (bottom).

the stock. Stir in honey and French mustard, bring to the boil and pour over the chops. Cover with foil and cook in a preheated oven, 180°C, 350°F, Gas Mark 4, for 45 minutes. Serve with peas and creamed potatoes.

Dublin Coddle

PREPARATION TIME: 30 minutes

COOKING TIME: 1 hour

SERVES: 4 persons

This was regarded as a Saturday night special in Dublin and it would always be served up with Guinness. I can always remember the sausages being boiled first, even if they were going to be fried or grilled later. I presume this was for reasons of hygiene, as sausages would be home made or made on nearby farms, where there would not necessarily be factory-like conditions of cleanliness.

1lb (450g) pork sausages
8oz (225g) thickly sliced bacon
1lb (450g) onions
1½lb (675g) potatoes
Salt and pepper to taste

Place the bacon and the sausages in a saucepan. Cover with boiling water. Return to the boil and simmer for 5 minutes. Drain off the liquid into a bowl and reserve. Peel and slice the potatoes and onions, and put them with the meat in a heavy saucepan or greased casserole. Cover with the stock, season with salt and pepper and cover with greaseproof paper before putting on the lid. Either simmer on top of the stove or in a moderate oven for about one hour.

Boiled Chicken and Parsley Sauce

PREPARATION TIME: 15 minutes

COOKING TIME: 3 hours 15 minutes

SERVES: 6-8 persons

In the days when most people living in the country in Ireland kept their own hens, if a letter was received announcing the imminent arrival of unexpected guests, the housewife didn't jump into the car and head for the supermarket – she went out and caught a hen which had finished laying, and wrung its neck. After plucking it and cleaning it, she would cook it slowly in a pot and serve it with parsley sauce. It would probably be accompanied by a piece of boiling bacon which, apart from helping the chicken to go further, provides an excellent contrast in flavour and colour, and of course cabbage and lovely floury potatoes boiled in their jackets.

1 large boiling fowl
1 onion
1 carrot
1 turnip
1 stick celery
A bouquet garni
Salt and Pepper

Parsley Sauce
2oz (60g) butter
2oz (60g) plain flour
½ pint (300ml) stock
½ pint (300ml) milk
Cupful chopped parsley

Put 2-3ozs (60-85g) of dripping in a large pan. Wash and dry the bird, inside and out, and season well with salt and pepper. Turn it in the fat to brown slightly, remove the bird and add the vegetables, chopped into large pieces. Turn them in the fat for a few minutes then put in the bird and cover with boiling water. Add salt, pepper and bouquet garni. Bring back to the boil, skim, then cover the pot and simmer the contents slowly for about three hours or 40 minutes to the pound (450g).
When the bird is cooked remove it from the pot and keep hot on a serving dish. Melt the butter in a saucepan, stir in the flour and cook for a minute. Remove from heat and gradually stir in ½ pint (300ml) of the strained chicken stock. Return to the heat and, when it has thickened, gradually add the milk and continue cooking until it boils up again. Lower heat and cook for a further 2 minutes; add parsley and season with salt and pepper. Serve separately in a sauce boat.

Spiced Beef

PREPARATION TIME: 1 week

COOKING TIME: 6 hours

At Christmas time in Ireland you will see spiced beef displayed in many butcher's shop windows. It will be attractively tied-up with red ribbons and decorated with holly to contrast with its dark and velvety exterior. The mixture of spices and saltpetre, which have been rubbed into it at regular intervals for a week or more, keep the beef inside its dark coating a spicy red. This, served cold and thinly sliced, is a great favourite in most Irish households at Christmas time. It is not difficult to prepare at home, although it does require quite a lot of time and care.

6lb (2.7kg) piece of brisket, silverside or topside

For the spicing:
3 bayleaves, finely chopped
1 tsp (5ml) powdered mace
6 finely ground cloves
1 tsp (5ml) crushed black peppercorns
Large clove garlic made into a paste with salt
1 tsp (5ml) allspice
2 tblsp (30ml) black treacle
2 heaped tblsp (40ml) brown sugar
1lb (450g) cooking salt
2 tsp (10ml) saltpetre

Mix all the spicing ingredients together. Place beef in a large dish and rub well all over with the mixture. Repeat this process every day for a week, turning the meat and rubbing in the spices which will now be mixed with the juices drawn from the meat.
Tie the meat up firmly and rub in a final tsp (5ml) of ground cloves. Cover with water and simmer slowly for six hours. When cool enough remove from the cooking liquid, place in a dish and cover with a weighted plate. Slice very thinly and serve.

Boiled Mutton

We rarely see mutton on sale these days, but it appeared regularly on the menu in Irish households in days gone by. The average leg of mutton weighed about 10lbs (4.5kg), which was not considered too large to boil for a typical household in the early part of this century. It was suggested that for a small family the leg could be divided into three parts; the shank for boiling, the fillet for roasting and the lap for Irish stew.
To boil a leg of mutton, or the shank end, allow 20 minutes to the pound (450g) and 20 minutes over. If using the whole leg, first skewer the lap into position then plunge the joint into enough boiling, salted water to cover it and

Dublin Coddle (right) and Boiled Chicken and Parsley Sauce (below right).

GUINNESS

boil for 4-5 minutes, then reduce the heat and simmer gently for the remainder of the cooking time. Serve with caper sauce, pouring a little over the joint which has been kept hot on a serving dish, and serve the remainder separately.

Caper Sauce

COOKING TIME: 15 minutes

2oz (60g) butter or dripping
2oz (60g) flour
½ pint (300ml) milk
½ pint (300ml) pot liquor
2 dsp (20ml) capers and a little of their preserving liquid
Salt and pepper

The sauce for pouring over the mutton should be thicker than that served in the sauce boat so that it will nicely coat the meat. Good dripping can be used instead of butter. Melt the butter in a heavy pan, stir in the flour and cook for a minute but do not allow to brown. Remove from heat and stir in a little of the milk, then gradually add rest of the milk over gentle heat, stirring all the time. Gradually add 8oz (250ml) of the hot cooking liquor and bring to the boil. Boil for 2-3 minutes, stirring constantly. Test for flavour and season with pepper and more salt, if necessary. If it seems of a good coating consistency, add the capers and a little of the preserving liquid but do not bring the sauce back to the boil or it will curdle. Pour a little of the sauce over the mutton on the serving dish. Measure out the other 2oz (50ml) of the hot stock and gradually add to the sauce in the pan. Pour into a sauce boat. Boiled white turnips and parsnips should be served around the meat and the dish garnished with parsley.

This page: Spiced Beef. Facing page: Marinated Pork Chops (top) and Boiled Mutton and Caper Sauce (bottom).

Beef Dishes

Chilli Beef

PREPARATION TIME: 30 minutes
COOKING TIME: 2 hours

675g (1½lb) minced beef
40g (1½oz) fat
1 medium onion, peeled and chopped
1 clove garlic, crushed
300ml (½ pint) stock
15ml (1 tblsp) flour
30ml (2 tblsp) chilli powder
2.5ml (½ tsp) oregano
1 bayleaf
Seasoning

Brown minced beef in hot fat. Remove to a casserole. Brown onion and garlic in remaining fat and add to meat. Pour in stock until just covered. Cover and cook in a slow oven, 150°C, 325°F, Gas Mark 2, for about 1 hour. Mix flour and chilli powder smoothly with a little stock or water and stir into casserole. Add red kidney beans if required. Add oregano, bayleaf and seasoning and continue cooking for a further 30 minutes-1 hour.

Southseas Meat Balls

PREPARATION TIME: 20 minutes
COOKING TIME: 10-20 minutes

450g (1lb) minced beef
1 egg, beaten
Seasoning
15ml (1 tblsp) oil
3 small shallots, chopped
15g (2 tblsp) flour
450g (1lb) pineapple chunks
15ml (1 tblsp) soy sauce
5ml (1 tsp) wine vinegar
½ green pepper, finely chopped
25g (1oz) blanched almonds

Blend the beef, egg and seasoning in a large bowl. Make the beef mixture into four flat balls, brush with oil and grill for 10-20 minutes. Keep warm. Heat the oil in a frying pan. Fry the shallots gently for 3 minutes. Take out. Stir in the flour and cook the roux for 3 minutes. Pour in the juice from the canned pineapple and bring to the boil, stirring. Add the soy sauce and vinegar. Season. Add the shallots, pineapple chunks, green pepper and almonds. Place the meatballs in the pan and heat through, spooning the sauce over.

Steak Diane

PREPARATION TIME: 20 minutes
COOKING TIME: from 5-20 minutes

1 onion, finely chopped
50-70g (2-3oz) butter
4 thin slices of sirloin steak
Worcestershire sauce
Brandy (optional)

Fry the onion in butter for a few minutes until soft. Add the steak and cook on both sides. Add Worcestershire sauce and the brandy to the butter. Ignite, if wished, and pour over the steaks. Garnish with chopped parsley.

Meat Roll

PREPARATION TIME: 30 minutes
COOKING TIME: 1 hour 30 minutes

450g (1lb) minced meat
100g (4oz) suet, finely chopped
1 onion, finely chopped
50g (2oz) fresh breadcrumbs
Seasoning
25g (1oz) dripping
Meat stock

For Coating
Beaten egg
Dry breadcrumbs

Mix the meat, suet, onion, fresh breadcrumbs and seasoning. If necessary add a little egg to bind. Shape into a thick roll, moulding out any cracks. Brush over with egg and coat with the dry breadcrumbs. Grease a piece of greaseproof paper with the dripping and wrap round the roll. Secure the ends and lay in a baking tin. Bake for 1¼-1½ hours at 220°C, 425°F, Gas Mark 7. Just before serving, brush over with a little meat stock.

Beef Stroganoff

PREPARATION TIME: 30 minutes
COOKING TIME: 50 minutes

670-900g (1½-2lb) lean beef, cut into long strips
100g (4oz) butter
15ml (1 tblsp) oil
Flour
2-3 onions, chopped
100g (4oz) mushrooms, sliced
45ml (3 tblsp) dry sherry
300-450ml (½-¾ pint) stock
Seasoning
200ml (6 fl oz) sour cream

Melt butter in an oiled frying pan. Dip the strips of meat into seasoned flour and fry for several minutes. Transfer meat to a casserole. Fry onions for 7-10 minutes in the same fat. Spread over meat in casserole. Fry mushrooms for a few minutes. Add to casserole. Moisten with sherry and stock. Adjust seasoning to taste. Cover casserole and place in a slow oven, 170°C, 325°F, Gas Mark 2, for 30 minutes or until meat is tender. Add sour cream and cover again until heated through.

This page: Southseas Meat Balls (top right), Chilli Beef (centre left) and Meat Roll (bottom).

Facing page: Steak Diane (top), Beef Stroganoff (centre) and Steak and Kidney Pudding (bottom).

Roasted Fore Rib

PREPARATION TIME: 20 minutes

COOKING TIME: 15 minutes per 450g (1lb), plus 15 minutes

Place meat in a roasting tin and spread with dripping or cooking fat and season. Place in the centre of a preheated oven 180°C, 350°F, Gas Mark 4. If a covered roasting tin is used, basting is not necessary, but if the joint is uncovered the meat should be basted every 20-30 minutes. The meat should be turned over, using 2 metal spoons, halfway through the cooking. When the meat is cooked, transfer to a large carving dish. Keep hot.

Meat Roll in Pastry Case

PREPARATION TIME: 45 minutes

COOKING TIME: 30 minutes

450g (1lb) minced meat
1 onion, finely minced
100g (4oz) suet, finely chopped
Seasoning
225g (8oz) shortcrust pastry
Egg or milk to glaze

Fry mince and onion till cooked. Remove from pan. Mix the meat, suet, onion and seasoning together. If necessary add a little egg to bind to a pliable, slightly moist, mixture. Shape into a thick roll, moulding out any cracks. Roll out a piece of pastry large enough to cover the roll. Brush with egg or milk to glaze. Lay meat roll in a loaf tin and cook at 200°C, 400°F, Gas Mark 6, for about 20 minutes until pastry is golden brown.

Silverside (Salted)

PREPARATION TIME: soak overnight

COOKING TIME: 20 minutes per 450g (1lb) plus 20 minutes

To prepare meat for cooking, soak meat overnight in cold water to remove excess salt. Put the joint into a pan and cover with cold water. Bring to the boil, then pour off the liquor. Cover again with cold water and bring to the boil. After 5 minutes, reduce the heat and allow to simmer for the appropriate length of time.

Meat Roll in Pastry Case (far left), Curried Shepherd's Pie (top centre), Roasted Fore Rib (bottom centre) and Monday Beef Casserole (bottom right).

Curried Shepherd's Pie

PREPARATION TIME: 20 minutes
COOKING TIME: 45 minutes

350g (12oz) minced beef
2 onions, finely chopped
25g (1oz) fat
15g (½oz) flour
15ml (1 tblsp) curry powder
300ml (½ pint) stock or a small tin of tomatoes and a little stock
Seasoning
15ml (1 tblsp) chutney
450g (1lb) mashed potatoes

Fry onions in hot fat. Add flour and curry powder. Add stock or tomatoes and stock. Bring to the boil and cook until thickened. Add the minced beef and cook gently, stirring from time to time. Break up any lumps in the mince. Add seasoning and chutney. When meat is tender put into a pie dish. Cover with the mashed potatoes. Brown in oven or under grill until crisp.

Beef Cobbler

PREPARATION TIME: 45 minutes
COOKING TIME: 2 hours 15 minutes

Stew
50g (2oz) fat
2 large onions, sliced
750g (1½lb) stewing steak, diced
15ml (1 tblsp) paprika
150ml (¼ pint) water
1 green pepper, seeded, cored and diced
4 tomatoes, skinned and quartered
Seasoning

Cobbler
175g (6oz) self-raising flour
Seasoning
40g (1½oz) margarine
Milk

Stew
Heat fat and fry the onions and diced meat until brown. Stir in paprika, blended with water, and the rest of the ingredients. Put into a covered casserole and cook for 2¼ hours at 150-170°C, 300-325°F, Gas Mark 2-3.

Cobbler
Sieve dry ingredients, rub in margarine and mix to a soft dough with milk. Cut into small rounds and put on top of beef mixture. Glaze with a little milk. Turn oven up to 220°C, 425°F, Gas Mark 7, until cobbler mixture is golden brown.

Monday Beef Casserole

PREPARATION TIME: 25 minutes
COOKING TIME: 10-20 minutes

2 cups mashed potato
1 egg, beaten
1.25ml (¼ tsp) salt
175g (6oz) cooked beef, chopped
½ cup celery, chopped
100g (4oz) milk
Salt to taste
Dash nutmeg
Margarine or butter

Beat potatoes with egg and salt. Put half the potatoes in the bottom of a greased casserole. Blend and add remaining ingredients, except butter, to casserole. Cover with remaining potatoes. Dot with butter and bake in oven at 190°C, 375°F, Gas Mark 5, until top is browned.

Topside of Beef

PREPARATION TIME: 5 minutes
COOKING TIME: 15 minutes per 450g (1lb) plus 15 minutes

Place meat in a roasting tin and spread with dripping or cooking fat and season. Place in the centre of a preheated oven at 180°C, 350°F, Gas Mark 4. If a covered roasting tin is used basting is not necessary. If the joint is uncovered, the meat should be basted every 20-30 minutes. The meat should be turned over, using two metal spoons, halfway through the cooking. When the meat is cooked, transfer to a large carving dish and keep hot.

Steak and Kidney Pudding

PREPARATION TIME: 30 minutes
COOKING TIME: 4 hours

675g (1½lb) stewing steak
2 lamb's kidneys
15ml (1 tblsp) flour
Seasoning
350g (12oz) suet crust pastry
150ml (¼ pint) stock

Cut steak and kidney into cubes and mix together. Put flour and seasoning onto a plate and toss meat in this. Line a pudding basin with the pastry. Put in meat, add enough stock to come two-thirds of the way up the basin. Roll out remaining pastry to make a lid and place on top of basin. Cover with greased paper. Fix firmly round the basin rim. Put the basin in a steamer. Stand this over a saucepan of boiling water. Steam for 4 hours. Allow water to boil rapidly for the first 2 hours, add more boiling water when necessary.

Steak Pie

PREPARATION TIME: 30 minutes
COOKING TIME: 2 hours 15 minutes

750g (1½lb) stewing steak
40g (1½oz) flour
Seasoning
50g (2oz) fat
2 onions, sliced and chopped
600ml (1 pint) brown stock
225g (8oz) flaky pastry

Prepare the steak, cutting it into pieces. Roll in seasoned flour and fry in hot fat for a few minutes in a saucepan. Add onions and turn in the fat for 2-3 minutes. Stir in the stock gradually, bring to the boil and cook until the sauce has thickened. Then lower the heat and simmer for 1½ hours. Put the steak into a pie dish. Roll out the pastry. Put a band of pastry round the moistened rim of the pie dish. Top with the rest of the pastry, seal the edges. Bake for 40-45 minutes at 230°C, 450°F, Gas Mark 8.

Swiss Steak

PREPARATION TIME: 25 minutes
COOKING TIME: 1 hour 30 minutes

450-670g (1-1½lb) thick slice of steak
15ml (1 tblsp) plain flour
Seasoning
Dripping or margarine
1 medium tin peeled tomatoes
1 onion, peeled and grated

Mix flour and seasoning together and rub well into the surface of the meat. Melt dripping in a saucepan and fry meat gently until brown. Rub tomatoes through a sieve and add to meat with grated onion. Place joint, onions and tomatoes in a casserole dish. Cover and simmer gently at 180°C, 350°F, Gas Mark 4, for 1½ hours.

Top Rib Pot Roast

PREPARATION TIME: 25 minutes
COOKING TIME: 30 minutes per 450g (1lb)

50g (2oz) good dripping
6 large onions, peeled
6 large carrots, peeled
3 large turnips, peeled
1-1.5kg (2-3lb) piece of top rib, boned and rolled
Seasoning

Melt dripping in a large pan and fry vegetables until a good brown colour, then take out of pan. Fry meat on all sides over a fierce heat to seal in juices. Return vegetables to pan, with just enough water to give about 3½cm (1½ inches) in depth. Season well. Put meat on top of vegetables and cover pan. The vegetables should not be too small, otherwise they may break during cooking. Reduce heat so the liquid simmers gently. Carve the meat as you would a roast joint. The liquid from the pan can be used for the gravy.

Stew and Dumplings

PREPARATION TIME: 30 minutes
COOKING TIME: 2 hours 20 minutes

500-750g (1-1½lb) beef steak
Seasoning
40g (1½oz) fat
2 onions, sliced
2 or 3 large carrots, sliced
450ml (¾ pint) water
½ bayleaf
Mixed herbs

For Dumplings
100g (4oz) self-raising flour
Seasoning
50g (2oz) shredded suet
Water to mix

Cut the meat into cubes, season, then brown in the fat. Add onions, carrots, water and herbs. Cover pan and cook slowly for 2 hours.

For Dumplings
Sieve the dry ingredients together, add the suet and mix to a dough with the water. Roll into balls with lightly-floured hands. Check there is sufficient liquid in the stew, then drop in the dumplings and cook for 15-20 minutes.

Facing page: Steak Pie (top), Beef Cobbler (centre left) and Stew and Dumplings (bottom right).

Peppered Steak

PREPARATION TIME: 15 minutes

COOKING TIME: from 5-25 minutes

4 rump or fillet steaks
Oil
30ml (2 tblsp) black hot peppers for steak
50g (2oz) butter
Salt
60ml (4 tblsp) brandy
45ml (3 tblsp) single cream
Watercress

Brush the steaks on both sides with oil, then coat with black hot peppers and crush into the steak with a steak hammer. Melt butter in a frying pan and cook steaks for about 1½ minutes on each side. Reduce heat and cook for about a further minute (for rare steak), 3 minutes (for medium steak) or 7 minutes (if a well-done steak is required). Season with salt. Warm brandy in a ladle near the heat. Set it alight and pour over steaks. Remove steaks and place on a warmed serving dish. Keep hot. Stir cream into the juices in the frying pan. Heat gently for a few minutes. Pour sauce over steaks and garnish with watercress.

Steak Française

PREPARATION TIME: 30 minutes

COOKING TIME: 30-40 minutes

450-750g (1-1¼lb) rump steak
Seasoning
45ml (3 tblsp) Pernod
2 onions, peeled and chopped
450g (1lb) tomatoes, skinned and chopped
25g (1oz) butter
2.5ml (½ tsp) marjoram

Cut steak into 1cm (½ inch) strips with a sharp knife. Place in a shallow dish. Sprinkle with seasoning and Pernod. Cover and

Steak Française (left), Peppered Steak (centre) and Beef in Cider (right).

leave on one side for 1 hour. Fry onions in melted butter until tender but not brown. Add tomatoes and stir well. Add onions and tomatoes to the steak mixture with the marjoram. Cook in an oven just above the centre at 180°C, 350°F, Gas Mark 4, for 30-40 minutes.

Beef in Cider

PREPARATION TIME: 30 minutes

COOKING TIME: 2 hours 30 minutes

450g (1lb) blade steak
25g (1oz) fat
3 medium onions, quartered
4 carrots, quartered
1 clove garlic, crushed
225g (8oz) tomatoes, sliced
Seasoning
600ml (1 pint) dry cider

Cut beef into cubes and brown lightly in fat. Brown the onions and carrots. Put meat into an overproof dish with onions, carrots, garlic and tomatoes. Add seasoning to taste and cover with cider. Put on lid and cook at 170°C, 325°F, Gas Mark 3, for 2½ hours.

Goulash

PREPARATION TIME: 25 minutes

COOKING TIME: 2 hours

675g (1½lb) stewing steak
25g (1oz) fat
2 onions, peeled and chopped
2 carrots, peeled and chopped
25g (1oz) flour
1 beef stock cube
45ml (3 tblsp) tomato purée
450ml (¾ pint) water
10ml (2 tsp) paprika
45ml (3 tblsp) yogurt

Cut meat into cubes and brown in hot fat. Remove to a casserole dish. Put onions and carrots into a pan and fry until lightly browned. Add to meat. Put flour, crumbled stock cube and tomato purée into pan and add a little more fat if necessary. Cook for a few minutes, then add paprika and water and stir until boiling. Pour into casserole, cover and cook in a slow oven, 150°C, 300°F, Gas Mark 2, for about 2 hours. Just before serving, adjust seasoning and stir in yogurt.

Beefburgers

PREPARATION TIME: 25 minutes

COOKING TIME: 10-20 minutes

1 large onion, finely chopped
450g (1lb) minced beef
45ml (3 tblsp) fresh breadcrumbs
60ml (4 tblsp) milk
Salt
Paprika
5ml (1 tsp) mustard powder
Oil
4 burger buns, sliced horizontally
4 tomatoes, sliced (optional)
4 slices of Cheddar cheese (optional)

Preheat the grill. Mix the onion, minced beef, breadcrumbs and milk in a large bowl. Season with salt, paprika and mustard. Leave for 10 minutes. Make four beefburgers from the mixture. Brush with oil. Cook for 5 minutes on both sides under the grill. Remove from heat. Top the burgers with tomato and cheese, if desired. Put back under the grill to melt cheese. Serve in warm buns.

Grilled Fillet Steak

PREPARATION TIME: 10 minutes

COOKING TIME: from 5-20 minutes

Fillet steak
Butter or oil

Preheat grill. Put steak on the grid of the grill pan and brush with melted butter or oil. Cook on one side, then turn over with tongs. Brush second side with butter or oil. Minute steak – 1 minute cooking each side. Under-done steak (rare) (¾ inch thick), 3-4 minutes. Medium-done steak – cook as under-done, then cook under lower heat for a further 3 minutes. Well-done steak – cook as under-done, then cook under lower heat for further 5-6 minutes.

Sausage and Egg Flan

PREPARATION TIME: 20 minutes

COOKING TIME: 30-40 minutes

175g (6oz) shortcrust pastry
450g (1lb) beef sausages
2 eggs
150ml (¼ pint) milk
1.25ml (¼ tsp) made mustard

Roll out pastry to line a deep flan case and prick the base. Fry sausages until cooked. Place in flan case. Whisk eggs. Add milk and mustard. Pour whisked mixture over the sausages. Place flan in oven, 230°C, 440°F, Gas Mark 8, for 15 minutes. Reduce temperature to 170°C, 325°F, Gas Mark 3, for a further 30 minutes, until pastry is cooked.

Cinnamon Roast

PREPARATION TIME: 30 minutes

COOKING TIME: 2 hours 30 minutes

1.5-2kg (3-4lb) brisket of beef
25g (1oz) flour
Seasoning
5ml (1 tsp) powdered cinnamon
25g (1oz) dripping
3-4 carrots, peeled and chopped
1 bayleaf
450ml (¾ pint) stock
1 onion

Coat joint with flour, seasoning and cinnamon. Melt fat in a pan and brown joint all over. Transfer joint to a dish. Fry onion and carrot until soft in the pan. Replace joint on top of vegetables. Put in bayleaf and add stock. Cover and simmer gently for 2-2½ hours. Thicken liquor with flour and serve separately.

This page: Cinnamon Roast (top), Curried Chuck Steak (centre left) and Swiss Steak (bottom right).

Facing page: Beefburgers (top left), Sliced Cold Beef and Bubble and Squeak (top right) and Grilled Fillet Steak (bottom).

Sausages in Tomato Sauce

PREPARATION TIME: 20 minutes
COOKING TIME: 25 minutes

450g (1lb) beef sausages
3 sticks celery, sliced
50g (2oz) salted peanuts

Tomato Sauce
15g (½oz) margarine
2 onions, finely chopped
2 carrots, finely chopped
1 stick celery, finely chopped
15g (½oz) flour
25g (1oz) tomato paste
50g (2oz) chopped red pepper
1 chicken stock cube
300ml (½ pint) boiling water
1 clove garlic, crushed
½ bayleaf
Sprig thyme
Seasoning
45ml (3 tblsp) medium sherry

Tomato Sauce
Put the margarine in a saucepan, add the onions, carrots and celery and brown slightly. Add the flour, stir and brown slightly, until the flour is sandy in colour. Add the tomato paste and red pepper. Stir well. Cool. Add the stock cube mixed with the boiling water, add garlic and herbs. Season and simmer for 1 hour, then check the seasoning. Sieve the sauce and stir in the sherry.

Sausages
Grill the sausages and keep them hot in a dish. Scald the celery sticks for 5 minutes in boiling water. Drain and add to the sausages. Pour the sauce over and keep hot. When ready to serve, garnish with salted peanuts.

Sliced Cold Beef and Bubble and Squeak

PREPARATION TIME: 20 minutes
COOKING TIME: 10-20 minutes

Sliced cold beef enough for 4 servings
½ medium cabbage
40g (1½oz) butter
1 small onion, finely chopped
Leftover mashed potato equal to the amount of cabbage

Bring a saucepan of water to the boil. Remove the core and any damaged leaves from the cabbage. Shred the cabbage. Put the cabbage into the water and cook for 6-7 minutes. Drain well. Heat the butter in a large frying pan. Fry the

onion gently until softened. Add the cabbage and stir over a low heat for 2 minutes. Fold in the mashed potato until it is completely mixed with the cabbage. Press the mixture lightly into the frying pan to form a large pancake. Cook for 5 minutes or until the underside is lightly browned. Turn and brown on the other side for 5 minutes. Serve very hot with the sliced cold meat.

Curried Chuck Steak

PREPARATION TIME: 35 minutes
COOKING TIME: 3 hours

750g (1¼lb) chuck steak, cut and diced
25g (1oz) fat
1 large onion, chopped
15-30ml (1-2 tblsp) curry powder
15ml (1 tblsp) paprika
50g (2oz) walnuts
50g (2oz) blanched almonds
25g (1oz) flour
450ml (¾ pint) stock
Seasoning
50g (2oz) desiccated coconut
50g (2oz) sultanas
15ml (1 tblsp) redcurrant jelly
15ml (1 tblsp) lemon juice
50g (2oz) mixed spice

Melt the fat and fry meat and onion until just brown. Add curry powder, paprika, walnuts and almonds and cook for 3 minutes. Stir in flour and cook gently for several minutes. Gradually blend in stock. Bring to boil and cook until thickened. Season and add coconut, sultanas, redcurrant jelly and lemon juice. Transfer mixture to a casserole, cover and cook at 170°C, 325°F, Gas Mark 3, for 2½-3 hours.

Sausage and Egg Flan (far left), Sausages in Tomato Sauce (bottom centre) and Goulash (top right).

Festive Leg of Lamb

PREPARATION TIME: 30 minutes
COOKING TIME: 30-35 minutes per 450g (1lb)

1 leg of lamb
225g (8oz) pineapple rings
Glacé cherries

Score the surface of the joint in a diamond pattern. Drain the pineapple and reserve the juice. Place the joint in a roasting tin and pour the pineapple juice over the scored surface. Roast at 180°C, 350°F, Gas Mark 4, basting occasionally. Cut pineapple rings in half. Garnish the joint with pieces of pineapple in a line down the length of the leg. Pin each piece in place with a cherry on a cocktail stick and serve.

Country Lamb Casserole

PREPARATION TIME: 30 minutes
COOKING TIME: 2 hours

1kg (2lb) best end of neck of lamb
225g (8oz) onions, peeled and chopped
450g (1lb) carrots, peeled and chopped
750g (1½lb) potatoes, peeled and thickly sliced
Seasoning
2.5ml (½ tsp) dried thyme
900ml (1½ pints) boiling water
Chopped parsley

Cut neck into chops and season well. Put alternating layers of vegetables and meat in a large casserole dish. Season well between the layers and sprinkle the herbs at the same time. Finish with a layer of potatoes. Pour the water over the meat, cover and cook in a slow oven 170°C, 325°F, Gas Mark 3, for about 2 hours. Just before serving, skim and sprinkle well with parsley.

Roast Herbed Leg of Mutton

PREPARATION TIME: 15 minutes
COOKING TIME: 30 minutes per 450g (1lb) plus 30 minutes

1 leg mutton
2-3 cloves garlic
2 bayleaves
100g (4oz) soft butter
225g (8oz) fresh breadcrumbs
5ml (1 tsp) thyme
5ml (1 tsp) rosemary
15ml (1 tblsp) chopped parsley
Juice of ½ lemon
Seasoning

Prepare a sheet of foil to wrap meat completely. Slice 1 or 2 of the garlic cloves and insert in small cuts on

This page: Roast Lamb with Rosemary (top right), Savoury Pudding (top left) and Lamb Kebab (bottom).

Facing page: Country Lamb Casserole (top left), Wagon Wheel Lamb (top right) and Roast Herbed Leg of Mutton (bottom).

underside of meat. Place meat on foil, with bayleaves underneath. Cream butter with rest of the ingredients and crushed garlic cloves. Spread over the surface of the meat. Cover with foil and roast in the centre of the oven at 200°C, 400°F, Gas Mark 6. Then uncover and baste with the butter that has run onto foil. Continue roasting, uncovered, for 30 minutes, until crust is brown and crisp.

Lancashire Hot Pot

PREPARATION TIME: 45 minutes
COOKING TIME: 2 hours 30 minutes

450g (1lb) middle or best end of neck, cut into cutlets
15ml (1 tblsp) seasoned flour
4 medium onions, sliced
2 lamb's kidneys, skinned, cored and sliced
225g (½lb) mushrooms, sliced
675g (1½lb) potatoes, sliced
450ml (¾ pint) stock
Chopped parsley

Trim the lamb of any excess fat and coat with seasoned flour. Place layers of lamb, onion, kidney, mushrooms and potatoes in a large casserole, finishing with a layer of potatoes. Add the stock, cover and bake in a moderate oven, 180°C, 350°F, Gas Mark 4, for 2 hours. Remove the lid and cook for a further ½ hour to brown the potatoes. Sprinkle with chopped parsley.

Lemon and Ginger Chops

PREPARATION TIME: 3 hours
COOKING TIME: 15 minutes

4 chump lamb chops

Marinade
60ml (4 tblsp) oil
Grated rind of 1 lemon
30ml (2 tblsp) lemon juice
15ml (1 tblsp) ground ginger
Seasoning

Mix all the marinade ingredients together. Place the chops in a shallow dish and pour the marinade over them. Leave for 2-3 hours, turning occasionally. Remove the chops and place under a hot grill for 15 minutes, turning the chops occasionally and basting them with the marinade. Serve at once.

Wagon Wheel Lamb

PREPARATION TIME: 30 minutes
COOKING TIME: 20 minutes per 450g (1lb)

1-1.5kg (2-2½lb) loin or best end of neck of lamb
25g (1oz) fat
Small tin pineapple rings, cut in halves
10-20ml (2-4 tsp) brown sugar
Juice of ½ lemon

Garnish
175g (6oz) wagon wheel pasta
1.5 litres (3 pints) water
Salt
25-50g (1-2oz) butter

Place meat into a roasting tin and brush lightly with melted fat. Roast for 20 minutes per 450g (1lb) at 220°C, 425°F, Gas Mark 7. 30 minutes before end of cooking time, remove joint from oven and make six slits in the fat and skin. Press one pineapple half into each slit, brush with melted fat. Return to oven for rest of cooking time. When cooking time is finished, place the meat onto a hot dish and pour off all but 15ml (1 tblsp) of the fat.

Garnish
Chop the rest of the pineapple, add to the fat with the pineapple syrup, sugar and lemon juice, and heat. Cook pasta in boiling, salted water, strain and toss in butter. Arrange pasta around the meat and serve the syrup in a sauceboat.

Roast Lamb with Rosemary

PREPARATION TIME: 20 minutes
COOKING TIME: 20 minutes per 450g (1lb) plus 20 minutes

½ leg lamb
50g (2oz) butter
Seasoning
Rosemary
1 clove garlic (optional)
1kg (2lb) potatoes, peeled and cut into thick slices

Spread butter over lamb and season well. Stick rosemary leaves into the fat of the meat. Insert a clove of garlic near the bone. Place joint on a rack in a roasting tin. Roast in the centre of the oven at 220°C, 425°F, Gas Mark 7. Place sliced potatoes under the meat after it has been cooking for 30 minutes. Baste joint from time to time.

Lamb Kebab

PREPARATION TIME: 15 minutes
COOKING TIME: 10-25 minutes

350g (¾lb) lean lamb, cut into bite-size pieces
450g (1lb) chipolata sausages, cut into halves
4 small tomatoes, halved or quartered

Thread a mixture of the lamb, tomatoes and sausages onto metal skewers. Brush with melted butter and cook under the grill, turning the skewers to make sure that the food is well cooked.

Cutlets and Tomato Dip

PREPARATION TIME: 30 minutes
COOKING TIME: 30-45 minutes

4 large or 8 small cutlets
1 egg, beaten
45ml (3 tblsp) crisp breadcrumbs
Fat for frying

For the Dip
1 medium onion, peeled and chopped
1 small apple, peeled and chopped
25g (1oz) butter or margarine
Small tin or tube tomato purée
5ml (1 tsp) cornflour
300ml (½ pint) water
Seasoning
Pinch sugar
Pinch garlic salt

Coat cutlets with beaten egg and breadcrumbs. Fry onions and apple in the hot butter for several minutes. Add the tomato purée and cornflour blended with the water. Bring the mixture to the boil and cook steadily, stirring well until it comes to the boil and thickens slightly. Add the rest of the ingredients, lower the heat and continue cooking until a thick dip is made. Fry the cutlets in hot fat until golden brown and drain on kitchen paper. Serve with the tomato dip.

Lancashire Hot Pot (top right), and Cutlets and Tomato Dip (above right) and Lemon and Ginger Chops (bottom right).

Rolled and Stuffed Breast of Lamb

PREPARATION TIME: 15 minutes
COOKING TIME: 25 minutes per 450g (1lb) plus 25 minutes

900g (2lb) breast of lamb, boned
Sage and onion stuffing
A little oil or fat
Seasoning

Spread the breast of lamb with stuffing and roll. Brush the lamb with oil or melted fat. Season. Allow 25 minutes per 450g (1lb) + 25 minutes cooking time – weigh after stuffing meat. Place in roasting tin and cook at 170°C, 325°F, Gas Mark 3.

Stuffed Lamb Chops

PREPARATION TIME: 40 minutes
COOKING TIME: 35 minutes

4 chump lamb chops

Stuffing
1 small onion, finely chopped
25g (1oz) butter
2 lamb's kidneys, skinned, cored and chopped
50g (2oz) mushrooms, chopped
25g (1oz) fresh breadcrumbs
15ml (1 tblsp) sherry
1 tsp chopped parsley
Seasoning
10ml (2 tsp) oil or melted fat

Garnish
50g (2oz) button mushrooms
2 small tomatoes, halved
Triangle of bread
Parsley
A little oil or fat

Using a sharp knife, cut each chop horizontally through the fat and meat to make a small pocket for stuffing.

Stuffing
Fry the onion in butter, add the kidneys and mushrooms and continue cooking gently for 5 minutes. Add the rest of the ingredients and mix well. Press a spoonful of the stuffing into the pocket of the chops. Brush chops with oil. Grill the chops under a medium heat for 8-10 minutes on each side, turning once, until cooked.

Garnish
Fry the button mushrooms, tomatoes and bread. Serve the chops on a hot dish garnished with the tomatoes, mushrooms and triangles of bread.

Lamb Chops and Mint Sauce

PREPARATION TIME: 10 minutes
COOKING TIME: 25 minutes

4 lamb chops

Mint Sauce
30ml (2 tblsp) mint leaves
10ml (2 tsp) sugar
30ml (2 tblsp) vinegar
7.5ml (½ tblsp) hot water

Grill chops until cooked and tender. Keep hot. Wash and dry the mint leaves. Place on a chopping board with 5ml (1 tsp) sugar. Chop until fine, then put into a sauceboat. Add the rest of the sugar, stir in the hot water and leave for a few minutes to dissolve sugar. Add the vinegar. Serve with the chops.

Moussaka

PREPARATION TIME: 45 minutes
COOKING TIME: 1 hour 20 minutes

450g (1lb) aubergines, thinly sliced
15g (½oz) oil
2 large onions, thinly sliced
1 clove garlic, crushed
450g (1lb) minced lamb
425g (15oz) tin tomatoes
30ml (2 tblsp) tomato purée
Seasoning
2 eggs
150g (5oz) single cream
50g (2oz) Cheddar cheese, grated
25g (1oz) Parmesan cheese, grated

Fry the aubergines in oil for 3-4 minutes. Remove and drain well. Fry the onions and garlic in 15ml (1 tblsp) oil until golden brown. Add the lamb and cook for about 10 minutes, stirring occasionally. Add the tomatoes and tomato purée. Mix well. Bring to the boil and simmer for 20-25 minutes, season. Arrange alternate layers of aubergines and the lamb mixture in a large soufflé dish or shallow casserole dish. Bake in oven, 180°C, 350°F, Gas Mark 4 for 35-40 minutes. Beat the eggs and cream together and stir in the cheese. Pour onto the moussaka and return to the oven for a further 15-20 minutes until the top is firm and golden brown.

Lamb and Kidney Pie

PREPARATION TIME: 50 minutes
COOKING TIME: 2 hours

1 large onion, thinly sliced
30ml (2 tblsp) oil
450g (1lb) lamb from leg or shoulder, cubed
15ml (1 tblsp) flour
225g (8oz) lamb's kidney, skinned, cored and chopped
100g (4oz) mushrooms, sliced
150ml (¼ pint) beef stock or red wine
Few drops of gravy browning
Seasoning
200g (7oz) packet frozen pastry, thawed
Beaten egg to glaze

Fry the onion in oil until soft, but not brown. Toss the lamb in the flour with the kidney. Add to the onion and fry for 5-10 minutes, stirring occasionally. Add the mushrooms, stock, gravy browning and seasoning. Bring to the boil, stirring. Cover and simmer for 1 hour. Cool. Transfer the lamb mixture to a pie dish, then roll out the pastry. First make a collar of pastry round the dish and cover the pie. Seal edges but make a small hole in centre to allow the steam to escape. Brush with beaten egg to glaze. Cook at 220°C, 425°F, Gas Mark 7, for 10-15 minutes. Reduce the heat to 190°C, 375°F, Gas Mark 5, for a further 25-30 minutes, until pastry is well risen and golden brown.

Noisettes Provençales

PREPARATION TIME: 40 minutes
COOKING TIME: 35 minutes

8 noisettes of lamb
50g (2oz) butter
15ml (1 tblsp) oil

Provençale Sauce
50g (2oz) butter
15ml (1 tblsp) oil
1 large onion, finely chopped
1 clove garlic, crushed
450g (1lb) tomatoes, skinned and chopped
15ml (1 tblsp) tomato purée
150ml (¼ pint) dry white wine
Seasoning

Sauté the noisettes in the butter and oil for about 15 minutes, turning occasionally to brown the lamb on both sides.

This page: Stuffed Lamb Chops (top right), Lamb Chops and Mint Sauce (centre left) and Lamb and Kidney Pie (bottom).

Facing page: Moussaka (top), Rolled and Stuffed Breast of Lamb (centre) and Noisettes Provençales (bottom).

Provençale Sauce
Meanwhile, heat the butter with the oil and add the onion and garlic. Fry gently until soft but not brown. Stir in tomatoes, tomato purée and white wine and bring to the boil, stirring. Allow to cook uncovered over a fairly brisk heat for 10-15 minutes, stirring occasionally. Season to taste. Serve the sauce with the noisettes.

Risotto

PREPARATION TIME: 35 minutes

COOKING TIME: 1 hour

25g (1oz) butter
30ml (2 tblsp) oil
1 large onion, finely chopped
1 clove garlic, crushed
225g (8oz) long grain rice
100g (4oz) button mushrooms, sliced
200g (7oz) tin sweet corn and peppers
100g (4oz) frozen peas
1 whole green or red pepper, seeded, cored and chopped
350g (12oz) cooked lamb (leg or shoulder)
600ml (1 pint) chicken stock

Melt the butter with the oil. Add the onion and garlic and fry gently for 10-15 minutes until soft and golden brown. Stir in the rice and cook for a further 3-4 minutes, stirring continuously. Add the mushrooms, sweet corn and peppers, peas and the chopped red or green peppers. Cut the lamb into small pieces, add to the saucepan and mix well. Add the stock and bring to the boil. Reduce heat, cover and simmer for 35-40 minutes until the rice is cooked and the stock has been absorbed.

Winter Lamb

PREPARATION TIME: 35 minutes

COOKING TIME: 1 hour 55 minutes

1kg (2lb) scrag or best end of neck of lamb
50g (2oz) flour
50g (2oz) fat
2-3 onions, cut into rings
750ml (1¼ pint) brown stock
4-6 carrots, peeled and sliced
Seasoning
2.5ml (½ tsp) chopped mint
4 firm tomatoes, quartered
50-100g (2-4oz) mushrooms, sliced
Chopped parsley

Coat the lamb in the seasoned flour and fry for 2-3 minutes, add onions and continue cooking for a further 3 minutes. Stir in the stock gradually, bring to the boil and cook until thickened. Add carrots, seasoning and mint. Put lid on pan and simmer gently for 1½ hours. Add tomatoes and mushrooms and cook for 15 minutes. Garnish with chopped parsley.

Crown Roast of Lamb

PREPARATION TIME: 20 minutes

COOKING TIME: 25 minutes per 450g (1lb) plus 25 minutes

2 best ends of neck of lamb, chined
Stuffing (optional)
225g (8oz) button mushrooms
50g (2oz) butter
Cutlet frills

Trim the fat and skin from the ends of the rib bones, so that 2.5cm (1 inch) of bone protrudes. Place the joints back-to-back and sew the ends together, using fine string and a trussing needle, with the cutlet bones curving up and outwards. Most butchers will make the crown for you if given notice. If a stuffed joint is preferred, use your favourite stuffing to fill the crown roast. Cover the top of the crown of lamb with foil to keep the stuffing moist and to prevent the bones from burning during cooking. Roast at 180°C, 350°F, Gas Mark 4. Fry mushrooms in butter for 5-6 minutes. Remove the foil and top the stuffing with the mushrooms. Place a cutlet frill on each bone and serve.

Scandinavian Lamb

PREPARATION TIME: 50 minutes

COOKING TIME: 1 hour 20 minutes

1 breast of lamb, boned and cubed
15ml (1 tblsp) oil
1 medium onion, sliced
300ml (½ pint) stock
5ml (1 tsp) rosemary
Seasoning
15ml (1 tblsp) cornflour
150g (5oz) carton sour cream
150g (5oz) cooked peas

Fry the lamb in oil for 15-20 minutes. Remove from the pan and drain off most of the fat. Fry the onion in the remaining fat until soft. Return the lamb to the pan and add the stock, seasoning and rosemary. Bring to the boil, cover and simmer for 1 hour. Remove from the heat and add the sour cream and peas. This dish goes well with boiled rice.

Savoury Pudding

PREPARATION TIME: 40 minutes

COOKING TIME: 2 hours 15 minutes

1 onion, finely chopped
15ml (1 tblsp) oil
225g (8oz) minced lamb
15ml (1 tblsp) tomato purée
2.5ml (½ tsp) thyme
Seasoning
450ml (¾ pint) stock
1 large carrot, grated
350g (12oz) suet pastry
25g (1oz) cornflour
Gravy browning

Fry the onion and minced lamb in oil for 5 minutes, until mince is brown. Stir in the tomato purée, thyme, seasoning and stock and simmer for 10 minutes. Drain, reserving the stock. Add the carrot to the lamb mixture. Divide the pastry into three, and place one layer in the bottom of a greased 1,200ml (2 pint) basin. Place half the lamb mixture on top and repeat, finishing with a layer of suet pastry. Cover with buttered greaseproof paper or foil and steam for 2 hours. Mix cornflour with 30ml (2 tblsp) of cold water and add to reserved stock with a few drops of gravy browning. Bring to the boil, stirring continuously, and serve with the pudding.

Lamb Chops in Wine Sauce

PREPARATION TIME: 40 minutes

COOKING TIME: 45 minutes

25g (1oz) margarine or butter
4 loin chops
1 onion, sliced
5-10ml (1-2 tsp) paprika
150ml (¼ pint) dry white wine
150ml (¼ pint) chicken stock
15ml (1 tblsp) medium sherry
Seasoning
5ml (1 tsp) cornflour
50g (2oz) button mushrooms, sliced
2 tomatoes, skinned
Chopped parsley

Heat fat and brown chops on both sides. Drain and leave on one side. Add onion to pan and cook, with the paprika, until soft. Allow to cool slightly then pour on wine, stock and sherry. Return chops to pan, season well, bring to the boil, reduce heat and simmer, covered, for about 30 minutes. Blend cornflour with a little cold water and stir into wine and stock, stirring all the time. Add the mushrooms and tomatoes. Adjust seasoning and simmer for a further 15 minutes. Place chops on a serving dish, spoon over sauce and garnish with chopped parsley.

Crown Roast of Lamb (right), Festive Leg of Lamb (below) and Risotto (bottom).

Lamb Chops Reform

PREPARATION TIME: 35 minutes
COOKING TIME: 1 hour 10 minutes

8 lamb chops
25g (1oz) flour, seasoned
Beaten egg and breadcrumbs for coating
Oil for deep frying

Reform Sauce
50g (2oz) butter
50g (2oz) streaky bacon, chopped
1 small onion, chopped
1 large tomato, quartered
1 small carrot, sliced
50g (2oz) plain flour
600ml (1 pint) brown stock
10ml (2 tsp) mushroom ketchup (optional)
1 bouquet garni
Seasoning
15ml (1 tblsp) redcurrant jelly
15ml (1 tblsp) port

Trim and wipe chops. Dip them in seasoned flour and coat with egg and breadcrumbs.

Reform Sauce
Melt the butter in a saucepan. Add bacon and fry for 10 minutes. Add sliced vegetables until golden brown, stirring occasionally. Add flour and continue to fry slowly until a rich, brown colour. Add stock, mushroom ketchup and bouquet garni and simmer, covered, for 40 minutes. Skim and sieve the sauce. Add the redcurrant jelly and heat gently until the jelly dissolves. Stir in the port and check seasoning.

To Fry the Crumbed Cutlets
Heat a pan of cooking oil until hot. Place chops in the hot oil and fry for 1 minute. Turn off heat and allow the chops to continue cooking in the oil for a further 5 minutes. Drain well and arrange on a serving dish. Serve with the reform sauce.

Lamb Provençale

PREPARATION TIME: 30 minutes
COOKING TIME: 1 hour

450g (1lb) lamb from a cooked leg
50g (2oz) butter
15ml (1 tblsp) oil
2 medium onions, chopped
1 clove garlic, crushed
400g (14oz) tin tomatoes
15ml (1 tblsp) tomato purée
300ml (½ pint) dry white wine
100g (4oz) mushrooms, sliced
1 large green pepper, seeded and sliced
Seasoning

Cut lamb into small cubes. Melt the butter with the oil and add onions and garlic. Fry gently for about 10-15 minutes until soft, but not brown. Stir in the tomatoes, tomato purée and wine. Bring to the boil and add the lamb. Simmer, covered, for 25 minutes. Add the mushrooms and green peppers and cook for a further 15 minutes, stirring occasionally.

This page: Spare Ribs and Sweet and Sour Sauce (top), Lamb à l'Orange (centre left), Lamb Provençale (centre right) and Lamb Chops Reform (bottom). Facing page: Winter Lamb (top left), Scandinavian Lamb (top right), Irish Stew with Parsley Dumplings (centre left) and Lamb Chops in Wine Sauce (bottom right).

Lamb à l'Orange

PREPARATION TIME: 20 minutes
COOKING TIME: 25 minutes

1 small onion, finely chopped
15ml (1 tblsp) oil
1 large orange
15ml (1 tblsp) redcurrant jelly
300ml (½ pint) stock
2.5ml (½ tsp) dry mustard
2.5ml (½ tsp) caster sugar
Pinch cayenne pepper
15ml (1 tblsp) cornflour

350g (12oz) cooked lamb, leg or shoulder

Fry onion gently in oil until soft, but not brown. Grate the orange rind. Cut three fine slices from the orange, trim the pith and reserve for garnish. Squeeze the juice from the remainder of the orange and add to the onion with the orange rind, redcurrant jelly and stock. Bring to the boil, reduce heat and cook, stirring, for 5 minutes. Blend the mustard, sugar, pepper and cornflour together with 30ml (2 tblsp) cold water and stir into the orange sauce. Slice the lamb, add to sauce and bring to the boil. Reduce heat and simmer for 15 minutes. When cooked, garnish with the reserved orange slices.

Irish Stew with Parsley Dumplings

PREPARATION TIME: 45 minutes

COOKING TIME: 2 hours 50 minutes

Irish Stew
1.3kg (3lb) middle neck lamb chops
15g (½oz) seasoned flour
30ml (2 tblsp) dried onion flakes
15ml (1 tblsp) pearl barley
10ml (2 tsp) casserole seasoning
1 bayleaf
600ml (1 pint) boiling water
225g (8oz) potatoes, cut into chunks

Dumplings
100g (4oz) self-raising flour
2.5ml (½ tsp) salt
1.25ml (¼ tsp) ground black pepper
50g (2oz) suet, finely shredded
10ml (2 tsp) chopped parsley
30ml (2 tblsp) cold water

Coat the chops with seasoned flour and put them into a saucepan. Add the onion flakes and pearl barley. Sprinkle on the casserole seasoning and tuck in the bayleaf. Pour over the water and bring to the boil. Skim off any scum that rises to the surface. Reduce the heat, cover, simmer gently for 1 hour, add the potatoes and cook for a further 1½ hours.

Dumplings
Sift flour and seasoning into a bowl. Stir in suet and parsley, then add enough water to bind to a dough. Divide the dough into 4 large portions and shape into balls. About 20 minutes before the lamb has finished cooking, check that the liquid is boiling and drop dumplings into the pan. Replace the lid and finish the cooking at boiling point. Discard the bayleaf, adjust the seasoning and serve.

Spare Ribs and Sweet and Sour Sauce

PREPARATION TIME: 30 minutes

COOKING TIME: 50 minutes

4-8 spare ribs

Sauce
15g (½oz) cornflour
150ml (¼ pint) water
30ml (2 tblsp) vinegar from mixed pickles
Seasoning
15ml (1 tblsp) Worcestershire sauce
10ml (2 tsp) brown sugar

Garnish
Cooked rice
Lemon wedges

Put meat into roasting tim. Cook at 200°C, 400°F, Gas Mark 6, for about 30 minutes. Pour off surplus fat and return to oven for a further 15-20 minutes, until chops are crisp and brown.

Sauce
Blend cornflour with water, place all sauce ingredients in a pan and cook until thickened.

Garnish
Make a wide border of rice on a warm dish and arrange the spare ribs on this. Pour sauce into centre and place lemon wedges round the edge.

Meals with Pork

Facing page: Roast Leg of Pork (top), Roast Half Leg of Pork (centre) and Savoury Bacon (bottom).

Piquant Pork Chops

PREPARATION TIME: 30 minutes
COOKING TIME: 1 hour 10 minutes

4 pork chops
15ml (1 tblsp) oil
1 small onion, peeled and chopped
15ml (1 tblsp) brown sugar
15ml (1 tblsp) dry mustard
10ml (1 dsp) tomato purée
1 beef stock cube
300ml (½ pint) water
15ml (1 tblsp) Worcestershire sauce
30ml (2 tblsp) lemon juice

Put the chops in a baking tin or a wide, shallow casserole and bake uncovered at 190°C, 375°F, Gas Mark 4, for about 20 minutes. Meanwhile, heat the oil, add the onion and fry until browned. Add the sugar, mustard, tomato purée and crumbled beef stock cube. Mix well, then add water and stir till boiling. Add the Worcestershire sauce and lemon juice and check seasoning. Pour off any excess fat from the chops and pour the sauce over them. Cover and continue cooking in the oven at 180°C, 350°F, Gas Mark 3, for about 40-45 minutes.

Pork Steaks and Apple Sauce

PREPARATION TIME: 20 minutes
COOKING TIME: 25 minutes

4 pork steaks
Seasoning

Apple Sauce
450g (1lb) apples
150ml (¼ pint) water
15ml (1 tblsp) sugar
15g (½oz) butter or margarine

Season the pork steaks and fry or grill until cooked, turning often to ensure that they are cooked all the way through. Peel, core and thinly slice the apples. Put into a pan with the water, sugar and butter or margarine. Cook gently until soft, then rub through a sieve. Serve the apple sauce with the cooked pork steaks.

Piquant Pork Chops (top left), Pork Steaks and Apple Sauce (top right) and Pork Chops and Apple Chips (bottom).

Roast Leg of Pork

PREPARATION TIME: 20 minutes
COOKING TIME: 30 minutes per 450g (1lb) plus 30 minutes

1.25kg (2½lb) leg of pork
25g (1oz) dripping or cooking fat

Place meat in a roasting tin, season, and spread with dripping or cooking fat. Place in the centre of a preheated oven, 180°C, 350°F, Gas Mark 4. If a covered roasting tin is used, basting is not necessary, but if the joint is uncovered the meat should be basted every 20-30 minutes. The meat should be turned over, using two metal spoons, halfway through the cooking. When the meat is cooked, transfer to a large carving dish and keep hot.

Roast Half Leg of Pork

PREPARATION TIME: 15 minutes
COOKING TIME: 30 minutes per 450g (1lb) plus 30 minutes

Place meat in a roasting tin, season, and spread with dripping or cooking fat. Place in the centre of a preheated oven, 180°C, 350°F, Gas Mark 4. If a covered tin is used, basting is not necessary, but if the joint is uncovered the meat should be basted every 20-30 minutes. The meat should be turned over, using two metal spoons, halfway through the cooking. When the meat is cooked, transfer to a large carving dish and keep hot.

Savoury Bacon

PREPARATION TIME: 30 minutes
COOKING TIME: 45 minutes

250g (8oz) diced bacon (gammon or back)
3 spring onions, chopped
3 eggs
300ml (½ pint) milk
2.5ml (½ tsp) powdered sage
Seasoning
675g (1½lb) creamed potatoes
75g (3oz) cheese, grated

P
S

Fry onion until crisp. Beat eggs and add milk, sage, onion and seasoning. Grease an ovenproof dish and pipe creamed potatoes round the edge. Put the bacon in the centre of dish and pour the egg mixture over the bacon. Sprinkle the top with cheese. Bake in the centre of the oven at 190°C, 375°F, Gas Mark 5, for about 30 minutes until set, and the potato border has browned.

Spicy Pork Meatballs

PREPARATION TIME: 50 minutes
COOKING TIME: 40 minutes

675g (1½lb) minced pork
1 large onion, grated
Pinch garlic granules
50g (2oz) ground almonds
50g (2oz) fresh breadcrumbs
1 small egg, beaten
5ml (1 tsp) chopped parsley
1.25ml (¼ tsp) ground cinnamon
2.5ml (½ tsp) salt
2.5ml (½ tsp) black pepper
30ml (2 tblsp) medium sherry
15g (½oz) butter
60ml (4 tblsp) oil

Sauce
1 small onion, finely chopped
Pinch garlic granules
7.5ml (1½ tsp) soft brown sugar
4 tomatoes, skinned and chopped
½ green pepper, cored, seeded and sliced
½ red pepper, cored, seeded and sliced
1.25ml (¼ tsp) crushed chillis
1.25ml (¼ tsp) cayenne pepper
5ml (1 tsp) paprika
5ml (1 tsp) chopped parsley
300ml (½ pint) beef stock
10ml (2 tsp) cornflour
60ml (4 tblsp) medium sherry

Meatballs
Mix together the pork, onion, garlic granules, almonds, breadcrumbs, egg, parsley, cinnamon, seasoning and sherry. Combine well, then shape into about 40 walnut-sized balls. Melt the butter with half the oil in a frying pan. Add the meatballs in batches and fry gently until browned on all sides, taking care not to break up the meatball shapes. Remove from the pan with a slotted spoon and drain on paper towels.

Sauce
Heat the remaining oil in a saucepan, add the onion, garlic granules and brown sugar to the pan and fry until the onion is soft. Stir in the tomatoes, green and red peppers, crushed chillis, cayenne pepper, paprika and parsley and cook for a further 3 minutes. Add stock and bring to the boil, stirring occasionally. Dissolve the cornflour in the sherry and add to the pan. Simmer, stirring, until thickened. Add the meatballs to the sauce and shake the pan to coat well. Cover the pan and cook gently for 20-25 minutes or until the meatballs are cooked through. Taste and adjust seasoning before serving.

Pork Chops and Apple Chips

PREPARATION TIME: 40 minutes
COOKING TIME: 30 minutes

4 pork chops
Fat for deep frying
2 large cooking apples
A little flour

Grill or fry the chops for 15-20 minutes, turning frequently. Peel and core the apples and cut them into chips. Roll the chips in flour and fry in deep fat until cooked. Serve with the chops, at once.

Minced Pork Loaf

PREPARATION TIME: 45 minutes
COOKING TIME: 1 hour 45 minutes

225g (½lb) aubergine
675g (1½lb) minced pork
1 onion, chopped
50g (2oz) fresh breadcrumbs
15ml (1 tblsp) chopped parsley
Seasoning
Pinch curry powder
Pinch garlic salt
1 egg, beaten

Preheat oven to 200°C, 400°F, Gas Mark 6. Bake the aubergine in its skin for 15 minutes. Cut in two and scoop out the pulp. Mix in a bowl with the meat, onion, breadcrumbs, parsley, seasoning, curry powder and garlic salt. Blend in the beaten egg. Place the meat mixture in a greased, oblong bread tin. Stand the tin on a baking tray half filled with water and bake for 1½ hours. Cool and turn out on to a dish.

Bacon and Onion Roll

PREPARATION TIME: 30 minutes
COOKING TIME: 2 hours 15 minutes

1 large onion, chopped
5ml (1 tsp) powdered sage
Seasoning
1 rounded teacup fresh white breadcrumbs
25g (1oz) margarine, melted
4 bacon rashers, trimmed

Spicy Pork Meatballs (above right), Bacon and Onion Roll (right) and Minced Pork Loaf (top right).

Suet Pastry
225g (8oz) self-raising flour
5ml (1 tsp) baking powder
2.5ml (½ tsp) salt
Pinch of pepper
100g (4oz) finely shredded suet
150ml (¼ pint) water

Mix together the onion, seasonings and breadcrumbs. Stir in the margarine. For the pastry: sift the flour, baking powder and seasonings into a mixing basin. Add suet and stir in enough water to mix to a firm dough. Turn out on to a floured board and roll out to an oblong. Arrange bacon rashers over surface and spread with stuffing to within 2.5cm (1 inch) of edges. Moisten pastry edges and roll into a roly-poly about 20cm (8 inches) long. Pinch edges to seal. Wrap in greased, double-thickness greaseproof paper, folding into a large pleat the length of the roll to allow for expansion. Wrap loosely in kitchen foil. Steam briskly for 2 hours.

Curried Pork

PREPARATION TIME: 25 minutes
COOKING TIME: 40 minutes

175g (6oz) pasta (macaroni or shaped pasta)
Salt
450g (1lb) frozen mixed vegetables
450g (1lb) pork fillet, diced
30ml (2 tblsp) oil
1 large onion, chopped
1 green pepper
15ml (1 tblsp) black treacle
5-10ml (1-2 tsp) curry powder
Seasoning
Butter
1 onion, sliced into rings

Cook the pasta in 1½ litres (3 pints) of boiling, salted water until tender; strain and keep half on one side for a garnish. Cook the frozen vegetables in a little salted water until they begin to soften; strain. Toss the pork in the hot oil for 5 minutes, add the onion, green pepper, treacle, curry powder and seasoning, then lower heat and continue to cook for a further 5 minutes. Stir in the vegetables and half the pasta. Heat gently for 10 minutes. Serve in a border of pasta tossed in a little butter and garnish with sliced, raw onion rings.

Pork Croquettes

PREPARATION TIME: 30 minutes
COOKING TIME: 15 minutes

350g (12oz) cooked pork, minced
25g (1oz) butter or margarine
25g (1oz) flour
150ml (¼ pint) milk
10ml (2 tsp) chopped parsley
10ml (2 tsp) chopped gherkins
75g (3oz) soft, fresh breadcrumbs
Seasoning
Oil or fat to fry

To Coat
1 egg, beaten
50g (2oz) crisp breadcrumbs

Make a thick sauce of the butter or margarine, flour and milk, and add the parsley, gherkins and meat. Blend well, then stir in the breadcrumbs and seasoning. Allow the mixture to cool, form into eight finger shapes, brush with egg and coat in breadcrumbs. Fry in hot fat or oil until crisp and brown. Drain well on kitchen paper. Serve hot.

Shepherd's Pie

PREPARATION TIME: 40 minutes
COOKING TIME: 30 minutes

225-350g (8-12oz) cooked minced pork
25g (1oz) dripping or fat
1 onion, finely chopped
2 tomatoes, skinned and chopped
Good pinch of mixed herbs
Seasoning
150-300ml (¼-½ pint) stock
450g (1lb) mashed potato
25g (1oz) butter or margarine

Heat the fat or dripping and fry the onion for 3 minutes. Add the tomatoes and the meat and heat together for 2-3 minutes. Stir in the herbs, seasoning and stock. Put into a pie dish and cover with the mashed potato, forking this neatly over, or piping it. Scatter pieces of butter on the potatoes to help the topping to brown. Bake in the centre of the oven at 190°C, 375°F, Gas Mark 5, until crisp and brown on top.

Pork Fillet with Apricots

PREPARATION TIME: 30 minutes
COOKING TIME: 40 minutes

450g (1lb) pork fillet, cut into bite-size pieces
30ml (2 tblsp) seasoned flour
50g (2oz) butter
400g (14oz) tin apricot halves, drained and juice retained
30ml (2 tblsp) Worcestershire sauce
30ml (2 tblsp) demerara sugar
10ml (2 tsp) vinegar
10ml (2 tsp) lemon juice
120ml (8 tblsp) water
225g (8oz) long grain rice

Toss the pork pieces in seasoned flour. Heat the butter and fry the pork until lightly browned. Chop all but three of the apricot halves. Mix 120ml (8 tblsp) apricot juice with the Worcestershire sauce, sugar, vinegar, lemon juice and water. Add any remaining flour to the pork and pour in the apricot sauce and chopped fruit. Bring to the boil, stirring. Reduce heat, cover and simmer for about 15 minutes. Spoon pork and sauce onto a serving dish. Cook the rice in boiling, salted water and arrange in a border around the meat. Garnish with remaining apricot halves.

Cranberry Ham

PREPARATION TIME: 25 minutes
COOKING TIME: 15 minutes

4 thick slices cooked ham
25g (1oz) fat
30ml (2 tblsp) cranberry jelly or sauce

Heat the ham for 2-3 minutes in the hot fat or brush with melted fat and heat under the grill. Spread with the sauce or jelly and leave under a hot grill until the sauce bubbles; serve at once.

Bacon Pancakes

PREPARATION TIME: 20 minutes
COOKING TIME: 30 minutes

8 bacon rashers, de-rinded

Batter
100g (4oz) flour, preferably plain
Pinch of salt
1 egg
300ml (½ pint) milk

Sieve the flour and salt into a large basin, big enough for beating in the liquid. Add the egg to the basin, then add about a quarter of the milk. Stir carefully with a wooden spoon until the flour is blended. Beat hard until smooth. Add the rest of the liquid. When the batter becomes thinner use a flat egg whisk to aerate the mixture. Cook pancakes in the usual way. Meanwhile, fry or grill the bacon rashers and cut into pieces. Sandwich the pancakes with really crisp bacon and serve hot.

This page: Stuffed Loin of Pork (top), Pork Fillet with Apricots (centre left) and Curried Pork (bottom). Facing page: Bacon Pancakes (top), Pork Croquettes (centre left), Shepherd's Pie (centre right) and Cranberry Ham (bottom).

Bacon Casserole

PREPARATION TIME: 30 minutes

COOKING TIME: 40 minutes per 450g (1lb) plus 5 minutes to thicken

175-250g (6-9oz) bacon or ham per person
Ground black pepper or peppercorns
450g (1lb) mixed vegetables

Soak the bacon in cold water. Put into the casserole and cover with cold water. Add pepper or peppercorns and cover. Allow about 40 minutes per 450g (1lb) for a wide, thin joint; a little longer if a thick joint is used. Bake at 170°C, 325°F, Gas Mark 3. Add vegetables during cooking.

Belly of Pork Casserole

PREPARATION TIME: 40 minutes

COOKING TIME: 2 hours 15 minutes

1 large onion, sliced
1 large cooking apple, peeled and sliced
675g (1½lb) belly of pork
30ml (2 tblsp) tomato purée
1 chicken stock cube
450ml (¾ pint) boiling water
A pinch of freshly-ground black pepper
A pinch of sage

Put the onion and apple into a casserole and put the meat on top. Mix the tomato purée and stock cube together, add boiling water and stir till stock cube has dissolved. Pour over meat in casserole, add pepper and sage. Cover and bake at 170°C, 325°F, Gas Mark 2, for about 2 hours.

Stuffed Loin of Pork

PREPARATION TIME: 40 minutes

COOKING TIME: 25 minutes per 450g (1lb) plus 25 minutes

1.5kg (3lb) loin of pork, boned

Stuffing
100g (4oz) soft breadcrumbs
50g (2oz) suet, finely shredded
30ml (2 tblsp) chopped parsley
15ml (1 tblsp) chopped chives or spring onions
Seasoning
1 egg
A little oil or fat

Score the fat on the meat with a knife. Blend the stuffing ingredients together and then spread the stuffing over the meat carefully and roll it up. Brush the scored fat with melted fat or oil and sprinkle lightly with salt. Weigh after stuffing meat. Cook in a roasting tin at 220°C, 425°F, Gas Mark 7. Remove the meat to a hot dish when cooked, pour off the surplus fat, leaving just 15ml (1 tblsp) in the roasting tin and make a gravy with this.

Fluffy Baked Eggs and Bacon

PREPARATION TIME: 15 minutes

COOKING TIME: 15 minutes

4 slices of bread
Butter
4 eggs
Seasoning
8 bacon rashers, de-rinded

Toast the bread and spread with butter. Separate the egg yolks and whites. Whisk the whites until very stiff, seasoning well. Make the egg white into a ring on each slice of toast, drop a yolk in the centre and bake until set in oven at 190°C, 375°F, Gas Mark 5. Serve with grilled bacon.

This page: Belly of Pork Casserole (top), Pork Chops and Frankfurters (centre right) and Bacon and Sausage Plait (bottom left). Facing page: Bacon Chops with Pears (top), Pork with Sweet and Sour Sauce (centre left), Bacon Casserole (centre right) and Fluffy Baked Eggs and Bacon (bottom).

Pork Kebabs

PREPARATION TIME: 25 minutes

COOKING TIME: 20 minutes

450g (1lb) lean pork, cut into bite-size pieces

Brush kebabs with melted butter and cook under the grill, turning the skewers to make sure that the food is well cooked. The food can be slipped from the skewer easily onto serving plates.

This is a most attractive way of serving grilled foods. You can thread a mixture of foods – kidneys, bacon, sausages, diced pork, mushrooms, onions, tomato halves, etc. – onto metal skewers.

Bacon Chops with Pears

PREPARATION TIME: 25 minutes
COOKING TIME: 20 minutes

6 gammon chops
3 dessert pears
25g (1oz) melted butter
15g (½oz) flour
1 egg, beaten
100g (4oz) breadcrumbs
Oil for deep frying

Brush the bacon with melted butter and grill for 4-5 minutes on both sides. Peel and core the pears and cut in halves. Coat pear halves with flour, then with egg and breadcrumbs. Fry in deep oil for 10 minutes until golden brown. Serve bacon with a pear half on each slice.

Bacon and Sausage Plait

PREPARATION TIME: 50 minutes
COOKING TIME: 30-40 minutes

350g (¾lb) rough-puff pastry, frozen

Filling
250g (8oz) pork sausage meat
250g (8oz) cooked bacon, chopped
2 hard-boiled eggs, roughly chopped
5ml (1 tsp) sage
Seasoning

Glaze
1 egg, beaten
A little salt

Roll the pastry out to a 25cm (10 inch) square. Mix all the ingredients together and place down the centre of the pastry, leaving equal sides of unfilled pastry. Cut the sides obliquely in 1cm (½ inch) strips and brush with beaten egg. Lift alternate strips over the sausage mixture to form a roll resembling a plait. Brush with egg and sprinkle with salt. Bake at 200°C, 400°F, Gas Mark 6, for about 15 minutes. Lower heat to 180°C, 350°F, Gas Mark 4, for a further 15 minutes.

Ham in Cider and Raisin Sauce

PREPARATION TIME: 45 minutes
COOKING TIME: 30 minutes per 450g (1lb) plus 30 minutes

2kg (4lb) forehock, ham or bacon
1 carrot, sliced
1 onion, sliced
Bouquet garni
3 whole cloves
600ml (1 pint) cider
600ml (1 pint) water

Cider and Raisin Sauce
100g (4oz) seedless raisins
300ml (½ pint) stock (from cooking bacon)
25g (1oz) brown sugar
2-3 drops gravy browning
Juice of ½ lemon
10ml (2 tsp) cornflour
30ml (2 tblsp) water

Put the ham, vegetables, herbs and cloves in the pan and add cider and water. Bring to the boil and cover. Simmer slowly, allowing 20 minutes per 450g (1lb) plus 20 minutes for ham, or 30 minutes per 450g (1lb) plus 30 minutes for forehock.

Cider and Raisin Sauce
Put all the sauce ingredients, except cornflour and water, into a saucepan. Cover and simmer for 10 minutes. Blend the cornflour with 30ml (2 tblsp) water. Stir into the sauce, simmer for a further 3 minutes. Serve sauce separately.

Pork Chops and Frankfurters

PREPARATION TIME: 30 minutes
COOKING TIME: 20 minutes

4 small pork chops (loin or spare ribs)
Seasoning
50-75g (2-3oz) melted butter
4-8 frankfurters
1 green pepper, cored and sliced
2 small eating apples, cored and sliced
350g (12oz) can sauerkraut
Parsley

Season pork chops. If they are lean, brush with a little melted butter and grill until tender, turning over and lowering the heat when browned on either side. Simmer the frankfurters in boiling water for 5 minutes; drain. Fry the green pepper and apples in the rest of the butter, add the sauerkraut and heat thoroughly. Put the apple mixture on to a hot dish, top with the chops and frankfurters and garnish with parsley.

Boiled Bacon and Pease Pudding

PREPARATION TIME: overnight plus 30 minutes
COOKING TIME: 2 hours

175-250g (6-9oz) bacon per person
Pepper

Pease Pudding
225g (8oz) dried split yellow peas
1 onion
2 cloves
Seasoning
100g (4oz) butter

Wash and soak salted bacon overnight, or for several hours, in cold water. Put soaked bacon into a saucepan, cover with cold water. Bring to the boil, skim, removing any greyish film floating on top. Add pepper, but no salt. Put a lid on the pan and cook slowly, allowing 30 minutes per 450g (1lb) for thinner joints, 35 minutes per 450g (1lb) for thicker joints.

Pease Pudding
Place split peas in a bowl, cover with cold water and soak for 3 hours. Rinse thoroughly. Peel the onion and press a clove into each end. Place the onion and split peas in boiling water. Do not salt. Simmer for ¾-1 hour or until peas are soft. Drain. Remove the cloves from the onion. Mash the peas and the onion together or pass them through a blender to form a smooth purée. Season well and beat in the butter.

Ham in Cider and Raisin Sauce (top left), Pork Kebabs (bottom left) and Boiled Bacon and Pease Pudding (left).

Cooking with Veal

Veal Casserole

PREPARATION TIME: 30 minutes
COOKING TIME: 50 minutes

675g (1½lb) veal shoulder, cubed
Seasoning
50ml (2oz) chicken stock
2 large carrots
2 sticks celery, chopped
15ml (1 tblsp) quick tapioca
15ml (1 tblsp) water
4 slices of bread
Margarine

Season the veal. Bring chicken stock to the boil, add the meat, carrots and celery, cover and let simmer for 45 minutes. Mix the tapioca with the water, stir into the meat and simmer until the sauce thickens. Transfer to a casserole. Spread the bread slices with margarine on both sides and place on top of the casserole. Put in a hot oven until bread is toasted.

Veal en Croûte

PREPARATION TIME: 30 minutes
COOKING TIME: 55 minutes

Shortcrust Pastry
200g (7oz) flour
Pinch of salt
90g (3½oz) fat
Water to mix

Filling
75g (3oz) mushrooms, finely chopped
50g (2oz) butter
Seasoning
450-675g (1-1½lb) veal (in one piece)

Pastry
Sieve flour and salt together, rub in fat, bind with water and roll out to a large oblong.

Filling
Blend mushrooms with the butter and seasoning and spread over the centre of the pastry, leaving the ends plain. Put the veal on top, season lightly and wrap pastry round this. Seal the edges with water. Cook on a greased baking sheet for 20-25 minutes, in the centre of the oven at 220-230°C, 425-450°F, Gas Mark 7-8. Lower heat to 180-190°C, 350-375°F, Gas Mark 4-5, for a further 30 minutes.

Veal Chops with Cheese

PREPARATION TIME: 35 minutes
COOKING TIME: 30 minutes

8 thick veal chops
100g (4oz) butter
Seasoning
400g (14oz) Gruyère cheese, grated
2 eggs
60ml (4 tblsp) double cream
Grated nutmeg
100ml (4 fl oz) white wine

Melt the butter in a large sauté pan with an ovenproof handle. Add the veal chops and sear them on both sides over a high heat. Reduce heat, season the chops, cover pan and cook gently for about 20 minutes, turning the chops once. In a bowl mix the cheese, eggs and cream. Season and add the nutmeg. Drain off the cooking butter from the pan and reserve it. Put some of the cheese mixture on each chop. Add the wine to the pan and place it, uncovered, in the oven, 190°C, 375°F, Gas Mark 5, for 10 minutes to finish the cooking. Baste the chops with the reserved cooking butter once or twice.

Fricassée of Veal

PREPARATION TIME: 25 minutes
COOKING TIME: 1 hour 20 minutes

675g (1½lb) veal cutlets
1 onion, stuck with cloves
Seasoning
Bouquet garni
25g (1oz) butter
25g (1oz) flour

Garnish
Bacon rolls
Lemon slices

Cut meat into small pieces and put in a saucepan, together with the onion, seasoning and bouquet garni. Cover with water, bring to the boil and simmer until the meat is tender (about 1 hour). Melt the butter in a pan, add the flour and stir well. Do not brown. Remove the bouquet garni and the onion from the veal. Add the liquid to the flour and fat, then add this to the veal. Cook gently for a further 10 minutes. Garnish with bacon rolls and lemon slices.

Veal and Mushroom Pie

PREPARATION TIME: 50 minutes
COOKING TIME: 2 hours 50 minutes

450g (1lb) veal, cubed
Seasoned flour
Butter or oil for frying
1 small bayleaf
175g (6oz) mushrooms, peeled and sliced
300ml (½ pint) stock
175g (6oz) shortcrust pastry
1 egg, beaten

Dust veal in seasoned flour. Fry until lightly brown. Add bayleaf and stock and bring to simmering point. Cover and cook in oven at 180°C, 350°F, Gas Mark 4, until tender (about 2 hours). Leave to cool. Roll pastry out to fit a large ovenproof plate. Put meat and mushrooms onto the plate, adding seasoning to taste. Cover with pastry. Brush with beaten egg to glaze. Bake at 230°C, 450°F, Gas Mark 8, for about 30 minutes.

This page: Veal and Mushroom Pie (top), Fricassée of Veal (centre left) and Veal en Croûte (bottom).

Facing page: Ragoût (top), Veal Chops with Mushrooms (centre right) and Veal Chops with Cheese (bottom).

Rolled Breast of Veal

PREPARATION TIME: 30 minutes
COOKING TIME: 1 hour 20 minutes

1.5kg (3lb) breast of veal, boned and trimmed
100g (4oz) smoked ham streaked with fat, finely chopped
50g (2oz) lard
90ml (6 tblsp) finely chopped parsley
1 garlic clove, crushed
Seasoning
200ml (7 fl oz) dry white wine

Score the inside of the breast crossways, in lines 3mm (⅛ inch) deep. Mix the smoked ham, 25g (1oz) of the lard, 60ml (4 tblsp) of the parsley, the garlic and 5ml (1 tsp) seasoning to make a paste. Spread the paste over the cut surface of the veal. Beginning at one of the narrow sides, roll up the veal tightly; skewer or tie with string. Season the surface of the meat. In a heavy pan, slowly brown the veal on all sides in the rest of the lard. Add the wine, cover and simmer for 1 hour or until tender. Remove the veal to a carving board and allow to stand for 10 minutes before cutting into slices. Skim any excess fat off the pan juices. Taste the juices, adjust the seasoning to taste, then reheat, adding the remaining parsley, and use as a sauce for the veal.

Veal Chops with Mushrooms

PREPARATION TIME: 45 minutes
COOKING TIME: 1 hour 10 minutes

4 veal chops
Seasoning
30ml (2 tblsp) oil
4 medium-sized carrots, sliced
100g (4oz) mushrooms, sliced
1 small onion, sliced
60ml (4 tblsp) white wine
2 tomatoes, peeled and sliced

Trim chops and season. Heat oil, brown chops on both sides, then transfer to a casserole. Add all other ingredients and cook in the oven at 170°C, 325°F, Gas Mark 3, for about 1 hour.

Fried Veal with Rice

PREPARATION TIME: 30 minutes
COOKING TIME: 1 hour

4 neck cutlets
Seasoned flour
1 small onion
1 small green pepper
1 stick celery
1 tomato
75g (3oz) fat or oil
150ml (¼ pint) stock
225g (8oz) rice

Toss the cutlets in seasoned flour. Peel and chop the onion and chop other vegetables. Melt 50g (2oz) fat and fry the veal until brown on both sides. Add the stock; simmer the meat until it is tender (45 minutes). Boil the rice. Melt 25g (1oz) fat and fry the onion, green pepper and celery. Stir in the cooked rice and add the tomato. Serve the cutlets on top of the rice mixture and pour over the juices from the frying pan.

Veal Chops with Wine (above), Fried Veal with Rice (right) and Roast Best End of Neck (far right).

Roast Best End of Neck

PREPARATION TIME: 10 minutes

COOKING TIME: 25 minutes per 450g (1lb) plus 25 minutes

Place joint in a roasting tin and spread with dripping or cooking fat and season. Place in the centre of a preheated oven. If a covered roasting tin is used, basting is not necessary, but if the joint is uncovered, the meat should be basted every 20-30 minutes. The meat should be turned over, using two metal spoons, halfway through the cooking. When the meat is cooked, transfer to a large carving dish and keep hot.

Veal Chops with Wine

PREPARATION TIME: 30 minutes

COOKING TIME: 1 hour 20 minutes

4 veal chops
40g (1½oz) flour
Seasoning
30ml (2 tblsp) oil
1 onion, chopped
100g (4oz) mushrooms, sliced
300ml (½ pint) white wine

Trim chops and coat with seasoned flour. Heat oil, brown chops on both sides, then transfer to a casserole. Add onion to remaining oil and cook till lightly brown. Add remaining flour and mix well. Add mushrooms and wine and bring to boiling point, stirring all the time. Pour sauce over chops in the casserole. Cover and cook for about 1 hour at 180°C, 350°F, Gas Mark 3.

Blanquette of Veal with Prunes

PREPARATION TIME: 20 minutes

COOKING TIME: 30 minutes

450g (1lb) veal, diced
2 onions, diced
1 sachet of bouquet garni
600ml (1 pint) white stock
50g (2oz) butter
50g (2oz) flour
150ml (¼ pint) cream or evaporated milk
1-2 egg yolks
15ml (1 tblsp) lemon juice

Garnish
Freshly cooked prunes
Freshly cooked vegetables

Put the veal, onions and herbs into a pan with the stock. Simmer gently until tender. Strain; keep the meat hot. Make a sauce with the butter, flour and stock; cook for 2 minutes. Add the cream or evaporated milk and reheat. Stir in the egg yolks and lemon juice. Reheat, but do not boil. Pour over the veal. Garnish with the prunes and vegetables.

Veal Roll with Prune and Apple Stuffing

PREPARATION TIME: 40 minutes
COOKING TIME: 1 hour 15 minutes

350g (12oz) shortcrust pastry
450-675g (1-1½lb) veal fillet

Stuffing
100g (4oz) bacon, de-rinded and chopped
100g (4oz) soft breadcrumbs
5ml (1 tsp) mixed herbs
175g (6oz) soaked prunes, drained well
1 medium dessert apple
Seasoning
1 egg yolk

Glaze
1 egg white

Roll out pastry to an oblong about 20x15cm (8x6 inches). Flatten veal with a rolling pin into an oblong about 5mm (¼ inch) thick. Fry bacon for about 5 minutes, then mix with other stuffing ingredients. Spread over veal, then roll. Lay onto the pastry, brush sides with water and roll. Seal edges firmly. Brush with leftover egg white to glaze. Cook on a baking sheet for 20-25 minutes at 220°C, 425°F, Gas Mark 7, then lower the heat to 180-190°C, 350-375°F, Gas Mark 4-5, for 45 minutes.

Veal Escalopes

PREPARATION TIME: 30 minutes
COOKING TIME: 15 minutes

4 thin slices veal, approx. 350g (12oz) each
1 egg, beaten
75g (3oz) white breadcrumbs
75g (3oz) Cheddar cheese, finely grated
Pinch of salt
Dash cayenne pepper
50g (2oz) vegetable shortening
50g (2oz) butter

Trim the veal slices to give neat shapes and dip them in the beaten egg. Mix the breadcrumbs and grated cheese together and season with salt and cayenne pepper. Use this to coat the veal. Fry the veal on both sides in hot vegetable shortening for about 10 minutes, till golden brown.

Veal Rolls

PREPARATION TIME: 30 minutes
COOKING TIME: 2 hours 15 minutes

4 veal escalopes
25g (1oz) melted butter
Seasoning
10ml (2 tsp) onion, finely chopped
5ml (1 tsp) grated lemon rind
10ml (2 tsp) parsley, finely chopped

Sauce
25g (1oz) butter
1 small onion, grated or finely chopped
½ small apple, peeled and grated
10ml (2 tsp) cornflour
1 small tin tomato purée
1 chicken stock cube
450ml (¾ pint) water

Brush the escalopes with a little butter and sprinkle with seasoning, onion, parsley and lemon, and roll up tightly. Secure with a small skewer or thin string. Put into a casserole. To make the sauce heat the butter, add the onion and apple, and sauté for a few minutes without browning. Stir in the cornflour, tomato purée and crumbled chicken stock cube and mix well together. Add the water and stir till boiling. Boil for 2 minutes, then pour over veal rolls. Cover and cook at 170°C, 325°F, Gas Mark 2, for about 2 hours.

This page: Ginger Veal Chops (top), Rolled Breast of Veal (centre left) and Veal Marengo (bottom right).

Facing page: Blanquette of Veal with Prunes (top right), Veal Rolls (centre left), Veal Casserole (centre right) and Veal Escalopes (bottom).

Veal Marengo

PREPARATION TIME: 30 minutes
COOKING TIME: 1 hour 20 minutes

450g (1lb) neck of veal
Seasoned flour
75g (3oz) butter
2 onions, chopped
300ml (½ pint) white stock
225g (8oz) tomatoes, skinned and chopped
50g (2oz) mushrooms, chopped
Seasoning

Garnish
4 slices of bread, cut into croûtons
Fat for frying
Parsley
Lemon

Cut the veal into cubes. Coat with seasoned flour and fry until golden brown in hot butter. Add the onion and fry until transparent. Add the stock, tomatoes and mushrooms. Season well. Simmer gently for about 1 hour. Serve garnished with croûtons of fried bread, parsley and lemon.

Ginger Veal Chops

PREPARATION TIME: 30 minutes
COOKING TIME: 30 minutes

4 veal chops
Meat tenderizer
30ml (2 tblsp) margarine
1 tin condensed cream of celery soup
1 small tin peas or mixed vegetables
4 slices mild cheese
2.5ml (½ tsp) ginger

Tenderize veal following package directions. In a covered pan slowly sauté veal in margarine, turning to brown on both sides. When meat is tender, add soup and vegetables to pan. When thoroughly heated, place a slice of cheese on each veal chop and sprinkle top with ginger. Place under grill, or cover pan and cook, until cheese melts.

Ragoût

PREPARATION TIME: 30 minutes
COOKING TIME: 1 hour 5 minutes

450g (1lb) stewing veal and kidney, diced
50g (2oz) dripping
2 onions, sliced
50g (2oz) mushrooms or 2 sliced, seeded red or green peppers
1 large tin cream of tomato soup
15ml (1 tsp) paprika
½ teacup water
Seasoning
Chopped parsley

Heat the dripping in a pan and fry the veal and kidney, onions and peppers for a few minutes. Cover with the tomato soup and the paprika blended with water. Add seasoning to taste, cover, and simmer for about 1 hour. Garnish with chopped parsley, if desired.

Offal

Calves' Brains

PREPARATION TIME: 10 minutes
COOKING TIME: 35 minutes

450g (1lb) calves' brains
15ml (1 tblsp) vinegar

White Sauce
25g (1oz) cornflour
600ml (1 pint) milk
45ml (3 tblsp) white wine

Soak brains in cold water for 1 hour. Remove skin and traces of blood. Place brains in fresh water, to which 15ml (1 tblsp) of vinegar has been added and boil for 15-20 minutes. Drain and put in cold water to cool. Dry and slice.

White Sauce
Put the cornflour into a basin. Blend it to a thin cream with some of the milk, using a wooden spoon. Rinse a saucepan with cold water; this prevents milk from sticking to the pan. Heat the milk to boiling point and pour over the blended cornflour, stirring all the time; add the white wine. Rinse the pan, return the mixture to the pan and boil for 3-5 minutes. Serve the brains with the white sauce, adding chopped carrot and runner beans if desired.

Liver and Onions

PREPARATION TIME: 15 minutes
COOKING TIME: 20 minutes

675g (1½lb) onions
6 slices of lamb's liver
Seasoning
45ml (3 tblsp) plain flour
75g (3oz) butter
30ml (2 tblsp) chopped parsley (optional)

Peel and slice the onions. Trim and wipe the liver. Season the flour and use it to coat the liver. Melt the butter in a large frying pan. Add the onions and fry till golden. Add the liver slices and fry for 3-10 minutes on each side. Stir in the parsley, if desired. Transfer to a warmed serving dish and top with fried onions. Spoon pan juices over.

Haggis

PREPARATION TIME: 50 minutes

COOKING TIME: 2 hours 40 minutes

225g (8oz) sheep's liver
100g (4oz) beef suet
2 onions
1 breakfast cup oatmeal
Seasoning

Cover the liver with water and boil for 40 minutes. Drain and keep the liquid. Mince the liver finely. Parboil the onions, then chop them finely with the suet. Brown the oatmeal by tossing it quickly in a thick pan. Combine the minced liver, suet, onions and oatmeal and season. Moisten with the liquor in which the liver was boiled. Turn into a greased bowl, cover with greaseproof paper and steam for 2 hours.

Calves' Brains (far left), Kidney and Sausage Casserole (centre) and Haggis (above).

Liver and Bacon Kebabs

PREPARATION TIME: 20 minutes

COOKING TIME: 5-10 minutes

350g (12oz) piece of lamb's liver
175g (6oz) piece of streaky bacon
100g (4oz) button mushrooms
50g (2oz) melted butter
50g (2oz) fine breadcrumbs
2.5ml (½ tsp) paprika
Salt

Wipe and trim the liver. Cut it into 2.5cm (1 inch) cubes. De-rind the bacon, cut it into thick rashers, then into squares. Wipe and trim mushrooms. Preheat the grill. Line the grill pan with foil. Thread the bacon, liver and mushrooms onto four skewers. Brush with melted butter. Mix the breadcrumbs, paprika and salt together on a plate. Turn the kebabs in the breadcrumbs till evenly coated. Arrange on the grill pan and grill for about 5 minutes, turning the kebabs frequently and brushing them with the fat that runs from the bacon.

Piquant Kidneys

PREPARATION TIME: 10 minutes

COOKING TIME: 15 minutes

450g (1lb) calves' kidneys
1 onion, finely chopped
50g (2oz) butter
30ml (2 tblsp) chopped parsley
15ml (1 tblsp) wine vinegar
Seasoning

Prepare and wash the kidneys. Slice very thinly. Melt the butter in a frying pan and cook the onion and parsley for 5 minutes. Add the kidneys and cook for a further 5-10 minutes, stirring occasionally. Stir in the vinegar and bring to the boil, then remove from heat immediately. Add seasoning to taste.

This page: Chicken Liver Omelette (top), Lambs' Hearts with Walnut Stuffing (bottom right) and Piquant Kidneys (bottom left).

Facing page: Liver and Bacon Kebabs (top), Sweetbread Fritters (centre left) and Liver, Bacon and Onion (bottom right).

Tongue and Lentil Casserole

PREPARATION TIME: 4 hours 30 minutes

COOKING TIME: 2 hours 45 minutes

225g (8oz) lentils, soaked overnight
4 sheep's tongues
25g (1oz) fat
2 onions, chopped
225g (8oz) carrots, chopped
Pinch of mixed herbs
Seasoning
1 clove garlic, crushed

Soak the sheep's tongues for 3-4 hours. Drain, cover with cold water and bring to the boil. Simmer for 10-15 minutes. Drain, cover with fresh, cold water and simmer for 1 hour. Pour off and retain water. Leave tongues to cool, then remove skin. Slice tongues and put into a casserole. Melt the fat, add the onions and fry till brown, then add to the tongues. Add the drained lentils and carrots to the fat and fry for a few minutes. Put into the casserole with the herbs, seasoning and garlic. Cover with stock. Cover the casserole and cook in oven at 170°C, 325°F, Gas Mark 3, for 1½ hours.

Lambs' Hearts with Walnut Stuffing

PREPARATION TIME: 30 minutes

COOKING TIME: 1 hour 25 minutes

4 lambs' hearts
4 large onions
Stock
Butter or margarine

Walnut Stuffing
50g (2oz) fresh breadcrumbs
50g (2oz) chopped walnuts
50g (2oz) fat bacon
Seasoning
Pinch mace
Egg to bind
150ml (¼ pint) stock
25g (1oz) butter or margarine
4 large onions

Put all the stuffing ingredients into a small basin and add sufficient egg to bind. Prepare the hearts by cutting away all tough skin, etc. Stuff the hearts and tie the ends with thread. Simmer gently for 1 hour in a little well-seasoned stock, with the onions. Place in a fireproof dish, pour over the remainder of the stock, place a little butter or margarine on top of the hearts and onions, cover with a lid. Roast at 190°C, 375°F, Gas Mark 5, for about 20 minutes. Cut away thread before serving.

Braised Oxtail

PREPARATION TIME: 30 minutes

COOKING TIME: 2 hours 45 minutes

1 oxtail
25g (1oz) margarine
2 carrots
2 large onions
1 rasher bacon
300ml (½ pint) stock
Seasoning

Wash the oxtail in cold water. Cut into sections. Fry the oxtail in melted margarine until browned. Prepare and slice the vegetables and arrange them in layers, alternately with the meat, finishing with a layer of vegetables. Season each layer. Pour the stock into the dish and braise slowly for about 2-2½ hours at 170°C, 325°F, Gas Mark 3.

Pig's Trotters

PREPARATION TIME: 10 minutes

COOKING TIME: 30-45 minutes

Cook the trotters in water with a bouquet garni. Simmer until tender. Drain well. Brush with melted butter, season and grill until golden brown. Serve with mashed potatoes and vegetables.

Sweetbread Fritters

PREPARATION TIME: 30 minutes

COOKING TIME: 10 minutes

450g (1lb) prepared lamb's sweetbreads
Seasoning
60ml (4 tblsp) plain flour
Oil for deep frying

Batter
2 egg whites
30ml (2 tblsp) arrowroot
5ml (1 tsp) chopped fresh chives
5ml (1 tsp) chopped fresh tarragon

Cut the sweetbreads in half lengthways. Season the flour and toss the sweetbreads in it till evenly coated. Shake off any excess flour. Heat the oil in a deep fryer to 170°C, 340°F. Put the egg whites into a bowl and whisk till soft peaks form. Add the arrowroot and herbs and fold in gently with a metal spoon. Fold in the floured sweetbreads till coated with batter. Using two spoons, lift a few of the sweetbreads out of the batter and lower into the oil. Fry for 5-6 minutes till crisp and golden. Drain on kitchen paper, keep hot while you cook the rest, and serve.

Kidney and Sausage Casserole

PREPARATION TIME: 30 minutes

COOKING TIME: 2 hours 50 minutes

675g (1½lb) ox kidney
225g (8oz) pork sausages
25g (1oz) flour
Seasoning
50g (2oz) fat
1 medium onion, sliced
2 carrots, sliced
1 bayleaf
2.5ml (½ tsp) sage, crushed
300ml (½ pint) stock

Trim and core the kidneys. Cover with cold, salted water and leave for 15 minutes. Drain and dry. Cut the sausages into pieces. Season the flour and coat the kidneys and sausages well. Heat the fat and fry the meat till brown. Remove to a casserole. Add the onion and carrots to the fat and brown well, then place in the casserole. Add the bayleaf and sage. Put the remaining flour with the sediment left in pan, mix well, add the stock and stir till boiling. Pour over the meat in the casserole. Cover and cook at 170°C, 325°F, Gas Mark 2, for about 2½ hours. Adjust seasoning before serving.

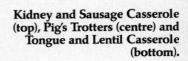

Kidney and Sausage Casserole (top), Pig's Trotters (centre) and Tongue and Lentil Casserole (bottom).

Tripe and Onion Pie

PREPARATION TIME: 45 minutes
COOKING TIME: 1 hour

450g (1lb) tripe
3 large onions, chopped
300ml (½ pint) water
25g (1oz) flour
30ml (2 tblsp) milk
Seasoning
25g (1oz) butter
225g (8oz) shortcrust pastry

Place the chopped onion in a pan, cover with water, season and simmer until tender. Wash the tripe and cut it into small pieces. Strain the onions; reserve half of the liquid. Replace the onions and liquid in the pan. Add the tripe. Simmer for 15 minutes. Blend the flour with a little cold milk, add to the saucepan, stir continually; add remaining milk and butter. Cook for 5 minutes. Line a dish or tin with half the pastry, put in the filling, cover with the remaining pastry. Cook at 220°C, 425°F, Gas Mark 7, for 25 minutes.

Savoury Sheeps' Hearts

PREPARATION TIME: 40 minutes
COOKING TIME: 2 hours 15 minutes

4 sheep's hearts

Stuffing
50g (2oz) butter
1 onion, chopped
1 stick celery, chopped
100g (4oz) breadcrumbs
1 orange
Seasoning
1 egg, beaten
2 onions, cut into quarters or eighths
2 carrots, cut into quarters
1 beef stock cube
600ml (1 pint) boiling water

Prepare the hearts carefully, removing all the veins and arteries, and wash them well in cold water. Melt the butter, add the onion and celery and cook for a few minutes. Add the breadcrumbs, grated orange rind and juice, and seasoning. Bind with the egg. Fill the hearts with this stuffing and sew up with needle and thread. Put into a casserole with the onion and carrot pieces. Dissolve the stock cube in boiling water and pour over the hearts. Cover and cook at 170°C, 325°F, Gas Mark 3, for 2 hours until tender. Remove thread before serving.

Chicken Liver Omelette

PREPARATION TIME: 20 minutes
COOKING TIME: 30 minutes

100g (4oz) chicken livers
100g (4oz) butter
2 sage leaves
Seasoning
45ml (3 tblsp) sherry
8 eggs
Parsley

Trim, wipe and finely chop the livers. Melt 25g (1oz) of the butter in a saucepan and add the livers. Stir fry for 5 minutes. Pour the sherry over and cook till it has almost evaporated. Remove pan from heat. Beat the eggs in a bowl with a little seasoning. Melt a quarter of the remaining butter in an omelette pan or small frying pan. When it begins to foam, pour in a quarter of the egg mixture. Tilt the pan so that the mixture runs evenly over the bottom. As the omelette begins to set underneath, place a quarter of the liver mixture along the centre and fold the sides of the mixture over the filling. Slide omelette onto a warmed serving dish and keep hot.

Braised Oxtail (top), Savoury Sheeps' Hearts (centre right) and Tripe and Onion Pie (bottom left).

Poultry and Game

Turkey Fries

PREPARATION TIME: 45 minutes
COOKING TIME: 1 hour 10 minutes

60ml (4 tblsp) oil
45ml (3 tblsp) lemon juice
Salt
8x125g (8x4oz) slices of turkey breast
20ml (4 tsp) Dijon mustard
2 eggs
225g (8oz) fresh breadcrumbs
50g (2oz) butter

Garnish
Chopped parsley
Lemon wedges

Mix half the oil with the lemon juice and a pinch of salt in a shallow dish. Add the turkey, mix well and leave to marinate for 1 hour. Drain the turkey and pat dry on kitchen paper. Spread thinly with the mustard. Beat the eggs lightly on a plate and use to coat turkey. Dip the turkey slices into the breadcrumbs, pressing on them gently. Melt the butter and remaining oil in a frying pan and gently fry the turkey for about 10 minutes on each side, till tender and golden brown. Drain. Garnish with chopped parsley and lemon wedges.

Roast Chicken Drumsticks

PREPARATION TIME: 10 minutes
COOKING TIME: 20-30 minutes

Place the chicken drumsticks in a roasting tin and spread with fat or oil. Season. Place in the oven at 180°C, 350°F, Gas Mark 4, for about 20-30 minutes until the juice runs clear and the skin is golden brown.

Turkey Roll (top) and Turkey Fries (bottom).

Roast Turkey

PREPARATION TIME: 10 minutes

COOKING TIME: 20 minutes per 450kg (1lb) plus 20 minutes

Place the turkey in a roasting tin. Brush with melted fat or oil. Season. Lightly cover the bird with foil or double greaseproof paper. The bird may be stuffed if desired but weigh it after stuffing to calculate cooking time. Place in the oven at 200°C, 400°F, Gas Mark 6, for the first 15 minutes, then lower to 180°C, 350°F, Gas Mark 4, for the remainder of the cooking time. Baste the turkey frequently. Remove covering for the last 20-30 minutes to allow the skin to brown. When the turkey is cooked, place it on a large carving dish and serve.

Chicken Casserole

PREPARATION TIME: 30 minutes

COOKING TIME: 2 hours 40 minutes

1 chicken, jointed
Seasoned flour
25g (1oz) dripping
1 carrot, sliced
1 turnip, sliced
1 onion, chopped
25g (1oz) flour
600ml (1 pint) stock
Bouquet garni
Seasoning

Toss the chicken joints in seasoned flour. Melt the dripping, brown the vegetables and the joints. Remove them from the pan. Add the flour but do not brown. Remove from heat and add stock. Return to heat and bring to the boil. Season to taste. Put vegetables and chicken in a casserole dish, pour sauce over, add the bouquet garni. Cook at 180°C, 325°F, Gas Mark 3, for about 2½ hours.

This page: Rabbit Casserole (top), Roast Guinea Fowl (bottom). Facing page: Roast Chicken Drumsticks (top right), Roast Turkey (centre) and Chicken Casserole (bottom right).

Chicken Pieces in Breadcrumbs

PREPARATION TIME: 30 minutes
COOKING TIME: 35-40 minutes

4 chicken quarters
Seasoning
50g (2oz) flour
1 egg
300ml (½ pint) milk
175g (6oz) breadcrumbs
45ml (3 tblsp) oil

Clean the chicken quarters and dredge with the seasoned flour. Beat the eggs in a bowl and mix in the milk. Dip the chicken pieces in the egg and milk and then coat with the breadcrumbs. Heat the oil in a frying pan and fry the chicken for 10 minutes or until browned on both sides. Reduce the heat, cover the pan and continue cooking gently for 25-30 minutes until the chicken is tender.

Roast Turkey Legs

PREPARATION TIME: 10 minutes
COOKING TIME: 30-40 minutes

Place the turkey legs in a roasting tin and spread with fat or oil. Season. Cook in the oven at 190°C, 375°F, Gas Mark 5, for about 30 minutes, until the juice runs clear and the skin is golden brown.

Roast Guinea Fowl

PREPARATION TIME: 10 minutes
COOKING TIME: 15 minutes per 450g (1lb)

Place the guinea fowl in a roasting tin and brush with melted fat or oil. Season. As guinea fowl can be very dry, be generous in the amount of fat used. Lightly cover the bird with foil or double greaseproof paper and cook at 200°C, 400°F, Gas Mark 6. Baste frequently. Remove the covering for the last 20-30 minutes to allow the skin to brown. When the bird is cooked, place it on a warm carving dish and serve.

Rabbit Casserole

PREPARATION TIME: 30 minutes
COOKING TIME: 2 hours 20 minutes

1.5kg (3lb) rabbit
25g (1oz) seasoned flour
50g (2oz) butter
100g (4oz) shallots, chopped
2 carrots, sliced
2 parsnips, sliced
1 small cooking apple, peeled, cored and chopped
600ml (1 pint) cider
15ml (1 tbsp) made mustard
10ml (2 tsp) casserole seasoning
2.5ml (½ tsp) thyme
Seasoning
1 bayleaf

Preheat the oven to 180°C, 350°F, Gas Mark 4. Cut the rabbit into six serving pieces. Coat with the seasoned flour. Melt the butter in a flameproof casserole. Add the rabbit and brown on all sides. Remove the rabbit from the pan, then add the shallots, carrots, parsnips and apple and fry until lightly coloured. Pour in the cider, stir in the mustard and casserole seasoning. Heat gently, stirring, until just simmering, then return the rabbit pieces to the pan. Add the thyme and the bayleaf, cover the casserole and place it in the oven. Cook for 1½-2 hours, until the rabbit is tender. Taste and adjust the seasoning and discard the bayleaf.

Roast Pheasant

PREPARATION TIME: 10 minutes
COOKING TIME: 40 minutes to 1 hour 30 minutes

Preheat the oven to 200°C, 400°F, Gas Mark 6. Stand prepared bird in a roasting tin, add a little dripping or oil. Cover roasting tin or wrap bird in foil. Roast a young bird for 40-50 minutes, an older bird for 1-1½ hours. Reduce the oven temperature to 180°C, 350°F, Gas Mark 4, after 10 minutes. If the bird is cooked in an open tin, baste frequently.

Game Pie

PREPARATION TIME: 40 minutes
COOKING TIME: 45 minutes

1 rabbit
4 bacon rashers, de-rinded
50g (2oz) dripping
2 onions, sliced
Seasoning
300ml (½ pint) stock
225g (8oz) flaky pastry
1 egg or milk to glaze

Soak the rabbit in warm water for about ½ hour. Wash well in cold water. Joint the rabbit into 6 pieces. Cut the bacon into large pieces. Melt the dripping in a saucepan. First brown the onions, then the bacon and pieces of rabbit. Season well. Add the stock and simmer gently for 1 hour until tender. Leave to cool. When cool, fill a pie dish with the meat and onions, add the liquid, then cover with the flaky pastry. Bake at 200°C, 400°F, Gas Mark 6, for ¾ hour. Brush with egg or milk during the last ½ hour.

Roast Turkey Legs (right), Chicken Pieces in Breadcrumbs (below).

S
P

Fricassée of Guinea Fowl

PREPARATION TIME: 30 minutes
COOKING TIME: 1 hour 30 minutes

1 guinea fowl
4 slices bacon
30ml (2 tbsp) flour
Seasoning
2 cups water

Clean the guinea fowl and joint into pieces. Fry the bacon, coat the pieces of fowl with seasoned flour and fry until brown. Remove the bacon and fowl from the pan, add the flour and stir, slowly adding the water. Bring to the boil. Replace the fowl and bacon, cover and simmer until tender (about 1½ hours).

Jugged Hare

PREPARATION TIME: 30 minutes
COOKING TIME: 3 hours 10 minutes

1 hare
1 onion, sliced
1 carrot, sliced
1 turnip, sliced
75g (3oz) fat
75g (3oz) flour
Seasoning
600ml (1 pint) stock
15ml (1 tbsp) port
Bouquet garni
Packet of sage and onion stuffing mix

Wash and joint hare. Fry the vegetables in fat. Remove vegetables from the pan, coat the hare in seasoned flour and fry. Add the stock and port, put into the casserole with the bouquet garni, cover and cook for about 3 hours at 180°C, 350°F, Gas Mark 4. Making stuffing as directed on packet and make into small balls. Add balls to casserole a quarter of an hour before serving.

This page: Jugged Hare (top) and Game Pie (bottom). Facing page: Roast Stuffed Pigeons (top right), Roast Pheasant (centre left) and Fricasée of Guinea Fowl (bottom right).

Roast Stuffed Pigeons

PREPARATION TIME: 30 minutes
COOKING TIME: 35 minutes to 1 hour 15 minutes

4 small pigeons
40-50g (1½-2oz) lard

For the Stuffing
2 hard-boiled eggs
75g (3oz) soft breadcrumbs
50g (2oz) suet
Seasoning
A little grated nutmeg
15ml (1 tbsp) chopped parsley
1 egg

To make the stuffing, chop the hard-boiled eggs and blend with the breadcrumbs, suet, seasoning, nutmeg and parsley, and bind with the egg. Put the stuffing into each of the pigeons, then cover the birds with the lard. If very young, roast in a hot oven for about 35 minutes at 200°C, 400°F, Gas Mark 6. Note that pigeons tend to have a fairly firm flesh and so it is better to roast for about 1¼ hours in a moderate oven 180°C, 350°F, Gas Mark 4. Baste the pigeons well during cooking or, if preferred, wrap each pigeon in foil after covering with lard and roast for about 1 hour 25 minutes at 180°C, 350°F, Gas Mark 4, opening the foil for the last 10-15 minutes.

This page: Duck with Orange Sauce (top left), Roast Duck (top right) and Roast Turkey Wings (bottom). Facing page: Chicken Pie (top left), Roast Poussin (centre right) and Mild Fruity Chicken Curry (bottom).

Duck with Orange Sauce

PREPARATION TIME: 30 minutes

COOKING TIME: 15 minutes per 450g (1lb) plus 15 minutes; 20 minutes for the sauce

1 duck

Orange Sauce
1 orange
150ml (¼ pint) water
300ml (½ pint) Espagnole sauce
15ml (1 tblsp) lemon juice
30ml (2 tblsp) port or claret

Place the duck in a roasting tin spread with fat or dripping. Season. Lightly cover the duck with foil or double greaseproof paper and place in the oven at 200°C, 400°F, Gas Mark 6. The duck should be basted frequently and the covering removed 20-30 minutes before the end of cooking time. After removing the covering, prick the breast all over to allow extra fat to run out and leave the breast crisp and succulent.

Orange Sauce
Pare the rind from the orange, discarding any white pith. Cut into wafer-thin strips and simmer these in water for about 10 minutes. Strain the Espagnole sauce, reheat with the orange rind, orange juice, lemon juice and wine. Serve the sauce with the cooked duck.

Mild Fruity Chicken Curry

PREPARATION TIME: 2 hours 30 minutes

COOKING TIME: 1 hour 15 minutes

150ml (5 fl oz) boiling water
150ml (5 fl oz) milk
100g (4oz) desiccated coconut
60ml (4 tblsp) oil
4 chicken pieces, skinned
30ml (2 tblsp) curry powder
25g (1oz) flour
300ml (½ pint) chicken stock
400g (14oz) tin pineapple chunks
15ml (1 tblsp) onion flakes
5ml (1 tsp) salt
30ml (2 tblsp) cream

Mix together the boiling water and milk in a bowl. Stir in the coconut and leave to infuse for about 2 hours. Strain liquid and discard the coconut. Heat half the oil in a large, heavy saucepan. Add the chicken pieces and fry until golden brown on all sides. Remove the chicken pieces from the pan with a slotted spoon. Heat the remaining oil in the pan. Stir the curry powder into the oil and fry for about ½ minute. Remove the pan from the heat and stir in the flour. Gradually stir in the stock, the strained coconut milk, the juice from the tin of pineapple and the onion flakes. Return the chicken to the pan with the salt. Bring to the boil, stirring occasionally. Cover and simmer for 1 hour, stirring occasionally. Stir in the pineapple chunks and heat through, then remove from the heat and stir in the cream. Taste and adjust the seasoning and serve with boiled rice.

Roast Turkey Wings

PREPARATION TIME: 10 minutes

COOKING TIME: 20 minutes

Put turkey wings into a roasting tin, spread with fat or oil and season. Place in the oven at 180°C, 350°F, Gas Mark 4, for about 20 minutes, until the juice runs clear and the skin is golden brown. Serve with a mixed salad, if desired.

Roast Duck

PREPARATION TIME: 10 minutes

COOKING TIME: 15 minutes per 450g (1lb) plus 15 minutes

Place the duck in a roasting tin, spread with fat or dripping and season. Lightly cover with foil or double greaseproof paper and place in the oven at 200°C, 400°F, Gas Mark 6. The duck should be basted frequently and the covering removed 20-30 minutes before the end of the cooking time. After removing the covering, prick the breast all over to allow extra fat to run out and leave the breast crisp and succulent. When the duck is cooked, transfer to a carving dish and serve.

Roast Poussin

PREPARATION TIME: 20 minutes

COOKING TIME: 30-40 minutes

2 poussins
1 packet sage and onion stuffing
A little fat

Make the stuffing as directed on the packet and stuff the birds. Place the poussins in a roasting tin with melted fat. Cook in the oven at 180°C, 350°F, Gas Mark 4, until tender.

Chicken Pie

PREPARATION TIME: 35 minutes

COOKING TIME: 45-50 minutes

450g (1lb) cooked chicken
50g (2oz) butter
50-100g (2-4oz) small mushrooms
50g (2oz) flour
300ml (½ pint) milk or 150ml (¼ pint) milk and 150ml (¼ pint) chicken stock
175g (6oz) shortcrust pastry
1 egg or milk to glaze

Cut the chicken into neat pieces. Heat half the butter and fry the mushrooms for a few minutes. Heat the other half of the butter, stir in the flour and cook for 2-3 minutes. Add the milk or milk and stock. Season. Bring to the boil and cook until thickened; add the chicken and mushrooms. Put into a 20cm (8 inch) pie plate. Cover with shortcrust pastry, brush with egg or milk. Bake at 200°C, 400°F, Gas Mark 5-6, for about 30 minutes or until the pastry is golden brown.

Chicken Liver Pâté

PREPARATION TIME: 30 minutes

COOKING TIME: 10 minutes

75g (3oz) butter
8 chicken livers
45ml (3 tblsp) cream
Good pinch of mixed herbs
Seasoning

Heat the butter in a frying pan and cook the livers gently until just tender. If you have an electric blender put them into this with the cream, herbs and seasoning. Switch on until smooth. Put into a buttered dish and allow to cool. When making a pâté by hand, rub the cooked livers through a sieve and then add the hot butter from the pan, cream, seasoning and herbs. Put into a buttered dish to cool.

Roast Chicken

PREPARATION TIME: 15 minutes

COOKING TIME: 15 minutes per 450g (1lb) plus 15 minutes

Place the chicken in a roasting tin, brush with melted fat or oil. Season. Lightly cover the bird with foil or double greaseproof paper The chicken may be stuffed, if desired, but weigh it after stuffing to determine cooking time. Cook at 200°C, 400°F, Gas Mark 6. Baste the chicken frequently. Remove the covering for the last 20-30 minutes to allow skin to brown. When the chicken is cooked, place it on a carving dish and serve.

Turkey Cutlets with Lemon Sauce

PREPARATION TIME: 30 minutes

COOKING TIME: 20 minutes

6 turkey cutlets
Seasoning
30ml (2 tblsp) plain flour
2 thick rashers of back bacon
15g (½oz) butter
150ml (¼ pint) chicken stock
30ml (2 tblsp) lemon juice
30ml (2 tblsp) chopped parsley

Garnish
Lemon slices
Sprigs of parsley

Season flour and coat the turkey cutlets. De-rind the bacon and cut it into strips. Melt the butter in a frying pan and cook the bacon for 5 minutes. Add the turkey pieces and fry for 3-5 minutes on each side. Remove the turkey and bacon and place on a warm plate. Keep hot. Add any remaining seasoned flour to the pan and stir well with a wooden spoon, scraping the sediment from the bottom of the pan. Gradually add the stock and bring to the boil; simmer for 5 minutes. Remove the pan from the heat and stir in the lemon juice and chopped parsley. Taste and adjust seasoning. Pour the sauce over the turkey cutlets and garnish with lemon slices and parsley sprigs.

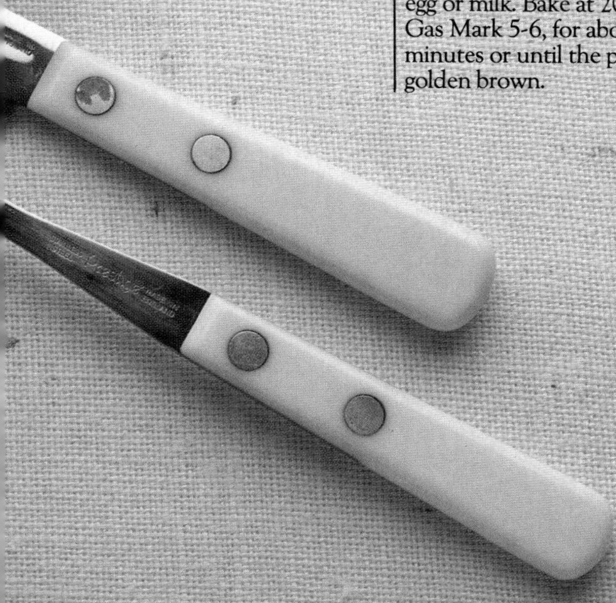

Turkey Cutlets with Lemon Sauce (top left), Chicken Liver Pâté (centre) and Roast Chicken (bottom left).

Vegetarian Fare

Macaroni Cheese

175g (6oz) quick cooking macaroni
1.75 litre (3 pints) water

Cheese Sauce
40g (1½oz) butter
40g (1½oz) flour
450ml (¾ pint) milk
Salt and pepper
100g (4oz) Cheddar cheese, grated

Topping
25-50g (1-2oz) Cheddar cheese, grated
25g (1oz) dried breadcrumbs

Garnish
1 tomato
Parsley

Boil the macaroni in salted water for about 7 minutes. Add a little pepper if desired. Melt the butter in a saucepan, stir in the flour and cook for 2 minutes. Cool. Gradually blend in the milk, bring to the boil and cook until thickened and smooth. Add seasoning, and the cheese. Strain the macaroni and blend with the sauce. Put into a 1.2 litre (2-pint) dish, top with the cheese and breadcrumbs and brown under a hot grill. Garnish with tomato and parsley.

Cheese and Potato Whirls

100g (¼lb) instant potato powder or 1lb of potatoes, cooked
25g (1oz) butter and a little milk, if using cooked potatoes
450g (1lb) grated cheese
1 egg
Salt and pepper
Mixed mustard
Egg, beaten to glaze

Rough Puff Pastry
225g (½lb) plain flour
2.5ml (½ tsp) salt
175g (6oz) margarine
10ml (2 tsp) wine vinegar or lemon juice
150ml (¼ pint) ice-cold water

First make the pastry. Sieve the flour and salt into a bowl. Cut margarine into 1cm (½") dice. Toss through the flour. Add vinegar or lemon juice to the water. Add to the flour and mix to a soft dough. Turn on to a floured board. Roll into a square. Fold the side edges to the middle, top and bottom to middle, then fold in half. Press gently together. Leave to rest in refrigerator for 15 minutes. Remove and roll the pastry once again into a square, fold the side edges to the middle, top and bottom to middle, then fold in half. Make the instant potato as directed on the tin or packet or mash the cooked potato with the butter and milk. Add the cheese, egg, seasoning and mustard. Roll the pastry into a square, spread with the cheese and potato mixture. Roll up as for a Swiss roll and brush with egg to glaze. Cut into the required number of slices and cook on a baking tray in the oven for 20-25 minutes at 230°C, 440°F, Gas Mark 8.

Cheese Crust Vegetable Pie

Cheese Pastry
175g (6oz) flour
Pinch of salt
100g (4oz) butter or margarine
75g (3oz) Cheddar cheese, grated
30-45ml (2-3 tblsp) cold water to mix

Filling
50g (2oz) butter
1 onion, peeled and sliced
200g (7oz) can sweet corn
3 carrots, peeled and sliced
50g (2oz) mushrooms, sliced
50g (2oz) packet of leek soup
2 sticks celery, scrubbed and sliced
Pepper
1 egg, beaten to glaze

Sift the flour and salt into a mixing bowl. Rub the butter or margarine into the flour and stir in the cheese. Bind together with the water. Melt the butter in a pan and fry the vegetables for a few minutes. Drain on paper towels. Make up the packet of leek soup as directed, but using only 600ml (1 pint) of water. Stir the vegetables into the leek soup, season with pepper and pour into a 900ml (1½ pint) pie dish. Roll out the pastry to top the pie. Trim and flute the edges. Use any leftover pastry to decorate the pie top. Brush with beaten egg. Cook in the oven for 15 minutes at 200°C, 400°F, Gas Mark 6. Reduce the heat to 180°C, 350°F, Gas Mark 4, and cook for a further 20 minutes. Serve with new potatoes.

Cheese Crust Vegetable Pie (top), Cheese and Potato Whirls (far left) and Macaroni Cheese (above left).

Corn Quiche

Pastry
175g (6oz) plain flour
Pinch of salt
75g (3oz) fat
30ml (2 tblsp) water to mix

Filling
200g (7oz) can sweet corn
2 eggs, beaten
300ml (½ pint) milk
100-175g (4-6oz) cheese, grated
Salt and pepper

Garnish
Parsley
Tomato

Sieve the flour and salt into a bowl. Cut the fat into pieces and rub in to the flour until it looks like breadcrumbs. Mix with enough water to make a dough. Roll out and use to line a flan ring. Drain the sweet corn and mix with the eggs. Add the milk, cheese and seasoning. Pour into the pastry case. Cook in a hot oven for 15 minutes at 220°C, 425°F, Gas Mark 7. Reduce the heat to 190°C, 375°F, Gas Mark 5 and cook for a further 10 minutes. Garnish with parsley and wedges of tomato. Serve hot or cold.

Cheese Crowns

600ml (1 pint) milk
100g (4oz) fine semolina
100g (4oz) Parmesan cheese
10ml (2 tsp) made mustard
15ml (1 tblsp) Worcestershire sauce
Dash of cayenne pepper
Lettuce to garnish

Coating
1 egg, beaten
75g (3oz) dried breadcrumbs
Fat for frying

Grease a sandwich tin and set aside. Heat the milk to near boiling point. Stir in the semolina, bring to the boil and cook, stirring vigorously, for 3-4 minutes. Remove the pan from the heat, add the remaining ingredients and pour into the prepared sandwich tin. When the mixture is cold, turn onto a floured board, and divide into 8 wedges. Brush with beaten egg and coat with breadcrumbs. Heat the fat, carefully add the wedges and shallow fry on both sides until crisp and golden brown. Drain on paper towels. To serve, stand on end, top with cutlet frills and serve on a bed of lettuce.

Savoury Egg Pie

Pastry
175g (6oz) plain flour
Pinch of salt
75g (3oz) fat
25ml (1½ tblsp) water

Filling
1 onion, peeled and chopped
25g (1oz) fat
450ml (¾ pint) milk
50g (2oz) soft, white breadcrumbs
3 large eggs, beaten
Few drops of Worcestershire sauce
Salt and pepper
Watercress to garnish

Sieve the flour and salt into a bowl. Cut the fat into pieces and rub in to flour until it looks like breadcrumbs. Mix with enough water to make a dough. Roll out the pastry and use to line a pie plate. Flute the edges. Fry the onion in the fat, and spread over the pastry. Warm the milk, add the breadcrumbs and eggs. Stir in the Worcestershire sauce and seasoning. Pour the mixture into the pastry case. Cook in the oven for about 20-25 minutes at 200°C, 400°F, Gas Mark 6, until the pastry is crisp and the filling is set. Garnish with watercress and serve hot or cold with salad.

Cheese Loaf

225g (8oz) self-raising flour
Pinch of salt
Pinch of dry mustard
50g (2oz) margarine
75g (3oz) cheese, grated
1 egg
85ml (3 fl oz) milk

Grease a small loaf tin and line the bottom with greaseproof paper. Sieve the flour, salt and mustard together and rub in the margarine. Add the cheese. Beat the egg and milk together and reserve a little to brush the top. Pour the rest into the dry ingredients and mix to a

soft dough. Shape into a loaf and put into the tin. Cook in the oven on a shelf above the centre for about 35 minutes at 200°C, 400°F, Gas Mark 6, until well risen and golden brown. Cool on a wire tray. Serve, sliced and buttered, the same day. If kept to the next day, serve toasted and buttered.

Egg and Potato Omelette

50g (2oz) butter
2 small cooked potatoes, diced
4 eggs
2.5ml (½ tsp) salt
Pinch of pepper

Heat the butter in a frying or omelette pan. Add the potatoes and cook until golden. Beat the eggs and season. Add the eggs to the potato and cook quickly until the mixture is set. Fold over and serve at once. Serve with a green vegetable.

Kedgeree Fish and Mushrooms

175g (6oz) cooked smoked haddock
1 hard-boiled egg, shelled
225g (8oz) cooked, long grain rice
Pinch of cayenne pepper
Pinch of salt
100g (4oz) mushrooms
A little butter
Chopped fresh parsley

Flake the fish coarsely with a fork. Chop the egg white, sieve the yolk and put the yolk to one side for garnishing. Using a fork mix the flaked fish, chopped egg white, cooked rice and seasoning in a saucepan over moderate heat until hot. Cook the mushrooms in a little butter. Pile the mixture into a hot dish and garnish with chopped parsley and sieved egg yolk. Serve at once with the cooked mushrooms.

Cheese Bread Pudding

4 large slices of buttered bread
100-175g (4-6oz) Cheddar cheese, grated
Salt and pepper
5ml (1 tsp) Worcestershire sauce
Pinch of dry mustard
2 eggs
450ml (¾ pint) milk

Cut the crusts off the bread and cut each slice into 6 squares. Fill a greased, 900ml (1½ pint) pie dish with layers of bread, cheese, seasoning, Worcestershire sauce and mustard. Reserve a little cheese. Beat together the eggs and milk and pour over the layers. Sprinkle the top with the reserved cheese and cook in the oven for 40-45 minutes at 160°C, 325°F, Gas Mark 3. Serve with potato croquettes.

Cheese Hot Pot

500g (1¼lb) potatoes
175g (6oz) onions
175g (6oz) carrots
250g (9oz) grated cheese
Salt and pepper
150ml (5 fl oz) water
Chopped parsley to garnish

Peel the potatoes, onions and carrots, and cut into thin slices. Put in layers into a deep dish, with the cheese and a little seasoning between layers. Continue until all the vegetables are used, finishing with a layer of cheese. Pour the water into the dish to moisten. Cover with a greased lid and cook in the oven for 30 minutes at 230°C, 450°F, Gas Mark 8. Reduce to 190°C, 375°F, Gas Mark 5, and cook for a further 1½ hours. Remove the lid and allow to brown for about 5 minutes. Garnish with chopped parsley.

Facing page: Cheese Hot Pot (top), Cheese Crowns (centre left), Corn Quiche (centre right) and Savoury Egg Pie (bottom).

This page: Kedgeree Fish and Mushrooms (top), Cheese Bread Pudding (centre left), Cheese Loaf (centre right) and Egg and Potato Omelette (bottom).

Section 4

SALADS AND VEGETABLES

Meals with Salads

French Dressing

15g (½oz) sugar
1.25ml (¼ tsp) salt
1.25ml (¼ tsp) dry mustard
150ml (¼ pint) vinegar
300ml (½ pint) corn oil

Blend the sugar, salt and mustard with the vinegar. Gradually beat or whisk in the oil, a little at a time. Taste and adjust the seasoning if necessary. Pour the dressing into a screw-topped jar. Shake vigorously before using, as the oil and vinegar will separate if left to stand.

Cheese and Ham Pie

Packet white sauce mix
100g (4oz) cheese, grated
100g (4oz) cooked ham, finely chopped
A little milk or beaten egg

Shortcrust Pastry
225g (8oz) flour
100g (4oz) margarine or fat
1 tsp salt
30ml (2 tblsp) cold water

First make the pastry. Sieve the flour and salt together in a bowl. Cut the fat into pieces and rub into the flour until it looks like breadcrumbs. Add the water to make a dough. Roll out enough pastry to line a shallow pie dish or tin. Make up the white sauce mix as directed on the packet. Mix the cheese and ham with the sauce and pour into the lined pie dish or tin. Roll out the remaining pastry to make a lid for the pie. Place on top, seal, and brush the top with milk or beaten egg. Place in the oven at 230°C, 450°F, Gas Mark 8 for 15 minutes. Reduce the temperature to 180°C, 350°F, Gas Mark 4, until cooked. Serve with a mixed salad.

Chunky Herrings

6-8 rollmop herrings
450g (1lb) small new potatoes, cooked
Small piece of cucumber, diced
Cooked peas
Sage or parsley to garnish

Vinaigrette Dressing
90ml (6 tblsp) oil
45ml (3 tblsp) wine vinegar
1.25ml (¼ tsp) chopped fresh herbs, e.g. tarragon, chervil
4-5 capers, chopped
Salt and pepper
Pinch of dry mustard

Remove the herrings from their liquid, drain well. Arrange the herrings on a flat dish. Blend together all the ingredients for the vinaigrette dressing. Mix the potatoes, cucumber and peas and toss with the dressing. Put the mixture round the herrings and garnish with sage or chopped parsley. Serve with a mixed salad. Serves six.

Mushroom Salad

Salt and pepper
Pinch of dry English mustard
135ml (4½ fl oz) oil
45ml (3 tblsp) wine vinegar
15ml (1 tblsp) chopped fresh parsley
1 garlic clove, peeled and crushed
350g (12oz) button mushrooms, sliced

Put the salt, pepper, mustard, oil, vinegar, parsley and garlic into a screw-topped jar and shake well. Pour over the mushrooms in a bowl. Leave to stand for 1 hour then serve.

Egg and Cheese Flan (far left), Chunky Herrings (centre) and Cheese and Ham Pie (above).

Egg and Cheese Flan

100g (4oz) cheese, grated
2 eggs
150ml (¼ pint) milk
1.25ml (¼ tsp) mixed mustard

Shortcrust Pastry
225g (8oz) flour
5ml (1 tsp) salt
100g (4oz) margarine or fat
30ml (2 tblsp) cold water

Make the shortcrust pastry. Sieve the flour and salt together into a bowl. Add the fat cut into pieces and rub into the flour until it is like breadcrumbs. Add the water to make a dough. Roll out and use to line a flan tin. Prick the base. Sprinkle with the cheese. Whisk the eggs, add the milk and mustard. Pour the egg mixture over the cheese. Cook the flan in the oven for 15 minutes at 230°C, 450°F, Gas Mark 8. Reduce the temperature to 160°C, 325°F, Gas Mark 3 and cook for about 30 minutes or until the flan is cooked. Serve with a mixed salad.

Dressed Crab

1 large cooked crab
Parsley to garnish

Pull off all the crab claws and wipe the shell. Turn the crab on to its back and firmly pull the body from the main shell. Remove and discard the stomach bag which lies behind the head and grey feathered gills or 'fingers' as these must not be eaten. Take out all the meat with a skewer or small spoon, putting dark and white into separate basins, then crack the top of the shell and remove pieces so there is a flat cavity to fill. Scrub inside the shell thoroughly under cold water. Dry and brush with oil. Crack the claws and remove the meat, adding it to the light meat. Arrange dark and light meat alternately in the shell and garnish with parsley. Serve with a mixed salad.

This page: Apple and Nut Salad (top), Kidney Beans and Onion (centre right) and Mushroom Salad (bottom). Facing page: Dressed Crab (top), Chicken Legs in Breadcrumbs (centre left), Tuna and Mackerel Loaf (centre right) and Chicken and Tomato Salad (bottom).

Kidney Beans and Onion

Salt and pepper
Pinch of dry English mustard
2.5ml (½ tsp) dried basil
1 garlic clove, peeled and crushed
45ml (3 tblsp) olive or corn oil
15ml (1 tblsp) wine vinegar
1 small onion, peeled and sliced
400g (14oz) can of red kidney beans, drained
Chopped parsley to garnish

Combine the salt, pepper, mustard, basil, garlic, oil and vinegar in a screw-topped jar. Lay the onion rings on a plate and sprinkle with salt. Leave for 30 minutes. Drain and rinse in cold water. Place the beans in a bowl, add the onion and toss in the dressing. Garnish with the chopped parsley and serve.

Chicken Legs in Breadcrumbs

Chicken legs as required
1 egg, beaten
Dried breadcrumbs
75g (3oz) oil or fat

Coat the chicken legs with the beaten egg and breadcrumbs. Heat the oil or fat in a pan. Fry the chicken fairly quickly until brown all over, then lower heat and cook slowly to cook right through. When pierced with a skewer the juices should run clear. Drain on crumpled paper towels. Serve with fried tomatoes and mushrooms and a green salad or other cooked vegetables.

Cucumber and Tomato Salad

450g (1lb) tomatoes, chopped
½ cucumber, finely diced
30ml (2 tblsp) French dressing
Watercress to garnish

Toss the cucumber and tomato in the French dressing. Garnish with watercress.

Tuna and Mackerel Loaf

1kg (2lb) sandwich loaf, one day old, refrigerated for 24 hours
50g (2oz) powdered gelatine
300ml (½ pint) white sauce
150g (5oz) canned tuna, drained
225g (8oz) mackerel fillets, drained
100g (4oz) cooked potato, diced
50g (2oz) cooked peas
50g (2oz) French beans, diced
50g (2oz) sweet corn
50g (2oz) cooked red peppers, diced
12 capers
25g (1oz) gherkins, diced
25g (1oz) chopped onion
Salt and pepper
Pinch of cayenne pepper
Juice and grated rind of ½ lemon
150ml (¼ pint) mayonnaise

Cut the crust off the loaf at one end and reserve. With a long bread knife cut round inside the crust and remove the bread from the centre. Scoop out any remaining crumbs. Dissolve the gelatine in 100ml (4 fl oz) hot water. Bring the white sauce to the boil, add the gelatine and simmer gently for 10 minutes until thick. Blend the tuna and mackerel fillets to a smooth paste. Add the paste to the thickened sauce and blend well. Mix in the rest of the ingredients except the mayonnaise. Cool and then add the mayonnaise. Fill the crust shell with the mixture. Replace the reserved crust, stand the loaf on a plate, place in the refrigerator and leave overnight to set. Serve by cutting into slices with a bread knife dipped in hot water. This is ideal for picnics or served with a mixed salad.

Bean Salad

175g (6oz) can kidney beans, drained
400g (14oz) can sliced green beans, drained
1 small onion, peeled and chopped
1 stalk celery, peeled and chopped
45ml (3 tblsp) wine vinegar
15ml (1 tblsp) oil
Few drops of sugar substitute
Salt and pepper

Mix the beans, chopped onion and chopped celery together. Mix the vinegar, oil, sugar substitute and seasoning together. Pour over the salad and leave to marinate in the dressing for a few hours, stirring occasionally. Serve well chilled with cold, lean meat.

Pineapple, Cheese and Celery Salad

120g (4oz) pineapple pieces
120g (4oz) cheese, diced
¼ head of celery, coarsely sliced
Salad cream for dressing
Lettuce
Watercress to garnish

Drain the pineapple and cut into small cubes. Toss with the other ingredients. Serve on a bed of lettuce, garnished with watercress.

Rice Salad

100g (4oz) patna rice
75g (3oz) pineapple pieces
150g (5oz) sweet corn
2 radishes, finely sliced
¼ red pepper, cored, seeded and finely sliced
¼ green pepper, cored, seeded and finely sliced
French dressing
Watercress or cucumber slices to garnish

Boil the rice in salted water for 15 minutes. Drain well and cool. Drain the pineapple thoroughly and cut into small cubes. Mix all the ingredients together in a bowl and toss in French dressing. Garnish with watercress or slices of cucumber.

Prawn Salad

90ml (6 tblsp) thick mayonnaise
15ml (1 tblsp) tomato purée
30ml (2 tblsp) lemon juice
15ml (1 tblsp) Worcestershire sauce
5ml (1 tsp) grated lemon rind
5ml (1 tsp) grated onion
10ml (2 tsp) chopped fresh parsley
Salt and pepper
About 100g (4oz) prawns

Mix the mayonnaise, tomato purée, lemon juice, Worcestershire sauce, lemon rind, onion, parsley and seasoning together thoroughly. Leave for 4 hours before using. Check the flavour before mixing the prawns with the sauce. Serve with a mixed salad.

Apple and Nut Salad

Salt and pepper
Pinch of dry mustard
45ml (3 tblsp) corn or olive oil
15ml (1 tblsp) wine vinegar
3 red eating apples, peeled and cored
8 sticks of celery, scrubbed and chopped
50g (2oz) chopped peanuts
Chopped fresh parsley to garnish

Put salt, pepper, mustard, oil and vinegar into a screw-topped jar and shake well. Put the apples and celery in a bowl with the chopped nuts. Pour the dressing over the apples and celery and toss well. Spoon into a serving dish and garnish with chopped parsley.

Chicken and Tomato Salad

1 lettuce, washed and cut into small pieces
2 cooked chicken breasts, sliced or 100g (4oz) bought sliced chicken
2 tomatoes, peeled and quartered
50g (2oz) frozen sweet corn, cooked and cooled
50g (2oz) frozen French beans, cooked and cooled

French Dressing
Salt and pepper
Pinch of dry English mustard
45ml (3 tblsp) olive oil
15ml (1 tblsp) wine vinegar

Make a French dressing by shaking together the salt, pepper, mustard, oil and vinegar in a screw-top jar. Place the lettuce pieces in a salad bowl, add the tomato, sweet corn and beans. Toss with the French dressing. Serve the chicken with the salad.

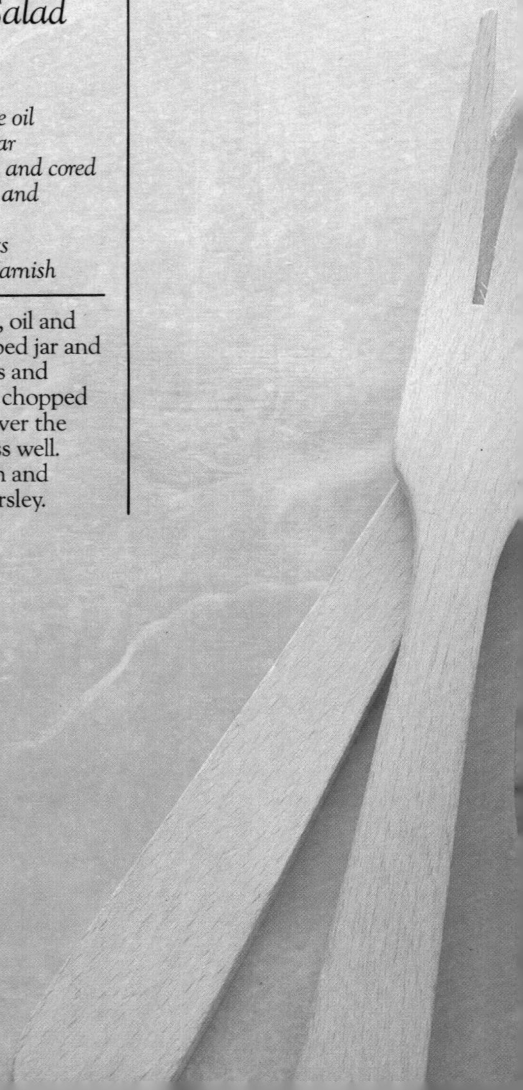

Cucumber and Tomato Salad (left), Rice Salad (below) and Pineapple, Cheese and Celery Salad (bottom).

Spanish Pâté

225g (8oz) chicken livers, minced
450g (1lb) pig's liver, minced
225g (8oz) minced beef
550g (1¼lb) pork, minced
350g (12oz) bacon fat, minced
15ml (1 tblsp) salt
Pepper
5ml (1 tsp) ground mace
15ml (1 tblsp) fresh mixed herbs, chopped
25ml (1 fl oz) sherry
50ml (2 fl oz) brandy
3 garlic cloves, peeled and crushed
75g (3oz) stuffed green olives

Mix together all the ingredients, except the olives, until well blended. Divide the pâté mixture between two well-greased terrines or loaf tins, adding the olives throughout the pâté, at different levels. Cover with foil and put in a roasting tin containing 5cm (2") water. Cook for 2 hours in the oven at 150°C, 300°F, Gas Mark 2. Leave to cool. Place the pâté in the refrigerater for 1-2 hours, then turn into a serving dish. Serve with a mixed salad.

Coleslaw

225g (8oz) Dutch cabbage, finely shredded
2 radishes, finely sliced
¼ cucumber, finely diced
1 stick celery, finely diced
¼ green pepper, cored, seeded and finely sliced
¼ red pepper, cored, seeded and finely sliced
1 apple, peeled and finely sliced
1 large carrot, peeled and coarsely grated
Mustard and cress or watercress
Salad cream for dressing

Mix the ingredients thoroughly together in a large bowl and dress with the salad cream. Garnish with mustard and cress or watercress.

Pasta Salad

100g (4oz) spaghetti
Knob of butter
2 carrots, peeled and coarsely grated
25g (1oz) raisins
6 radishes, finely sliced
¼ green pepper, cored, seeded and finely sliced
¼ red pepper, cored, seeded and finely sliced
30ml (2 tblsp) French dressing
Watercress or mustard and cress to garnish

Boil the spaghetti in salted water for 10-15 minutes. Drain well, toss in the butter and leave to cool. Put all vegetables and raisins together in a bowl and mix well. Toss in the French dressing. Garnish with watercress or mustard and cress.

Winter Salami Risotto

225g (8oz) salami, thinly sliced
100-175g (4-6oz) liver sausage, garlic sausage and luncheon meat, thinly sliced
2 green peppers
1 red pepper
4 large, ripe tomatoes
100g (4oz) green beans, cooked
8 stuffed olives
100-150g (4-5oz) medium or long grain rice, cooked
45-60ml (3-4 tblsp) vinaigrette dressing

Chop some of the meats and roll the remainder. Chop most of the vegetables, leaving a few large pieces for garnish. Slice the stuffed olives. Blend the rice with the vinaigrette dressing, chopped meat, vegetables and olives and put in the bottom of a shallow dish. Top with the larger pieces of vegetables and rolls of meat. Serve with a green salad.

This page: Bean Salad (top right), Coleslaw (centre left) and Pasta Salad (bottom). Facing page: Winter Salami Risotto (top), Prawn Salad (centre left) and Spanish Pâté (bottom).

Cooking Vegetables

for about 15 minutes at 200-220°C, 400-425°F, Gas Mark 6-7, until brown and crisp on the edges. An alternative to duchesse potatoes is to make birds' nests. Pipe the potato into rings and cook the same as for duchesse potatoes. Fill with vegetables.

Baked Potatoes

Peel potatoes and cut out any eyes and green parts. Cut into slices. Melt fat in an ovenproof dish and place potatoes in the dish. Cook in the oven at 220°C, 425°F, Gas Mark 7 for about 1 hour. Serve as required.

Potato

Potatoes (boiled)
New potatoes

Scrub potatoes well, then scrape. Cook in salted water for 10-20 minutes according to size. Drain well, toss in butter and serve.

Creamed Potatoes

Peel potatoes and cut out any eyes and any green parts. Cook in salted water for 15-20 minutes. When cooked, drain well. Using a potato masher or a fork, mash the potatoes in a pan until smooth and free of lumps. To each pound of potatoes add 25g (1oz) butter, a little milk and seasoning. Beat the mixture until light and fluffy. Serve as required.

Sauté Potatoes

Peel potatoes and cut out eyes and any green parts. Cook in salted water until they are almost cooked, drain well and allow to cool slightly. Cut into slices. Fry the potato slices in hot fat, turning them until crisp and golden brown on both sides. Serve as required.

Duchesse Potatoes

450g (1lb) cooked potatoes
25g (1oz) butter
1-2 egg yolks, beaten
A little hot milk if the egg yolks are small
10ml (2 tsp) salt
Pinch of pepper
A little egg and water mixed together to glaze

Put the hot, cooked potato through a sieve. Melt the butter in a saucepan. Add the beaten egg yolks and hot milk, if used. Beat well and add seasoning. Allow to cool slightly. Put into a piping bag with a star vegetable nozzle. Pipe in crowns on to a greased baking sheet. Brush with egg and water glaze. Cook in the top of the oven

This page: Baked Potatoes (top left), Creamed Potatoes (centre right) and Sauté Potatoes (bottom).

Facing page: Boiled Potatoes (top left), Duchesse Potatoes (top right), Birdsnest Potatoes (centre) and Potato Croquettes (bottom).

Potato Croquettes

450g (1lb) cooked potato
25g (1oz) butter
A little milk
10ml (2 tsp) salt
Pepper to taste
1 beaten egg
Breadcrumbs

Mash the cooked potato with the butter and a little milk. Add seasoning and leave to cool. Divide the mixture into even-sized portions. Roll each portion into a ball, using a little flour on the hands to prevent sticking. Using a palette knife and the hand, shape the balls into cork shapes, with flat ends. Coat with beaten egg and breadcrumbs. Fry in deep, hot fat until golden.

Old Potatoes

Peel potatoes and cut out any eyes and any green parts. Cook in salted water for 15-20 minutes until soft. Drain well and serve.

Bubble and Squeak

675g (1½lb) potatoes, peeled
A little milk
Knob of butter
450g (1lb) green cabbage, trimmed and roughly chopped
1 small onion, peeled and chopped
Salt and pepper
1 egg

Cook the potatoes in salted water until soft. Drain and mash with a little milk and butter. Plunge the cabbage into boiling, salted water. Cook for 5 minutes, drain well and finely chop. Mix the potato and cabbage with the onion, add seasoning and the egg. Put the mixture in a frying pan and fry in a little fat until golden brown.

This page: Bubble and Squeak (top), Potatoes Normandie (centre) and Jacket Potatoes (bottom).

Facing page: Brussels Sprouts (top), Mushrooms (centre left) and Glazed Carrots (bottom right).

Beetroot (Boiled)

Boil beetroot in a saucepan for 1-1½ hours. Do not damage the skin before cooking. The skin will peel off easily once the beetroot is cooked.

Braised Celery

25g (1oz) butter
2 medium-sized carrots, peeled and diced
8 sticks celery, scrubbed, trimmed and cut in half lengthways
300ml (½ pint) chicken stock
Salt and pepper
Chopped parsley to garnish

Heat the butter and fry the carrots for a few minutes. Add the celery and cook for a further 2 minutes. Place the vegetables in an ovenproof dish and pour on the stock. Season well. Cover and cook in the oven for about 1-1¼ hours at 180°C, 350°F, Gas Mark 4. Garnish with chopped parsley.

Spring Greens

Wash well. Shred finely before cooking in boiling, salted water for 10-15 minutes. When cooked, drain well. Toss in butter, if liked, and serve.

Leeks

675g (1½lb) fresh leeks, washed, trimmed and halved
Butter
Pepper

Cook the prepared leeks in boiling, salted water for 10 minutes. Drain and toss in butter and add pepper.

Roast Parsnips

450g (1lb) parsnips, peeled, quartered and sliced

Garnish
Chopped fresh parsley

Cook the prepared parsnips in boiling, salted water for about 5 minutes. Drain well. Place in the fat around the joint and cook for about 45 minutes. Garnish with chopped parsley.

Brussels Sprouts

Cut a cross in the stalks and remove the outer leaves. Cook in boiling, salted water for between 7-15 minutes. When cooked, drain, toss in butter and serve.

Corn on the Cob

Strip off the husks and remove the silky threads. Cook the corn on the cob in boiling water for about 10-15 minutes, adding a little salt at the end of the cooking time. When cooked, drain. Serve with melted butter.

Broccoli

Thoroughly wash the broccoli and remove any withered leaves. Cook in boiling, salted water for 25-30 minutes. When cooked, drain and serve as required.

This page: Leeks (top), Roast Parsnips (centre left), Boiled Beetroot (centre right) and Broccoli (bottom).

Facing page: Braised Celery (top left), Spring Greens (top right) and Corn on the Cob (bottom).

Pasta Salads

Bean Salad

PREPARATION TIME: 10 minutes
COOKING TIME: 15 minutes
SERVES: 4 people

225g (8oz) macaroni
425g (15oz) can red kidney beans, drained
60g (2oz) bacon, rind removed, and sliced
1 onion, peeled and chopped
2 sticks celery, sliced diagonally
15-30ml (1-2 tbsps) wine vinegar
45-60ml (3-4 tbsps) olive oil
1 tsp chopped parsley
Salt
Pepper

Cook macaroni in plenty of salted boiling water for 10 minutes, or until tender but still firm. Rinse in cold water and drain well.
Heat frying pan, and sauté bacon in its own fat until crisp. Add onion, and cook until soft. Mix vinegar, oil and parsley, and season well. Add bacon, onion, kidney beans and celery to macaroni. Pour over dressing, and toss together.

Niçoise Salad

PREPARATION TIME: 15 minutes
COOKING TIME: 15 minutes
SERVES: 4 people

225g (8oz) penne
3 tomatoes, quartered
115g (4oz) French beans, cooked
½ cucumber, cut into batons
200g (7oz) can tuna fish, drained and flaked
12 black olives, halved, with stones removed
45g (1½oz) can anchovy fillets, drained, and soaked in milk if desired
120ml (4 fl oz) bottled French dressing

Nicoise Salad (far left), Bean Salad (left) and Tuna and Tomato Salad (below).

Cook penne in lots of boiling salted water until tender but still firm. Rinse in cold water; drain, and leave to dry. Put flaked tuna in the base of a salad dish. Toss pasta together with tomatoes, cucumber, French beans, olives, and anchovies, and then pour over French dressing. Mix together well.

Tuna and Tomato Salad

PREPARATION TIME: 10 minutes
COOKING TIME: 15 minutes
SERVES: 4 people

225g (8oz) pasta shells
200g (7oz) can tuna fish, flaked
6 tomatoes
1 tbsp fresh chopped basil or marjoram, or 1 tsp dried basil or oregano
90ml (6 tbsps) French dressing

Mix herbs with French dressing. Cook pasta shells in a large saucepan of boiling salted water until tender – about 10 minutes. Rinse with cold water, and drain, shaking off excess water. Toss with 3 tablespoons of French dressing. Leave to cool. Meanwhile, slice enough of the tomatoes to arrange around the outside of the serving-dish. Chop the rest, and pour the remaining French dressing over them, and place in the centre of the dish. Add tuna to the pasta shells, and toss gently. Serve in the centre of the dish over the chopped tomatoes.

Stuffed Aubergine (Eggplant)

PREPARATION TIME: 15 minutes
COOKING TIME: 1 hour
OVEN: 180°C, 350°F, Gas Mark 4
200°C, 400°F, Gas Mark 6

4 small or 2 large aubergines
60g (2oz) soup macaroni
200g (7oz) bacon, rind removed, and diced
1 green pepper, cored and diced
1 yellow pepper, cored and diced
2 tomatoes, skin removed, chopped and seeds removed
30g (1oz) butter
½ tsp chilli powder
1 tbsp tomato purée
1 small onion, peeled and chopped
1 clove garlic, crushed
60g (2oz) Gruyère or Cheddar cheese, grated
1 tbsp breadcrumbs
Salt and pepper

Cook macaroni in plenty of boiling, salted water for 10 minutes, or until tender but still firm. Rinse in cold water, and drain well. Wrap aubergines in baking foil, and bake in a moderate oven (180°C, 350°F, Gas Mark 4) for 30 minutes. Cut aubergines in half lengthways. Scoop out the pulp, leaving 1.5cm (½ inch) of thickness on the skin. Chop pulp. Heat butter in a pan. Add onion and garlic, and cook until transparent. Add bacon and peppers and fry for 5 minutes. Then add aubergine pulp, tomato, tomato purée, chilli powder, and salt and pepper. Cook a further 3 minutes. Stir in macaroni, and fill the scooped-out aubergine halves with the mixture. Top with grated cheese and breadcrumbs, and brown under a grill or in a quick oven (200°C, 400°F, Gas Mark 6). Serve immediately.

Gianfottere Salad

PREPARATION TIME: 40 minutes
COOKING TIME: 30 minutes
SERVES: 4 people

225g (8oz) pasta spirals
1 aubergine (egg plant)
1 courgette (zucchini)
1 red pepper
1 green pepper
2 tomatoes
1 onion
60ml (4 tbsps) olive oil
1 clove garlic
Salt
Pepper

This page: Gianfottere Salad.

Facing page: Stuffed Aubergine (Eggplant).

Cut aubergine into 1cm (½") slices. Sprinkle with salt and leave for 30 minutes. Skin the tomatoes by putting them into boiling water for 20 seconds, and then rinsing in cold water, and peeling skins off. Chop roughly. Cut courgette into 1cm (½") slices. Remove cores and seeds from peppers, and chop roughly. Peel and chop onion. Heat 45ml (3 tbsps) olive oil in pan, and fry onion gently until transparent, but not coloured. Meanwhile, rinse salt from aubergine, and pat dry with absorbent paper. Chop roughly. Add aubergine, courgette, peppers, tomatoes and garlic to onion, and fry gently for 20 minutes. Season with salt and pepper. Allow to cool. Meanwhile, cook pasta spirals in a lot of boiling salted water for 10 minutes, or until tender but still firm. Rinse in cold water and drain well, and toss in remaining 15ml (1 tbsp) olive oil. Toss vegetables together with pasta spirals.

Stuffed Courgettes (Zucchini)

PREPARATION TIME: 15 minutes

COOKING TIME: 30 minutes

OVEN: 200°C, 400°F, Gas Mark 7

4 courgettes
60g (2oz) soup pasta
2 tomatoes, skin removed, chopped, and seeds removed
30g (1oz) butter or margarine
115g (4oz) minced beef
1 small onion, peeled and chopped
2 cloves garlic, crushed
60g (2oz) Gruyère or Cheddar cheese, grated
1 tbsp breadcrumbs
1 tsp tomato purée
Salt and pepper

Cook pasta in lots of boiling salted water for 5 minutes or until tender. Rinse in cold water and drain well. Meanwhile, put courgettes in a pan and cover with cold water. Bring to the boil and cook gently for 3 minutes. Rinse under cold water. Cut courgettes in half lengthways. Carefully scoop out the pulp, leaving 1.5cm (½ inch) thickness on skin. Chop pulp. Heat butter in a frying-pan. Add garlic and onion, and fry gently until transparent. Increase heat and add minced beef. Cook for 5 minutes, turning often until meat is well browned. Stir in tomato purée and salt and pepper to taste. Add courgette pulp, tomatoes and pasta, and cook for 2 minutes. Spoon into courgette shells. Sprinkle top with grated cheese and breadcrumbs, and brown under a hot grill or in a quick oven. Serve immediately.

Stuffed Tomatoes

PREPARATION TIME: 10 minutes

COOKING TIME: 20 minutes

OVEN: 180°C, 350°F, Gas Mark 4

4 large ripe tomatoes
450g (1lb) fresh spinach
¼ tsp grated nutmeg
30g (1oz) butter, creamed
60g (2oz) soup pasta
15ml (1 tbsp) double cream
1 clove garlic, crushed
15g (½oz) Gruyère or Cheddar cheese, grated
4 anchovy fillets, sliced
Salt and pepper

Cut tops off tomatoes, and carefully scoop out the insides with a teaspoon. Wash spinach well and remove stalks. Cook gently in a large saucepan, without added water, until spinach is soft. Chop very finely, or blend in a food processor. Meanwhile, cook pasta for 5 minutes, or until tender. Rinse and drain well. Mix with the spinach. Add butter, cream, nutmeg and garlic, and season well. Fill each tomato and top with cheese and anchovy fillets. Bake in a moderate oven for 10 minutes. Serve immediately.

Mushroom Salad

PREPARATION TIME: 1 hour 10 minutes

COOKING TIME: 15 minutes

SERVES: 4 people

225g (8oz) farfalle (pasta butterflies/bows)
225g (8oz) mushrooms (button or cup), sliced
75ml (5 tbsps) olive oil
Juice of 2 lemons
1 tsp fresh chopped basil
1 tsp fresh chopped parsley
Salt
Pepper

Mix oil together with lemon juice and fresh herbs. Put the sliced mushrooms into a bowl, and pour over 60ml (4 tbsps) of the dressing. Leave for 1 hour. Cook the pasta in a large saucepan of boiling salted water for 10 minutes, or until tender. Rinse in cold water, and drain. Toss with the rest of the dressing, and leave to cool. Fold mushrooms and pasta together gently, adding salt and freshly-ground black pepper to taste. Sprinkle with parsley.

Prawn Salad

PREPARATION TIME: 10 minutes

COOKING TIME: 15 minutes

SERVES: 4 people

225g (8oz) pasta shells
225g (8oz) prawns or shrimps, shelled and de-veined
150ml (¼ pint) mayonnaise
Juice of 1 lemon
1 tsp paprika
Salt
Pepper
1 lettuce
1 cucumber, sliced

Cook the pasta in plenty of boiling salted water for 10 minutes, or until tender. Drain, and rinse under cold water. Shake off excess water; put into a bowl, and pour over lemon juice. Leave to cool. Mix paprika into mayonnaise. Add to prawns, and toss. Arrange a bed of lettuce leaves and sliced cucumber in a dish, and pile pasta in centre. Pile prawns on top.
(This can also be made with flaked crab meat or salmon).

Stuffed Courgettes (Zucchini) (above right) and Stuffed Tomatoes (top).

Prawn Salad (left) and Mushroom Salad (far left).

Curried Prawn Salad

PREPARATION TIME: 10 minutes
COOKING TIME: 20 minutes
SERVES: 4 people

225g (8oz) soup pasta
225g (8oz) prawns or shrimps, shelled and de-veined
1 tsp paprika
Juice of ½ a lemon
1 dsp curry powder
1 tsp tomato purée
30ml (2 tbsps) olive oil
1 small onion, peeled and chopped
1 clove garlic, crushed
150ml (¼ pint) water
2 slices lemon
1 tsp apricot jam
300ml (½ pint) mayonnaise
Salt
Pepper

Heat oil, and fry garlic and onion gently until soft but not coloured. Add curry powder and paprika, and cook for 2 minutes. Stir in tomato purée and water. Add lemon slices, and salt and pepper to taste. Cook slowly for 10 minutes; stir in jam, and bring to the boil, simmering for 2 minutes. Strain and leave to cool. Add mayonnaise. Meanwhile, cook pasta in plenty of boiling salted water for 10 minutes, or until tender but still firm. Rinse under cold water and drain well. Toss in lemon juice, and put in serving-dish. Arrange prawns on top, and pour over curry sauce. Toss well. Sprinkle with paprika.

Courgette (Zucchini) Salad

PREPARATION TIME: 15 minutes
COOKING TIME: 15 minutes
SERVES: 4 people

225g (8oz) elbow macaroni
4 courgettes, sliced thinly
2 tomatoes, chopped
8 stuffed green olives, sliced
90ml (6 tbsps) French dressing

Cook pasta in lots of boiling salted water for 10 minutes, or until tender but still firm. Rinse in cold water, and drain well. Mix with 3 tablespoons French dressing. Leave to cool. Meanwhile, cook the courgettes gently in boiling, lightly-salted water, until just tender but still crisp. Drain, and flush with cold water. Leave to cool. Mix together pasta, courgettes, tomatoes and stuffed olives, and 3 tablespoons French dressing. Serve chilled.

Mexican Chicken Salad

PREPARATION TIME: 10 minutes
COOKING TIME: 15 minutes
SERVES: 4 people

225g (8oz) soup pasta shells
225g (8oz) cooked chicken, shredded
200g (7oz) can sweetcorn kernels, drained
1 stick celery, sliced
1 red pepper, cored, seeds removed, and diced
1 green pepper, cored, seeds removed, and diced

Dressing:
15ml (1 tbsp) mayonnaise
30ml (2 tbsps) vinegar
Salt
Pepper

Cook pasta in plenty of boiling salted water until just tender. Drain well, and leave to cool. Meanwhile, combine mayonnaise with vinegar and salt and pepper to taste. When the pasta is cool, add chicken, sweetcorn, celery and peppers. Toss well and serve with dressing.

This page: Mexican Chicken Salad.

Facing page: Curried Prawn Salad (top) and Courgette (Zucchini) Salad (bottom).

Oriental Vegetables and Pulses

Narangi Piyaz Salad
(ONION AND ORANGE SALAD)

PREPARATION TIME: 15 minutes

2 large seedless oranges or
4 satsumas
6 spring onions, finely chopped, including green leaves
Salt
10ml (2 tsp) lemon juice
1.25ml (¼ tsp) ground black pepper
2.5ml (½ tsp) sugar
10ml (2 tsp) salad oil

Peel oranges and separate into segments. Cut each segment in two. Add onions, salt, lemon juice, pepper, sugar and oil. Gently toss to mix. Serve as a side salad.

Channa
(CHICKPEA)

PREPARATION TIME: soaking overnight
COOKING TIME: 20-30 minutes

225g (8oz) chickpea
1.3 litres (2¼ pints) water
5ml (1 tsp) bicarbonate of soda
50g (2oz) ghee or
45ml (3 tblsp) oil
1 onion, peeled and chopped
1 bayleaf
2.5cm (1 inch) cinnamon stick
4 black cardamoms
5ml (1 tsp) ginger paste
5ml (1 tsp) garlic paste
5ml (1 tsp) ground coriander
5ml (1 tsp) chilli powder
1.25ml (¼ tsp) turmeric
5 fresh tomatoes, chopped or
5 canned tomatoes, chopped
1-2 green chillis, cut in half
Salt to taste
2 sprigs fresh coriander, chopped

Soak chickpeas overnight in 750ml (1¼ pints) water with the bicarbonate of soda. Drain chickpeas and boil in 600ml (1 pint) of water for 10-12 minutes in a pressure cooker. Strain and save the liquid. Heat ghee or oil and add onion, bayleaf, cinnamon and cardamoms. Fry for 1-2 minutes. Add ginger and garlic pastes. Fry for 1 minute. Sprinkle with coriander, chilli and turmeric powder. Mix well and fry for half a minute. Add tomatoes, green chillis and chickpeas. Mix well and add 175-250ml (6-8 fl oz) cooking liquid. Add extra water if insufficient liquid. Cover and gently simmer for 10-15 minutes. Add salt and green coriander. The chickpeas should disintegrate when pressed between thumb and index finger. If not fully tender add extra water and cook further. Channa is a thick, moist dish. Serve with kulcha or nan.

Kassi Mooli
(GRATED MOOLI)

PREPARATION TIME: 10 minutes

225g (8oz) mooli
Salt to taste
Juice of 1 lemon
1 green chilli, finely chopped
1 sprig fresh coriander leaves, chopped

Wash and scrape mooli. Wash again and grate. Keep on sieve and let some of the liquid pass through. Press and squeeze gently and put in a dish. Sprinkle with salt and lemon juice and mix in green chilli and fresh coriander leaves. Serve with daal and roti. Caution: mooli has a strong smell therefore always store well wrapped in cling film, in refrigerator.

Red Cabbage and Carrot Salad

PREPARATION TIME: 10 minutes

½ small red cabbage, finely chopped
2-3 carrots, peeled and grated
50g (2oz) raisins
5ml (1 tsp) sugar
1.25ml (¼ tsp) salt or to taste
150ml (¼ pint) soured cream
10ml (2 tsp) lemon juice

Mix cabbage, carrots and raisins. Sprinkle with sugar and salt and pour over the well-stirred soured cream. Sprinkle with lemon juice and mix well. Serve with any meal as a side salad. In place of soured cream, plain salad cream may be used.

Lobia Curry
(BLACK EYED LOBIA BEAN CURRY)

PREPARATION TIME: soak overnight and 10 minutes
COOKING TIME: 30-40 minutes

225g (8oz) lobia beans, washed and soaked overnight in water
600ml (1 pint) water
1 onion, peeled and chopped
50g (2oz) ghee or
45ml (3 tblsp) oil
1 bayleaf
2.5 (1 inch) cinnamon stick
5ml (1 tsp) ginger paste
5ml (1 tsp) garlic paste
1.25ml (¼ tsp) turmeric powder
5ml (1 tsp) ground coriander
5ml (1 tsp) chilli powder
4-5 canned tomatoes, crushed or
4 fresh tomatoes, chopped
Salt to taste
2 green chillis, halved and chopped
2 sprigs fresh coriander leaves, chopped

Boil presoaked lobia beans in 600ml (1 pint) water for 20 minutes. Cool. Fry onion in ghee or oil for 3-4 minutes. Add bayleaf, cinnamon, ginger and garlic paste and fry for 2 minutes. Add turmeric, ground coriander, chilli powder and stir the mixture well. Add boiled lobia and tomatoes. Add salt, chopped chilli and fresh coriander leaves. Cover and cook for 10-15 minutes on gentle heat. The gravy should be of thick consistency. Serve with rice or rotis.

This page: Narangi Piyaz Salad (top) and Red Cabbage and Carrot Salad (bottom) with Kassi Mooli.

Facing page: Lobia Curry (top), Razma (centre right) and Channa (bottom).

Aloo Methi
(POTATO AND FRESH FENUGREEK LEAVES)

PREPARATION TIME: 10 minutes

COOKING TIME: 10 minutes

50g (2oz) ghee or
45ml (3 tblsp) oil
5ml (1 tsp) cumin seed
1 pinch asafoetida (hing)
3 medium potatoes, peeled and cut into chunks
1 bunch fresh methi leaves, chopped
5ml (1 tsp) chilli powder
5ml (1 tsp) coriander powder
Salt
1.25ml (¼ tsp) turmeric powder
Juice of 1 lemon

Heat ghee or oil and add cumin seed and hing. When seeds begin to crackle, add potatoes. Fry and cook potatoes for 3-4 minutes then add methi leaves. Mix well and sprinkle with chilli powder, coriander, salt and turmeric powder. Stir the mixture to distribute spices evenly. Cover and cook on low heat for 6-8 minutes. Add lemon juice before serving.

Kachhoomar
(SHREDDED ONION SALAD)

PREPARATION TIME: 20-25 minutes

1 large Spanish onion, finely sliced into rings
1.25ml (¼ tsp) salt
1.25ml (¼ tsp) chilli powder
1 sprig fresh green coriander, chopped

Aloo Gajjar (left), Toorai Tarkari (centre) and Aloo Methi (right).

1 green chilli, chopped
15ml (1 tblsp) lemon juice
2 fresh tomatoes, chopped (optional)

In a dish put onion slices, salt, chilli powder, fresh coriander, green chilli and lemon juice. Mix well so as to release onion juice. Add tomatoes and mix well. Serve with meal or with kebabs.

Aloo Gajjar
(POTATO AND CARROTS)

PREPARATION TIME: 10 minutes
COOKING TIME: 10-15 minutes

50g (2oz) ghee or
30ml (2 tblsp) oil
5ml (1 tsp) cumin seeds
2 medium potatoes, peeled and cut into 1cm (½ inch) cubes
3 medium carrots, scraped and cubed
5ml (1 tsp) chilli powder
5ml (1 tsp) ground coriander
1.25ml (¼ tsp) turmeric powder
Salt to taste
Juice of half a lemon

Heat ghee or oil and add cumin seeds. When they begin to crackle, add potatoes. Fry for 3-4 minutes then add carrots. Stir the mixture and sprinkle with chilli, coriander, turmeric powder and salt. Stir fry the mixture for 1-2 minutes then cover and cook on low heat for 8-10 minutes. Sprinkle with a little water to help cook carrots. Sprinkle with lemon juice before serving.

Razma
(RED KIDNEY BEAN CURRY)

PREPARATION TIME: razma to be soaked overnight
COOKING TIME: 40-50 minutes

225g (8oz) red kidney beans, washed
600ml (1 pint) water
5ml (1 tsp) bicarbonate of soda
50g (2oz) ghee or
45ml (3 tblsp) oil
1 onion, peeled and chopped
2.5cm (1 inch) cinnamon stick
1 bayleaf
3 black cardamoms
5ml (1 tsp) ginger paste
5ml (1 tsp) garlic paste
5ml (1 tsp) chilli powder
5ml (1 tsp) ground coriander
5ml (1 tsp) garam masala powder
1.25ml (¼ tsp) turmeric
200g (7-8oz) canned tomatoes, crushed
Salt to taste
2 green chillis, halved
2 sprigs fresh coriander leaves, chopped

Soak kidney beans in 600ml (1 pint) water with bicarbonate of soda overnight. Next day pressure-cook in 450ml (¾ pint) fresh water (add extra water if some has been absorbed by the beans) for 5-8 minutes. Cool and strain, retaining the liquid. Heat ghee or oil and fry onion for 2-3 minutes. Add cinnamon, bayleaf, cardamoms, ginger and garlic pastes. Cook for 1 minute. Add chilli powder, ground coriander, garam masala and turmeric. Stir the spices well. Add tomatoes and salt. Add kidney beans and fry the mixture for 2-3 minutes. Add 175-250ml (6-8 fl oz) cooking liquid. Sprinkle with green chilli and fresh coriander leaves. Simmer for 15-20 minutes. Add liquid if gravy is too thick. Remove from heat and serve.

Saag Bhaji
(BRUSSELS SPROUT BHAJI)

PREPARATION TIME: 6 minutes

COOKING TIME: 10 minutes

50g (2oz) ghee or
45ml (3 tblsp) oil
5ml (1 tsp) five spice mixture (panchphoran)
1 bayleaf
2.5cm (1 inch) cinnamon stick
450g (1lb) Brussels sprouts cut in half
5ml (1 tsp) chilli powder
7.5ml (1½ tsp) ground coriander
1.25ml (¼ tsp) turmeric powder
Salt
5ml (1 tsp) sugar
4 cloves, ground
Juice of 1 lemon

Heat ghee or oil and add five spice mixture. Add bayleaf, cinnamon stick and fry for half a minute. Add Brussels sprouts. Mix well and sprinkle with chilli powder, coriander and turmeric. Add salt to taste and stir well to blend all the spices. Cover and cook on gentle heat for 8-10 minutes, stirring the mixture occasionally. Sprinkle with sugar and ground cloves. Mix well. Cover and cook for another 2-3 minutes. Sprinkle with lemon juice before serving.

Toorai Tarkari
(COURGETTE CURRY)

PREPARATION TIME: 10 minutes

COOKING TIME: 15 minutes

22ml (1½ tblsp) oil
5ml (1 tsp) cumin seeds
225g (½lb) courgettes, peeled and sliced into quarter inch thick rounds
2.5ml (½ tsp) chilli powder
5ml (1 tsp) ground coriander
1.25ml (¼ tsp) turmeric powder
3-4 fresh or canned tomatoes, chopped
Salt to taste
1 green chilli, halved
1 sprig fresh coriander leaves, chopped

Heat oil and add cumin seeds. When they crackle, add courgette slices. Stir and sprinkle with chilli, coriander and turmeric powder. Mix well and add chopped tomatoes. Sprinkle with salt, green chilli and fresh coriander. Cover and cook for 10-12 minutes.

Pochari Kosambri (top left), Kachhoomar (top right) and Phalon-Ka-Chaat (bottom).

Phalon-Ka-Chaat
(SWEET AND SOUR FRUIT SALAD)

PREPARATION TIME: 20-25 minutes

2 bananas, peeled and sliced
1 large guava, chopped
1 pear, peeled and chopped
225-275g (8-10oz) canned peaches, chopped, discard syrup
225-275g (8-10oz) canned pineapple chunks, discard syrup
1 small fresh pawpaw, peeled, seeded and cut into chunks
A few grapes, seeded
1 apple, peeled, cored and chopped
10ml (2 tsp) lemon juice
Salt
1.25ml (¼ tsp) ground black pepper
1.25ml (¼ tsp) chilli powder
Pinch of black rock salt (kala namak)

Put all the fruits into a large bowl. Sprinkle with lemon juice, salt, pepper and chilli. Mix well. Add pinch of ground black rock salt. (kala namak). Mix and serve as a starter, side salad or snack. Note: many other fruits may be added e.g. mango, kiwi, plum, lychees, melons, etc.

Baigan Dahivaley
(AUBERGINE SLICES IN YOGURT)

PREPARATION TIME: 10 minutes

COOKING TIME: 10-15 minutes

5ml (1 tsp) chilli powder
1.25ml (¼ tsp) turmeric powder
1 large aubergine, cut into 5mm (¼ inch) thick round slices
Oil for deep frying
225-275g (8-10oz) natural yogurt
5ml (1 tsp) garam masala powder
1.25ml (¼ tsp) salt
1 green chilli, chopped
1 sprig fresh green coriander leaves, chopped

Rub chilli and turmeric into aubergine and deep fry aubergine slices in oil, 1-2 minutes each side, and drain on kitchen paper. Beat yogurt and add garam masala powder, salt, green chilli and fresh coriander. Mix well. Arrange aubergine on a flat serving plate or dish. Pour yogurt over evenly. Serve as a side dish.

Pachari Kosambri
(VEGETABLE, NUT AND COCONUT SALAD)

PREPARATION TIME: 20-25 minutes

100g (4oz) grated white cabbage
1 small onion, peeled and finely chopped
1 small apple, grated
1 raw mango, peeled and grated
Juice of 1 lemon
1.25ml (¼ tsp) salt
50g (2oz) fresh, grated coconut
1 green chilli, chopped
2 sprigs fresh coriander, chopped
50g (2oz) bean sprouts
½ cucumber, grated
50g (2oz) unsalted peanuts, skin removed

Put grated cabbage, onion, apple and mango into a bowl. Mix well, squeeze and discard excess juice. Drain well. Sprinkle with lemon juice, salt, coconut, green chilli and fresh coriander. Add bean sprouts and cucumber and mix gently. Add lightly roasted and coarsely ground peanuts. Mix and serve. Note: other nuts, like cashews, chiroli, pecan, walnut and hazelnuts may be used. Grated carrots may also be included if desired.

Green Bean Bhaji

PREPARATION TIME: 10 minutes

COOKING TIME: 10-12 minutes

45ml (3 tblsp) oil or melted ghee
5ml (1 tsp) urid daal
2-3 green chillis
6-8 fresh curry leaves
350g (12oz) frozen sliced green beans, unthawed
Salt to taste
15ml (1 tblsp) desiccated coconut

Heat oil or ghee and add urid daal, green chilli and curry leaves. Stir fry for half a minute. Add beans and sprinkle with salt. Cover and cook for 6-8 minutes. Sprinkle with coconut and mix well. Cover and cook for 3-4 minutes. Serve with chapatis.

Mattar Paneer (top left), Saag Bhaji (top right) and Baigan Dahivaley (bottom).

Mushroom Aloo Bhaji
(POTATO AND MUSHROOM BHAJI)

PREPARATION TIME: 5-6 minutes

COOKING TIME: 10-12 minutes

50g (2oz) ghee or
45ml (3 tblsp) oil
1 onion, peeled and chopped
450g (1lb) medium potato, peeled and cubed
2.5ml (½ tsp) salt to taste
30ml (2 tblsp) garam masala powder
225g (½lb) button mushrooms, sliced
Lemon juice

Heat ghee or oil and fry onion until tender (2-3 minutes). Add potatoes and fry for 5-6 minutes. Sprinkle with salt and garam masala. Mix well and cover. Cook for 4-5 minutes until potatoes are tender. Add mushrooms. Stir well. Cover and cook for 2-3 minutes. Sprinkle with lemon juice to taste. Remove from heat and serve.

Mili-Juli Sabzi
(MIXED VEGETABLE BHAJI)

PREPARATION TIME: 15 minutes

COOKING TIME: 10-15 minutes

50g (2oz) ghee or
45ml (3 tblsp) oil
1 onion, peeled and chopped
5ml (1 tsp) cumin seeds
1 medium potato, peeled and chopped
3 cauliflower florets, cut into small pieces
1 small aubergine, cubed
1 medium green pepper, seeded and cubed
225g (½lb) mixed frozen vegetables
Salt to taste
5ml (1 tsp) turmeric powder
5ml (1 tsp) ground coriander
5ml (1 tsp) chilli powder
3-4 fresh tomatoes, chopped
2 sprigs green fresh coriander leaves, chopped
1-2 green chillis, chopped

Heat ghee or oil and fry onion and cumin seeds for 2-3 minutes. Add potatoes and stir fry for 4-5 minutes. Add cauliflower, aubergine and green pepper and cook for 4 minutes. Add mixed vegetables. Stir to mix well. Sprinkle with salt, turmeric, coriander and chilli powder. Add chopped tomato. Stir and cover. Cook on low heat for 5-6 minutes. Add fresh coriander and chopped chilli. Mix and serve. To make moist curry add 150ml (¼ pint) water after tomatoes are added.

Dum Aloo
(SPICED POTATO CURRY)

PREPARATION TIME: 10 minutes

COOKING TIME: 15 minutes

50g (2oz) ghee or
45ml (3 tblsp) oil
1 bayleaf
1 onion, minced finely
2.5ml (½ tsp) ginger paste
2.5ml (½ tsp) garlic paste
2.5ml (½ tsp) whole mustard seed
2.5ml (½ tsp) cumin seed
450g (1lb) small potatoes, with skins, washed and dried or
450g (1lb) potatoes, peeled and cut into chunks
1.25ml (¼ tsp) turmeric powder
10ml (2 tsp) ground coriander
7.5ml (1½ tsp) chilli powder
150ml (¼ pint) natural yogurt
1.25ml (¼ tsp) salt

Heat ghee or oil and add bayleaf and onion. Fry for 3-4 minutes. Add ginger and garlic and fry for 1 minute. Add mustard and cumin seed. Add potatoes, mix well and cook for 4-5 minutes, stirring constantly to avoid burning. Sprinkle with turmeric, coriander and chilli powder. Add yogurt and salt to taste. Mix gently, cover and cook for 8-10 minutes until potatoes are tender and most of the liquid has evaporated. Sprinkle with a little water if potatoes are not quite tender. Dum aloo is a dry dish with potatoes covered with spices. Serve with puri.

Khata-Meetha Kaddu
(SWEET AND SOUR PUMPKIN)

PREPARATION TIME: 10 minutes
COOKING TIME: 15-20 minutes

50g (2oz) ghee or
45ml (3 tblsp) oil
1 bayleaf
2.5cm (1 inch) cinnamon stick
6 green cardamoms
6 cloves
5ml (1 tsp) five spice mixture (panch-phoran)
2 medium potatoes, peeled and cut into chunks
450g (1lb) pumpkin, peeled and cut into chunks
5ml (1 tsp) chilli powder
7.5ml (1½ tsp) ground coriander
1.25ml (¼ tsp) turmeric powder
2.5ml (½ tsp) salt
10ml (2 tsp) sugar
15ml (1 tblsp) tamarind pulp
45ml (3 tblsp) water

Heat oil and add bayleaf, cinnamon, cardamom, cloves and five spice mixture and fry for half a minute. Add potatoes and fry for 4 minutes. Add pumpkin. Stir vegetables and cook for 3 minutes. Sprinkle with chilli powder, coriander, turmeric, salt and sugar. Stir the mixture to blend the spices. Add tamarind pulp and water. Cover and cook on gentle heat for 8-10 minutes until potatoes are tender. This is a moist curry without gravy. Serve with paratha or puri.

Palak Paneer
(PANEER AND SPINACH)

PREPARATION TIME: 20 minutes and overnight for paneer. Follow paneer making recipe.
COOKING TIME: 10 minutes

450g (1lb) fresh spinach leaf (or well-drained, canned or frozen spinach)
50g (2oz) ghee or
45ml (3 tblsp) oil
225g (8oz) paneer, cut into cubes
1 onion, peeled and finely chopped
2.5cm (1 inch) ginger root, peeled and finely chopped
4 fresh tomatoes or
4-5 canned tomatoes, chopped
5ml (1 tsp) chilli powder
15ml (1 tblsp) lemon juice
5ml (1 tsp) ground coriander
25g (1oz) unsalted butter
1.25ml (¼ tsp) turmeric powder
1.25ml (¼ tsp) salt

Boil fresh spinach in 600ml (1 pint) water for 5 minutes. Drain and save water. Mash or purée spinach and keep aside. If canned or thawed frozen spinach is used, save liquid. Heat ghee or oil and fry paneer pieces until light brown. Remove. In the same oil fry onion and ginger for 3-4 minutes. Add tomatoes and sprinkle with chilli, coriander, turmeric and salt to taste. Cover and cook for 2-3 minutes. Add paneer, puréed spinach and lemon juice. If too dry use 45ml (2-3 tblsp) spinach water to moisten the curry. Remove from heat and serve with butter. This is a thick, moist curry.

Daal Pulses

PREPARATION TIME: 5 minutes
COOKING TIME: 10 minutes

225g (8oz) split or dehusked moong daal washed in 2-3 changes of water
600ml (1 pint) water
1.25ml (¼ tsp) turmeric powder
5ml (1 tsp) ground coriander
Salt to taste
1 small onion, peeled and chopped
50g (2oz) unsalted butter or clarified butter
1 green chilli, chopped
2 cloves garlic, peeled and chopped

To garnish
1 sprig fresh coriander leaves, chopped

Boil moong daal in water until tender and soft. Drain. Mash the daal with a potato masher or egg beater. Add turmeric and ground coriander and salt to taste. Simmer

This page: Khata-Meetha Kaddu (top), Palak Paneer (right), Dum Aloo (bottom).

Facing page: Green Bean Bhaji (top), Mili-Juli Sabzi (right) and Mushroom Aloo Bhaji (bottom).

until volume is reduced by ⅓rd. Fry onion in butter until golden brown, add chilli and garlic. Fry until garlic is browned. Pour over daal. Garnish with chopped fresh coriander. Serve with rice or chapatis.

Khari Urid Daal
(DRY URID DAAL)

PREPARATION TIME: 5 minutes

COOKING TIME: 10-15 minutes

225g (8oz) white dehusked urid daal washed in 3-4 changes of water
Salt to taste
200ml (⅓ pint) water

For garnish
1 onion, peeled and sliced
50g (2oz) unsalted butter
1 green chilli, chopped
2.5cm (1 inch) ginger root, peeled and sliced
1 sprig fresh coriander, chopped

Boil urid daal covered in water, with salt to taste, on low heat until water has evaporated. Fry onion in butter until golden brown. Add chopped chilli and ginger and fry for 2-3 minutes. Pour over dry daal. Garnish with chopped coriander. Serve with roti or paratha.

Masoor Daal
(RED LENTIL)

PREPARATION TIME: 6 minutes

COOKING TIME: 20-25 minutes

225g (8oz) red lentils
600ml (1 pint) water
5ml (1 tsp) chilli powder
10ml (2 tsp) ground coriander
1.25ml (¼ tsp) turmeric powder
1.25ml (¼ tsp) salt
1 sprig fresh coriander leaves, chopped
4 fresh tomatoes, chopped or
5 canned tomatoes, crushed
1 onion, peeled and chopped
50g (2oz) butter
1 green chilli, halved and chopped

Wash lentils in 4-5 changes of water, until water is clear. Drain. Add 600ml (1 pint) water and cover and simmer gently, without stirring, for 10-15 minutes until lentils are thoroughly cooked. Blend with a masher or beat with an egg beater. Add chilli powder, ground coriander, turmeric, salt, fresh coriander and tomatoes. Cover and simmer for 6-8 minutes. Remove from heat. Fry onion in butter and when brown pour over daal. Garnish with chopped chilli. Serve with rice or chapati.

Sambhar (top), Masoor Daal (centre) and Arhar Toor Daal (bottom).

Arhar Toor Daal
(YELLOW LENTIL)

PREPARATION TIME: 5-6 minutes

COOKING TIME: 20-25 minutes

225g (8oz) toor daal
600ml (1 pint) water
1.25ml (¼ tsp) turmeric powder
5ml (1 tsp) ground coriander
1.25ml (¼ tsp) salt
6 curry leaves
1 green chilli, split in half
15ml (1 tblsp) fresh or desiccated coconut
1 sprig green fresh coriander, chopped
5ml (1 tsp) mustard seed
50g (2oz) butter

Wash toor daal in 4-5 changes of water. Drain. Add 600ml (1 pint) water, turmeric, salt and coriander. Cover and simmer gently for 10-15 minutes until daal is well cooked and soft. Blend with the aid of a masher or an egg whisk. Add curry leaves, coconut, chilli and coriander leaves. Cover and cook for further 8-10 minutes. Heat butter and fry mustard seed for half a minute. Pour over daal. Serve with rice or rotis. Toor daal should have a smooth, thick consistency.

Sabut Masoor
(WHOLE LENTIL)

PREPARATION TIME: 5 minutes

COOKING TIME: 20-25 minutes

50g (2oz) butter
1 onion, peeled and chopped
1 bayleaf
2.5cm (1 inch) cinnamon stick
5ml (1 tsp) ginger paste
5ml (1 tsp) garlic paste
225g (8oz) daal washed in 3-4 changes of water
450ml (¾ pint) water
5ml (1 tsp) ground coriander
2.5ml (½ tsp) chilli powder
1.25ml (¼ tsp) turmeric powder
3 fresh tomatoes, chopped or
3 canned tomatoes, chopped
1 green chilli, chopped
1 sprig fresh coriander, chopped
Salt to taste

Heat butter and fry onion until golden brown. Add bayleaf, cinnamon stick, ginger and garlic pastes and fry for 1 minute. Add drained daal and water. Cover and simmer gently for 12-15 minutes. The daal should be well cooked. Beat with a potato masher or egg beater to blend. Sprinkle with coriander, chilli and turmeric powder. Add tomatoes, green chilli and fresh coriander leaves. Season with salt. Mix well and cover and cook gently for 7-10 minutes. Remove from heat and serve with rice or chapatis. The daal should have gravy of medium consistency. If too dry, add a little water and boil for 2-3 minutes.

Sambhar
(DAAL AND VEGETABLE)

PREPARATION TIME: 10 minutes

COOKING TIME: 20-30 minutes

225g (8oz) toor daal
600ml (1 pint) water
1 carrot, peeled and sliced
1 potato, peeled and cubed
6-8 okra (bhindi), topped and tailed and cut into 2.5cm (1 inch) pieces
1 small courgette, sliced
1 small aubergine, halved and sliced
6 curry leaves
30ml (2 tblsp) tamarind pulp
1 green chilli, slit in half
Salt to taste
1 sprig fresh green coriander
15ml (1 tblsp) oil
2.5ml (½ tsp) mustard seed
1.25ml (¼ tsp) asafoetida (hing)

The following spices should be dry roasted and ground into a powder:
5ml (1 tsp) coriander seed
5ml (1 tsp) cumin seed
2 whole dry red chilli
10ml (2 tsp) channa daal
1.25ml (¼ tsp) fenugreek seed (methi)

Wash toor daal in 4-5 changes of water until water is clear. Drain. Add 300ml (½ pint) water, cover and simmer gently for 6-10 minutes. Remove any froth that forms. When daal is soft, beat with a potato masher or whisk. In a separate pan, boil all the vegetables: carrots, potatoes, aubergine, okra, courgette, with the ground, roasted spice and remaining water, for 4-5 minutes. Mix daal and vegetables along with liquid and stir gently to form an

Sabut Masoor (top), Khari Urid Daal (right) and Lal Mireh Aur Moong Phali (bottom).

even mixture. Add curry leaves, tamarind pulp, salt, chopped chilli and fresh coriander. Simmer for 10-15 minutes. Remove to a serving dish. For tempering, heat oil and fry mustard seed and asafoetida for half a minute and pour over sambhar. Serve with boiled rice.

Butter Beans and Green Capsicum

PREPARATION TIME: 10 minutes

COOKING TIME: 10 minutes

15ml (1 tblsp) oil
1 onion, peeled and chopped
225g (8oz) butter beans or broad beans
1 large green pepper, seeded and chopped
1.25ml (¼ tsp) turmeric
2.5ml (½ tsp) chilli powder
5ml (1 tsp) ground coriander
Salt to taste
4-5 fresh or canned tomatoes, chopped
1 green chilli, chopped
1 sprig fresh coriander leaves, chopped

Heat oil and fry onion for 3-4 minutes. Add beans and green pepper. Cook for 4-5 minutes. Sprinkle with turmeric, chilli and ground coriander. Add salt and tomatoes. Mix well. Cover and cook for 5-6 minutes on low heat. Add green chilli and fresh coriander. Cook covered for 2-3 minutes. If too dry add 30ml (2 tblsp) water. This is a dry dish.

Stuffed Peppers

PREPARATION TIME: 20 minutes

COOKING TIME: 30-35 minutes

50g (2oz) ghee or
45ml (3 tblsp) oil
1 onion, peeled and finely chopped
1 potato, peeled and diced
225g (8oz) mixed frozen vegetables
5ml (1 tsp) garam masala powder
2.5ml (½ tsp) chilli powder
10ml (2 tsp) dried mango powder
Salt to taste
6-8 small green peppers
Oil

Heat ghee or oil and fry onion until tender (3-4 minutes). Add potatoes and cook for 4-5 minutes. Add mixed vegetables, and sprinkle with garam masala, chilli powder, mango powder and salt to taste. Cover and cook gently until potatoes are tender. Remove from heat and cool. Wash and wipe dry green peppers. Remove top by slicing across to form a lid. Remove pith and seeds. Heat 45ml (3 tblsp) oil and fry peppers laid sideways, for 1-2 minutes, cooking on all sides. Drain well. Fill each pepper with filling and arrange them on a baking tray and bake in preheated oven, Gas Mark 3 (160°C or 325°F) for 20 minutes. Serve.

Aloo Gobi

PREPARATION TIME: 10 minutes

COOKING TIME: 10-12 minutes

1 large onion, peeled and chopped
75g (3oz) ghee or
45ml (3 tblsp) oil
2 medium potatoes, peeled and cut into chunks
1 medium cauliflower, cut into small florets
2-3 green chillis, chopped
2 sprigs fresh coriander leaves, chopped
3.75cm (1½ inch) ginger root, peeled and finely chopped
Salt to taste
Juice of 1 lemon
10ml (2 tsp) garam masala

Fry onion in ghee or oil until just tender, 2-3 minutes. Add potatoes and fry for 2-3 minutes. Add cauliflower and stir fry for 4-5 minutes. Add green chillis, coriander, ginger and salt. Mix well. Cover and cook for 5-6 minutes on low heat, or until potatoes are tender. Sprinkle with lemon juice and garam masala before serving. Serve with parathas.

Nau-Rattan Chutney
(NINE JEWELLED CHUTNEY)

PREPARATION TIME: 20 minutes
COOKING TIME: 20-30 minutes

1 banana, peeled and sliced
1 apple, cored and chopped
1 large mango, peeled, stoned and sliced
3 rings of canned pineapple, chopped
200-225g (7-8oz) canned peaches, chopped
100g (4oz) dates, pitted and sliced
50g (2oz) ginger root, peeled and chopped
50g (2oz) raisins
175-200g (6-7oz) brown sugar or jaggery
2-3 dry red chillis
175ml (6 fl oz) malt vinegar
5ml (1 tsp) salt
2.5ml (½ tsp) cumin seed
2.5ml (½ tsp) coriander seed
2.5ml (½ tsp) onion seed
2.5ml (½ tsp) aniseed seed
50g (2oz) almonds, chopped

In a saucepan put all the fruits, dates, ginger, raisins, sugar, chillis and malt vinegar. Add salt and simmer gently for 10-15 minutes. Add coarsely ground, dry roasted cumin, coriander, onion seed, aniseed and almonds. Mix well and cook for 5-6 minutes. Cool and bottle. Chutney should be thick and sticky.

Lal Mireh Aur Moong Phali Chutney
(RED-HOT CHUTNEY)

PREPARATION TIME: 5 minutes

1 large red pepper
3-4 whole dry red chillis
50g (2oz) unsalted peanuts
1cm (½ inch) ginger root, peeled and sliced
Juice of 3 lemons
Salt

Halve red pepper, remove pith and seed. In a liquidiser, blend red pepper, chillis, peanuts and ginger. A few spoons of lemon juice may be needed to blend the mixture. Pour into a bowl. Add salt and the lemon juice. Mix well and serve. Red-hot chutney can be frozen. Freeze in small tubs in small quantities. Can be kept refrigerated in sealed bottles for up to 2 months.

Dahi-Podina Chutney
(YOGURT AND MINT CHUTNEY)

PREPARATION TIME: 5-6 minutes

150ml (¼ pint) natural yogurt
20ml (4 tsp) sugar
10ml (2 tsp) dry mint powder or 2-3 sprigs mint leaves, chopped
Salt

Put yogurt, sugar and mint into a liquidiser and blend for 1-2 minutes. Add salt and mix. Serve with kebabs, samosa and pakoras. Alternatively, blend in a bowl with an egg beater. Ready made concentrated mint sauce may be used in place of dry or fresh mint leaves.

Inset illustration, far left: Meethi Tomatar Chutney (top), Tmali Ki Chutney (right) and Dahi-Podina Chutney (bottom).

Main illustration: Chutneys. Adrak Khajoor Ki Khati Mithi (top), Nau-Rattan (right), Coriander, Green Chili and Coconut (bottom), Coconut and Urid Daal (left) and Red Pepper and Peanut (centre).

Tmali Ki Chutney (TAMARIND CHUTNEY)

PREPARATION TIME: 6 minutes

COOKING TIME: 10-12 minutes

225g (½lb) dry tamarind pods
100-175g (4-6oz) sugar or jaggery
1.25ml (¼ tsp) salt
5ml (1 tsp) chilli powder
5ml (1 tsp) cumin seed
5ml (1 tsp) coriander seed

Soak tamarind pods in 150ml (¼ pint) of boiling water for 5 minutes. Squeeze pods to remove soft pulp. Strain through sieve or squeeze by hand. Add little fresh warm water to the pulp and repeat, taking 3 extracts. The first one is the thickest and subsequent ones will be low in strength. Take 250-265ml (8-9 fl oz) thick tamarind extract. Discard the pods. Add to this extract sugar, salt, chilli powder and lightly ground, roasted cumin and coriander seed. Mix well. Adjust sugar and salt if necessary. Serve with kebabs. Tamarind chutney can be kept refrigerated for up to 1 month.

Adrak Khajoor Ki Khati Mithi Chutney (DATE AND GINGER CHUTNEY)

PREPARATION TIME: 20-30 minutes

100g (4oz) dates, sliced and stoned
50g (2oz) fresh ginger, peeled and cut into matchstick-size strips
100g (4oz) fresh, unripe mango, peeled and thinly sliced or
50g (2oz) dry mango pieces (aanchoor)
50g (2oz) raisins and currants mixed
25g (1oz) almonds, chopped
200ml (⅓ pint) water
175g (6oz) sugar or jaggery
1.25ml (¼ tsp) salt
5ml (1 tsp) red chilli powder

Put dates, ginger, fresh or dry mango, currants and almonds into a saucepan. Add water. Keep aside for 6-8 minutes. Add sugar or grated jaggery, salt and chilli powder and simmer gently. Cook for 15-20 minutes until chutney is thick and sticky. Remove, cool and serve. It can be bottled and kept with or without refrigeration for up to 3 months.

Meethi Tomatar Chutney (SWEET TOMATO CHUTNEY)

PREPARATION TIME: 5-6 minutes

COOKING TIME: 10-15 minutes

25g (1oz) ghee or
15ml (1 tblsp) oil
2.5cm (1 inch) cinnamon stick
1 bayleaf
6 cloves
2.5ml (1 tsp) mustard seed
5ml (1 tsp) chilli powder
1.25ml (¼ tsp) turmeric powder
50g (2oz) sugar
450g (1lb) fresh or canned tomatoes
50g (2oz) raisins
2.5ml (½ tsp) salt

Heat ghee or oil and fry cinnamon, bayleaf and cloves for 1 minute. Add mustard seed. When they begin to crackle, add chilli, turmeric and sugar. Mix well and add tomato. Mix well and add raisins and salt. Cover and simmer for 8-10 minutes. Add a little water if liquid thickens. Tomato chutney should have medium consistency. Serve hot or cold. Once cooked it can be bottled or kept in refrigerator for 4-6 weeks.

Aloo-Mattar and Mirchi Bhaji
(POTATO, PEA AND GREEN PEPPER CURRY)

PREPARATION TIME: 15 minutes

COOKING TIME: 10 minutes

1 onion, peeled and chopped
50g (2oz) ghee or
30ml (2 tblsp) oil
2 medium potatoes, peeled and cut into chunks
5ml (1 tsp) ground coriander
5ml (1 tsp) chilli powder
1.25ml (¼ tsp) turmeric powder
225g (8oz) frozen green peas
1 green pepper, seeded and cut into chunks
225g (8oz) canned tomatoes, crushed
Salt to taste
2 green chillis, cut into quarters
2 sprigs fresh green coriander leaves, chopped
120ml (4 fl oz) water

Fry onion in ghee or oil until just tender (2-3 minutes). Add potatoes and fry for 5-6 minutes. Sprinkle with ground coriander, chilli powder and turmeric powder. Mix well and add peas and green pepper. Stir and add tomato and season with salt. Add chopped green chilli and fresh coriander. Add water, cover and cook for 5-6 minutes until potatoes are tender. The dish should have a thick gravy.

Bharey Bhindi
(WHOLE STUFFED OKRA)

PREPARATION TIME: 20-30 minutes

COOKING TIME: 15-20 minutes

225g (½lb) bhindi (okra), washed, dried, topped and tailed
1 large onion, peeled and thickly sliced
75g (3oz) ghee or
60ml (4 tblsp) oil
10ml (2 tsp) ground coriander
10ml (2 tsp) ground cumin
5ml (1 tsp) turmeric powder
5ml (1 tsp) chilli powder
Salt to taste
15ml (1 tblsp) dry mango powder
15ml (1 tblsp) aniseed (sauf) powder

Split okra or bhindi halfway down. Fry onion for half a minute in 1oz ghee or 1 tablespoon of oil and remove. Mix coriander, cumin, turmeric and chilli powder, and put a little of this spice mixture into the split okras. Heat the remaining oil in a frying pan or wok. Add stuffed okras. Sprinkle with salt and stir well. Cover and cook on low heat for 5-6 minutes. Add fried onions, then sprinkle with mango and aniseed powder. Cover and cook for 3-4 minutes. Serve with roti.

Tendli Bhaji with Cashew Nuts

Tendli is an Asian vegetable that looks like a gooseberry and tastes like courgette.

PREPARATION TIME: 10 minutes

COOKING TIME: 12-15 minutes

30ml (2 tblsp) oil
50g (2oz) cashew nuts
3-4 cloves of garlic, peeled and crushed
2.5ml (½ tsp) mustard seed
6-8 curry leaves
2-3 dry red chilli or fresh green chilli
225g (½lb) tendli, washed, dried and cut in half lengthways
Salt to taste
10ml (2 tsp) desiccated coconut
1.25ml (¼ tsp) turmeric powder

Heat oil and fry cashew nuts until light brown. Remove, then fry garlic until light brown. Add mustard seed, curry leaves and red or green chilli. Fry for half a minute. Add tendli, sprinkle with salt and stir the mixture. Sprinkle with desiccated coconut, turmeric and fried cashew nuts. Cover and cook on low heat for 10-12 minutes or until tendli is tender.

This page: Aloo-Mattar and Mirchi Bhaji (left), Bharey Bhindi (centre) and Tendli Bhaji with Cashew Nuts (right).

Facing page: Butter Beans and Green Capsicum (top), Aloo Gobi (left) and Stuffed Peppers (bottom).

Section 5

MEALS WITH FLAIR

An Introduction to Wok Cooking

The wok is an ancient Chinese cooking utensil known for its versatility. It can be used for stir-frying, deep frying, steaming, boiling and braising a wide variety of food.

The traditional wok is made of heavy gauge carbon steel which conducts heat well, giving a quick high temperature. However, this medium will rust if not oiled and given proper care. Lengthy cooking in liquid may impart a metallic taste to the food or may cause the discolouration of white liquids or food. Aluminium and stainless steel woks are also available and are a good choice, particularly if steaming, braising, boiling, or cooking for a long time. These woks need no seasoning but do not heat as efficiently as carbon steel.

Cooking times in the next five chapters are only a guide, as actual times will vary with the kind of wok you use and the intensity of the heat source. There are three types of wok: round bottomed, for use on gas burners – with the use of a ring base for stability; flat bottomed, for electric ranges; and electric woks, which can be used to cook at the table or anywhere there is a power point. Other equipment that may be needed includes a curved, long-handled spatula, and curved slotted spoon (which fit into the curved shape of the wok), a domed lid, a metal trivet or bamboo steamer and a deep fat frying thermometer.

Stir-frying, a fuel and timesaver. It is unique to wok cooking, where small pieces of food are toss-cooked in minutes over intense heat, in a very small amount of oil. The shape of the wok allows for tossing with abandon. Food is cooked in a matter of minutes and the flavours and juices are sealed in, resulting in succulent meat, poultry and seafood, and tender and crisp vegetables. Nutritional values are retained, as are the fresh and bright colours of vegetables.

A number of steps followed will lead to ease of cooking and best results:

☆ Heat wok before adding oil.

☆ Have all ingredients needed for the recipe prepared and to hand before beginning to cook. Care should be taken in the preparation of the food so that everything cooks in a short time and adds to the appearance of the final dish.

☆ Any sauces or seasonings should generally be prepared in advance.

☆ Slice meat and poultry very thinly and evenly (it will slice easier if partially frozen and a very sharp knife is used).

☆ Ingredients that take the longest to cook should be put into the wok first.

☆ Add a small amount of food at a time – in batches if necessary.

☆ Ensure everything is ready for serving, including family or guests, as the food must be eaten immediately it is cooked. It is not the sort of cooking that can be done ahead of time.

Deep frying. Points to note when cooking with oil:

☆ Care must be taken not to move or tilt the wok when it contains hot oil.

☆ Ensure wok is uncovered when heating oil.

☆ Ensure handles are not sticking over edge of stove.

☆ Be careful if adding moist food as it tends to spatter.

☆ After cooking, allow oil to cool before pouring out or returning to its container.

Steaming and Braising. Points to note when steaming and braising:

☆ During cooking some steam will condense and form drops of water under the domed lid. To shield the food, cover with a piece of greaseproof paper.

☆ Check the water level once in a while and top up as needed.

A few well-chosen ingredients, now readily available, will give you the authentic flavours for many a delicious Oriental dish, enabling you to savour the pleasures of exotic Eastern cuisine.

Though the wok is primarily an Oriental utensil, I have interspersed the Eastern dishes with a variety of Western-style recipes, since wok cooking adapts well to many types of cuisine.

Wok Soups and Starters

Wonton Soup

PREPARATION TIME: 15 minutes

COOKING TIME: 15 minutes

SERVES: 4 people

225g (8oz) minced pork
4 spring onions, chopped finely
½ tsp finely chopped root ginger
15ml (1 tbsp) light soy sauce
115g (4oz) wonton wrappers
1 tsp cornflour
5ml (1 tsp) sesame oil
5ml (1 tsp) Chinese wine, or dry sherry
1 tsp sugar
Salt
Pepper
1 litre (2 pints) chicken stock
2.5ml (½ tsp) sesame oil

Garnish

Coriander, or finely chopped spring onion

Place in a bowl the minced pork, spring onions, ginger, soy sauce, 5ml (1 tsp) sesame oil, Chinese wine, sugar, cornflour, salt and pepper. Mix together well and set aside. Heat stock in wok and bring to the boil. Season with salt and pepper. Wrap ½ teaspoon of pork mixture into each wonton wrapper. Close tightly and drop into stock. Cook for 5 minutes. Wontons will usually rise to the surface when cooked. Add 2.5ml (½ tsp) sesame oil and stir in. Garnish with spring onion or fresh coriander. Serve hot.

Chinese Combination Soup

PREPARATION TIME: 30 minutes

COOKING TIME: 20 minutes

SERVES: 4 people

4 dried Chinese mushrooms
225g (8oz) chicken
115g (4oz) fine/thread egg noodles
1 clove garlic, sliced thinly
1 tsp finely sliced root ginger
¼ small cabbage, shredded
600ml (1 pint) chicken stock
15ml (1 tbsp) peanut oil
2 eggs, beaten
15ml (1 tbsp) dark soy sauce
15ml (1 tbsp) sherry
15ml (1 tbsp) water
1 tsp cornflour
2 shallots, peeled and sliced finely

Soak mushrooms in hot water for 20 minutes. Remove and discard stems. Slice mushroom caps thinly. Soak noodles in boiling salted water for 2 minutes. Rinse in cold water. Drain. Slice chicken finely. Heat wok and add peanut oil. Add garlic and ginger, and fry gently for 5 minutes, then discard. Add chicken, and fry for a few minutes until meat has turned white. Add mushrooms, shallots, cabbage and stock. Bring to the boil and simmer for 5 minutes. Gradually pour in eggs and stir so that they cook in shreds. Mix cornflour with 15ml (1 tbsp) of water, and pour into soup, stirring continuously. Cook for 2 minutes or until soup thickens. Add noodles, soy sauce and sherry. Serve immediately.

This page: Wonton Soup (top) and Curry Soup with Meatballs (bottom).

Facing page: Chinese Combination Soup (top) and Eggflower Soup (bottom).

Curry Soup with Meatballs

PREPARATION TIME: 30 minutes
COOKING TIME: 20 minutes
SERVES: 4 people

Meatballs
225g (8oz) lean minced beef
1 clove garlic, crushed
1 onion, peeled and chopped finely
½ tsp salt
½ tsp curry powder, or ¼ tsp curry paste
½ tsp ground cinnamon
½ tsp ground cloves
½ tsp ground pepper
30g (1oz) breadcrumbs
1 small egg, lightly beaten

Broth
1 tsp garam masala
1 tsp turmeric
600ml (1 pint) water
1 clove garlic, crushed
1 onion, peeled and finely chopped
1 tsp curry leaves
½ cup desiccated coconut, soaked in 1 cup hot water for 15 minutes
30ml (2 tbsps) peanut oil

Mix together meatball ingredients, and form into small balls about the size of walnuts. Heat wok, add oil and, when hot, fry meatballs. When browned well all over, remove with a slotted spoon, and drain on absorbent paper. Carefully drain oil from wok. Add 5ml (1 tsp) of oil, and fry spices for 30 seconds. Add onion, curry leaves, and garlic, and cook together for 3 minutes. Meanwhile, strain coconut in a sieve, press out as much liquid as possible, and discard the pulp. Add water and coconut milk to the wok and simmer together for 5 minutes. Adjust seasoning. Strain soup and return to wok. Add meatballs and simmer a further 5 minutes. Serve hot.

Hot and Sour Soup

PREPARATION TIME: 30 minutes
COOKING TIME: 30 minutes
SERVES: 4 people

115g (4oz) lean pork fillet
4 dried Chinese mushrooms
60g (2oz) bamboo shoots, sliced
1 square beancurd, diced
30ml (2 tbsps) sunflower or vegetable oil
1 litre (2 pints) light, clear stock, or hot water plus 2 chicken stock cubes
1 tsp cornflour
30ml (2 tbsps) cold water
5ml (1 tsp) sesame oil

Marinade
15ml (1 tbsp) light soy sauce
45ml (3 tbsps) brown vinegar
30ml (2 tbsps) water
5ml (1 tsp) sesame oil
Salt
Pepper

Garnish
Fresh coriander

Soak Chinese mushrooms for 20 minutes in hot water. Meanwhile, slice pork into thin slivers. Make the marinade by combining light soy sauce, brown vinegar, water, sesame oil, and salt and pepper. Pour over pork and leave for 30 minutes. Drain mushrooms. Remove and discard stalks. Slice caps very finely. Remove pork from marinade, and reserve marinade. Heat wok, and add sunflower or vegetable oil. When hot, stir-fry pork, mushrooms and bamboo shoots for 2 minutes. Add stock and bring to the boil. Simmer for 10 minutes. Add beancurd, marinade, and salt and pepper to taste. Slake cornflour in 30ml (2 tbsps) of cold water. Add to soup and allow to simmer for 5 minutes. Add sesame oil and sprinkle with fresh coriander. Serve hot.

Chicken and Asparagus Soup

PREPARATION TIME: 10 minutes
COOKING TIME: 45 minutes
SERVES: 4 people

450g (1lb) chicken pieces
1 onion, peeled and chopped roughly
1 carrot, chopped roughly
1 stick celery, chopped roughly
4 peppercorns
300g (10oz) can asparagus pieces
1 litre (2 pints) water
Salt
Pepper

Garnish
Chopped parsley

Remove chicken meat from bones and cut into fine shreds. Put chicken bones, onion, carrot, celery, peppercorns and water in wok, and season with salt and pepper. Bring to the boil, reduce heat, and simmer for 30 minutes. Strain and return stock to wok. Add chicken shreds, and simmer until chicken is cooked. Add undrained asparagus pieces. Adjust seasoning. Serve sprinkled with chopped parsley.

Eggflower Soup

PREPARATION TIME: 10 minutes
COOKING TIME: 10 minutes
SERVES: 4 people

600ml (1 pint) chicken stock
2 eggs, lightly beaten
15ml (1 tbsp) light soy sauce
400g (14oz) can plum tomatoes
2 spring onions, chopped finely

Drain and chop tomatoes, removing pips, and reserve juice. Bring soy sauce, tomato juice and stock to the boil in the wok. Add tomatoes and half the spring onions, and cook for 2 minutes. Dribble beaten eggs in gradually, stirring continuously. Serve immediately, sprinkled with remaining spring onions.

Chicken and Asparagus Soup (below) and Hot and Sour Soup (right).

Poppadums

COOKING TIME: 5 minutes

Poppadums
Oil for deep frying

Heat oil in wok. When oil is hot, deep fry 1 poppadum at a time for 2-3 seconds, holding edges apart with forks. They will puff up, and should be pale golden in colour. If browning, reduce heat of oil. If not cooking quickly enough, increase heat. Remove, shaking off excess oil, and drain on absorbent paper. They may be eaten straight away, or when cool may be kept in an airtight container until needed.

Fried Bananas

PREPARATION TIME: 5 minutes
COOKING TIME: 10 minutes
SERVES: 4 people

3-4 bananas
15ml (1 tbsp) lemon juice
30ml (2 tbsps) oil
Salt

Peel bananas and slice diagonally. Heat wok and add oil. When hot, add bananas. Fry, turning carefully until browned well all over. Sprinkle with lemon juice and a pinch of salt, and serve as an accompaniment to a curry.

Prawn Crisps/Crackers (Krupuk)

COOKING TIME: 5 minutes

Prawn Crisps
Oil for deep frying

Heat oil in wok, and make sure the oil is hot, but not too hot. It should be hot enough to puff the prawn crisps in 2-3 seconds: if they brown, the oil is too hot. If it is not hot enough, they will take too long to cook, and will be tough and chewy. A few can be fried together, but do not put too many in as they need to be removed quickly before over-cooking. Use a slotted spoon to remove, and drain on absorbent paper. If necessary, store in an airtight container until needed.

Chicken Liver Pâté

PREPARATION TIME: 20 minutes
COOKING TIME: 20 minutes
SERVES: 4 people as a starter

225g (8oz) chicken livers, trimmed
115g (4oz) butter
1 medium onion, peeled and chopped finely
1 bay leaf
1 clove garlic, crushed
15ml (1 tbsp) brandy
5ml (1 tsp) Worcestershire sauce
Salt
Pepper

Garnish
Sprig of parsley

Heat wok and add half of the butter. Add onion, garlic and bay leaf, and fry gently until onion is soft but not coloured. Increase heat, and add chicken livers and salt and freshly-ground black pepper to taste, and fry for 5 minutes, turning regularly. Add Worcestershire sauce and stir well. Remove from heat, and set aside to cool. Meanwhile, cream remaining butter. Remove bay leaf and chop liver finely – this can be done in a blender. Push through a sieve; beat in creamed butter and stir in brandy. Fill into individual ramekin dishes or into a china dish. If keeping, smooth over surface and cover with clarified butter. Garnish with a sprig of parsley.

Cheese Nibbles

PREPARATION TIME: 20 minutes
COOKING TIME: 20 minutes
MAKES: 40 pieces

60g (2oz) Gruyère cheese
60g (2oz) Emmenthal cheese
1 egg, lightly beaten
30ml (2 tbsps) milk
1 tsp dry English mustard
1 clove garlic, crushed

This page: Prawn Crisps/Crackers (top left), Fried Bananas (centre right) and Poppadums (bottom).

Facing page: Chicken Liver Pâté (top) and Cheese Nibbles (bottom).

30g (1oz) plain flour
1 tsp baking powder
Salt
Pepper
10 slices stale brown bread
Oil for deep frying

Sift together flour, baking powder, mustard, and a pinch of salt and pepper. Grate cheese. Mix together cheese, egg, milk, garlic and flour mixture. Beat together well. Trim off bread-crusts, and cut each slice diagonally into 4 triangles. Spread one heaped teaspoon of mixture on each triangle of bread to cover well. Heat oil in wok. When hot, carefully fry in batches with bread side up first. Deep fry until golden brown on both sides. Remove and drain on absorbent paper. Keep hot until all frying is completed. Serve hot.

Seafood Hot and Sour Soup

PREPARATION TIME: 20 minutes
COOKING TIME: 20 minutes
SERVES: 4 people

2 dried Chinese mushrooms
1 cake fresh beancurd, diced
115g (4oz) prawns or shrimps, shelled and de-veined
600ml (1 pint) light stock, preferably fish stock
60g (2oz) crab meat, or 2 crab-sticks, cut into 1.5cm (½") slices
1 tbsp oyster sauce
15ml (1 tbsp) light soy sauce
15ml (1 tbsp) lemon juice
½ tsp lemon rind, cut into slivers
15ml (1 tbsp) vegetable oil
1 red chilli, seeds removed, and finely sliced
2 spring onions, sliced
Salt
Pepper
5ml (1 tsp) sesame oil

Garnish
Fresh coriander, if desired

Soak mushrooms in hot water and set aside for 20 minutes. Heat wok, add vegetable oil and, when hot, stir-fry prawns, chilli, lemon rind and spring onions. Add stock, oyster sauce and light soy sauce, and bring to the boil. Reduce heat and simmer for 5 minutes. Add salt and pepper to taste. Remove hard stalks from mushrooms and slice caps finely. Add crab meat, beancurd and Chinese mushrooms to wok, and cook a further 5 minutes. Stir in lemon juice and sesame oil. Adjust seasoning, and serve sprinkled with fresh coriander leaves if desired.

Spring Rolls

PREPARATION TIME: 20 minutes
COOKING TIME: 30 minutes
MAKES: 12 rolls

225g (8oz) finely minced pork
1 red chilli, seeds removed, and sliced finely
10 canned water chestnuts, chopped
1 onion, peeled and chopped finely
1 clove garlic, crushed
½ tsp grated root ginger
1 tsp ground turmeric
30ml (2 tbsps) peanut oil
12 spring roll wrappers
Salt
Pepper
Peanut or vegetable oil for deep frying

Heat wok, add 30ml (2 tbsps) of peanut oil, and fry garlic, ginger,

Facing page: Seafood Hot and Sour Soup (top) and Sweetcorn and Chicken Soup (bottom).

This page: Prawn Toast (top) and Spring Rolls (right).

ground turmeric and onion for 3 minutes. Add pork, and stir-fry until pork is browning. Add water chestnuts and chilli, and salt and pepper to taste, and fry for a further 2 minutes. Remove from wok, and set aside to cool. Place spring roll wrapper with one corner pointing towards you. Spoon some of the mixture just in front of the centre. Fold over the corner nearest to you, and roll to centre. Fold the two side points into the centre and finish rolling up. They may be sealed with a paste of water and flour if necessary. Refrigerate until needed. Heat oil for deep frying in wok, and deep fry spring rolls in batches just before needed. Drain on absorbent paper, and serve warm with chilli or sweet-and-sour sauce.

Prawn Toast

PREPARATION TIME: 15 minutes
COOKING TIME: 15 minutes
MAKES: approximately 20 pieces

225g (8oz) prawns or shrimps, shelled and de-veined, and chopped finely
1 small egg, beaten
10ml (2 tsps) sherry
2 tsps oyster sauce
½ tsp grated root ginger
2 tsp cornflour
Salt
5 slices white bread
Oil for deep frying

Combine prawns, beaten egg, sherry, oyster sauce, grated ginger, cornflour and a pinch of salt. Using a 4cm (1½") round pastry cutter, cut out circles of bread. Spread mixture on each piece of bread to cover well. Heat oil in wok for deep frying. Fry in batches with bread side up first, until bread is golden brown. Remove and drain on absorbent paper. Keep hot until all frying is completed.

Sweetcorn and Chicken Soup

PREPARATION TIME: 15 minutes
COOKING TIME: 45 minutes
SERVES: 4 people

1 chicken, with giblets
225g (8oz) can creamy sweetcorn
1 onion, peeled and chopped roughly
1 carrot, scraped and chopped roughly

1 stick celery, chopped
6 peppercorns
Parsley stalks
1 bay leaf
1 litre (2 pints) water
Salt
Pepper

Garnish
Chopped parsley or chives

Clean chicken, and cut into quarters. Put into wok with giblets, chopped vegetables, peppercorns, bay leaf, parsley stalks, seasoning and water. Bring to the boil. Reduce heat and simmer for 30 minutes. Strain and return stock to wok. Remove meat from chicken and cut into fine shreds. Add undrained sweetcorn to stock, and bring to boil. Simmer for 5 minutes. Add chicken and cook for 1 minute. Sprinkle with chopped parsley or chives. Serve hot.

Rice Paper Prawn Parcels

PREPARATION TIME: 15 minutes
COOKING TIME: 15 minutes
MAKES: about 20 parcels

225g (8oz) prawns or shrimps, shelled and de-veined
6 spring onions, sliced finely
1 packet rice paper
1 egg white
½ tsp cornflour
150ml (¼ pint) peanut oil
5ml (1 tsp) Chinese wine, or 10ml (2 tsps) dry sherry
5ml (1 tsp) light soy sauce
1 tsp sugar
Salt
Pepper

Dry prepared prawns on absorbent paper. Mix egg white, cornflour, wine, sugar, soy sauce, spring onions and seasoning together. Mix in prawns. Heat peanut oil in wok until hot. Wrap five or six prawns in each piece of rice paper. Gently drop in rice paper parcels and deep fry for about 5 minutes. Serve hot.

Crab Rolls

PREPARATION TIME: 20 minutes
COOKING TIME: 20 minutes
MAKES: 12 rolls

175g (6oz) crab meat, fresh or canned
3 spring onions, finely sliced
12 spring roll wrappers
30g (1oz) cellophane noodles
¼ tsp grated root ginger
1 tsp oyster sauce
2 tbsps finely chopped bamboo shoots
Salt
Vegetable or peanut oil for deep frying

Soak cellophane noodles in hot water for 8 minutes, or as directed, and drain. Flake crab meat, and drain if necessary. Combine crab meat with spring onions, noodles, ginger, bamboo shoots, oyster sauce, and salt to taste. Place spring roll wrappers with one corner pointing towards you. Spoon some of the mixture just before the centre. Fold over the corner nearest you and roll to centre. Fold the two side points into the centre, and roll up completely. They may be sealed with a paste of flour and water if necessary. Refrigerate until needed. Heat oil in wok and deep fry batches of spring rolls just before serving. Drain on absorbent paper. Serve warm with ginger sauce or sweet-and-sour sauce.

This page: Crab Rolls (top) and Rice Paper Prawn Parcels (bottom).

Facing page: Ginger Scallops in Oyster Sauce (top) and Crispy Fish with Chilli (bottom).

Wok Seafood Recipes

Crispy Fish with Chilli

PREPARATION TIME: 40 minutes
COOKING TIME: 30 minutes
SERVES: 4 people

450g (1lb) fish fillets, skinned, bones removed, and cut into 2.5cm (1") cubes

Batter
60g (2oz) plain flour
1 egg, separated
15ml (1 tbsp) oil
75ml (5 tbsps) milk
Salt

Sauce
1 tsp grated root ginger
¼ tsp chilli powder
2 tbsps tomato purée
2 tbsps tomato chutney
30ml (2 tbsps) dark soy sauce
30ml (2 tbsps) Chinese wine or dry sherry
30ml (2 tbsps) water
1 tsp sugar
1 red chilli, seeds removed, and sliced finely
1 clove garlic, crushed
Salt
Pepper
Oil for deep frying

Sift the flour with a pinch of salt. Make a well in the centre, and drop in the egg yolk and oil. Mix to a smooth batter with the milk, gradually incorporating the flour. Beat well. Cover and set aside in a cool place for 30 minutes. Whisk egg white until stiff, and fold into batter just before using. Heat oil in wok. Dip fish pieces into batter and coat completely. When oil is hot, carefully lower fish pieces in and cook until cooked through and golden brown – about 10 minutes. Remove with a slotted spoon. Reheat oil and refry each fish piece for 2 minutes. Remove with a slotted spoon and drain on absorbent paper. Carefully remove all but 15ml (1 tbsp) of oil from wok. Heat oil, and add chilli, ginger, garlic, chilli powder, tomato purée, tomato chutney, soy sauce, sugar, wine and water, and salt and pepper to taste. Stir well over heat for 3 minutes. Increase heat and toss in fish pieces. Coat with sauce and, when heated through, serve immediately.

continuously. Return squid and cook until heated through. Place in a warm serving dish and serve hot with rice.

Squid with Broccoli and Cauliflower

PREPARATION TIME: 15 minutes

COOKING TIME: 20 minutes

SERVES: 4 people

450g (1lb) squid, cleaned
1 onion, peeled and chopped roughly
225g (8oz) fresh broccoli florets
225g (8oz) fresh cauliflower florets
2 sticks celery, sliced diagonally
½ tsp grated root ginger
1 tbsp cornflour
30ml (2 tbsps) water
30ml (2 tbsps) light soy sauce
30ml (2 tbsps) Chinese wine, or dry sherry
2 tbsps oyster sauce
2.5ml (½ tsp) sesame oil
½ tsp sugar
150ml (¼ pint) oil, for deep frying
Salt
Pepper

Cut cleaned squid lengthways down centre. Flatten out with inside uppermost. With a sharp knife make a lattice design, cutting deep into squid flesh (to tenderise and make squid curl when cooking). Heat oil in wok. Add squid and cook until it curls. Remove from pan and drain on absorbent paper. Carefully pour off all but 15ml (1 tbsp) of oil. Add onion, celery, broccoli, cauliflower and ginger, and stir-fry for 3 minutes. Slake cornflour with water, and add soy sauce, wine, oyster sauce, sesame oil, sugar, and salt and pepper to taste. Mix well and add to wok. Bring to the boil and simmer for 3 minutes, stirring continuously. Return squid and cook until heated through. Place in a warm serving dish and serve hot with rice.

Ginger Scallops in Oyster Sauce

PREPARATION TIME: 10 minutes

COOKING TIME: 15 minutes

SERVES: 4 people

450g (1lb) scallops, cleaned, dried on absorbent paper, and sliced
10 spring onions, sliced diagonally into 2.5cm (1") slices
2.5cm (1") green ginger, peeled and sliced very thinly
Salt
30ml (2 tbsps) vegetable oil

Sauce
1 tbsp oyster sauce
15ml (1 tbsp) light soy sauce
2.5ml (½ tsp) sesame oil
1 tsp grated root ginger
1 tsp cornflour
75ml (5 tbsps) light stock, or 75ml (5 tbsps) hot water and half a chicken stock cube
Pinch of sugar

Combine oyster sauce, soy sauce, sesame oil, cornflour, sugar and grated ginger and set aside. Sprinkle the scallops with a pinch of salt. Heat wok, and add oil. Add sliced ginger and spring onions, and stir-fry gently for 1 minute. Raise heat to high. Add scallops and stir-fry for 1 minute. Add sauce mixture and stir in. Remove from heat, and stir in stock gradually. Return to heat and bring to the boil, stirring continuously. Simmer gently for 3 minutes, until sauce is slightly thickened. Adjust seasoning. Serve immediately with boiled rice.

Steamed Fish with Black Beans

PREPARATION TIME: 15 minutes

COOKING TIME: 15 minutes

SERVES: 4 people

1kg (2lbs) whole snapper, bass or bream, cleaned and scaled
1 tbsp salted black beans
2 cloves garlic, crushed
15ml (1 tbsp) light soy sauce
5ml (1 tsp) Chinese wine, or 10ml (2 tsps) dry sherry
1 tsp sugar
½ tsp cornflour
5ml (1 tsp) sesame oil
½ can bamboo shoots, cut into shreds
Salt
Pepper

Facing page: Squid with Broccoli and Cauliflower.

This page: Singapore Fried Noodles (below) and Steamed Fish with Black Beans (bottom).

Wash and clean fish well and dry with absorbent paper. Make 3 or 4 diagonal cuts in flesh of fish on each side. Rub garlic into cuts and place fish on a heat-proof dish. Rinse black beans in cold water, then crush with the back of a spoon. Add cornflour, sesame oil, soy sauce, sugar and wine, and salt and pepper and mix together well. Pour over fish. Sprinkle bamboo shoots on top of fish. Put plate on top of a bamboo steamer or metal trivet standing in wok. Add water, ensuring the level is below the level of the plate. Cover and bring to the boil. Steam for about 10 minutes after boiling point is reached. Ensure that the fish is cooked, but do not oversteam. Serve hot.

Stir-Fried Prawns and Mangetout

PREPARATION TIME: 5 minutes
COOKING TIME: 5 minutes
SERVES: 4 people

225g (8oz) prawns or shrimps, shelled and de-veined
115g (4oz) mangetout, trimmed
60ml (4 tbsps) peanut oil
30ml (2 tbsps) dry white wine
Juice of half a lemon
15ml (1 tbsp) light soy sauce
Pinch of salt
Black pepper

Garnish
Parsley

Blanch mangetout in boiling salted water for 1 minute. Drain and set aside. Heat wok, add the peanut oil, and stir-fry prawns for 30 seconds. Add mangetout, dry white wine, lemon juice, soy sauce, and salt and pepper, and toss together until heated through. Adjust seasoning and garnish with parsley. Serve immediately with boiled rice.

Seafood Combination

PREPARATION TIME: 20 minutes
COOKING TIME: 20 minutes
SERVES: 4 people

225g (8oz) prawns or shrimps, shelled and de-veined
115g (4oz) squid, cleaned, cut into 2.5cm (1") rings, opened up, and scored with lattice design
115g (4oz) mangetout, trimmed
115g (4oz) white fish fillets, cut into 2.5cm (1") cubes
1 stick celery, sliced diagonally
1 carrot, scraped and cut into matchstick strips
1 tsp grated root ginger
½ tsp salt
15ml (1 tbsp) dry white wine
1 egg white
1 tsp cornflour
Oil for deep frying

Combine wine, salt, egg white, grated ginger and cornflour, and mix well. Add prawns and fish, and toss well. Drain prawns and fish, reserving sauce. Blanch mangetout in boiling water for 1 minute. Drain. Heat oil in wok. Deep fry prawns, fish and squid for 2 minutes. Remove from pan and drain on

This page: Seafood Combination.

Facing page: Mediterranean Fish Stew (top) and Stir-Fried Prawns and Mangetout (bottom).

absorbent paper. Carefully remove oil from wok, reserving 15ml (1 tbsp) of oil in wok. Heat oil. Stir-fry carrot and celery for 3 minutes. Add mangetout and stir-fry a further 3 minutes. Add any remaining sauce and stir. Add seafood and toss well until heated through.

Honey Sesame Prawns

PREPARATION TIME: 20 minutes

COOKING TIME: 20 minutes

SERVES: 4 people

450g (1lb) prawns or shrimps, shelled and de-veined
2 tbsps cornflour
115g (4oz) self-raising flour
1 egg, lightly beaten
Pinch of salt
Pepper
150ml (¼ pint) water
Oil for deep frying
2 tbsps honey
1 tbsp sesame seeds
15ml (1 tbsp) sesame oil

Sift flour and salt and pepper into a bowl. Make a well in the centre and add egg and water, gradually bringing in the flour. Beat to a smooth batter and set aside for 10 minutes. Meanwhile, toss prawns in cornflour and coat well. Shake off any excess cornflour. Add prawns to batter and coat well. Heat oil in wok, and add prawns, a few at a time. Cook until batter is golden. Remove and drain on absorbent paper, and keep warm. Repeat until all prawns have been fried. Carefully remove hot oil from wok. Gently heat sesame oil in pan. Add honey and stir until mixed well and heated through. Add prawns to mixture and toss well. Sprinkle over sesame seeds and again toss well. Serve immediately.

Steamed Fish in Ginger

PREPARATION TIME: 20 minutes

COOKING TIME: 15 minutes

SERVES: 4 people

1.5kg (3lbs) whole snapper, bass or bream, cleaned and scaled

Stuffing

½ cup cooked rice
1 tsp grated root ginger
3 spring onions, sliced finely
10ml (2 tsps) light soy sauce
6 spring onions, cut into 5cm (2") lengths, then into fine shreds
3 pieces green ginger, cut into fine shreds

Garnish

Lemon slices and parsley, if desired

Mix together rice, grated ginger, sliced spring onion and soy sauce. Stuff rice mixture into cleaned fish cavity, packing in well. Place fish on a heat-proof plate, and arrange strips of spring onion and green ginger on top of fish. Put the plate on top of a bamboo steamer or metal trivet standing in wok. Add water, ensuring the water level is not up to the plate. Cover and bring to the boil. Steam for 10 minutes from boiling point. Ensure that the fish is cooked, but be sure not to oversteam the fish. Serve hot, garnished with lemon slices and parsley, if desired.

Singapore Fried Noodles

PREPARATION TIME: 20 minutes

COOKING TIME: 25 minutes

SERVES: 4 people

225g (8oz) packet egg noodles
225g (8oz) prawns or shrimps, shelled and de-veined
1 chicken breast, cut into shreds
115g (4oz) bean sprouts
2 cloves garlic, crushed
3 sticks celery, sliced diagonally
2 spring onions, sliced
1 red chilli, seeds removed, and sliced
1 green chilli, seeds removed, and sliced
1 tsp chilli powder
2 eggs, lightly beaten
45ml (3 tbsps) oil
Salt
Pepper

Garnish

Chilli flowers (carefully cut end of chilli into shreds, and soak in cold water until flower opens)

Soak noodles in boiling water for 8 minutes, or as directed. Drain noodles on absorbent paper and leave to dry. Heat wok, and add 15ml (1 tbsp) of oil. Add lightly beaten eggs, and salt and pepper to taste. Stir gently and cook until set. Remove from wok, and cut into thin strips and keep warm. Add remaining oil to wok. When hot, add garlic and chilli powder and fry for 30 seconds. Add chicken, celery, spring onions and red and green chillies, and stir-fry for 8 minutes or until chicken has cooked through. Add noodles, prawns and bean sprouts, and toss until well mixed and heated through. Serve with scrambled egg strips on top and garnish with chilli flowers.

Mediterranean Fish Stew

PREPARATION TIME: 20 minutes

COOKING TIME: 30 minutes

SERVES: 4 people

450g (1lb) white fish fillets, cut into 5cm (2") cubes
30ml (2 tbsps) olive oil
2 cloves garlic, crushed
1 onion, peeled and sliced finely
2 sticks celery, sliced
1 tbsp chopped parsley
1 tsp oregano
2 tbsps tomato purée
150ml (¼ pint) fish stock or water
30ml (2 tbsps) sweet Italian vermouth, or sweet sherry
115g (4oz) squid (optional), cleaned
2 leeks, white parts sliced finely
400g (14oz) can plum tomatoes
115g (4oz) flat mushrooms, sliced
Salt
Pepper

Garnish

Lemon slices
Parsley

Heat wok, and add oil. Add garlic, onion, celery, leeks, oregano, parsley and squid. Cover and cook gently for 10 minutes, stirring once or twice. Add tomato purée, stock or water, wine, undrained tomatoes, mushrooms, fish, and salt and pepper to taste. Bring to the boil, then cover and simmer gently for 15 minutes. Ensure fish is cooked through (it will be opaque all the way through, and will flake easily). Garnish with lemon slices and parsley. Serve immediately.

Honey Sesame Prawns (top) and Steamed Fish in Ginger (right).

Wok Meat Dishes

Pork with Black Bean Sauce

PREPARATION TIME: 40 minutes

COOKING TIME: 45 minutes

SERVES: 4 people

225g (8oz) lean pork, cut into 2.5cm (1") cubes
15ml (1 tbsp) oil
1 red pepper, cored, seeds removed, and sliced

Sauce

3 tbsps black beans, rinsed in cold water and crushed with back of a spoon
30ml (2 tbsps) Chinese wine, or dry sherry
1 tsp grated ginger
30ml (2 tbsps) light soy sauce
3 cloves garlic, crushed
1 tbsp cornflour
150ml (¼ pint) water

Mix together black beans, wine, ginger, soy sauce and garlic. Blend cornflour with 30ml (2 tbsps) of water and add to mixture. Place pork in a bowl, and pour over sauce. Toss together well. Leave for at least 30 minutes. Heat wok, add oil and stir-fry red pepper for 3 minutes. Remove and set aside. Add pork, reserving marinade sauce. Stir-fry pork until browned well all over. Add marinade sauce and remaining water. Bring to the boil. Reduce heat, cover, and gently simmer for about 30 minutes, until pork is tender, stirring occasionally. Add more water if necessary. Just before serving, add red pepper and heat through. Serve with plain white rice.

Lamb Meatballs with Yogurt

PREPARATION TIME: 15 minutes

COOKING TIME: 30 minutes

SERVES: 4 people

450g (1lb) lean minced lamb
2 cloves garlic, crushed
1 small onion, peeled and grated
½ tsp chilli powder
1 tsp garam masala
1 tbsp chopped mint
30g (1oz) breadcrumbs
1 egg, lightly beaten
30ml (2 tbsps) oil
75ml (5 tbsps) plain yogurt
Small pinch of saffron strands, or ¼ tsp ground turmeric
30ml (2 tbsps) boiling water
Salt
Pepper

Garnish

Fresh coriander or mint

This page: Beef and Oyster Sauce.
Facing page: Lamb Meatballs with Yogurt (top) and Pork with Black Bean Sauce (bottom).

In a bowl, mix together minced lamb, garlic, onion, chilli powder, garam masala, mint and breadcrumbs. Add lightly beaten egg to bind ingredients together. Add salt and pepper to taste. Wet hands. Take a teaspoon of mixture, and roll between palms, forming small balls. Heat wok and add oil. Add meatballs, shake wok to make meatballs roll around, and fry until browned well all over. Add saffron or turmeric to 30ml (2 tbsps) boiling water. Leave for 5 minutes. Add water to yogurt, and stir in until evenly mixed. Reheat meatballs and serve on yogurt. Garnish with mint or fresh coriander. Serve with rice.

Beef and Oyster Sauce

PREPARATION TIME: 30 minutes

COOKING TIME: 20 minutes

SERVES: 4 people

450g (1lb) fillet or rump steak, sliced into thin strips
115g (4oz) bean sprouts
115g (4oz) button mushrooms
1 red pepper, cored, seeds removed, and chopped roughly
2 sticks celery, sliced diagonally
2 onions, peeled and quartered
30ml (2 tbsps) light soy sauce
30ml (2 tbsps) peanut or vegetable oil

Oyster Sauce
3 tbsps oyster sauce
1 chicken stock cube dissolved in 30ml (2 tbsps) boiling water
15ml (1 tbsp) dark soy sauce
15ml (1 tbsp) Chinese wine or dry sherry
1 tbsp cornflour
30ml (2 tbsps) cold water
Salt
Pepper

Place steak in a bowl and pour over 30ml (2 tbsps) light soy sauce. Toss together well and set aside for at least 30 minutes. Meanwhile, mix together oyster sauce, chicken stock, dark soy sauce and wine. Blend together cornflour and cold water, and set aside. Heat wok, and add oil. Add onion, celery, mushrooms and red pepper, and stir-fry for 5 minutes. Remove from wok and set aside. Reheat oil and, when hot, toss in steak. Brown well all over, then add sauce and fried vegetables. Add cornflour mixture and bring to the boil, tossing continuously. Add salt and pepper to taste. Finally, add bean sprouts and simmer gently for 3 minutes. Serve hot with noodles or rice.

Sweet and Sour Pork with Peppers

PREPARATION TIME: 1 hour 15 minutes

COOKING TIME: 30 minutes

SERVES: 4 people

450g (1lb) pork fillets, cut into 2.5cm (1") cubes
1 large green pepper, cored, seeds removed, and chopped roughly
1 large yellow or red pepper, cored, seeds removed, and chopped roughly
1 small can or jar of Chinese mixed pickle
1 large onion, peeled and chopped finely
300ml (½ pint) peanut oil

Batter
1 egg
5ml (1 tsp) peanut oil
4 tbsps cornflour
4 tbsps self-raising flour
Water

Marinade
15ml (1 tbsp) peanut oil
2.5ml (½ tsp) light soy sauce
10ml (2 tsps) Chinese wine, or 15ml (1 tbsp) dry sherry
1 tsp cornflour
1 tsp sugar
Pinch of salt
Pinch of pepper

Sauce
4 tbsps sugar
100ml (⅙ pint) wine vinegar
100ml (⅙ pint) water
1 tbsp tomato purée
Pinch of salt
1 tsp cornflour
Small pinch of red food colouring (if desired)

Mix together marinade ingredients. Pour over pork pieces and leave for about 1 hour, turning occasionally. Mix together batter ingredients, with enough water to form batter. Add pork. Heat peanut oil in wok. When hot, deep-fry pork pieces in small batches, so that they do not stick together. Remove when golden brown, using a slotted spoon, and set aside. Continue until all battered pork pieces are cooked. Heat oil again and repeat process, cooking pork for 5 minutes to make batter nice and crisp. Keep warm. Carefully drain off all but 15ml (1 tbsp) of oil. Heat, and add onion, peppers and Chinese mixed pickle. Cover and cook for 3 minutes. Remove and set aside. Heat vinegar, water, sugar, tomato purée, red food colouring and salt. Slake cornflour with 15ml (1 tbsp) of water. Stir into sauce. Bring to the boil and cook for 3 minutes. Add pork and vegetables to sauce. Serve hot with rice.

Beef Worcestershire

PREPARATION TIME: 40 minutes

COOKING TIME: 20 minutes

SERVES: 4 people

450g (1lb) fillet or rump steak, cut into 4cm (1½") cubes
60g (2oz) wonton wrappers
150ml (¼ pint) oil for deep frying

Sauce
30ml (2 tbsps) Worcestershire sauce
15ml (1 tbsp) dark soy sauce
1 tbsp sugar
Pinch of salt
Pinch of pepper
½ tsp cornflour

Mix together ingredients for sauce, and pour over steak. Toss well. Leave for at least 30 minutes, turning occasionally. Meanwhile, heat oil in wok. Fold wonton wrappers in half diagonally and seal open corners with water and press

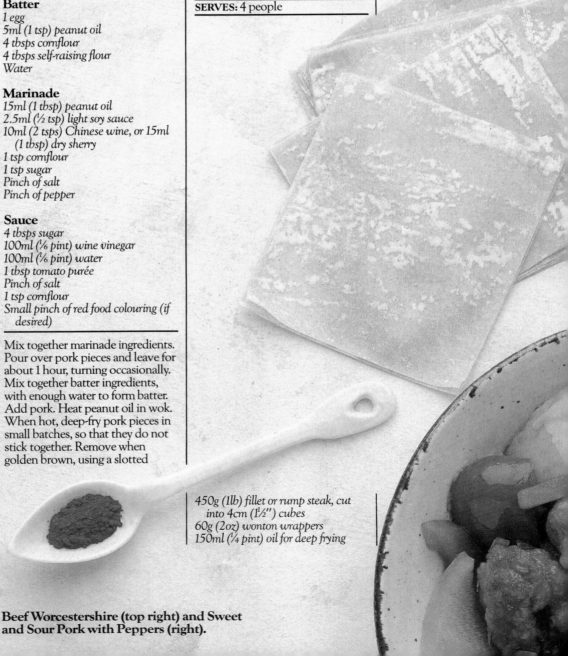

Beef Worcestershire (top right) and Sweet and Sour Pork with Peppers (right).

together. Deep fry a few wonton wrappers at a time until golden brown. Remove with a slotted spoon and drain on absorbent paper. Repeat until there are enough wonton wrappers to go around the edge of the serving dish. Carefully remove all but 30ml (2 tbsps) of oil from wok. Remove steak from sauce mixture and reserve. Heat wok, and when oil is hot, add steak and stir-fry until well browned. Pour over sauce and bring to the boil. Reduce heat and simmer, stirring continuously. When sauce thickens, and will coat steak well, place in warm serving dish and garnish with wonton wrappers. Serve immediately with boiled rice.

Pork with Plum Sauce

PREPARATION TIME: 40 minutes

COOKING TIME: 30 minutes

SERVES: 4 people

450g (1lb) lean pork fillet, cut into 2.5cm (1") cubes
1 tbsp cornflour

This page: Beef with Mango.

Facing page: Pork with Plum Sauce (top) and Stir-Fried Leeks and Lamb (bottom).

5ml (1 tsp) sesame oil
15ml (1 tbsp) light soy sauce
15ml (1 tbsp) sherry
1 tbsp brown sugar
½ tsp cinnamon
1 clove garlic, crushed
1 spring onion, sliced finely
30ml (2 tbsps) peanut oil
4 tbsps bottled plum sauce
60ml (4 tbsps) water
Salt
Pepper

Garnish
Spring onion flowers

Mix together cornflour, sesame oil, light soy sauce, sherry, brown sugar, cinnamon and salt. Pour over pork, and toss together. Leave for at least 30 minutes. Remove pork and reserve marinade. Heat wok and add peanut oil. Add pork, and stir-fry until golden brown all over. Add spring onion, plum sauce and water to wok, and mix together well. Bring to boil, cover, and simmer gently for 15 minutes, or until pork is tender, stirring occasionally. Add marinade, and bring to boil. Simmer gently for a further 5 minutes. Garnish with spring onion flowers. (To make these, cut spring onion into 5cm (2") lengths. Carefully cut lengths into fine shreds, keeping one end intact, and then soak in cold water until curling.) Serve hot with boiled rice.

Guy's Curry (Hot)

PREPARATION TIME: 40 minutes

COOKING TIME: 2 hours 15 minutes

SERVES: 4 people

1kg (2lbs) steak, skirt or rump, cut into 1.5cm (½") cubes
1½ cups coconut cream
1 onion, peeled and finely chopped
3 cloves garlic, chopped
2 tbsps sultanas
1 tbsp curry leaves
1 dsp cumin
1 dsp coriander
1 tbsp vindaloo curry paste (or milder curry paste if a curry less hot than vindaloo is desired)
1 carrot, grated
2 apples, chopped finely
1 banana, sliced finely
2 tomatoes, chopped finely
1 red pepper, cored, seeds removed, and chopped finely
6 small pieces lemon rind
2 tbsps desiccated coconut
1 dsp sugar
1 cup water
150ml (¼ pint) safflower or vegetable oil

Accompaniments
1 apple, chopped finely
1 banana, sliced
1 red pepper, cored, seeds removed, and chopped finely
1 carrot, grated
1 tomato, chopped finely
2 tbsps sultanas
2 tbsps desiccated coconut
Half a cucumber, sliced, in 2 tbsps natural yogurt

Prepare fruit and vegetables. Heat wok, add oil and heat until warm. Add onion and garlic, and fry until golden brown. Remove garlic, and discard. Add steak and stir-fry until well browned all over. Add sultanas and stir in well. Add curry leaves, stir in, and cook for 5 minutes. Add cumin and coriander and stir. Cook a further 5 minutes. Add curry paste and cook for 10 minutes. Add grated carrot, red pepper, apples, tomatoes, lemon rind and banana and mix in well. Add water. Cover and cook for 30 minutes. Stir in desiccated coconut and cook for a further 30 minutes. Add sugar and cook for another 20 minutes. Add more water as necessary. Add coconut cream and cook a further 20 minutes. Serve hot with boiled rice and accompaniments.

Stir-Fried Leeks and Lamb

PREPARATION TIME: 10 minutes

COOKING TIME: 30 minutes

SERVES: 4 people

450g (1lb) lamb, cut into 2.5cm (1") cubes
450g (1lb) leeks, cut into 2.5cm (1") slices
1 tsp rosemary
1 tsp redcurrant jelly
1 tbsp chopped mint
1 tsp basil
400g (14oz) can plum tomatoes
15ml (1 tbsp) oil
Salt
Pepper

Garnish
Fresh mint

Heat wok, and add oil. Add rosemary, basil and leeks, and stir-fry gently for 3 minutes. Remove from wok, and increase heat. Add lamb and stir-fry until well-browned all over. Return leeks to wok. Add undrained tomatoes, redcurrant jelly, mint, and salt and pepper to taste. Cover and simmer for 20 minutes, adding water if necessary. Serve hot, garnished with fresh mint.

Right: Guy's Curry (Hot).

Steak with Black Bean Sauce

PREPARATION TIME: 1 hour 15 minutes

COOKING TIME: 20 minutes

SERVES: 4 people

225g (8oz) fillet or rump steak, thinly sliced
1 large onion, peeled and chopped
1 large green pepper, cored, seeds removed, and diced
3 cloves garlic, crushed
1 tsp grated root ginger
1 small can sliced bamboo shoots, drained
3 tsps black beans
30ml (2 tbsps) light soy sauce
60ml (4 tbsps) peanut oil
5ml (1 tsp) Chinese wine, or 10ml (2 tsps) dry sherry
3 tsps sugar
1 tsp cornflour
5ml (1 tsp) sesame oil
Pinch of bicarbonate of soda
Salt
Pepper

Put sliced steak into a bowl, and sprinkle over bicarbonate of soda. Add 15ml (1 tbsp) of light soy sauce, 1 tsp of sugar, wine, sesame oil, salt and pepper, and leave to marinate for at least 1 hour. Heat wok and add 30ml (2 tbsps) peanut oil. When hot, add steak and fry quickly. Remove from heat, and remove steak. Set aside. Add onion, green pepper, bamboo shoots, and a pinch of salt to wok. Cover and cook for 3 minutes. Remove and set aside. Make black bean sauce by crushing black beans and mixing with garlic, ginger, 1 tsp of sugar and 15ml (1 tbsp) of peanut oil. Heat wok, add 15ml (1 tbsp) of oil and pour in black bean mixture. Add steak and vegetables and mix well. Make seasoning sauce by mixing cornflour with remaining 15ml (1 tbsp) of light soy sauce, and adding 1 tsp of sugar. When well mixed, pour into wok and stir. Bring to the boil and cook for 3 minutes. Serve hot with rice.

Braised Pork with Spinach and Mushrooms

PREPARATION TIME: 20 minutes

COOKING TIME: 30 minutes

SERVES: 4 people

450g (1lb) lean pork fillet, cut into thin strips
225g (8oz) spinach leaves, washed, hard stalks removed, and shredded
4 dried Chinese mushrooms, soaked in hot water for 20 minutes, stems discarded, and caps sliced finely
½ tsp ground nutmeg
30ml (2 tbsps) water
30ml (2 tbsps) peanut oil
1 onion, peeled and quartered
1 clove garlic, crushed
1 tbsp flour
Salt
Pepper

Heat wok, add 5ml (1 tsp) of oil, and roll it around to coat the surface. Put nutmeg and spinach in wok, and cook gently for 5 minutes. Remove from pan. Add remaining oil to wok and fry garlic and onion over gentle heat for 5 minutes. Remove from wok. Meanwhile, add a good pinch of salt and freshly-ground black pepper to the flour and toss in the pork, coating well. Fry pork until each piece is browned all over. Add water and mushrooms, and return onion mixture to wok. Cover and simmer gently for 10 minutes, stirring occasionally. Add spinach and salt and pepper to taste, and cook, uncovered, for 2 minutes. Serve hot with steamed rice.

This page: Braised Pork with Spinach and Mushrooms (top) and Steak with Black Bean Sauce (bottom).

Facing page: Fillet Steak Chinese Style (top) and Lamb Curry (Mild) (bottom).

sauce, and add soy sauce to sauce mixture. Toss pork in cornflour, coating well. When oil is hot, brown pork well all over. Remove from pan and reduce heat. Fry garlic and ginger for 30 seconds. Add water. Bring to the boil, then return pork to wok. Reduce heat; cover and simmer for 15 minutes, stirring occasionally. Add sauce mixture and pineapple, and simmer for a further 15 minutes. Garnish with coriander. Serve hot with rice or noodles.

Lamb Curry (Mild)

PREPARATION TIME: 45 minutes

COOKING TIME: 1 hour

SERVES: 4 people

1kg (2lb) leg of lamb
2 tbsps natural yogurt
15ml (1 tbsp) sesame oil
2 tsps garam masala
4 cloves garlic, crushed
1 tsp grated ginger
2 tsps curry powder
½ tsp ground black pepper
2 tbsps desiccated coconut
1 onion, peeled and sliced finely
1 tsp curry leaves
3 ripe tomatoes, chopped roughly
30g (1oz) sultanas
1 potato, peeled and chopped into 1.5cm (½") cubes
1 tsp sambal oelek
3 cups lamb stock
15ml (1 tbsp) peanut oil
Salt
Pepper

Garnish
1 tbsp desiccated coconut

Cut lamb into 2.5cm (1") cubes. Put bones in pan, cover with water, and bring to the boil. Simmer for 10 minutes. Strain and discard bones. Mix together yogurt, sesame oil, garam masala, garlic, ginger, curry powder, pepper and sambal oelek. Add lamb and toss well. Leave to marinate for 30 minutes. Heat wok, and add peanut oil. Fry onion and curry leaves. When softened, increase heat and add lamb and marinade. Brown lamb well. Add lamb stock, potato, tomatoes, desiccated coconut, sultanas, and salt and pepper to taste. Bring to the boil. Reduce heat and cover, and cook gently for 20 minutes. Ensure potato is covered with liquid (add water if necessary). Remove cover, and cook for a further 15 minutes. Serve hot, sprinkled with desiccated coconut. Serve with boiled rice and poppadums.

Pork Chow Mein

PREPARATION TIME: 20 minutes

COOKING TIME: 20 minutes

SERVES: 4 people

300g (10oz) egg noodles
450g (1lb) pork, sliced thinly
15ml (1 tbsp) Chinese wine, or dry sherry
1 tsp grated root ginger
1 leek, sliced
1 red pepper, cored, seeds removed, and cut into strips
1 stick celery, sliced diagonally
30g (1oz) peas
150ml (¼ pint) chicken or light stock
15ml (1 tbsp) light soy sauce
1 tsp sugar
1 tsp cornflour
15ml (1 tbsp) water
1 small can bamboo shoots, sliced
45ml (3 tbsps) oil
Salt
Pepper

Soak noodles in hot water for 8 minutes, or as directed. Rinse in cold water, and drain. Combine wine, soy sauce and sugar, and pour over pork. Toss together and set aside for at least 15 minutes. Heat wok and add oil. Add ginger, celery and leek, and stir-fry for 2 minutes. Add red pepper and bamboo shoots, and stir-fry for a further 2 minutes. Remove from wok. Increase heat, and add pork, reserving marinade. Stir-fry over high heat for 4 minutes. Return vegetables to wok. Add chicken stock gradually and stir well. Add peas and cook for 2 minutes. Blend cornflour with water. Mix into marinade sauce and stir well. Add noodles and sauce to wok and toss together, heating through as sauce thickens. Add salt and pepper to taste. Simmer for 3 minutes. Serve hot.

Pork Chow Mein (right).

Kidneys with Bacon

PREPARATION TIME: 20 minutes
COOKING TIME: 25 minutes
SERVES: 4 people

450g (1lb) lambs' kidneys
1 tbsp tomato chutney
8 rashers streaky bacon, diced
1 onion, peeled and quartered
3 cloves garlic, crushed
30ml (2 tbsps) oil
15ml (1 tbsp) light soy sauce
1 tbsp cornflour
45ml (3 tbsps) sherry
1 tbsp chopped parsley
30ml (2 tbsps) water
Salt
Pepper

Garnish
Sprig of parsley

Cut kidneys in half and remove hard core with a sharp knife or scissors. Cut a lattice design on back of kidneys. Pour over sherry, and set aside for 15 minutes. Heat wok and add oil. Add bacon, onion and garlic, and stir-fry for 5 minutes. Remove from wok. Add kidneys, reserving sherry, and fry for 3 minutes. Stir in tomato chutney. Add soy sauce and water to wok, and return bacon and onion mixture. Add salt and pepper to taste. Cover and simmer gently for 10 minutes. Meanwhile, blend cornflour with sherry marinade. Add parsley and cornflour mixture, and stir, cooking gently until sauce thickens. Garnish with parsley. Serve hot with rice.

Lamb with Cherries

PREPARATION TIME: 15 minutes
COOKING TIME: 1 hour 15 minutes
SERVES: 4 people

450g (1lb) boneless lamb from leg, cut into 2.5cm (1") cubes
60g (2oz) butter or margarine
1 onion, peeled and chopped finely
½ tsp turmeric
½ tsp cinnamon
½ tsp ground nutmeg
1 tsp brown sugar
1 can black cherries, pips removed
15ml (1 tbsp) lemon juice
1 tbsp arrowroot
150ml (¼ pint) water
Salt
Pepper

Heat half butter in wok. Add lamb and fry quickly to brown well all over. Remove from wok and set aside. Add remaining butter and onion and fry for 2 minutes. Add turmeric, cinnamon, nutmeg and brown sugar, and fry for a further 1 minute. Add salt and pepper to taste. Return lamb to wok and add water. Cover and gently simmer for 45 minutes to 1 hour, until lamb is tender. And undrained cherries. Blend arrowroot with lemon juice and stir into mixture. Bring to boil and simmer for 4 minutes or until sauce has thickened. Serve hot with rice.

Mee Goreng

PREPARATION TIME: 20 minutes
COOKING TIME: 15 minutes
SERVES: 4 people

225g (8oz) fine egg noodles
60ml (4 tbsps) peanut oil
1 onion, peeled and chopped finely
115g (4oz) pork, finely sliced
115g (4oz) prawns or shrimps, shelled and de-veined
2 cloves garlic, crushed
15ml (1 tbsp) light soy sauce
1 tsp sambal manis or sambal oelek
¼ cabbage, shredded
1 green chilli, seeds removed, and sliced
2 sticks celery, sliced
Salt
Pepper

Garnish
Sliced cucumber
Sliced spring onions

Soak noodles in hot water for 8 minutes, or boil until cooked. Rinse in cold water. Drain in a colander. Set aside. Heat wok and add oil. Stir-fry onion, garlic and chilli until onion starts to colour. Add sambal manis or sambal oelek. Add pork, celery, cabbage and salt and pepper, and stir-fry for 3 minutes. Add soy sauce, noodles and prawns, and toss mixture to heat through well. Place in a warm serving dish, surrounded with sliced cucumber and sprinkled with spring onions on top.

Five-Spice Beef with Broccoli

PREPARATION TIME: 15 minutes
COOKING TIME: 15 minutes
SERVES: 4 people

225g (8oz) fillet or rump steak
1 clove garlic, crushed
½ tsp finely grated ginger
½ tsp five-spice powder
115g (4oz) broccoli florets
Bunch of chives, snipped into 2.5cm (1") lengths
30ml (2 tbsps) peanut oil
½ tsp salt
15ml (1 tbsp) dark soy sauce
½ cup hot water
2 tsps cornflour, slaked in 15ml (1 tbsp) cold water

Cut steak into thin slices, then into narrow strips. Mix together with garlic, ginger, and five-spice powder. Heat wok, add 15ml (1 tbsp) of oil, and stir-fry broccoli for 8 minutes. Remove broccoli and add remaining oil. Add meat, and stir-fry for 3 minutes. Add broccoli, soy sauce, salt and water, and heat to simmering point. Mix cornflour with cold water, and pour into wok, stirring continuously until liquid thickens. Toss in chives, stir, and serve immediately with boiled rice.

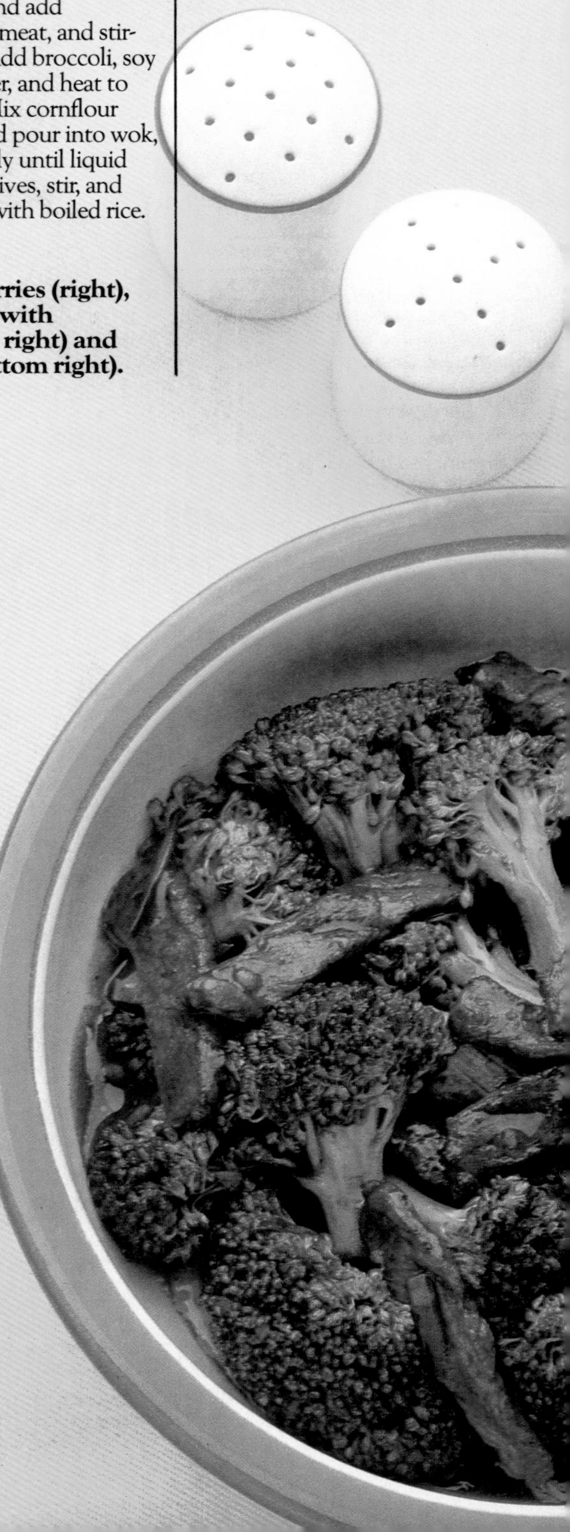

Lamb with Cherries (right), Five-Spice Beef with Broccoli (below right) and Boiled Rice (bottom right).

Beef with Pineapple and Peppers

PREPARATION TIME: 40 minutes

COOKING TIME: 15 minutes

SERVES: 4 people

450g (1lb) fillet or rump steak, sliced thinly
1 can pineapple slices, drained and chopped
1 green pepper, cored, seeds removed, and chopped roughly
1 red pepper, cored, seeds removed, and chopped roughly
2 cloves garlic, crushed
1 tsp chopped root ginger

1 onion, peeled and chopped roughly
30ml (2 tbsps) light soy sauce
1 tsp sugar
2 tsps cornflour
30ml (2 tbsps) water
15ml (1 tbsp) peanut oil

Sauce
1 tbsp plum sauce
15ml (1 tbsp) dark soy sauce
1 tsp sugar
5ml (1 tsp) sesame oil
1 tsp cornflour
60ml (4 tbsps) water
Salt
Pepper

Combine 30ml (2 tbsps) of light soy sauce with 1 tsp of sugar, 2 tsps of cornflour and 30ml (2 tbsps) of water. Mix well and pour over steak. Toss together well, and put aside for at least 30 minutes, turning occasionally. Heat wok and add peanut oil. Add ginger, garlic, onion and peppers, and stir-fry for 3 minutes. Remove from wok and set aside. Add extra oil if necessary and stir-fry beef, well separated, for 2 minutes. Remove from wok. Mix together all sauce ingredients in wok, and heat until sauce begins to thicken. Add vegetables, beef and pineapple, and toss together over a high heat until heated through. Serve with boiled rice.

This page: Beef with Pineapple and Peppers.

Facing page: Duck with Orange.

Wok Poultry Cuisine

Duck with Orange

PREPARATION TIME: 30 minutes
COOKING TIME: 50 minutes
SERVES: 4 people

1 small duck
15g (½ oz) butter or margarine
15ml (1 tbsp) oil
3 oranges
300ml (½ pint) light chicken stock
100ml (⅙ pint) red wine
2 tbsps redcurrant jelly
1 tsp arrowroot
15ml (1 tbsp) cold water
Salt
Pepper

Garnish
Watercress
Slivers of orange peel

Pare the rind of 2 oranges and cut into fine shreds. Blanch in hot water and set aside for garnish. Extract juice from 2 oranges. Cut peel and pith from 1 orange, and then slice into rounds, or cut flesh into sections if preferred. Wash duck and dry well with absorbent paper. Heat wok, and add oil and butter. When hot, add duck, and brown all over. Remove from wok and, using poultry shears or a chopper, cut duck in half lengthways, and then cut each half into 2.5cm (1") strips. Return duck to wok, and add stock, red wine, redcurrant jelly, orange juice and rind, and salt and pepper to taste. Bring to boil, reduce heat, cover and simmer gently for 20 minutes. Add orange slices, and simmer a further 10 minutes, or until duck is cooked. If sauce needs to be thickened, mix arrowroot with cold water and add to sauce. Bring to the boil, and simmer for 3 minutes. Garnish with slivers of orange peel and watercress.

Chicken and Cashews

PREPARATION TIME: 15 minutes
COOKING TIME: 40 minutes
SERVES: 4 people

450g (1lb) chicken breasts, skinned, boned, and cut into shreds
4 tsps cornflour
15ml (1 tbsp) light soy sauce
60ml (4 tbsps) peanut oil
30ml (2 tbsps) water
1 stick celery, sliced thinly
½ cup roasted cashews
115g (4oz) green beans, trimmed and sliced
1 clove garlic, crushed
1 onion, peeled and sliced
1 carrot, cut into matchstick strips
2 spring onions, sliced
½ cup chicken stock, made from chicken bones, or ½ cup of hot water plus 1 chicken stock cube
½ tsp five-spice powder
Salt
Pepper

Simmer chicken bones in a little water to make chicken stock, or dissolve chicken stock cube in hot water. Set aside to cool. Combine half the cornflour, the five-spice powder, and a pinch of salt. Toss in chicken and mix well. Heat wok, add peanut oil and, when hot, add chicken pieces a few at a time, tossing well. Stir-fry until chicken just starts to change colour – about 3 minutes. Lift out with a slotted spoon, and drain on absorbent paper. Repeat until all chicken is done. Carefully pour off all but 15ml (1 tbsp) of oil. Add onion and garlic, and cook for 2 minutes. Add celery, beans, carrot, and spring onions, and stir-fry for 2 minutes. Add strained chicken stock, and cook for 3 minutes until vegetables are tender but still crisp. Slake remaining cornflour with 30ml (2 tbsps) of water. Add soy sauce, and pour into wok. Adjust seasoning if necessary. Bring back to the boil and let simmer for 3 minutes. Add chicken and heat through. Remove from heat. Stir in cashews, and serve at once with noodles or rice.

Chicken with Mango

PREPARATION TIME: 5 minutes
COOKING TIME: 30 minutes
SERVES: 4 people

4 chicken breasts, cut into shreds
2 ripe mangoes, sliced, or 1 can sliced mangoes, drained
4 spring onions, sliced diagonally
½ tsp ground cinnamon
1 tsp grated ginger
15ml (1 tbsp) light soy sauce
1 chicken stock cube
150ml (¼ pint) water
30ml (2 tbsps) oil
30ml (2 tbsps) sweet sherry
1 tsp sugar
Salt
Pepper

Heat wok and add oil. Add ginger and cinnamon, and fry for 30 seconds. Add chicken and spring onions, and stir-fry for 5 minutes. Add light soy sauce, crumbled chicken stock cube, water and sugar, and bring to boil. Add salt and pepper to taste, and simmer for 15 minutes. Add mangoes and sherry, and simmer, uncovered, until sauce has reduced and thickened. Serve hot with boiled rice.

Stir-Fried Chicken with Yellow Bean Paste

PREPARATION TIME: 1 hour 10 minutes
COOKING TIME: 20 minutes
SERVES: 4 people

450g (1lb) chicken breasts, sliced thinly
30ml (2 tbsps) oil
2 tbsps yellow bean paste
1 tsp sugar
1 egg white, lightly beaten
15ml (1 tbsp) rice vinegar
15ml (1 tbsp) light soy sauce
1 tbsp cornflour
Salt
Pepper

Garnish
Spring onion flowers (cut spring onions into 5cm (2") lengths. Carefully cut into fine shreds, keeping one end intact, and then soak in cold water until curling).

Mix together lightly beaten egg white, cornflour, and salt and pepper. Place chicken in a bowl and pour over mixture. Toss together to coat well. Set aside in a cool place for at least 1 hour. Combine vinegar, soy sauce and sugar. Remove chicken, and set egg mixture aside. Heat wok, and add oil. When hot, stir-fry chicken until lightly browned. Remove from wok. Add bean paste to wok and stir-fry for 1 minute. Add vinegar mixture and stir in well. Return chicken to pan, and fry gently for 2 minutes. Finally, add egg mixture, and simmer until sauce thickens, stirring all the time. Garnish with spring onion flowers. Serve immediately with boiled rice.

Soy Chicken Wings

PREPARATION TIME: 1 hour 10 minutes
COOKING TIME: 20 minutes
SERVES: 4 people

1kg (2lbs) chicken wings
½ tsp crushed root ginger
15ml (1 tbsp) Chinese wine, or 30ml (2 tbsps) dry sherry
15ml (1 tbsp) light soy sauce
15ml (1 tbsp) dark soy sauce
1 tbsp sugar
30ml (2 tbsps) peanut oil
1 tsp cornflour
10ml (2 tsps) sesame oil
1 star anise
2 spring onions, sliced
45ml (3 tbsps) water
Salt
Pepper

Wash chicken wings, and dry on absorbent paper. Mix together ginger, light soy sauce, sugar, cornflour, sesame oil, wine, and seasoning. Pour marinade over chicken wings and leave for at least 1 hour, turning occasionally. Heat peanut oil until very hot. Add spring onions and chicken wings,

Chicken with Mango (left) and Stir-Fried Chicken with Yellow Bean Paste (below).

and fry until chicken has browned well on all sides. Add dark soy sauce, star anise and water. Bring to the boil, and simmer for 15 minutes. Remove star anise. Serve hot or cold.

Chicken Livers with Peppers

PREPARATION TIME: 30 minutes

COOKING TIME: 15 minutes

SERVES: 4 people

450g (1lb) chicken livers
4 Chinese mushrooms
1 green pepper
1 red pepper
15ml (1 tbsp) rice vinegar
2 tsps sugar
30g (1oz) fresh ginger
1 small leek
45ml (3 tbsps) vegetable oil
1 onion

Garnish

2 spring onion flowers (trim and slice lengthways, keep one end intact, and leave in cold water in refrigerator until curling)

Soak mushrooms in hot water for 20 minutes. Clean and trim chicken livers, and blanch in boiling water for 3 minutes. Drain and slice. Peel

and finely slice ginger. Mix vinegar and sugar, and add ginger, and set aside. Clean and trim leek and cut into thin rings. Peel and slice onion and cut into strips. Core and remove seeds from peppers, and cut into strips. Drain mushrooms, remove hard stalks, and cut caps into thin slices. Heat wok, add oil, and, when hot, add mushrooms, onion, leek and peppers, and stir-fry for 5 minutes. Remove and set aside. Add liver and ginger mixture. Stir-fry for a further 5 minutes, return vegetable mixture to wok and heat through. Serve garnished with spring onion flowers.

This page: Chicken with Cashews (top) and Soy Chicken Wings (bottom), and Chicken Livers with Peppers (right).

brown. Increase heat and add curry powder. Fry for 30 seconds. Add salt and vinegar, and cook for 1 minute. Add chicken, and turn so that mixture coats chicken well. Add coconut cream and milk, and simmer gently over a low heat for 20 minutes. Serve with boiled rice.

Honey Soy Chicken Wings

PREPARATION TIME: 5 minutes

COOKING TIME: 30 minutes

SERVES: 4 people

450g (1lb) chicken wings
½ tsp salt
30ml (2 tbsps) peanut oil
60ml (4 tbsps) light soy sauce
30ml (2 tbsps) clear honey
1 clove garlic, crushed
1 tsp ginger, freshly grated
1 tsp sesame seeds

Heat wok, add oil, and when hot, add chicken wings and fry for 10 minutes. Pour off excess oil carefully. Add soy sauce, honey, sesame seeds, garlic, grated ginger and salt. Reduce heat, and gently simmer for 20 minutes, turning occasionally. Serve hot or cold with rice.

Sesame Fried Chicken

PREPARATION TIME: 10 minutes

COOKING TIME: 30 minutes

SERVES: 4 people

450g (1lb) chicken breasts, or 4 good-sized pieces
115g (4oz) plain flour
1 tsp salt
1 tsp pepper
60g (2oz) sesame seeds
2 tsps paprika
1 egg, beaten, with 15ml (1 tbsp) water
45ml (3 tbsps) olive oil

Sift flour onto a sheet of grease-proof paper and stir in salt, pepper, paprika and sesame seeds. Dip chicken breasts in egg and water mixture, then coat well in seasoned

Chicken Curry (Mild)

PREPARATION TIME: 10 minutes

COOKING TIME: 40 minutes

SERVES: 4 people

1½kgs (3lbs) chicken
15ml (1 tbsp) peanut oil
1 onion, peeled and finely chopped
2 cloves garlic, crushed
½ tsp grated ginger
2 tsps curry powder
½ tsp salt
15ml (1 tbsp) vinegar
150ml (¼ pint) milk
150ml (¼ pint) coconut cream

Cut chicken into small pieces: breast-meat into 4 pieces, thigh-meat into 2 pieces, and wings separated at joints. Heat oil until hot. Reduce heat. Add onion, garlic and ginger and cook gently, stirring continuously. Cook for 10 minutes, or until onion is soft and a golden

This page: Chilli Sichuan Chicken (top) and Honey Soy Chicken Wings (bottom).

Facing page: Chicken Curry (Mild) (top) and Sesame Fried Chicken (bottom).

Wok Vegetables and Sauces

Sweet and Sour Cabbage

PREPARATION TIME: 5 minutes
COOKING TIME: 20 minutes
SERVES: 4 people as a vegetable

Half a small cabbage
30g (1oz) butter or margarine
45ml (3 tbsps) vinegar
2 tbsps sugar
45ml (3 tbsps) water
Salt
Pepper

Slice cabbage into shreds. Melt butter in wok. Put cabbage into wok with other ingredients and set over a moderate heat. Stir until hot, then cover and simmer for 15 minutes. Adjust seasoning if necessary. Serve hot. Good with sausages and mashed potato.

Gado Gado

PREPARATION TIME: 20 minutes
COOKING TIME: 30 minutes
SERVES: 4 people as a vegetable

115g (4oz) bean-sprouts
115g (4oz) Chinese cabbage, shredded
115g (4oz) green beans, trimmed
Half a cucumber, cut into batons
1 carrot, peeled and cut into thin strips
1 potato, peeled and cut into thin strips
15ml (1 tbsp) peanut oil

Peanut Sauce
30ml (2 tbsps) peanut oil
60g (2oz) raw shelled peanuts
2 red chillies, seeds removed, and chopped finely, or 1 tsp chilli powder
2 shallots, peeled and chopped finely
1 clove garlic, crushed
1 tsp brown sugar
Juice of half a lemon
100ml (1/6 pint) coconut milk
150ml (1/4 pint) water
Salt

Garnish
Sliced hard-boiled eggs
Sliced cucumber

Heat wok and add 15ml (1 tbsp) peanut oil. When hot, toss in carrot and potato. Stir-fry for 2 minutes and add green beans and cabbage. Cook for a further 3 minutes. Add bean-sprouts and cucumber, and stir-fry for 2 minutes. Place in a serving dish.

Make peanut sauce. Heat wok, add 30ml (2 tbsps) peanut oil, and fry peanuts for 2-3 minutes. Remove and drain on absorbent paper. Blend or pound chillies, shallots and garlic to a smooth paste. Grind or blend peanuts to a powder. Heat

This page: Gado Gado with Peanut Sauce.

Facing page: Stir-Fried Vegetable Medley (top) and Sweet and Sour Cabbage (bottom).

oil and fry chilli paste for 2 minutes. Add water, and bring to the boil. Add peanuts, brown sugar, lemon juice, and salt to taste. Stir until sauce is thick – about 10 minutes – and add coconut milk. Garnish vegetable dish with slices of hard-boiled egg, and cucumber and serve with peanut sauce.

Sweet and Sour Sauce

PREPARATION TIME: 10 minutes

COOKING TIME: 10 minutes

Juice of 2 oranges
30ml (2 tbsps) lemon juice
30ml (2 tbsps) white wine vinegar
1 tbsp sugar
1 tbsp tomato purée
15ml (1 tbsp) light soy sauce
½ tsp salt
1 tbsp cornflour
30ml (2 tbsps) water
Pinch of red food dye if desired

Combine orange and lemon juice, sugar, vinegar, tomato purée, soy sauce, salt, and red dye (if desired). Place in wok and heat gently. Blend cornflour with water, and stir into sauce. Bring to boil and simmer for 3 minutes, stirring continuously. Good with fish, pork, wontons and spring rolls.

Mango Chutney

PREPARATION TIME: 5 minutes

COOKING TIME: 20 minutes

1 can mango slices, drained and chopped
1 cup white wine vinegar
2 cloves garlic, crushed
1 tsp chopped root ginger
½ tsp five-spice powder
1 tsp salt
60g (2oz) sugar
30g (1oz) sultanas
Pinch chilli powder (optional)

Place vinegar, salt, garlic, ginger, five-spice powder, chilli powder and sugar in wok. Bring to boil, and simmer, uncovered, for 10 minutes. Add mango and sultanas, and simmer gently until sauce is thick. Serve cool as an accompaniment to a curry.

Left: Sweet and Sour Sauce (top), Mango Sauce (centre) and Chilli Sauce (bottom). Tomato Chutney (right) and Mango Chutney (bottom).

Ginger Sauce

PREPARATION TIME: 5 minutes

COOKING TIME: 10 minutes

1 tbsp grated root ginger
30ml (2 tbsps) light soy sauce
15ml (1 tbsp) Chinese wine, or dry sherry
1 tsp sugar
1 tsp cornflour
30ml (2 tbsps) water
15ml (1 tbsp) oil

Heat wok, add oil and gently fry ginger. Mix together soy sauce, wine and sugar. Blend cornflour with water, and add to soy/wine mixture. Pour into wok and bring to the boil. Simmer for 3 minutes, stirring continuously. Strain through sieve. Good with sea-food, pork, beef and crab rolls.

Brinjal Bhartha

PREPARATION TIME: 20 minutes

COOKING TIME: 30 minutes

SERVES: 4 people as a vegetable

2 large aubergines, cut into 2·5cm (1") slices
45ml (3 tbsps) oil
150ml (¼ pint) water
1 onion, peeled and chopped finely
2 green chillies, seeds removed, and sliced very thinly
½ tsp ground cumin
Pinch of sugar
10ml (2 tsps) lemon juice
Salt

Slice aubergines and sprinkle with salt. Set aside for 15 minutes. Rinse off salt and dry with absorbent paper. Heat wok and add 30ml (2 tbsps) of oil. Fry aubergines in hot oil, browning lightly on both sides. When all oil has been absorbed, add water. Cover and simmer for 15 minutes, or until aubergines are soft. Remove from wok, and drain. Heat remaining oil in wok. Add onion, ground cumin and chillies, and cook gently for 5 minutes without colouring onion. Meanwhile skin aubergines, and push flesh through a sieve or blend. Add onion mixture to aubergines. Add sugar, lemon juice and salt to taste.

Special Fried Rice

PREPARATION TIME: 15 minutes

COOKING TIME: 20 minutes

SERVES: 4 people

2 cups boiled rice
115g (4oz) prawns or shrimps, shelled and de-veined
225g (8oz) Chinese barbecued pork, or cooked ham, diced or cut into small pieces
115g (4oz) bean-sprouts
115g (4oz) frozen peas
2 spring onions, sliced diagonally
15ml (1 tbsp) light soy sauce
5ml (1 tsp) dark soy sauce
30ml (2 tbsps) peanut oil
Salt
Pepper

Pancake
2 eggs, beaten
Salt

Garnish
2 spring onion flowers (trim spring onions, slice lengthways, leaving one end intact and leave in cold water in refrigerator until curling).

Heat wok and add 15ml (1 tbsp) of peanut oil. Roll oil around surface. Make pancake by mixing beaten eggs with a pinch of salt and 5ml (1 tsp) of oil. Add egg mixture to wok, and move wok back and forth so that the mixture spreads over the surface. When lightly browned on the underside, turn over and

This page: Special Fried Rice (top) and Ginger Sauce (bottom).

Facing page: Brinjal Bhartha (top) and Okra and Tomatoes (bottom).

cook on other side. Set aside to cool. Heat remaining oil in wok. When hot, add spring onions and peas and cook, covered, for 2 minutes. With a slotted spoon, remove and set aside. Re-heat oil and add rice. Stir continuously over a low heat until rice is heated through. Add soy sauces and mix well. Add peas, spring onions, bean-sprouts, meat, prawns, and salt and pepper to taste. Mix thoroughly. Serve hot, garnished with pancake and spring onion flowers. The pancake may be sliced very finely and mixed in if desired.

Julienne of Vegetables

PREPARATION TIME: 20 minutes
COOKING TIME: 15 minutes
SERVES: 4 people as a vegetable

2 medium onions, peeled and cut into matchstick strips
2 carrots, scraped and cut into matchstick strips
1 parsnip, scraped and cut into matchstick strips
2 sticks celery, cut into matchstick strips
1 turnip, peeled and cut into matchstick strips
15ml (1 tbsp) oil
30ml (2 tbsps) water
15g (½oz) butter
Salt
Pepper

Prepare vegetables. Heat wok and add oil. Stir-fry vegetable strips over gentle heat for 5 minutes. Add water and salt to taste, and increase heat. Cook for a further 5 minutes over high heat. Drain any liquid from wok. Add butter and freshly-ground black pepper, and toss to coat well.

Mango Sauce

PREPARATION TIME: 5 minutes
COOKING TIME: 20 minutes

1 can sliced mangoes
150ml (¼ pint) malt vinegar
½ tsp garam masala
1 tsp grated root ginger
1 tbsp sugar
5ml (1 tsp) oil
Salt

Heat wok and add oil. Add garam masala and ginger, and cook for 1 minute. Add undrained mangoes, vinegar and sugar, and salt to taste. Simmer, uncovered, for 15 minutes. Blend and push through a sieve. Good with chicken, beef and spring rolls.

Stir-Fried Vegetable Medley

PREPARATION TIME: 20 minutes
COOKING TIME: 10 minutes
SERVES: 4 people as a vegetable

2 carrots, cut into flowers (slice strips out lengthways to produce flowers when cut across into rounds)
1 can baby sweetcorn, drained
2 cups broccoli florets (slit stems to ensure quick cooking)
1 onion, peeled and sliced in julienne strips
2 sticks celery, with tough strings removed, sliced diagonally in half-moon shapes
1 courgette, sliced diagonally
1 clove garlic, crushed
15ml (1 tbsp) light soy sauce
¼ tsp finely-grated ginger
30ml (2 tbsps) oil
Salt
Pepper

Prepare all ingredients before starting to cook. Heat wok and add oil. Add ginger, garlic, onion, carrots, broccoli and courgette, and toss in oil for 2-3 minutes. Add celery and baby sweetcorn, and toss 1-2 minutes longer. Season with soy sauce, and salt and pepper if desired. Add cornflour to thicken vegetable juices if necessary.

Ratatouille

PREPARATION TIME: 30 minutes
COOKING TIME: 30 minutes
SERVES: 4 people as a vegetable

1 aubergine, sliced into 2·5cm (1") slices
2 courgettes, sliced diagonally
4 tomatoes, chopped roughly
2 onions, peeled and quartered
1 red pepper, cored, seeds removed, and chopped roughly
1 green pepper, cored, seeds removed, and chopped roughly
3 cloves garlic, crushed
1 tsp dry basil
60ml (4 tbsps) olive oil
Salt
Pepper

Slice aubergine and sprinkle with salt. Leave for 20 minutes. Rinse in water, and dry on absorbent paper. Chop roughly. Heat wok and add oil. Add onions, garlic and basil. Cover and cook gently until onion is soft but not coloured. Add peppers, courgettes and aubergine. Cover and fry gently for 15 minutes stirring occasionally. Add tomatoes and salt and pepper to taste and cook covered for a further 10 minutes. Serve hot or chilled.

Tomato Chutney

PREPARATION TIME: 5 minutes
COOKING TIME: 15 minutes

4-6 ripe tomatoes, chopped roughly
1 cup white wine vinegar
½ tsp garam masala
1 tsp salt
30g (1oz) sugar
2 green chillies, seeds removed, and chopped finely
1 tsp chopped root ginger
Pinch chilli powder (optional)

Place tomatoes, vinegar, salt, garam masala, chilli powder, chillies, sugar and ginger in wok. Bring to boil, and simmer, uncovered, for 15 minutes or until thickened. Serve cool as an accompaniment to a curry.

Okra and Tomatoes

PREPARATION TIME: 15 minutes
COOKING TIME: 10 minutes
SERVES: 4 people as a vegetable

225g (8oz) okra, sliced into 1·5cm (½") pieces
1 onion, peeled and chopped
2 tomatoes, chopped
1 red chilli, seeds removed, and sliced finely
¼ tsp turmeric
¼ tsp chilli powder
½ tsp garam masala
15ml (1 tbsp) oil or ghee
150ml (¼ pint) water
Salt

Heat wok and add oil or ghee. When hot, add turmeric, chilli powder and garam masala, and fry for 30 seconds. Add onion, okra and red chilli, and stir-fry for 3 minutes. Add tomatoes, water, and salt to taste, and cook uncovered for 5 minutes or until sauce thickens.

Chilli Sauce

PREPARATION TIME: 5 minutes
COOKING TIME: 10 minutes

4 tbsps tomato purée
½ tsp chilli powder
30ml (2 tbsps) Chinese wine, or dry sherry
30ml (2 tbsps) white wine vinegar
150ml (¼ pint) water
1 tsp cornflour
2 cloves garlic, crushed
1 tsp grated root ginger
15ml (1 tbsp) dark soy sauce
15ml (1 tbsp) sesame oil

Ratatouille (right) and Julienne of Vegetables (bottom right).

Heat wok and add oil. When hot, add garlic and ginger and fry for 1 minute. Mix together tomato purée, chilli powder, wine, soy sauce and vinegar. Add to wok. Blend cornflour with 15ml (1 tbsp) of water and add to wok with remaining water. Bring to the boil and simmer for 3 minutes, stirring continuously. Good with sea-food, beef, vegetables and spring rolls.

Indian Cuisine

Bhoona Gosht

PREPARATION TIME: 15 minutes
COOKING TIME: 1 hour

1 onion, peeled and chopped
45ml (3 tblsp) oil or
40g (1½oz) ghee
2.5cm (1 inch) cinnamon stick
6 small cardamoms
1 bayleaf
6 cloves
3 large cardamoms
5ml (1 tsp) ginger paste
5ml (1 tsp) garlic paste
450g (1lb) braising steak or lamb or beef, cubed
10ml (2 tsp) ground coriander
10ml (2 tsp) ground cumin
5ml (1 tsp) chilli powder
1.25ml (¼ tsp) turmeric powder
4 fresh tomatoes or
1 small can of tomatoes
250ml (8 fl oz) water
Salt to taste
2 green chillis, chopped
2 sprigs fresh coriander, chopped

Fry onions in oil or ghee until light brown. Add cinnamon, cardamoms, cloves, bayleaf. Fry for one minute. Add ginger and garlic pastes and fry for further one minute. Add meat and sprinkle with coriander, cumin, chilli and turmeric powder. Mix well and fry for 10 minutes. Add chopped fresh or canned tomatoes. Season with salt and add water. Cover and cook for 40-45 minutes on low heat, until meat is tender. Add chopped chillis and coriander.

Kofta Curry

PREPARATION TIME: 15 minutes
COOKING TIME: 30 minutes

450g (1lb) lean minced meat
2.5ml (½ tsp) ginger paste
5ml (1 tsp) garlic paste
1 egg
5ml (1 tsp) ground garam masala
2.5ml (½ tsp) chilli powder

For sauce
1 onion, peeled and finely chopped
30-40g (about 1½oz) ghee or
2-3 tblsp oil
6 small cardamoms
2.5cm (1 inch) stick cinnamon
6 cloves
1 bayleaf
5ml (1 tsp) garlic paste
5ml (1 tsp) ginger paste
5ml (1 tsp) ground cumin
2.5ml (½ tsp) chilli powder
1.25ml (¼ tsp) turmeric powder
10ml (2 tsp) ground coriander
Salt to taste
150ml (¼ pint) plain, natural yogurt or
30ml (2 tblsp) tomato purée
600ml (1 pint) water

For garnish
2 green chillis, chopped
2 sprigs fresh coriander, finely chopped

Mix mince with ginger, garlic paste and egg. Add garam masala and chilli powder. Mix well and make 16-20 even-sized balls. Keep in a cool place.

Sauce
Fry onion in ghee for 4 minutes until light golden brown. Add cardamom, cinnamon, cloves and bayleaf. Stir fry for one minute. Add garlic and ginger pastes and fry for another minute. Sprinkle with cumin, chilli, turmeric and coriander. Stir well and add yogurt or tomato purée. If yogurt is used, fry the spices until yogurt is dry and oil separates (5-7 minutes). Add water, cover and bring to boil. Add salt. Slide mince balls one at a time into the saucepan. Shake the saucepan to settle the mince balls; do not stir or else the balls will break. Cover and gently simmer for 20 minutes. Garnish with chopped chillis and coriander leaves. Serve with rice or chapatis.

Keema Methi

PREPARATION TIME: 30 minutes
COOKING TIME: 30 minutes

1 onion, peeled and chopped
25g (1oz) ghee or
2 tblsp oil
4 small green cardamoms
2.5cm (1 inch) cinnamon stick
1 bayleaf
6 cloves
5ml (1 tsp) ginger paste
5ml (1 tsp) garlic paste
450g (1lb) lamb or beef mince
5ml (1 tsp) powder chilli
10ml (2 tsp) ground coriander
10ml (2 tsp) ground cumin
1.25ml (¼ tsp) turmeric powder
150ml (¼ pint) natural yogurt
Salt to taste
1 bunch fresh methi leaves, stemmed and chopped or
15ml (1 tblsp) dry kasuri methi leaves

Fry onion in oil till just tender. Add cardamoms, cinnamon stick, bayleaf, cloves and fry for one minute. Add ginger and garlic pastes and cook for one minute. Add mince. Stir the mixture and sprinkle with chilli, coriander, cumin and turmeric. Mix well and cook for 5 minutes. Add well-stirred yogurt and fresh methi leaves or dry methi. Cover and cook till liquid is absorbed. Season with salt. Serve with chapati or rice.

Dam Ke Kebab
(BAKED KEBAB)

PREPARATION TIME: 30 minutes
COOKING TIME: 1 hour

450g (1lb) lean mince
5ml (1 tsp) ginger paste
5ml (1 tsp) garlic paste
2 green chillis, ground or finely chopped
10ml (2 tsp) garam masala
150ml (¼ pint) natural yogurt
1.25ml (¼ tsp) meat tenderiser
2 sprigs green coriander, finely chopped
5ml (1 tsp) chilli powder
2 eggs
1 onion, peeled, thinly sliced and fried until crisp
Salt to taste
2 green chillis, chopped
Juice of 1 lemon
Oil

Mix together the mince, ginger, garlic paste, ground chilli, garam masala, yogurt, meat tenderiser, half finely chopped coriander, chilli powder, eggs and crisply fried onions. Mix well and season with salt. In a well-greased baking tray, spread mince to 1cm (½ inch) thick. Brush with oil and bake in a preheated oven Gas Mark 4 (180°C or 350°F) for 20 minutes. Reduce temperature to Gas Mark 2 (150°C or 300°F) for a further 20-30 minutes or until liquid has evaporated. Cut into 5cm (2 inch) squares. Garnish with chopped chillis and remaining fresh coriander leaves. Sprinkle with lemon juice before serving.

Boti-Kebab

PREPARATION TIME: 6 minutes and 3-4 hours to marinate
COOKING TIME: 30 minutes

450g (1lb) shoulder or leg of lamb, cut into bite size pieces
5ml (1 tsp) ginger paste
5ml (1 tsp) garlic paste
5ml (1 tsp) chilli powder
1.25ml (¼ tsp) salt
30ml (2 tblsp) malt vinegar
Juice of ½ a lemon
Oil for basting
1 green pepper
1 large onion, cut into 2.5cm (1 inch) pieces
3-4 tomatoes, quartered
6-8 skewers

Mix meat with ginger, garlic, chilli powder, salt and vinegar and leave to marinate for 3-4 hours. Sprinkle with lemon juice and rub spices well into meat; keep aside. Heat grill. Thread pieces of meat onto skewers, alternating them with tomato, green pepper and onion. Brush with oil and cook under grill for 3-4 minutes turning frequently to cook all sides. Sprinkle with lemon juice and serve with mixed salad.

Facing page: Bhoona Gosht (top left), Kofta Curry (centre right) and Keema Methi (bottom).

coriander and cumin. Fry for 5-6 minutes. Add water and salt to taste. Cook covered for 30-40 minutes on low heat until meat is cooked and liquid has evaporated. Add onion rings. They can be fried in a little extra oil if desired. Stir the meat, cover and cook for a further 10-15 minutes. The onions should be tender. Sprinkle with lemon juice and add green chillis and coriander. This is a dry dish. Serve with pulas or puri.

Meat Palak
(SPINACH MEAT)

PREPARATION TIME: 30-45 minutes

COOKING TIME: 1 hour

50-75g (2-3oz) ghee or
60ml (4 tblsp) oil
1 medium onion, peeled and chopped
1 bayleaf
2.5cm (1 inch) cinnamon stick
4 small cardamoms
6 cloves
2.5cm (1 inch) of root ginger, crushed
3-4 cloves of garlic, crushed
450g lamb or beef, cubed
150ml (¼ pint) natural yogurt
5ml (1 tsp) chilli powder
2.5ml (½ tsp) turmeric powder
10ml (2 tsp) ground coriander
2 green chillis, chopped (optional)
2 sprigs of fresh green coriander, chopped (optional)
450g (1lb) leaf spinach, boiled and puréed (or canned or frozen spinach purée)
Salt to taste

Heat oil and fry onions until light golden brown. Add bayleaf, cinnamon, cardamoms and cloves. Fry for one minute. Add ginger and garlic paste and fry for a further minute. Add meat and yogurt and sprinkle with chilli, turmeric and coriander. Season with salt and cook with the lid on until moisture evaporates (30-40 minutes). Add puréed or canned spinach, mix well and cook for a further 15-20 minutes on a low heat until oil rises to the top. Garnish with chopped chilli and coriander.

Chicken Masala

PREPARATION TIME: 10 minutes and marinate overnight

COOKING TIME: 40-50 minutes plus 10 minutes

1½kg (3lb) chicken, cut into 8-10 pieces
30ml (2 tblsp) oil
150ml (¼ pint) natural yogurt
5ml (1 tsp) ginger
5ml (1 tsp) garlic
10ml (2 tsp) ground cumin
10ml (2 tsp) garam masala powder
5ml (1 tsp) salt
Juice of 1 lemon
10ml (2 tsp) ground black pepper
10ml (2 tsp) ground mango
5ml (1 tsp) kasuri methi
5ml (1 tsp) dry mint powder

Marinate chicken pieces overnight in a well-mixed marinade made from the oil, yogurt, ginger, garlic, cumin, garam masala, salt and lemon juice. Roast chicken with marinade wrapped in baking foil in preheated oven Gas Mark 5 (190°C or 375°F) for 40-50 minutes. Save the liquid and mix with the black pepper, mango powder, methi and mint. Mix well and keep aside. Cool chicken slightly and cut into bite size pieces. Pour in the liquid mixture and mix well. Transfer onto baking tray and bake for further 10-15 minutes until the chicken pieces are dry. Serve as snack or with cocktails.

Meat Madras

PREPARATION TIME: 10 minutes

COOKING TIME: 1 hour

1 onion, peeled and chopped
40g (1½oz) ghee or
45ml (3 tblsp) oil
2cm (¾ inch) cinnamon stick
4 small cardamoms
2 bayleaves
6 fresh curry leaves
6 cloves
15ml (1 tblsp) fresh or desiccated coconut
1.25ml (¼ tsp) fenugreek seeds, crushed
3 cloves garlic, peeled and chopped
2.5cm (1 inch) ginger root, peeled and sliced
450g (1lb) braising steak or lamb, cut into cubes
Salt to taste
5ml (1 tsp) chilli powder
10ml (2 tsp) ground coriander
10ml (2 tsp) ground cumin
1.25ml (¼ tsp) turmeric powder
4 tomatoes, quartered
250ml (8 fl oz) water
2 green chillis, quartered (optional)
2 sprigs fresh green coriander, chopped
Juice of 1 lemon

Fry onion in ghee or oil until just tender (2-3 minutes). Add cinnamon, cardamoms, bayleaves, curry leaves, cloves, coconut, fenugreek seeds, garlic and ginger and fry for 1-2 minutes. Add meat and fry for 3 minutes. Sprinkle with chilli, coriander, cumin, and turmeric. Stir well and add water. Cover and cook for 20 minutes. Add salt, and cook for a further 15-20 minutes until liquid has evaporated. Add tomatoes, chilli and coriander leaves. Cover and cook for 10 minutes on a low heat. Sprinkle with lemon juice. Serve with parathas.

Chicken Tomato

PREPARATION TIME: 30 minutes

COOKING TIME: 40-50 minutes

1 onion, peeled and chopped
45ml (3 tblsp) oil or
40g (1½oz) ghee
2.5cm (1 inch) cinnamon stick
1 bayleaf
6 cloves
6 green cardamoms
2.5cm (1 inch) ginger root, peeled and sliced
4 cloves garlic, peeled and chopped
1½kg (3lb) roasting chicken cut into 8-10 pieces
5ml (1 tsp) chilli powder
5ml (1 tsp) ground cumin
5ml (1 tsp) ground coriander
400g (14oz) canned tomatoes, crushed
5ml (1 tsp) salt
2 sprigs fresh coriander leaves, chopped
2 green chillis, halved

Fry onion for 2 minutes in oil or ghee. Add the cinnamon, bayleaf, cloves, cardamoms for 1 minute then add ginger and garlic. Fry for half a minute. Add chicken pieces. Sprinkle with chilli powder, cumin, coriander. Fry for 2-3 minutes, add crushed tomatoes. Season with salt and add chopped green coriander and chillis. Stir chicken to mix well. Cover and cook for 40-45 minutes until chicken is tender.

Chicken Tandoori

Although the true taste of tandoori (clay oven) is not achieved, a very good result is obtained by baking in an oven.

PREPARATION TIME: 10 minutes and marinate overnight

COOKING TIME: 30-40 minutes

1½kg (3lb) chicken, cut into 8-10 clean pieces
5ml (1 tsp) garlic paste
5ml (1 tsp) ginger paste
5ml (1 tsp) ground black pepper
5ml (1 tsp) paprika
1.25ml (¼ tsp) red food colouring
5ml (1 tsp) salt
45ml (3 tblsp) malt vinegar
Juice of 1 lemon
150ml (¼ pint) natural yogurt
5ml (1 tsp) dry mint powder
Oil
1 lemon, cut into wedges

Mix all the ingredients, apart from the lemon wedges and oil, and marinate chicken pieces in it overnight. Arrange chicken pieces on baking tray. Brush with oil and bake in preheated oven Gas Mark 5 (190°C or 375°F) for 40 minutes, turning them over to achieve even baking. Bake until dry and well browned. Serve with lemon wedges.

Korma

PREPARATION TIME: 15 minutes

COOKING TIME: 40-50 minutes

40g (1½oz) ghee or
45ml (3 tblsp) oil
1 medium onion, peeled and thinly sliced
2.5cm (1 inch) cinnamon stick
6 cloves
6 small cardamoms
1 bayleaf
5ml (1 tsp) small black whole cumin seeds
10ml (2 tsp) ginger paste
5ml (1 tsp) garlic paste
450g (1lb) shoulder of lamb, cubed
5ml (1 tsp) chilli powder
5ml (1 tsp) ground coriander
10ml (2tsp) ground cumin
1.25 ml (¼ tsp) turmeric powder
150ml (¼ pint) natural yogurt
175ml (6 fl oz) water
Salt to taste
2 sprigs fresh coriander, chopped
2 green chillis, halved
15ml (1 tblsp) ground almonds

Facing page: Chicken Tandoori (top), Chicken Tomato (centre right) and Chicken Masala (bottom).

Fry onion in oil or ghee until golden brown. Add cinnamon, cloves, cardamoms, bayleaf and black cumin. Fry for 1 minute, add ginger and garlic paste. Stir for half a minute. Add meat and sprinkle with chilli, coriander, cumin and turmeric powders. Mix well and add yogurt. Cover and cook for 10-15 minutes, occasionally stirring the mixture. Add water, salt to taste and cover. Cook on low temperature for 30-40 minutes or until meat is tender. Korma should have medium-thick gravy. Add ground almonds, green chillis and coriander leaves. Add extra water if needed. Serve with rice or chapatis.

Pork Vindaloo

PREPARATION TIME: 15 minutes
COOKING TIME: 1-1¼ hours

1 large onion, peeled and chopped
50g (2oz) ghee or
45ml (3 tblsp) oil
2.5cm (1 inch) cinnamon stick
6 cloves
6 green cardamoms
5ml (1 tsp) ginger paste
5ml (1 tsp) garlic paste
450g (1lb) lean pork, cut into cubes
45ml (3 tblsp) malt vinegar
5ml (1 tsp) chilli powder
5ml (1 tsp) ground cumin
10ml (2 tsp) ground coriander
30ml (2 tblsp) tamarind pulp
10ml (2 tsp) tomato purée
10ml (2 tsp) sugar
Water
2 sprigs fresh green coriander leaves, chopped
1-2 green chillis, chopped
Salt to taste
15ml (1 tblsp) oil for tempering
6-8 curry leaves

Fry onion in ghee or oil until light brown. Add cinnamon stick, cloves and cardamoms. Fry for half a minute. Add ginger, garlic pastes and pork and fry for 5 minutes or until liquid from pork is dry. Add vinegar and chilli, cumin, coriander, tamarind pulp, tomato purée and sugar. Cover and cook for 10-15 minutes. Add a little water if mixture is dry. Sprinkle with coriander leaves and chopped chilli. Cook on low heat for 30-40 minutes or until pork is tender. The dish should have a rich gravy. Heat tempering oil and add the curry leaves. When leaves turn crisp and dark, pour the flavoured oil over the curry and cover. Mix well before serving. Serve with boiled rice.

Chicken Dhansak

PREPARATION TIME: 20 minutes
COOKING TIME: 40-50 minutes

50g (2oz) ghee or
45ml (3 tblsp) oil
1 onion, peeled and chopped
4 cloves garlic, chopped
2.5cm (1 inch) ginger paste
1.25ml (¼ tsp) turmeric powder
5ml (1 tsp) chilli powder
10ml (2 tsp) ground cumin
10ml (2 tsp) ground coriander
4 green cardamoms, ground
8 peppercorns, ground
2.5cm (1 inch) cinnamon stick, ground
2 tomatoes, quartered
1½kg (3lb) chicken cut into 10-12 pieces, ribcage discarded
65g (2½oz) toor daal (yellow lentil), washed in few changes of water
65g (2½oz) moong daal, washed in few changes of water
65g (2½oz) masoor daal (red lentil) washed in few changes of water
1 medium aubergine cut into 1cm (½ inch) cubes
100g (4oz) red pumpkin, peeled and cut into 2.5cm (1 inch) cubes
4 sprigs fresh methi leaves, chopped or
100g (¼lb) spinach leaves, chopped
2 sprigs fresh coriander leaves, chopped
45ml (3 tblsp) oil or melted ghee
900ml (1½ pints) water
Salt to taste
15ml (1 tblsp) brown sugar or grated jaggery
30ml (2 tblsp) tamarind pulp concentrate
1 onion, sliced and fried brown
1 lemon, sliced

Heat the ghee or oil in a deep pan and fry onion until light brown. Add garlic, ginger, turmeric, chilli, cumin, coriander, ground cardamom, peppercorn and cinnamon stick and stir fry for 1 minute. Add tomatoes and cook for 2-3 minutes. Add chicken and cook until liquid from chicken has evaporated (10-15 minutes). Add lentil, moong and toor daals,

This page: Chicken Makhani (left), Dum Ka Murgh (centre) and Chicken Dhansak (right).

Facing page: Goan Curry (top) and Pork Vindaloo (bottom).

has evaporated. Add tamarind pulp, yogurt, turmeric, black pepper, cumin, coriander, sugar, coconut and salt to taste. Mix well, cover and cook for 20-30 minutes. Add water if the mixture is too dry. Add green coriander and chilli. Cover and cook for 20-25 minutes or until pork is tender. The dish should have a smooth gravy. Serve with plain boiled rice.

Dum Ka Murgh
(WHOLE CHICKEN OR CHICKEN JOINTS)

The recipe can be used for both jointed and whole chicken.

PREPARATION TIME: 30 minutes
COOKING TIME: 1 hour

1 onion, finely minced
10ml (2 tsp) ground coriander
5ml (1 tsp) chilli powder
1.25ml (¼ tsp) turmeric powder
15ml (1 tblsp) tomato purée
5ml (1 tsp) ginger paste
5ml (1 tsp) garlic paste
2.5ml (½ tsp) salt
150ml (¼ pint) natural yogurt
1½kg (3lb) chicken, cut into 8-10 pieces
Oil

Mix onion, coriander, chilli, turmeric, tomato, ginger, garlic and salt with yogurt. Rub the mixture onto the chicken pieces. Brush with oil and bake in an oven at Gas Mark 5 (190°C or 375°F) for 50 minutes – 1 hour, brushing with oil frequently, until the liquid has evaporated and chicken is cooked. For whole chicken, bake with above spices wrapped in baking foil for 1½ to 1¾ hours, then evaporate the liquid.

aubergine, pumpkin, methi leaves and fresh coriander. Mix well and add the water. Add salt. Cover and cook on low heat until chicken is tender (20-30 minutes). Remove from heat and take chicken pieces out. Mash daal with the aid of a masher or beat with an egg whisk until daal blends with water to form a smooth, greenish gravy. Add chicken and sprinkle with sugar or jaggery and tamarind pulp. Cover and cook for 10 minutes. Before serving, a little extra water may be used to thin down the gravy if it is thick. Before serving, garnish dhansak with onion rings and lemon slices. Serve with rice.

Goan Curry

PREPARATION TIME: 20 minutes
COOKING TIME: 1 hour

50g (2oz) ghee or
45ml (3 tblsp) oil
1 large onion, peeled and chopped
1 bayleaf
2.5cm (1 inch) cinnamon stick
5 green cardamoms
6 cloves
7.5ml (1½ tsp) garlic paste
5ml (1 tsp) ginger paste
8 curry leaves
450g (1lb) lean pork, cut into cubes
15ml (1 tblsp) tamarind pulp
150ml (¼ pint) natural yogurt
1.25ml (¼ tsp) turmeric powder
5ml (1 tsp) ground black pepper
5ml (1 tsp) ground cumin
5ml (1 tsp) ground coriander
2.5ml (½ tsp) sugar
15ml (1 tblsp) desiccated coconut
Salt to taste
150ml (¼ pint) water
2 sprigs fresh coriander, chopped
2 green chillis, chopped

Heat oil and fry onion until golden brown. Add bayleaf, cinnamon, cardamoms, cloves, garlic, ginger and curry leaves and fry for 1-2 minutes. Add pork and fry for 5-7 minutes or until liquid from pork

Chicken Makhani
(BUTTER CHICKEN)

PREPARATION TIME: 20 minutes
COOKING TIME: 1 hour

150ml (¼ pint) natural yogurt
5ml (1 tsp) ginger paste
5ml (1 tsp) salt
1.25ml (¼ tsp) red or orange food colouring
1-1½ kg (3lb) chicken, cut into 8-10 pieces with skin removed
Oil
50g (2oz) butter
2.5cm (1 inch) cinnamon stick

6 cloves
6 green cardamoms
1 bayleaf
150ml (¼ pint) soured cream
1.25ml (¼ tsp) saffron, crushed
150ml (¼ pint) single cream
Salt to taste
10ml (2 tsp) ground almonds
1.25ml (¼ tsp) cornflour
15ml (1 tblsp) water

Mix yogurt, ginger paste, salt and red colouring and rub into chicken. Let it marinate overnight. Place in an ovenproof dish and brush with oil. Bake in oven Gas Mark 5 (190°C or 375°F) for 40-50 minutes. Save the liquid, if any. In a saucepan melt butter and fry cinnamon, cloves, cardamoms and bayleaf for 1 minute. Add soured cream and chicken liquid. Add crushed saffron, and single cream. Cover and simmer gently for 5-6 minutes. Add chicken pieces and adjust seasoning. Add ground almonds. Dissolve cornflour in water and add to the chicken. Let it thicken. Cover and simmer for 3-4 minutes. Remove from heat. Serve with nan.

Malabari Chicken

PREPARATION TIME: 20 minutes
COOKING TIME: 40-50 minutes

1 large onion, peeled and chopped
50g (2oz) ghee or
45ml (3 tblsp) oil
2.5cm (1 inch) cinnamon stick
6 green cardamoms
6 cloves
1 bayleaf
5ml (1 tsp) ginger paste
5ml (1 tsp) garlic paste
1½kg (3lb) chicken cut into 10-12 pieces
5ml (1 tsp) chilli powder
5ml (1 tsp) ground cumin
5ml (1 tsp) ground coriander
150ml (¼ pint) natural yogurt
5ml (1 tsp) salt
15g (½oz) coconut milk or cream
15g (½oz) blanched and sliced almonds
15g (½oz) raisins
120ml (4 fl oz) water
30ml (2 tblsp) evaporated milk
2 sprigs fresh coriander leaves, chopped (optional)
2 green chillis, chopped (optional)
225-240g (7-8oz) pineapple chunks

Fry onion in ghee or oil until tender (3-4 minutes). Add cinnamon, cardamoms, cloves, bayleaf and fry for one minute.

Then add ginger and garlic paste. Stir fry for half a minute. Add chicken. Stir and cook for 2-3 minutes. Sprinkle with chilli, cumin and coriander. Stir and mix well. Add yogurt and salt. Cover and cook for 10 minutes or until yogurt is dry and oil separates. Add coconut cream, almonds, raisins and water. Cover and cook for 20-30 minutes. Add evaporated milk and cook for 5 minutes. Add coriander leaves and green chillis and pineapple chunks. Mix gently and cook for another 5 minutes. Malabari chicken is a moist curry with thick, rich sauce. It is served with pulao rice.

Chicken Tikka

PREPARATION TIME: 10 minutes
COOKING TIME: 30 minutes

150ml (¼ pint) natural yogurt
5ml (1 tsp) chilli powder
10ml (2 tsp) ginger and garlic paste
10ml (2 tsp) garam masala powder
2.5ml (½ tsp) salt
1.25ml (¼ tsp) red food colouring
1½kg (3lb) chicken, cut into 6cm (2½ inch) pieces
Juice of 1 lemon
Oil
1 lemon cut into wedges

Mix yogurt with chilli powder, ginger and garlic, garam masala, salt and red food colouring. Pour over chicken pieces and mix well. Sprinkle with lemon juice. Mix well. Line the grill with baking foil. Arrange chicken pieces. Brush with oil and cook them under the grill for 4-5 minutes on each side. Brush with oil occasionally. Serve with wedges of lemon and a crisp lettuce salad.

Maach Bhaja
(MACKEREL FRY)

PREPARATION TIME: 10 minutes
COOKING TIME: 15 minutes

2 large mackerel, gutted and cut into 2.5cm (1 inch) thick slices
5ml (1 tsp) chilli powder
5ml (1 tsp) turmeric powder
5ml (1 tsp) salt
Oil for frying
Lemon juice

Wash fish thoroughly. Drain and dry well. Sprinkle with chilli powder, turmeric and salt. Rub in well. Heat oil and fry fish, a few pieces at a time, 3-4 minutes on each side. Drain on kitchen paper. Serve with lemon juice sprinkled over fish.

Sprat Fry

PREPARATION TIME: 10 minutes
COOKING TIME: 15-20 minutes

225g (8oz) cleaned sprats, washed and dried
1.25ml (¼ tsp) turmeric
5ml (1 tsp) chilli powder
5ml (1 tsp) salt
Oil for deep frying
Lemon juice

Rub sprats well with turmeric, chilli powder and salt. Gently heat oil and fry fish for 6-8 minutes, a few at a time, until crisp. Drain on kitchen paper. Sprinkle with lemon juice and serve.

Masala Fish
(WHOLE FRIED FISH)

PREPARATION TIME: 10 minutes
COOKING TIME: 15 minutes

5ml (1 tsp) ginger paste
5ml (1 tsp) garlic paste
5ml (1 tsp) salt
3 sprigs fresh coriander leaves, crushed
2 green chillis, crushed
5ml (1 tsp) ground black pepper
1.25ml (¼ tsp) turmeric powder
10ml (2 tsp) water
4-6 herring or rainbow trout, gutted, washed and dried
Oil
Lemon slices

Make 3 slanting slits on fish. Mix together the ginger, garlic, salt, coriander, chilli, ground pepper and turmeric powder. Add the water. Rub spices over fish and inside the cuts. Bake under grill for 10-15 minutes, brushing with oil and turning the fish occasionally until cooked. Garnish with lemon slices.

This page: Malabari Chicken (top) and Chicken Tikka (bottom).

Facing page: Main dish – top to bottom – Masala Fish, Maach Bhaja, Sprat Fry and Cod Roe Fry.

Cod Curry

PREPARATION TIME: 15 minutes
COOKING TIME: 20 minutes

50g (2oz) ghee or
45ml (3 tblsp) oil
1 large onion, peeled and chopped
2.5cm (1 inch) cinnamon stick
1 bayleaf
5ml (1 tsp) ginger paste
5ml (1 tsp) garlic paste
5ml (1 tsp) chilli powder
5ml (1 tsp) ground cumin
5ml (1 tsp) ground coriander
1.25ml (¼ tsp) turmeric powder
150ml (¼ pint) natural yogurt or
225g (8oz) canned tomatoes, crushed
1-2 green chillis, chopped
2 sprigs fresh coriander leaves, chopped
5ml (1 tsp) salt
450g (1lb) cod cutlets or fillet, cut into 5cm (2 inch) pieces

Melt ghee or oil and fry onion until golden brown. Add cinnamon, bayleaf, ginger and garlic paste. Fry for 1 minute. Add chilli, cumin, coriander powder and turmeric powder. Fry for 1 minute. Add either yogurt or tomatoes, chopped green chilli and fresh coriander leaves. Add salt and cover. Simmer for 2-3 minutes. Add 150ml (¼ pint) water. Bring to boil. Add cod. Cover and cook gently for 15-18 minutes. If tomato is used do not add any water. Serve with rice.

Prawn Curry

PREPARATION TIME: 15 minutes
COOKING TIME: 20 minutes

1 large onion, peeled and chopped
50g (2oz) ghee or
45ml (3 tblsp) oil
2.5cm (1 inch) cinnamon stick
6 green cardamoms
6 cloves
1 bayleaf
5ml (1 tsp) ginger paste
5ml (1 tsp) garlic paste
5ml (1 tsp) chilli powder
5ml (1 tsp) ground cumin
5ml (1 tsp) ground coriander
2.5ml (½ tsp) salt
1 green pepper, chopped into 1cm (½ inch) pieces
225-270g (8-10oz) canned tomatoes, crushed
450g (1lb) large prawns, peeled
2 green chillis, chopped
2 sprigs fresh coriander leaves, chopped

Prawn Curry (left), Cod Curry (centre), and Fish Kebab (right).

Fry onions in oil until just tender (3-4 minutes). Add cinnamon, cardamoms, cloves and bayleaf. Fry for 1 minute and then add ginger and garlic paste. Add chilli, cumin, coriander and salt. Fry for half a minute. Add chopped green pepper and tomatoes, then bring to boil. Add prawns, cover, and bring to boil. Cook for 10-15 minutes. Add chopped green coriander leaves and chopped chillis. Serve with plain boiled rice.

Cod Roe Fry

PREPARATION TIME: 5 minutes
COOKING TIME: 15 minutes

225g (½lb) soft cod roes
1.25ml (¼ tsp) turmeric powder
5ml (1 tsp) chilli powder
2.5ml (½ tsp) salt
15ml (1 tblsp) plain flour

For batter
100g (4oz) baisen flour, sifted
1.25ml (¼ tsp) salt
1 egg, beaten
Water
Oil for deep frying

Put cod roes in a mixing bowl. Sprinkle with spices, one at a time, and add salt. Rub well so as to coat the roes thoroughly, then roll them in flour and keep aside. In a separate bowl mix baisen flour, salt, egg and a little water to make a smooth coating batter. Heat oil gently. Fry roes, a few at a time, well coated in batter, until crisp and golden. Drain on kitchen paper and serve hot.

Fish Kebab

PREPARATION TIME: 20 minutes
COOKING TIME: 15 minutes

275g (10oz) whiting or coley fillet
1 onion, peeled and chopped
2.5cm (1 inch) ginger root, peeled and finely chopped
1 green chilli, finely chopped
2 sprigs fresh coriander leaves, finely chopped
1 egg, beaten
10ml (2 tsp) garam masala powder
Salt to taste
5ml (1 tsp) ground black pepper
Juice of 1 lemon
Oil

Boil fish in water for 8-10 minutes. Cool and drain. Remove skin and bones and mash fish flesh. Add chopped onion, ginger, chilli, coriander leaves, egg, garam masala, salt, black pepper and lemon juice. Beat or grind into smooth paste. Make 10-12 equal-sized portions and pat each portion into a flat burger shape. Heat oil and shallow fry on each side for 3-4 minutes. Serve with onion salad.

Facing page: Farfalle with Beef, Mushroom and Soured Cream (top), Tagliatelle Carbonara (centre left) and Pasta Spirals with Spinach and Bacon (bottom).

Tortiglioni alla Puttanesca

PREPARATION TIME: 10 minutes
COOKING TIME: 15 minutes
SERVES: 4 people

300g (10oz) tortiglioni, spiral pasta
200g (7oz) can plum tomatoes, drained
45g (1½oz) can anchovy fillets, drained
30ml (2 tbsps) olive oil
2 cloves garlic, crushed
½ tsp basil
Pinch chilli powder
115g (4oz) black olives, stoned and chopped
2 tbsps chopped parsley
Salt
Pepper

Chop tomatoes and remove seeds, and chop anchovies. Cook pasta in plenty of boiling salted water for 10 minutes, or until tender but still firm. Rinse in hot water, and drain. Pour into a warmed bowl. Meanwhile, heat oil in pan, add garlic, chilli powder and basil, and cook for 1 minute. Add tomatoes, parsley, olives and anchovies, and cook for a few minutes. Season with salt and pepper. Pour sauce over pasta, and mix together thoroughly. Serve immediately.

Pasta Spirals with Spinach and Bacon

PREPARATION TIME: 15 minutes
COOKING TIME: 15 minutes

300g (10oz) pasta spirals
225g (8oz) spinach
90g (3oz) bacon
1 clove garlic, crushed
1 small red chilli
½ small red pepper
1 small onion
45ml (3 tbsps) olive oil
Salt and pepper

Wash spinach, remove stalks and cut into thin shreds. Core and seed pepper, and slice half finely. Peel onion and chop finely. Remove rind from bacon and chop: Remove seeds from chilli, and slice thinly. Cook pasta spirals in plenty of boiling salted water for 10 minutes, or until tender but still firm. Drain. Meanwhile, heat oil in pan, and add garlic, onion, bacon, chilli and red pepper. Fry for 2 minutes, add spinach, and fry for a further 2 minutes, stirring continuously. Season with salt and pepper to taste. Toss with pasta spirals. Serve immediately.

Tagliatelle Carbonara

PREPARATION TIME: 10 minutes
COOKING TIME: 15 minutes

300g (10oz) tagliatelle
30g (1oz) butter or margarine
115g (4oz) streaky bacon rashers, rind removed, and shredded
15ml (1 tbsp) olive oil
60ml (4 tbsps) single cream
Pinch of paprika
60g (2oz) Parmesan cheese, grated
2 eggs
Salt and pepper

This page: Tortiglioni alla Puttanesca.

Purée tomatoes, and push through a sieve into a saucepan. Add oregano, salami and olives, and heat gently. Add salt and pepper to taste. Meanwhile, cook spaghetti in plenty of boiling salted water for 10 minutes, or until tender but still firm. Drain well. Heat olive oil and freshly-ground black pepper in the pan used to cook the spaghetti. Add spaghetti, and pour the sauce over. Toss well. Serve immediately with pecorino cheese.

Farfalle with Creamy Cheese Sauce

PREPARATION TIME: 5 minutes

COOKING TIME: 15 minutes

SERVES: 4 people

300g (10oz) farfalle (pasta butterflies /bows)
15g (½ oz) butter or margarine
15g (½ oz) flour
300ml (½ pint) milk
60g (2oz) Gruyère or Cheddar cheese, grated
½ tsp French mustard
1 tbsp grated Parmesan cheese

Heat butter in pan. Stir in flour and cook for 1 minute. Remove from heat and gradually stir in milk. Return to heat and stir continuously. Boil for 3 minutes. Stir in Gruyère or Cheddar cheese, and mustard; do not reboil. Meanwhile, cook the pasta in lots of boiling salted water for 10 minutes, or until tender but still firm. Rinse in hot water and drain well. Pour over cheese sauce, and toss. Top with a sprinkling of Parmesan cheese. Serve immediately.

Pasta with Tomato and Yogurt Sauce

PREPARATION TIME: 5 minutes

COOKING TIME: 40 minutes

300g (10oz) pasta shells
45ml (3 tbsps) plain yogurt
15g (½oz) butter or magarine
15g (½oz) flour
150ml (¼ pint) beef stock
400g (14oz) can plum tomatoes
1 bay leaf
Sprig of thyme
Parsley stalks
Salt and pepper

Melt butter in a pan. Stir in the flour, and pour in the stock gradually. Add undrained tomatoes, bay leaf, thyme and parsley stalks. Season with salt and pepper. Bring to the boil, and simmer for 30 minutes. Strain and push through a sieve, adjust seasoning, and re-heat. Meanwhile, cook pasta in plenty of boiling salted water for 10 minutes, or until tender but still firm. Rinse in hot water and drain well. Place in warmed serving dish; pour over tomato sauce, then yogurt. (Yogurt may be marbled through tomato sauce). Serve immediately.

Penne with Chilli Sauce

PREPARATION TIME: 40 minutes

COOKING TIME: 20 minutes

300g (10oz) penne
1 clove garlic, crushed
1 onion, peeled and chopped
450g (1lb) ripe tomatoes
1 aubergine
1 red chilli
30ml (2 tbsps) oil
60g (2oz) pecorino cheese, grated

Trim and cut aubergine into 1.5cm (½ inch) slices, and salt lightly. Leave for 30 minutes. Rinse and wipe dry with absorbent paper. Meanwhile, heat oil in a frying-pan over a moderate heat, and fry garlic and onion until lightly coloured. Peel and seed tomatoes, and chop roughly. Seed chilli, and chop finely. Cut aubergine roughly and add to onion. Fry together for 5 minutes. Add tomatoes and chilli, and mix well. Simmer sauce gently, uncovered, for 5 minutes, stirring occasionally. Meanwhile, cook pasta in lots of boiling salted water for 10 minutes, or until tender but still firm, stirring occasionally. Rinse in hot water, and drain well. Place in a warmed serving dish. Add hot sauce and toss well. Serve immediately with side dish of grated pecorino cheese.

Penne with Chilli Sauce (above) and Pasta with Tomato and Yogurt Sauce (left).

Pasta Spirals with Creamy Parsley Sauce

PREPARATION TIME: 5 minutes

COOKING TIME: 15 minutes

300g (10oz) pasta spirals
30g (1oz) butter or margarine
15g (½oz) flour
300ml (½ pint) milk
1 tbsp chopped parsley
1 tbsp lemon juice, or ½ tbsp vinegar

Heat butter in pan; when melted, stir in flour. Cook for 1 minute. Remove from heat, and gradually stir in milk. Return to heat, and stir continuously until boiling. Cook for 2 minutes. Meanwhile, cook pasta spirals in lots of boiling salted water for 10 minutes, or until tender but still firm. Rinse in hot water, and drain well. Just before serving, add lemon juice and parsley to sauce, and pour over pasta. Serve immediately.

Spaghetti Bolognese

PREPARATION TIME: 10 minutes

COOKING TIME: 1 hour 15 minutes

300g (10oz) spaghetti
30g (1oz) butter or margarine
15ml (1 tbsp) olive oil
2 onions, peeled and chopped finely
225g (8oz) minced beef
1 carrot, scraped and chopped finely
1 115g (4oz) can tomato purée
300ml (½ pint) brown stock
30ml (2 tbsps) sherry
Salt and pepper
Parmesan cheese, grated

Heat the butter and oil in a pan and fry the onions and carrot slowly until soft. Increase heat and add the minced beef. Fry for a few minutes, then stir, cooking until meat is browned all over. Add the tomato purée, salt and pepper to taste, and the stock, and simmer gently for about ¾ hour, until the mixture thickens, stirring occasionally. Add 2 tablespoons sherry, and cook for a further 5 minutes. Meanwhile, place the spaghetti in lots of boiling salted water, and cook for 10 minutes, or until tender but still firm. Drain. Serve with Bolognese sauce on top, and sprinkle with Parmesan cheese.

Fish Ravioli

PREPARATION TIME: 30 minutes

COOKING TIME: 30 minutes

OVEN: 180°C, 350°F, Gas Mark 4

SERVES: 4 people

Dough:
275g (9oz) strong plain flour
Pinch of salt
3 eggs

Filling:
225g (8oz) sole fillets, or other flat fish, skinned and boned
2 tbsps breadcrumbs
2 eggs, beaten
1 spring onion, finely chopped
1 slice of onion
1 slice of lemon
6 peppercorns
1 bay leaf
1 tbsp lemon juice
300ml (½ pint) water

Lemon sauce:
30g (1oz) butter or margarine
30g (1oz) flour
300ml (½ pint) strained cooking liquid from fish
2 tbsps double cream
2 tbsps lemon juice
Salt
Pepper

To make filling:
Pre-heat oven. Wash and dry fish. Place in oven-proof dish with slice of onion, slice of lemon, peppercorns, bay leaf, lemon juice and water. Cover and cook in oven for 20 minutes. Remove fish from liquid, and allow to drain. Strain liquid, and set aside. When fish is cool, beat with the back of a spoon to a pulp. Add eggs, breadcrumbs and spring onion, and salt and pepper to taste. Mix well.

This page: Fish Ravioli.

Facing page: Spaghetti Bolognese (top) and Pasta Spirals with Creamy Parsley Sauce (bottom).

To make dough:
Sift flour into a bowl. Make a well in the centre, and add the eggs. Work the flour and eggs together with a spoon, and then knead by hand, until a smooth dough is formed. Leave to rest for 15 minutes. Lightly flour board, and roll out dough thinly into a rectangle. Cut dough in half. Shape the filling into small balls, and set them about 4cm (1½") apart on one half of the dough. Place the other half on top, and cut with a ravioli cutter or small pastry cutter. Seal the edges. Cook in batches in a large, wide pan with plenty of boiling salted water until tender – about 8 minutes. Remove carefully with a perforated spoon. Meanwhile, make sauce.

To make sauce:
Melt butter in pan. Stir in flour, and cook for 30 seconds. Draw off heat, and gradually stir in liquid from cooked fish. Return to heat and bring to boil. Simmer for 4 minutes, stirring continuously. Add cream and mix well. Season to taste. Remove from heat, and gradually stir in lemon juice. Do not reboil.

Pour sauce over ravioli and serve immediately.

Ravioli with Ricotta Cheese

PREPARATION TIME: 30 minutes
COOKING TIME: 20 minutes
SERVES: 4 people

Dough:
275g (9oz) strong plain flour
Pinch of salt
3 eggs

Filling:
30g (1oz) butter or margarine
225g (8oz) ricotta cheese
60g (2oz) Parmesan cheese, grated
1 egg yolk
2 tbsps chopped parsley
Salt
Pepper

Tomato sauce:
400g (14oz) can plum tomatoes
1 tsp basil
15ml (1 tbsp) olive oil
30g (1oz) bacon
15ml (1 tbsp) double cream
1 small onion, peeled and chopped
1 bay leaf
1 tbsp flour
Salt
Pepper

To make filling:
Beat the butter to a cream, add egg yolk, and blend well. Beat ricotta cheese to a cream, and add butter-egg mixture gradually until smooth. Add Parmesan cheese and parsley, and salt and pepper to taste. Set aside.

To make dough:
Sift flour in a bowl. Make a well in the centre, and add the eggs. Work flour and eggs together with a spoon, and then knead by hand, until a smooth dough is formed. Leave to rest for 15 minutes. Lightly flour board, and roll dough out thinly into a rectangle. Cut dough in half. Shape the filling into small balls and set them about 4cm (1½") apart on one half of the dough. Place the other half on top and cut with a ravioli cutter or small pastry cutter. Seal the edges. Cook in batches in a large, wide pan with plenty of boiling salted water until tender – about 8 minutes. Remove carefully with a perforated spoon. Meanwhile, make sauce.

To make sauce:
Heat oil, and fry bacon and onion until golden. Add bay leaf and basil, and stir in flour. Cook for 1 minute, draw off heat, and add tomatoes gradually, stirring continuously. Add salt and pepper to taste. Return to heat and bring to boil. Cook for 5 minutes, then push through a sieve. Stir in cream, and adjust seasoning.

Pour sauce over ravioli. Serve immediately.

Wholemeal Spaghetti with Walnut and Parsley

PREPARATION TIME: 10 minutes
COOKING TIME: 10 minutes

300g (10oz) wholemeal spaghetti
4 tbsps parsley
2 tbsps walnuts
60ml (4 tbsps) olive oil
2 cloves garlic, peeled
Salt and pepper
3 tbsps grated Parmesan or pecorino cheese

Fry garlic gently in oil for 2 minutes. Set oil aside to cool. Wash parsley and remove stalks. Finely chop parsley, walnuts and garlic in a food processor with a metal blade, or in a blender. When chopped well, add cooled oil in a thin stream. Turn mixture into a bowl, mix in grated cheese, and add salt and pepper to taste. Cook spaghetti in a large pan of boiling salted water for 10 minutes or until tender but still firm. Drain. Serve with sauce tossed through. Serve with a side dish of grated Parmesan or pecorino cheese.

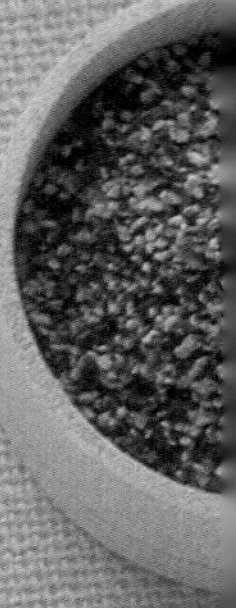

Tagliatelle with Bacon and Tomato Sauce

PREPARATION TIME: 15 minutes
COOKING TIME: 15 minutes

300g (10oz) red tagliatelle
1 onion, peeled and finely chopped
6 rashers of bacon, rind removed, and cut into strips

400g (14oz) can plum tomatoes, drained, seeds removed, and chopped roughly
2 tbsps chopped parsley
15ml (1 tbsp) olive oil
1 tbsp dry basil
60g (2oz) pecorino cheese, grated
Salt and pepper

Heat oil in pan. Add onion and bacon, and cook over gentle heat until onion is transparent but not coloured. Add parsley, basil and tomato. Simmer gently for 5 minutes, stirring occasionally. Add salt and pepper to taste. Meanwhile, cook tagliatelle in a large pan with plenty of boiling salted water. Cook for about 10 minutes, unil tender but still firm. Drain and return to the pan. Add sauce and toss through. Serve with grated pecorino cheese.

Tagliatelle with Bacon and Tomato Sauce (left) and Wholemeal Spaghetti with Walnut and Parsley (below).

Pasta Shells with Gorgonzola Cheese Sauce

PREPARATION TIME: 5 minutes

COOKING TIME: 15 minutes

175g (6oz) gorgonzola cheese
60ml (4 tbsps) milk
30g (1oz) butter or margarine
45ml (3 tbsps) double cream
300g (10oz) shell pasta
Salt
Parmesan cheese, grated

Heat gorgonzola cheese, milk and butter gently in a pan. Stir to a sauce with a wooden spoon. Stir in double cream. Add salt if necessary. Meanwhile, cook shells in plenty of boiling salted water for 10 minutes, or until shells are tender but still firm. Drain, shaking colander to remove excess water. Add shells to hot sauce and toss to coat well. Serve immediately with grated Parmesan cheese on the side.

Meat Ravioli

PREPARATION TIME: 30 minutes

COOKING TIME: 30 minutes

SERVES: 4 people

Dough:
275g (9oz) strong plain flour
Pinch of salt
3 eggs

Filling:
60g (2oz) butter or margarine
225g (8oz) minced beef
115g (4oz) cooked spinach, chopped
2 tbsps breadcrumbs
2 eggs, beaten
75ml (5 tbsps) red wine
1 onion, peeled and grated
1 clove garlic, crushed
Salt
Pepper

Sauce:
400g (14oz) can plum tomatoes
1 small onion, peeled and grated
1 small carrot, diced finely
1 bay leaf
3 parsley stalks
Salt
Pepper

60g (2oz) Parmesan cheese, grated

To make filling:
Heat butter in pan. Add garlic and onion, and fry gently for 1 minute. Add minced beef, and fry until browned. Add red wine, and salt and pepper to taste, and cook uncovered for 15 minutes. Strain juices and reserve them for sauce. Allow to cool. Add breadcrumbs, chopped spinach, and beaten eggs to bind. Adjust salt and pepper to taste.

To make dough:
Sift flour in a bowl. Make a well in the centre and add the eggs. Work flour and eggs together with a spoon, then knead by hand, until a smooth dough is formed. Leave dough to rest for 15 minutes. Lightly flour board, and roll out dough thinly into a rectangle. Cut dough in half. Shape the filling into small balls, and set them about 4cm (1½") apart on one half of the dough. Place the other half on top, and cut with a ravioli cutter or small pastry cutter. Seal the edges. Cook in batches in a large, wide pan with plenty of boiling salted

This page: Pasta Shells with Gorgonzola Cheese Sauce (top) and Spaghetti Amatriciana (bottom).

Facing page: Spinach Ravioli (top) and Meat Ravioli (bottom).

water until tender – about 8 minutes. Remove carefully with a perforated spoon. Meanwhile, make sauce.

To make sauce:
Put all ingredients in a saucepan. Add juice from cooked meat, and bring to boil. Simmer for 10 minutes. Push through a sieve, and return smooth sauce to pan. Adjust seasoning.

Put ravioli in a warm dish and cover with tomato sauce. Serve immediately, with grated Parmesan cheese.

Spaghetti Amatriciana

PREPARATION TIME: 10 minutes
COOKING TIME: 20 minutes

300g (10oz) spaghetti
1 onion, peeled and chopped finely
6 rashers bacon, rind removed, and cut into strips
1 400g (14oz) can plum tomatoes, drained, seeds removed, and chopped roughly
1 red chilli, seeds removed, and chopped finely
30ml (2 tbsps) olive oil
60g (2oz) pecorino cheese, grated

Heat oil in pan. Add onion and bacon, and cook over gentle heat until onion is soft but not coloured. Drain off surplus fat. Add tomato and chilli. Stir. Simmer gently for 5 minutes, stirring occasionally. Meanwhile, cook spaghetti in lots of boiling salted water for about 10 minutes, or until tender but still firm. Drain and return to pan. Add sauce and stir through. Serve with grated pecorino cheese.

Carrettiera with Pasta Rings

PREPARATION TIME: 5 minutes
COOKING TIME: 15 minutes
SERVES: 4 people

300g (10oz) pasta rings
200g (7oz) can tuna fish, flaked
115g (4oz) mushrooms, cleaned and sliced
30g (1oz) butter or margarine

Heat butter in pan, and cook mushrooms. Add tuna to warm through. Meanwhile, cook pasta in plenty of boiling salted water for 10 minutes, or until tender but still firm. Rinse under hot water. Drain well. Pour over mushroom and tuna, and toss together. Serve immediately.

Hare Sauce with Wholemeal Spaghetti

PREPARATION TIME: 10 minutes
COOKING TIME: 1 hour 15 minutes
SERVES: 4 people

300g (10oz) wholemeal spaghetti
225g (8oz) hare, cut into small pieces
115g (4oz) streaky bacon rashers, rind removed, and diced
2 onions, peeled and sliced
1 clove garlic, crushed
30ml (2 tbsps) olive oil
½ tsp oregano
15g (½ oz) flour
150ml (¼ pint) red wine

Heat oil in heavy pan. Lightly brown hare pieces. Remove hare pieces and put aside. Add onion, bacon, garlic and oregano to oil,

Ravioli with Ricotta Cheese (above), Brasciole with Tagliatelle (right) and Hare Sauce with Wholemeal Spaghetti (top right).

and fry until lightly coloured. Draw off heat, and stir in flour with a metal spoon. Return to heat and cook for 2 minutes. Remove from heat, and add wine, and return to heat, stirring until boiling. Add hare, cover pan, and simmer gently for about 1 hour, until hare is tender. Add salt and pepper to taste. When sauce is ready, cook spaghetti in lots of boiling salted water for about 10 minutes, or until tender but still firm. Rinse in hot water, and drain. Serve with hare sauce on top. Serve immediately.

Brasciole with Tagliatelle

PREPARATION TIME: 15 minutes
COOKING TIME: 25 minutes
SERVES: 4 people

225g (8oz) tagliatelle
4 veal steaks
4 thin slices ham
4 tbsps grated Parmesan cheese
30g (1oz) butter or margarine
400g (14oz) can plum tomatoes
Salt
Pepper

Push tomatoes and their juice through a sieve. Pound veal steaks out thinly. Place a slice of ham on the top of each steak. Sprinkle a tablespoon of the Parmesan cheese over each steak, and freshly-ground black pepper. Roll up, and tie gently with string at each end and in the middle. Heat butter in a pan, and add veal rolls. Cook gently until lightly browned all over. Add puréed tomatoes, and cover. Cook for 15 minutes. Meanwhile, cook tagliatelle in plenty of boiling salted water for 10 minutes, or until tender but still firm. Rinse in hot water, and drain. Cut veal rolls into 2.5cm (1") rounds. Toss tagliatelle together with tomato sauce, and top with veal rolls and grated Parmesan cheese. Serve immediately.

Tagliatelle with Garlic and Oil

PREPARATION TIME: 5 minutes

COOKING TIME: 10 minutes

300g (10oz) green tagliatelle
150ml (¼ pint) olive oil
3 cloves garlic, crushed
2 tbsps chopped parsley
Salt and pepper

Cook the tagliatelle in lots of boiling salted water for 10 minutes, or until tender but still firm, stirring occasionally. Meanwhile, make the sauce. Heat the oil in a pan and, when warm, add peeled, crushed garlic. Fry gently until golden brown. Add chopped parsley, and salt and pepper to taste. Drain tagliatelle. Add sauce, and toss to coat well. Serve hot.

Farfalle with Tomato Sauce

PREPARATION TIME: 10 minutes

COOKING TIME: 30 minutes

300g (10oz) farfalle
2 400g (14oz) can plum tomatoes, chopped
15ml (1 tbsp) olive oil
1 onion, peeled and sliced
2 cloves garlic, crushed
½ tsp dry basil
Salt and pepper
2 tbsps chopped fresh basil or chopped parsley
Parmesan cheese, grated

Heat oil in a deep pan. Add garlic and onion, and cook until softened. Add dry basil, and cook for 30 seconds. Add undrained tomatoes; season with salt and pepper. Bring to the boil, reduce heat, and simmer, uncovered, for about 20 minutes, or until sauce is reduced by half. Meanwhile, cook the pasta in a large pan of boiling salted water, until tender but still firm – about 10 minutes. Rinse in hot water, and drain well. Put sauce through a sieve, and stir in the fresh parsley or basil. Toss sauce through pasta. Serve with grated Parmesan cheese. Serve immediately.

This page: Tagliatelle with Garlic and Oil (top) and Spaghetti with Basil Sauce (Pesto) (bottom).

Facing page: Pasta Shells with Mushroom Sauce (top) and Farfalle with Tomato Sauce (bottom).

Pasta Shells with Mushroom Sauce

PREPARATION TIME: 5 minutes

COOKING TIME: 15 minutes

300g (10oz) pasta shells
225g (8oz) button mushrooms
30g (1oz) butter or margarine
15g (½oz) flour
600ml (1 pint) milk
Salt and pepper

Rinse the mushrooms and chop them roughly. Melt butter in a saucepan and add mushrooms. Fry for 5 minutes, stirring occasionally. Stir in the flour and cook for 1 minute. Draw off the heat, and add milk gradually, stirring continuously. Bring to the boil and cook for 3 minutes. Season with salt and pepper. Meanwhile, cook the pasta shells in lots of boiling salted water for 10 minutes, or until tender but still firm. Rinse in hot water and drain well. Place in a warmed serving dish, and pour over mushroom sauce. Serve immediately.

CINNAMON
PEPPER

Tortellini

PREPARATION TIME: 30 minutes

COOKING TIME: 15 minutes

SERVES: 4 people

Dough:

300g (10oz) strong plain flour
Pinch of salt
3 eggs
15ml (1 tbsp) water
15ml (1 tbsp) oil

Filling:

1 cooked chicken breast, finely diced
2 spinach leaves, stalks removed, cooked and chopped finely
30g (1oz) ham, finely diced
1 tbsp grated Parmesan cheese
30g (1oz) cream cheese
1 egg, beaten
Salt
Pepper

Sauce:

300ml (½ pint) single cream
60g (2oz) mushrooms, cleaned and sliced
60g (2oz) Parmesan cheese, grated
1 tbsp chopped parsley
Salt
Pepper

To make filling:
Beat the cream cheese until soft and smooth. Add chicken, ham, spinach and Parmesan cheese, and mix well. Add egg gradually, and salt and pepper to taste. Set aside.

To make dough:
Sift flour and salt onto a board. Make a well in the centre. Mix water, oil and lightly-beaten egg together, and gradually pour into well, working in the flour with the other hand, a little at a time. Continue until the mixture comes together in a firm ball of dough. Knead on a lightly-floured board for 5 minutes, or until smooth and elastic. Put into a bowl, cover with a cloth, and let stand for 15 minutes. Roll dough out on a lightly-floured board as thinly as possible. Using a 5cm (2") cutter, cut out rounds. Put ½ teaspoon of filling into the centre of each round. Fold in half, pressing edges together firmly. Wrap around forefinger, and press ends together. Cook in batches in a large pan, in plenty of boiling salted water for about 10 minutes until tender, stirring occasionally.

To make sauce:
Meanwhile, gently heat cream in a pan. Add mushrooms, Parmesan cheese, parsley, and salt and pepper to taste. Gently cook for 3 minutes.

Toss sauce together with tortellini. Serve immediately, sprinkled with parsley.

Pasta Shells with Walnuts and Cream Cheese

PREPARATION TIME: 5 minutes

COOKING TIME: 15 minutes

300g (10oz) pasta shells
15ml (1 tbsp) olive oil
1 clove garlic, crushed
1 tbsp oregano
30g (1oz) butter or margarine
60ml (4 tbsps) milk
115g (4oz) packet cream cheese
115g (4oz) walnuts, chopped very finely (keep a few aside to decorate)
60ml (4 tbsps) cream
Parmesan cheese, grated
Salt and pepper

Heat oil in a pan. Add crushed garlic and oregano, and cook for 1 minute. Add butter, cream cheese, chopped walnuts, and salt and pepper to taste. Stir, and leave to simmer gently for 5 minutes. Meanwhile, cook pasta shells in plenty of boiling salted water for 10 minutes, or until shells are tender but still firm. Drain in a colander, shaking to remove any trapped water. Put into warmed serving dish. Remove sauce from heat; add cream, and stir. Pour over shells, and toss to coat evenly. Garnish with walnut halves. Serve immediately with grated Parmesan cheese.

Spinach Ravioli

PREPARATION TIME: 30 minutes

COOKING TIME: 20 minutes

SERVES: 4 people

Dough:

275g (9oz) strong plain flour
Pinch of salt
3 eggs

Filling:

225g (8oz) cooked spinach
30g (1oz) butter or margarine
60g (2oz) Parmesan cheese, grated
Pinch of grated nutmeg
1 egg, beaten
Salt
Pepper

Cream cheese sauce:

30g (1oz) butter or margarine
15g (½ oz) flour
300ml (½ pint) milk
1 tsp French mustard
2 tbsps grated Parmesan cheese

To make filling:
Chop spinach and heat in a pan. Beat butter into spinach. Add Parmesan cheese, nutmeg, and salt and freshly-ground black pepper to taste. Finally mix in the beaten egg well.

To make dough:
Sift flour in a bowl; make a well in the centre, and add the eggs. Work flour and eggs together with a spoon, and then knead by hand, until a smooth dough is formed. Leave to rest for 15 minutes. Lightly flour board, and roll out dough thinly into a rectangle. Cut dough in half. Shape the filling into small balls, and set them about 4cm (1½") apart on one half of the dough. Place the other half on top, and cut with a ravioli cutter or small pastry cutter. Seal the edges.

Cook in batches in a large, wide pan with plenty of boiling salted water until tender – about 8 minutes. Remove carefully with a perforated spoon. Meanwhile, make sauce.

To make sauce:
Heat butter in pan. Stir in flour and cook for 30 seconds. Draw off heat, and stir milk in gradually. Bring to boil and simmer for 3 minutes, stirring continuously. Add mustard, and half the cheese, and seasoning to taste.

Pour sauce over ravioli, and serve immediately with remaining cheese sprinkled over the top.

Spaghetti with Basil Sauce (Pesto)

PREPARATION TIME: 5 minutes

COOKING TIME: 15 minutes

300g (10oz) spaghetti
2 cups fresh basil leaves

Tagliatelle with Butter and Cheese (top) and Pasta Shells with Walnuts and Cream Sauce (right).

2 tbsps pine nuts
75ml (5 tbsps) olive oil
2 cloves garlic, peeled
Salt and pepper
3 tbsps Parmesan or pecorino cheese, grated

Garnish:
Fresh basil

Wash basil and remove leaves, discarding stems. Heat 1 tablespoon of oil over a low temperature. Add garlic and pine nuts, and cook until pine nuts are a light golden brown. Drain. Finely chop basil leaves, pine nuts and garlic in a food processor with a metal blade, or in a blender. When smooth, add remaining oil in a thin stream, blending continuously. Turn mixture into a bowl; mix in grated cheese, and add salt and pepper to taste. Meanwhile, cook spaghetti in a large pan of boiling salted water for 10 minutes, or until just tender. Drain, and serve with basil sauce tossed through. Serve with side dish of grated cheese. Garnish with fresh basil.

Penne with Spicy Chilli Sauce

PREPARATION TIME: 15 minutes
COOKING TIME: 40 minutes

300g (10oz) penne
1 onion, peeled and chopped
400g (14oz) can plum tomatoes
2 red chillies, seeds removed, and chopped finely
2 cloves garlic, crushed
15ml (1 tbsp) olive oil
115g (4oz) bacon, rind removed, and diced
60g (2oz) pecorino cheese, grated
2 spring onions, chopped
Salt and pepper

Garnish:
4 spring onions (cut into 5cm [2 inch] strips. Keeping one end intact, cut into strips. Soak in chilled water until the flower has opened).

Chop tomatoes, removing seeds by straining juice. Heat oil in a pan, and fry garlic, onion and bacon gently for 10 minutes. Add tomato, chillies and chopped spring onions, and half the cheese, and salt and pepper to taste. Cook, uncovered, for 20 minutes. 10 minutes before sauce is ready, cook the penne in lots of boiling salted water for 10 minutes, or until tender but still firm. Rinse under hot water, and drain well. Put into a warmed serving dish, and toss together with half the sauce. Pour remaining sauce on top, and garnish with spring onion flowers, and remaining cheese if desired. Serve at once.

Tagliatelle with Butter and Cheese

PREPARATION TIME: 5 minutes
COOKING TIME: 15 minutes

300g (10oz) tagliatelle – 100g (3½oz) each yellow, green and red tagliatelle
90g (3oz) butter
60g (2oz) Parmesan cheese, grated
90ml (6 tbsps) double cream
Salt and pepper

Cook the tagliatelle in a large pan of boiling salted water for 10 minutes, or until just tender. Drain. Meanwhile, put the butter and cream in a pan, and stir over a low heat until butter has melted. Remove from heat, add half the grated cheese, and salt and pepper to taste. Stir into tagliatelle and serve immediately with remaining cheese on top.

Pasta Spirals with Peas and Tomatoes

PREPARATION TIME: 5 minutes
COOKING TIME: 15 minutes

300g (10oz) pasta spirals
350g (12oz) peas
1 tsp sugar
400g (14oz) can plum tomatoes, chopped
1 tsp basil
60g (2oz) butter or margarine
Salt and pepper

Cook pasta spirals in plenty of boiling salted water for 10 minutes or until tender. Drain. Meanwhile, cook peas in boiling water with a pinch of salt and a teaspoon of sugar. Melt butter in a pan. Add basil, and cook for 30 seconds. Add tomatoes and their juice. When hot, add pasta spirals and peas, and salt and pepper to taste. Toss together. Serve immediately.

Spaghetti with Egg, Bacon and Mushroom

PREPARATION TIME: 10 minutes
COOKING TIME: 15 minutes

300g (10oz) spaghetti
225g (8oz) mushrooms, sliced
115g (4oz) bacon rashers, rind removed, and diced
60g (2oz) butter or margarine
60g (2oz) Parmesan cheese, grated
2 eggs, hard-boiled and chopped finely
1 tbsp chopped parsley
Salt and pepper

Melt half the butter in a frying-pan. Add mushrooms and bacon, and cook for 10 minutes over a moderate heat, until bacon is crisp. Meanwhile, cook the spaghetti in lots of boiling salted water until tender but still firm – about 10 minutes. Drain. Return to pan. Add rest of butter, salt and lots of freshly-ground black pepper, and the mushroom and bacon. Toss together. Serve with hard-boiled eggs sprinkled on top, and parsley if desired. Serve grated Parmesan cheese separately.

This page: Pasta Spirals with Peas and Tomatoes.

Facing page: Spaghetti with Egg, Bacon and Mushroom (top) and Penne with Spicy Chilli Sauce (bottom).

Baked and Grilled Pasta

Cannelloni

PREPARATION TIME: 10 minutes
COOKING TIME: 1 hour
OVEN: 180°C, 350°F, Gas Mark 4
SERVES: 4 people

12 cannelloni shells
2 tbsps Parmesan cheese, grated
15ml (1 tbsp) oil

Filling:
450g (1lb) minced beef
15ml (1 tbsp) olive oil
1 onion, peeled and chopped
2 cloves garlic, crushed
225g (8oz) packet frozen spinach, thawed
½ tsp oregano
½ tsp basil
1 tsp tomato purée
60ml (4 tbsps) cream
1 egg, lightly beaten
Salt and pepper to taste

Tomato sauce:
15ml (1 tbsp) olive oil
1 onion, peeled and chopped
1 clove garlic, crushed
400g (14oz) can plum tomatoes
2 tbsps tomato purée
Salt
Pepper

Béchamel sauce:
1 slice of onion
3 peppercorns
1 small bay leaf
300ml (½ pint) milk
30g (1oz) butter or margarine
30g (1oz) flour
Salt
Pepper

To make filling:
Heat oil in pan, and fry garlic and onion gently until soft and transparent. Add meat and cook, stirring continuously, until well browned. Drain off any fat, add tomato purée, basil and oregano, and cook gently for 15 minutes. Add spinach, egg and cream, and salt and pepper to taste. Cook cannelloni in a large pan of boiling salted water for 15-20 minutes, until tender. Rinse in hot water and drain. Fill carefully with meat mixture, using a piping bag with a wide, plain nozzle, or a teaspoon.

To make tomato sauce:
Heat oil in pan. Add onion and garlic, and cook gently until transparent. Push tomatoes through a sieve, and add to the pan with tomato purée and salt and pepper to taste. Bring to boil, and then simmer for 5 minutes. Set aside.

To make Béchamel sauce:
Put milk in pan with onion, peppercorns and bay leaf. Heat gently for 1 minute, taking care not to boil, and set aside to cool for 5 minutes. Strain. Melt butter in

This page: Prawn Crespelle.

Facing page: Cannelloni with Tomato and Cheese (top) and Cannelloni (bottom).

Crespelle with Tuna (left) and Crespelle with Chicken and Tongue (below).

pan. Remove from heat and stir in flour. Gradually add cool milk, and bring to boil, stirring continuously, until sauce thickens. Add seasoning.

Spread tomato sauce on the base of an oven-proof dish. Lay cannelloni on top, and cover with Béchamel sauce. Sprinkle with grated cheese, and bake in a moderate oven for 30 minutes. Serve immediately.

Prawn Crespelle

PREPARATION TIME: 40 minutes
COOKING TIME: 30 minutes
OVEN: 190°C, 375°F, Gas Mark 5
SERVES: 4 people

12 crespelle:
3 eggs
115g (4oz) plain flour
Pinch of salt
200ml (8 fl oz) water
8ml (½ tbsp) olive oil
30g (1oz) butter or margarine, melted

Filling:
225g (8oz) prawns or shrimps, washed, peeled and de-veined
30g (1oz) butter or margarine
15g (½oz) flour
300ml (½ pint) milk
Juice of 1 lemon
Salt
Pepper

Garnish:
1 lemon, cut into slices

To make crespelle:
Sift flour with a pinch of salt. Break eggs into a bowl, and whisk. Add flour gradually, whisking all the time until the mixture is smooth. Add water, and stir in well. Add oil, and mix. Cover bowl with damp cloth, and leave in a cool place for 30 minutes.
Heat a crêpe pan or 19cm (7″) frying pan. Grease lightly with melted butter, and put a tablespoon of batter in the centre. Roll the pan to coat the surface evenly. Fry until crespelle is brown on the underside. Loosen edge with a palette knife; turn over and brown the other side. Stack and wrap in a clean cloth until needed.

To make filling:
Heat butter in pan; stir in flour, and cook for 1 minute. Remove from heat, and gradually stir in milk. Return to heat, and bring to the boil. Allow to simmer for 3 minutes. Stir in lemon juice and add salt and pepper to taste. Add half the sauce to prawns. Place one crespelle in an oven-proof dish, and add a spoon of prawn mixture. Cover with one crespelle, and repeat, finishing with a crespelle on top. Bake in a pre-heated oven for 10 minutes. When ready to serve, cover with remaining sauce. Garnish with lemon slices. Serve immediately.

Crespelle with Chicken and Tongue

PREPARATION TIME: 40 minutes
COOKING TIME: 20 minutes
OVEN: 230°C, 450°F, Gas Mark 8
SERVES: 4 people

10 crespelle:
3 eggs
115g (4oz) plain flour
Pinch of salt
200ml (8 fl oz) water
8ml (½ tsp) olive oil
30g (1oz) butter or margarine, melted

Filling:
115g (4oz) chicken, cooked and shredded
115g (4oz) tongue, cut into strips

Béchamel sauce:
30g (1oz) butter or margarine
15g (½oz) flour
300ml (½ pint) milk
To infuse:
4 peppercorns
1 bay leaf
Slice of onion
Salt
Pepper

To make crespelle:
Sift flour with a pinch of salt. Break eggs into a bowl, and whisk. Add flour gradually, whisking all the time until the mixture is smooth. Add water and stir in well. Add oil, and mix. Cover bowl with a damp cloth, and leave in a cool place for 30 minutes.
Heat a crêpe pan, or 19cm (7″) frying pan. Grease lightly with melted butter, and put a good tablespoon of batter in the centre. Roll the pan to coat the surface evenly. Fry until crespelle is brown on the underside. Loosen edge with a palette knife; turn over and brown the other side. Stack and wrap in a clean cloth until needed.

To make Béchamel sauce:
Warm milk with peppercorns, bay leaf and slice of onion. Remove from heat, and let stand for 5 minutes. Strain. Heat butter in pan. Stir in flour and cook for 1 minute. Remove from heat, and gradually stir in two-thirds (200ml) of the milk. Return to heat, and stir continuously until boiling. Simmer for 3 minutes. Add salt and pepper to taste. Put half of the sauce in a bowl, and add the chicken and tongue. Mix together. Beat remaining milk (100ml) into remaining sauce.

Lay 1 crespelle on a plate, and top with a layer of chicken and tongue. Cover with another crespelle, and continue, finishing with a crespelle. Pour over sauce, and bake in pre-heated oven for 10 minutes. Serve immediately.

Crespelle with Tuna

PREPARATION TIME: 40 minutes
COOKING TIME: 30 minutes
SERVES: 4 people

12 crespelle:
3 eggs
115g (4oz) plain flour
Pinch of salt
200ml (8 fl oz) water
8ml (½ tbsp) olive oil
30g (1oz) butter or margarine, melted

Filling:
270g (9oz) can tuna fish, drained
3 tbsps mayonnaise
1 tbsp tomato purée

Tomato sauce:
400g (14oz) can plum tomatoes
½ tsp basil
1 clove garlic, crushed
1 onion, peeled and chopped
15g (½oz) butter or margarine
2 tbsps chopped parsley
Salt
Pepper

To make crespelle:
Sift the flour with a pinch of salt. Break eggs into a bowl, and whisk. Add flour gradually, whisking all the time, until the mixture is smooth. Stir in water, and mix oil in well. Cover bowl with a damp cloth, and leave in a cool place for 30 minutes.
Heat a crêpe pan, or 19cm (7″) frying pan. Grease lightly with melted butter, and put a good tablespoon of batter in the centre. Roll the pan to coat the surface evenly. Fry until crespelle is brown on the underside. Loosen edge with a palette knife; turn over and brown on the other side. Stack and wrap in a clean cloth until needed.

To make sauce:
Heat butter in pan, and gently fry garlic and basil for 30 seconds. Add onion, and fry until transparent. Add tomatoes, and cook for 10 minutes. Push through a sieve, and return to pan. Add salt, and freshly-ground black pepper, to taste, and parsley if desired.

To make filling:
Flake tuna fish, and put into a bowl. Mix mayonnaise and tomato purée, and stir into tuna fish. Divide mixture equally between crespelle, placing mixture at one end, and rolling up. Place in an oven-proof dish. Pour over tomato sauce, and cook under a hot grill for 5 minutes. Serve immediately.

Cook the macaroni in plenty of boiling salted water for 10 minutes, or until tender but still firm. Rinse in hot water and drain well. Meanwhile, melt the butter in a pan. Stir in the flour and cook for 1 minute. Remove from heat, and gradually stir in the milk. Return to heat and bring to the boil. Simmer for 3 minutes, stirring continuously. Stir in the mustard, anchovies, and half the cheese. Season with salt and pepper to taste. Stir in the macaroni, and pour into an oven-proof dish. Sprinkle the remaining cheese over the top, and make a latticework with the remaining anchovies. Brown under a hot grill. Serve immediately.

Macaroni with Creamy Chicken Sauce

PREPARATION TIME: 5 minutes

COOKING TIME: 20 minutes

SERVES: 4 people

225g (8oz) macaroni
60g (2oz) butter or margarine
30g (1oz) flour
600ml (1 pint) milk
115g (4oz) chicken breasts
15ml (1 tbsp) olive oil
115g (4oz) Cheddar cheese, grated
Salt
Pepper

Heat oil in a frying pan, and gently fry chicken for 10 minutes, or until cooked through. When cool, shred chicken. Cook macaroni in plenty of boiling salted water for 10 minutes, or until tender but still firm. Rinse in hot water. Drain well. Meanwhile, heat the butter in a pan, and stir in the flour, and cook for 1 minute. Draw off the heat and gradually add the milk, stirring all the time. Bring the sauce to the boil, stirring continuously, and cook for 3 minutes. Add the chicken, macaroni, and salt and pepper to taste, and mix well. Pour mixture into an oven-proof dish, and sprinkle with cheese on top. Cook under a pre-heated grill until golden brown. Serve immediately.

Macaroni Cheese with Anchovies

PREPARATION TIME: 5 minutes

COOKING TIME: 15 minutes

SERVES: 4 people

225g (8oz) macaroni
60g (2oz) butter or margarine
60g (2oz) flour
600ml (1 pint) milk
½ tsp dry mustard
175g (6oz) Gruyère or Cheddar cheese, grated
60g (2oz) can anchovy fillets
Salt
Pepper

Drain anchovies, and set enough aside to slice to make a thin lattice over the dish. Chop the rest finely.

This page: Macaroni Cheese with Anchovies.

Facing page: Macaroni with Creamy Chicken Sauce (top) and Italian Casserole (bottom).

Italian Casserole

PREPARATION TIME: 15 minutes
COOKING TIME: 40 minutes
OVEN: 180°C, 350°F, Gas Mark 4
SERVES: 4 people

90g (3oz) small macaroni
60g (2oz) butter or margarine
1 clove garlic, crushed
1 onion, peeled and chopped
2 400g (14oz) cans plum tomatoes
1 tbsp tomato purée
1 red pepper, cored, seeds removed, and chopped roughly
1 green pepper, cored, seeds removed, and chopped roughly
10 black olives, halved, and stones removed
115g (4oz) Mozzarella cheese, sliced thinly
225g (8oz) salami, cut into chunks
Salt
Pepper

Cook the macaroni in plenty of boiling salted water for 10 minutes, or until tender but still firm. Rinse under hot water and drain well. Place in a shallow, oven-proof dish. Meanwhile, heat butter in pan, and fry onion and garlic gently until soft. Add undrained tomatoes, tomato purée, red and green peppers, salami and olives, and stir well. Simmer uncovered for 5 minutes. Season with salt and pepper. Pour over the macaroni, stir, and cover with the sliced cheese. Bake uncovered in a moderate oven for 20 minutes, until cheese has melted. Serve immediately.

Macaroni Cheese with Sausage

PREPARATION TIME: 10 minutes
COOKING TIME: 20 minutes
SERVES: 4 people

225g (8oz) macaroni
60g (2oz) butter or margarine
60g (2oz) flour
600ml (1 pint) milk
1 tsp dry mustard
175g (6oz) Cheddar cheese, grated
8 Frankfurter sausages, or 400g (14oz) can hot-dog sausages
Salt
Pepper

Garnish:
1 pimento, cut into strips

Poach the Frankfurter sausages for 5-8 minutes. Remove skins and, when cold, cut into diagonal slices. (If using hot-dog sausages, just cut as required). Cook macaroni in plenty of boiling salted water for about 10 minutes, or until tender but still firm. Rinse in hot water, and drain well. Meanwhile, melt the butter in a pan. Stir in the flour, and cook for 1 minute. Draw off heat, and gradually add milk, stirring all the time. Bring to the boil, stirring continuously, and cook for 3 minutes. Add sausages, grated cheese, mustard, and salt and pepper to taste. Stir well. Add macaroni, and mix in well. Pour mixture into an oven-proof dish, and sprinkle the remaining cheese over the top. Make a lattice of pimento, and cook under a pre-heated grill until golden brown. Serve immediately.

Pastitsio

PREPARATION TIME: 10 minutes
COOKING TIME: 1 hour
OVEN: 190°C, 375°F, Gas Mark 5
SERVES: 4 people

225g (8oz) macaroni
90g (3oz) butter or margarine
60g (2oz) Parmesan cheese, grated
Pinch of grated nutmeg
2 eggs, beaten
1 medium onion, peeled and chopped
1 clove garlic, crushed
450g (1lb) minced beef
30ml (2 tbsps) tomato purée
60ml (4 tbsps) red wine
90ml (6 tbsps) beef stock
2 tbsps chopped parsley
30g (1oz) plain flour
300ml (½ pint) milk
Salt
Pepper

Set oven. Cook macaroni in plenty of boiling salted water for 10 minutes, or until tender but still firm. Rinse under hot water. Drain. Put one-third of the butter in the pan and return macaroni to it. Add half the cheese, nutmeg, and salt and pepper to taste. Leave to cool. Mix in half the beaten egg, and put aside. Melt half of the remaining butter in a pan, and fry onion and garlic gently until onion is soft. Increase temperature and add meat, and fry until browned. Add tomato purée, stock, parsley and wine, and season with salt and pepper. Simmer for 20 minutes. In a small pan, melt the rest of the butter. Stir in the flour and cook for 30 seconds. Remove from heat, and stir in milk. Bring to boil, stirring continuously, until the sauce thickens. Beat in the remaining egg and season to taste. Spoon half the macaroni into a serving-dish and cover with the meat sauce. Put on another layer of macaroni and smooth over. Pour over white sauce, and sprinkle with remaining cheese, and bake in the oven for 30 minutes until golden brown. Serve immediately.

Cannelloni with Tomato and Cheese

PREPARATION TIME: 10 minutes
COOKING TIME: 40 minutes
OVEN: 210°C, 400°F, Gas Mark 7
SERVES: 4 people

12 cannelloni shells

Filling:
400g (14oz) can plum tomatoes
1 tsp tomato purée
1 tsp oregano or basil
115g (4oz) ricotta cheese
115g (4oz) Parmesan cheese, grated
Salt
Pepper

Sauce:
400g (14oz) can plum tomatoes
1 onion, peeled and chopped
15ml (1 tbsp) olive oil
1 tbsp grated Parmesan cheese
1 tbsp cornflour
Salt
Pepper

Cook cannelloni shells in a large pan of boiling salted water for 15-20 minutes until tender. Rinse in hot water and drain well.

Pastitsio (above) and Macaroni Cheese with Sausage (right).

90g (3oz) mushrooms, cleaned and chopped
15g (½oz) flour
1 tsp curry powder
150ml (¼ pint) milk
60ml (4 tbsps) soured cream
60ml (4 tbsps) mayonnaise
1 egg, lightly beaten
175g (6oz) can tuna fish
3 shallots, peeled and chopped
Salt
Pepper

Topping:
4 tbsps breadcrumbs
60g (2oz) Cheddar cheese, grated
30g (1oz) butter or margarine

Cook cannelloni shells in a large pan of boiling salted water for 15-20 minutes until tender. Rinse in hot water and drain well. Meanwhile, melt butter in saucepan. Fry onion until transparent, add mushrooms and celery, and fry for 5 minutes. Add curry powder and flour, and fry until light golden brown. Draw off the heat, and gradually add milk, stirring continuously. Return to heat and bring to the boil. Cook for 3 minutes, stirring all the time. Add soured cream, mayonnaise, and undrained flaked tuna. Season with salt and pepper and stir until sauce boils. Simmer for 3 minutes. Add shallots and egg, and mix well. Spoon mixture into cannelloni shells, and place in an oven-proof dish. Sprinkle over a mixture of breadcrumbs and cheese, and dot with butter or margarine. Bake in a moderate oven for 20 minutes. Serve immediately.

Crab Cannelloni

PREPARATION TIME: 10 minutes
COOKING TIME: 40 minutes
OVEN: 200°C, 400°F, Gas Mark 7
SERVES: 4 people

This page: Spinach Lasagne.

Facing page: Curried Tuna Cannelloni (top) and Crab Cannelloni (bottom).

12 cannelloni shells

Filling:
225g (8oz) fresh crab meat (or frozen crab meat, thawed)
30g (1oz) butter or margarine
3 shallots, peeled and chopped

½ tsp Worcestershire sauce
1 tsp Dijon mustard
Salt
Pepper

Mornay sauce:
2 tbsps butter or margarine
2 tbsps flour
1¼ cups milk
¼ cup Cheddar or Parmesan cheese, grated
Salt
Pepper

Cook cannelloni shells in a large pan of boiling salted water for 15-20 minutes until tender. Rinse in hot water and drain well. Meanwhile, heat butter in pan. Add shallots, crab meat, Worcestershire sauce, mustard, salt and pepper, and stir until heated through. Fill cannelloni shells with crab mixture, using a pastry bag with a wide, plain tube, or a teaspoon. Place in an oven-proof dish.

To make Mornay sauce:
Heat butter in pan, and stir in flour. Remove from heat and gradually add milk. Return to heat, and bring to boil. Cook for 3 minutes, stirring continuously. Stir in half the cheese until it melts. Do not reboil. Season with salt and pepper. Pour over the cannelloni and sprinkle with remaining cheese. Place in a hot oven, or under a broiler until golden brown. Serve immediately.

Lasagne Rolls

PREPARATION TIME: 5 minutes
COOKING TIME: 15 minutes
SERVES: 4 people

8 lasagne noodles
½ pound boned chicken breasts
2 tbsps butter or margarine
¼ cup Gruyère or Cheddar cheese, grated
1 tbsp flour
½ cup milk
¼ cup mushrooms, sliced
2 tsps oil
Salt
Pepper

In a large saucepan, fill two-thirds with boiling salted water and 2 teaspoons oil. Bring to the boil. Add 1 sheet of lasagne; wait about 2 minutes, and add another sheet. Only cook a few at a time. When tender, remove, and rinse under cold water, and leave to drain. Repeat until all the lasagne is cooked. Meanwhile, wash and slice mushrooms, and slice chicken. Put half the butter in a small frying pan, and fry the mushrooms and chicken. In a small saucepan, melt the rest of the butter. Add the flour, and cook for a minute. Remove from the heat, and add the milk. Mix well and bring to the boil. Cook for 3 minutes. Add sauce to chicken and mushrooms, and add half the cheese, mixing well. Add salt and pepper to taste. Spread out lasagne, and spread one-eighth mixture at one end of each. Roll up each piece of lasagne, and put into an oven-proof dish. Sprinkle with remaining cheese, and put under a broiler until golden brown. Serve immediately.

Lasagne

PREPARATION TIME: 10 minutes
COOKING TIME: 45 minutes
OVEN: 400°F (200°C)
SERVES: 4 people

8 lasagne noodles

Meat sauce:
4 tbsps butter or margarine
1 carrot, diced
1 celery stick, diced
1 onion, peeled and diced
¼ pound ground beef
1 tsp marjoram
1 tbsp flour
1 tbsp tomato paste
½ cup beef stock
Salt
Pepper

Béchamel sauce:
2 tbsps butter or margarine
2 tbsps flour
1 cup milk
6 peppercorns
1 bay leaf
Slice of onion
Parsley stalks

To make meat sauce:
Heat butter in pan and add onion, celery and carrot. Cook until golden. Add ground beef, and brown well. Stir in flour; add tomato paste, beef stock, marjoram, and salt and pepper. Cook for 15 minutes.

Meanwhile, cook the lasagne in lots of boiling salted water for 10 minutes, or until tender. Rinse in cold water and drain carefully. Lay out on a clean cloth to dry.

To make Béchamel sauce:
Heat milk in a saucepan with peppercorns, slice of onion, bay leaf and parsley stalks. Bring to simmering point and remove from heat. Allow to cool for 5 minutes. Strain. Melt butter in a saucepan. Stir in flour and cook for 30 seconds. Remove from heat and gradually add milk, stirring continuously. Cook for 3 minutes.

Grease an oven-proof baking dish. Line base with a layer of lasagne sheets. Cover with a layer of meat sauce, and a layer of Béchamel sauce. Place another layer of lasagne, repeating until all the ingredients are used, finishing with a layer of lasagne and a layer of Béchamel sauce. Bake in a hot oven until the top is golden. Serve immediately.

Lasagne Rolls (above right) and Lasagne (below right).

Springtime Desserts

Savarin Chantilly (top), Individual Banana Tarts (centre) and Coffee Pecan Pie (bottom).

Individual Banana Tarts

PREPARATION TIME: 30 minutes
COOKING TIME: 15 minutes
OVEN: 200°C (400°F) Gas Mark 6

Pastry
75g (3oz) butter
175g (6oz) plain flour
2 tablespoons caster sugar
1 egg yolk
1 tablespoon water

Filling
2 firm bananas
1 teaspoon lemon juice
150ml (5 fl oz) double cream
6oz apricot jam to glaze

Pastry
Place the butter and flour into a bowl and rub to form a breadcrumb-like mixture. Stir in the sugar. Beat together the egg yolk and water and add to flour to form a stiff dough. Lightly knead and chill for ½ hour. Roll out pastry and using a 7.5cm (3 inch) fluted cutter. Press into tartlet tins and bake until golden brown.

Filling
Slice the bananas and sprinkle with the lemon juice. Whisk the cream and fill the pastry cases. Lay the sliced banana in a circle to cover the cream. Melt the apricot jam in a small saucepan and pour over tartlet pastry cases, making sure all the bananas are glazed. Serve cold.

Coffee Pecan Pie

PREPARATION TIME: 20 minutes plus chilling

175g (6oz) digestive biscuits
75g (3oz) butter, melted
25g (1oz) soft brown sugar
75g (3oz) pecan nut halves
225g (8oz) marshmallows
300ml (½ pint) strong black coffee
15g (½oz) gelatine
3 tablespoons hot water
150ml (5 fl oz) double cream
1 teaspoon ground coffee

Crush the biscuits and mix together with the butter and sugar. Press the mixture onto the base and up the sides of an 18cm (7 inch) spring-form cake tin. Chill. Reserve 8 halves of pecan nuts for decoration and chop the remainder. In a large saucepan dissolve the marshmallows in the coffee, heating gently and stirring frequently. Dissolve the gelatine in the hot water and stir into the marshmallow mixture. Leave to cool until almost set. Whisk the cream until it peaks and fold into the coffee mixture. Add the chopped nuts. Pour onto the crushed biscuit base and chill until set. Remove from the tin and decorate with the nut halves. Sprinkle with the ground coffee.

Savarin Chantilly

PREPARATION TIME: 35 minutes plus chilling
COOKING TIME: 30 minutes
OVEN: 200°C (400°F) Gas Mark 6

Savarin
150g (6oz) strong white flour
½ teaspoon salt
6 tablespoons milk
2 level teaspoons dried yeast
1 level teaspoon caster sugar
2 eggs
75g (3oz) butter

Syrup
150g (6oz) caster sugar
250ml (½ pint) water
Pared rind of ½ lemon and juice of 1 lemon
3 tablespoons rum

Filling
125ml (¼ pint) single cream
125ml (¼ pint) double cream
400g (1lb) tinned or fresh fruit

Savarin
Butter and sprinkle with flour a 20cm (8 inch) ring mould. Sift the flour and salt into a mixing bowl. Heat the milk in a small saucepan and add the dried yeast and sugar (do not boil the milk). Leave in a warm place for 20 minutes or until the mixture looks frothy. Mix the eggs into the yeast mixture and pour into the flour. Stir with a wooden spoon to form a smooth batter. Melt the butter and allow it to cool slightly. Pour into the batter and stir. Pour the batter into the ring mould and spread evenly. Put the mould into a polythene bag but leave room for the mixture to rise. Leave in a warm place. When the mixture has risen to the top of the tin bake in a preheated oven for half an hour until golden brown and firm to the touch.

Syrup
While the savarin is baking, add the sugar and water to a saucepan and finely pare the lemon rind. Stir over a low heat until the sugar has dissolved. Bring the mixture to the boil and simmer for 5 minutes. Remove from the heat and add the lemon juice and rum. When the savarin has cooled in the tin for five minutes remove it from the tin. Wash and dry the baking mould and pour the hot syrup evenly round the mould. Replace the savarin so that it floats in the syrup.

Filling
The savarin will soak up the syrup so that it can be turned out. Turn out the savarin and refrigerate overnight. Place savarin on a serving dish and whip the single and double cream. Spoon into the centre and top with fruit (apricot, mango, oranges or stoned cherries make a suitable decoration).

Mont Blanc

PREPARATION TIME: 20 minutes plus chilling
COOKING TIME: 1¼ hours
OVEN: 120°C (250°F) Gas Mark ½

2 egg whites
185g (6oz) caster sugar
½ teaspoon vanilla essence
225ml (7½ fl oz) double cream
1½ tablespoons icing sugar
277g (8oz) can chestnut purée
1 tablespoon brandy
25g (1oz) plain chocolate, grated or chopped nuts

Whisk the egg whites until they peak, adding the sugar and vanilla essence. Fill a piping bag with the meringue mixture and fit a 1cm (½ inch) plain nozzle. Draw six circles 7.5cm (3 inches) diameter on a baking sheet lined with non-stick silicone paper and cover with the meringue. Bake in a very cool oven until firm but not brown. Cool. Whip the cream until it peaks and fold in the icing sugar. Mix the chestnut purée with the brandy and spoon the mixture into a piping bag fitted with a 3mm (⅛ inch) nozzle and pipe round the edge of the meringue bases. Top with cream and chocolate or nuts to decorate. Serve chilled.

Mango Soufflé

PREPARATION TIME: 20 minutes plus chilling

1 tablespoon water
Juice of one lemon
75g (3oz) caster sugar
15g (½oz) gelatine
3 eggs (separated)
1 mango peeled and stoned
140ml (5 fl oz) double cream

To decorate
25g (1oz) toasted chopped nuts
140ml (5 fl oz) whipping cream, whipped
Caramel chips (see quick garnishes)

Prepare a 12.5cm (5 inch) freezerproof soufflé dish. Cut a double strip of lightly oiled greaseproof paper 50 x 12.5cm (20 x 5 inches) and tie securely round the dish. Put the water and lemon juice in a small pan and sprinkle in the gelatine. Heat to dissolve the gelatine and cool. Whisk the egg yolks and sugar until thick. Purée the mango and mix with the gelatine into the egg mixture. Fold in the stiffly whisked egg white with cream. Pour into the prepared dish and chill.

To decorate
Carefully remove the paper and press the nuts into the sides. Decorate with whipped cream. Another method of decoration is to use caramel chips.

Red Fruit Compote

PREPARATION TIME: 10 minutes plus chilling

100g (4oz) granulated sugar
300ml (½ pint) water
150g (6oz) redcurrants, stalks removed
225g (8oz) raspberries, hulled
225g (8oz) strawberries, hulled
2 tablespoons Cointreau or orange liqueur
Single cream

Boil the sugar and water in a pan till the sugar dissolves. This should take about 5 minutes. Remove from heat and cool. Put all the fruits in a serving dish and pour over the Cointreau and leave to stand for an hour and a half. Stir carefully from time to time. Pour the cold syrup over the fruits and serve chilled with cream.

Individual Fruit Salad

PREPARATION TIME: 20 minutes plus chilling

3 bananas
2 oranges
100g (4oz) strawberries
50g (2oz) redcurrants

Passion Fruit Sauce
3 passion fruits
3 tablespoons clear honey
Juice of one lime
2 tablespoons dark rum

Peel and slice horizontally the bananas and oranges. Hull and halve the strawberries and arrange on individual plates and chill.

Passion Fruit Sauce
Spoon out the seeds and flesh of the passion fruits and boil with the honey and lime juice. Add two tablespoons of dark rum and chill. Pour the passion fruit sauce over the fruit and serve. Decorate with the redcurrants.

Almond Cream Flan

PREPARATION TIME: 20 minutes
COOKING TIME: 35 minutes
OVEN: 200°C (400°F) Gas Mark 6

Flan
50g (2oz) plain flour
50g (2oz) caster sugar
2 eggs

Filling
150ml (5 fl oz) double cream
1 level tablespoon sieved icing sugar
25g (1oz) ground almonds
350g (12oz) strawberries, hulled and sliced; keep one whole strawberry for decoration

Glaze
3 tablespoons water
75g (3oz) caster sugar
Whipped cream and strawberry leaves (optional)

Flan
Grease a 20cm (8 inch) flan tin. Line the base with a circle of greaseproof paper. Sieve the flour into a bowl. Put the caster sugar and eggs into another bowl and whisk for 12 minutes over a saucepan of hot water, off the heat. The mixture should thicken and pale. Remove from the pan and whisk for another 5 minutes. If using an electric whisk, omit the whisking over hot water. Sieve the flour a little at a time over the mixture and fold in with a metal spoon. Pour mixture into prepared tin and cook in a hot oven until firm. When cooked, leave to cool in the tin for a few minutes then turn onto a wire rack.

Filling
Whip the cream stiffly, adding the icing sugar slowly. Fold in the almonds and spoon this mixture into the flan base. Arrange the strawberries on top.

Glaze
Place water and sugar in a pan and slowly bring to the boil. The sugar should be dissolved. Stir the rapidly boiling mixture constantly. Boil for 2 minutes. Allow the glaze to cool and brush over the strawberries. Decorate with whipped cream and strawberry leaves if available.

Red Fruit Compote (far left), Individual Fruit Salad with Passion Fruit Sauce (centre) and Almond Cream Flan (left).

Petits Pots de Café

PREPARATION TIME: 10 minutes plus cooling

3 tablespoons caster sugar
40g (1½oz) butter
1½ tablespoons rum
3 teaspoons instant coffee powder (granules should be crushed)
3 eggs, separated
120ml (4 fl oz) double cream, whipped
Walnut halves

Mix the sugar, butter, rum and coffee in a bowl over a pan of hot water, and stir until melted. Add the egg yolks and mix well. Leave to cook for 5 minutes over the hot water and remove from the heat. When the mixture has cooled, whisk the egg whites until stiff and fold into the coffee mixture. Spoon into individual ranekins and decorate with whipped cream and nuts if available.

Fruit Coupelles with Dried Fruit Compote

PREPARATION TIME: 20 minutes
COOKING TIME: 7 minutes
OVEN: 200°C (400°F) Gas Mark 6

100g (4oz) dried apricots
50g (2oz) dried apple
100g (4oz) prunes
50g (2oz) raisins
50g (2oz) sultanas
50g (2oz) currants
500ml (1 pint) strong black coffee

Coupelles
2 egg whites
65g (2½oz) caster sugar
50g (2oz) plain flour
50g (2oz) butter, melted and cooled

Place all the fruit ingredients in a saucepan and cover with the coffee. Boil rapidly then reduce heat to simmer for 3 minutes. Pour into a bowl and leave to cool for at least 10 hours. Whisk the egg whites until frothy. Add the sugar slowly. The mixture should be very stiff. Fold in the flour and melted butter. Grease a baking sheet. Drop the mixture onto the baking sheet to form 10cm (4 inch) rounds (the mixture makes 8). Cook in a preheated moderate oven until the edges are golden brown. Remove from the baking sheet one at a time. Mould over an inverted ramekin to form a cup shape.

When set remove from the dish and leave to cool on a wire rack. To serve fill the coupelles with the fruit compote.

Loganberries and Hazelnut Galette

PREPARATION TIME: 35 minutes
COOKING TIME: 20 minutes
OVEN: 190°C (375°F) Gas Mark 5

100g (4oz) hazelnuts, shelled
100g (4oz) softened butter
75g (3oz) caster sugar
1 egg yolk, lightly beaten
A few drops of vanilla essence
150g (6oz) plain flour
A pinch of salt
150g (6oz) plain flour
425ml (15 fl oz) double cream
1 level tablespoon caster sugar
450g (1lb) loganberries, hulled

Lightly grease three baking trays and dust with flour. Roast the hazelnuts in a hot oven 220°C (425°F) Gas Mark 7, or under the grill until the skin is split. Rub off the skins using kitchen paper and chop the nuts finely. Whisk the sugar and butter until fluffy and beat in the egg yolk and vanilla essence. Sieve the flour and salt and stir into the mixture adding the hazelnuts. Knead the mixture till it forms a smooth dough. Wrap in clear film and chill for 30 minutes. Divide the dough into 3 pieces and roll on a lightly floured surface to form 17.5cm (7 inch) rounds. Place each round onto the previously greased baking sheet. Cook one at a time in a moderately heated oven until lightly golden. Cut one round into 8 equal portions while still hot and leave the remaining 2 to cool for 10 minutes. Whip the cream until thick and add the sugar. Put half the mixture into a piping bag and save eight loganberries for decoration. Mix the remaining berries with the cream. Carefully position one galette on a serving plate. Cover with loganberry cream mixture and top with the remaining galette. Pipe eight swirls of cream on top and arrange the galette triangles on their edges supported by the cream swirls. Decorate with the reserved loganberries.

Pears in Wine

PREPARATION TIME: 15 minutes plus chilling
COOKING TIME: 30 minutes

250g (12oz) granulated sugar
125ml (¼ pint) water
6 large pears, peeled
225ml (7½ fl oz) dry red wine

Gently heat the sugar and water until the sugar has dissolved. Add the pears and cover. Then simmer for 15 minutes. Stir in the wine and continue to simmer uncovered for another 15 minutes. Remove the pears from the saucepan and arrange in a serving dish. Bring the wine syrup back to the boil until thick. Pour over the pears and allow to cool. Serve chilled.

Strawberry and Peach Heart

PREPARATION TIME: 20 minutes plus chilling

3 passion fruit
4 fl oz white wine
75g (3oz) caster sugar
3 tablespoons Cointreau or orange liqueur
100g (4oz) strawberries, hulled
3 peaches, halved and stoned
3 tablespoons strawberry jam
3 kumquats
3 kiwi fruit
3 tablespoons clear honey
1 teaspoon lime juice

Poach the flesh with the seeds of the passion fruit in the white wine until just tender. Add the sugar and continue to poach for a further four minutes. Sieve the mixture. Add the Cointreau and the strawberries and leave to cool. In a large saucepan filled with boiling water quickly submerge the

This page: Mango Soufflé (top), Mont Blanc (centre) and Petits Pots de Café (bottom).

Facing page: Loganberries and Hazelnut Galette (top), Fruit Coupelles with Dried Fruit Salad (centre) and Pears in Wine (bottom).

peaches and halve, removing the stone. Sieve the strawberry jam and using a writing nozzle fill a piping bag, and reserve in the refrigerator. Slice the kumquats. To make the kiwi fruit sauce, peel the kiwi fruit and purée them. Pass them through a sieve and stir in the honey and lime juice. Using the sieved strawberry jam reserved in piping bag, pipe heart shapes on each of the individual plates making sure not to break the line of strawberry jam. Fill the outline with the fruit, placing the peach half to one side and fill the hole left by removing stone with the strawberries. Pour over the kiwi fruit sauce and decorate with leaves. Serve chilled.

Chocolate and Brandy Cheesecake

PREPARATION TIME: 30 minutes plus chilling

COOKING TIME: 1 hour

OVEN: 160°C (325°F) Gas Mark 3

175g (6oz) plain chocolate digestives
75g (3oz) butter, melted
175g (6oz) plain chocolate
2 tablespoons brandy
2 eggs, lightly beaten
100g (4oz) soft brown sugar
350g (12oz) cream cheese
2 tablespoons cornflour

To decorate
Icing sugar

Crush the biscuits and mix them with the melted butter. Butter the sides and base of a loose-bottomed 18cm (7 inch) cake tin. Spoon the biscuit mixture into the cake tin, press onto the sides and base, and refrigerate for half an hour. Melt 100g (4oz) of the chocolate in a heatproof bowl over a pan of water and stir in the brandy. Beat together the eggs and sugar until thick. Add the cheese and continue to beat until the mixture is soft. Stir in the melted chocolate and cornflour. Pour the mixture into the cake tin and stand it on a baking sheet. Bake until it sets. Remove from the oven and cool, then chill for 4 hours before serving. To serve: remove the cheesecake from the cake tin and grate the remaining chocolate on top. Sift with a little icing sugar and serve.

Peach Brûlée

PREPARATION TIME: 20 minutes

GRILL SETTING: high

8 egg yolks
75g (3oz) caster sugar
1½ teaspoons vanilla essence
6 peach halves tinned or fresh
75g (3oz) soft brown sugar
Double cream

Beat the egg yolks and caster sugar until smooth and thick. Beat in the cream and pour the mixture into a saucepan. Cook over a low heat. Stir frequently until the mixture is thick enough to coat the back of a wooden spoon. Beat for 2 minutes off the heat. Stir in the vanilla essence and pour the mixture into a heatproof serving dish. When cool, arrange the peach halves on top of the custard (cut side down). Chill for 1 hour. Sprinkle the soft brown sugar over the peaches and place the dish under a hot grill. When the sugar melts and starts to caramelise remove the dish from the grill and serve at once.

This page: Summer Pudding (left) and Strawberry and Peach Heart (right).

Facing page: Apricot Cream Cheese Dessert (top left), Peach Brûlée (top right) and Chocolate Brandy Cheesecake (bottom).

Summer Pudding

PREPARATION TIME: 10 minutes plus chilling

750g (1lb 8oz) fresh soft fruit
175g (6oz) granulated sugar
9 slices of white bread (use thick slices and remove the crusts)
Whipped cream

Put all the fruit into a saucepan with the sugar and heat until the sugar is dissolved. Shake the pan so that the fruit will stay whole. Remove from heat and cool. Line the base and sides of a 900ml (1½ pint) pudding basin with the slices of bread trying not to leave any gaps. Pour the fruit juice into the centre of the pudding and cover the top completely with bread and press down firmly. Place a saucer or small plate on top of the pudding and weigh down. Chill in the fridge overnight. Turn out and decorate with whipped cream.

Almond Pear

PREPARATION TIME: 20 minutes plus chilling
COOKING TIME: 1 hour
OVEN: 150°C (300°F) Gas Mark 2

600ml (1 pint) double cream
6 egg yolks
50g (2oz) caster sugar
½ teaspoon almond essence
100g (4oz) granulated sugar
150ml (¼ pint) water
4 large pears peeled, stoned and sliced thinly
175g (6oz) soft brown sugar
Lemon juice to sprinkle on pears

Pour the cream into a saucepan and heat (do not allow the cream to boil). Put the egg yolks, caster sugar and almond essence into a bowl and stir well. Slowly pour into the heated cream. Pour the mixture into a 900ml (1½ pint) baking dish and stand the dish in a roasting tin half filled with water (this is known as a *bain marie*). Loosely cover with foil and bake until set. Remove the dish from the bain marie and leave until cold. Refrigerate overnight. Put the granulated sugar and water in a saucepan and heat gently until the sugar has dissolved. Bring to the boil until thick and golden in colour. Oil a shallow cake tin and pour the caramelised sugar in. When the caramel has set, crack into small pieces with a rolling pin. Arrange the pear slices on top of the baked cream and sprinkle with demerara sugar, and lemon juice. Grill until the sugar has dissolved and the juice is bubbling. Leave to cool and return to the fridge for half an hour. Sprinkle with caramel chips before serving.

Apricot Cream Cheese Dessert

PREPARATION TIME: 20 minutes plus chilling
GRILL SETTING: high

225g (8oz) crushed brandy snaps
½ teaspoon ground ginger
125g (4oz) butter, melted
450g (1lb) cream cheese
50g (2oz) caster sugar
125ml (4 fl oz) single cream
2 tablespoons lemon juice
1 tablespoon gelatine dissolved in 2 tablespoons hot water
450g (1lb) can of apricot halves, drained
50g (2oz) preserved stem ginger, drained and chopped
40ml (15 fl oz) double cream
50g (2oz) soft brown sugar

Grease a 23cm (9 inch) loose-bottomed cake tin with a little butter. In a large mixing bowl crush the brandy snaps, ground ginger and butter and spoon into the base of the cake tin, pressing down with the back of a spoon. Place the cream cheese and caster sugar into a bowl and beat with a wooden spoon until the mixture is smooth. Stir in the single cream, lemon juice and dissolved gelatine. Beat well so that all the mixture is blended together. Spoon the mixture into the tin and refrigerate for 40 minutes. When the filling is set, remove the tin and arrange the apricot halves on top of the filling. Sprinkle over the preserved ginger and soft brown sugar. Grill for three minutes until the sugar has caramelised. Remove the dessert from the tin and serve.

Orange and Lemon Chiffon Flan

PREPARATION TIME: 45 minutes
COOKING TIME: 20 minutes
OVEN: 200°C (400°F) Gas Mark 6

Pastry Case
175g (6oz) plain flour
Pinch of salt
90g (3½oz) butter
25g (1oz) caster sugar
1 egg yolk

Filling
3 eggs, separated
75g (3oz) caster sugar
2 large oranges
1 large lemon
1 tablespoon gelatine
Warm water

For decoration
Sliced orange and lemon fan
150ml (5 fl oz) whipped cream

Pastry Case
Sieve the flour and salt into a bowl and rub in the fat. Add the sugar and mix well. Mix to a stiff paste with the egg yolk to form a pliable dough. Turn onto a floured board and roll out. Use to line a 20cm (8 inch) flan ring. Cut a circle from non-stick silicone baking paper and lay on top of pastry. Sprinkle with baking beans or crusts of bread (baking blind). Bake for about 20 minutes at 200°C (400°F) Gas Mark 6. Remove the baking beans and paper and return to the oven for 5 minutes.

Filling
Whisk the egg yolks, sugar and grated rind of two oranges and one lemon until thick. Dissolve the gelatine in a little warm water and make up to 300ml (½ pint) with orange juice and water. Pour the gelatine mixture into the egg mixture and whisk until it starts to thicken. Lightly fold in the stiffly beaten egg white, pile into the flan case and leave to set. Decorate with whipped cream and slices of orange.

Gateau American

PREPARATION TIME: 10 minutes
COOKING TIME: 20 minutes
OVEN: 200°C (400°F) Gas Mark 6

75g (3oz) granulated sugar
10g (½ oz) butter
75g (3oz) breadcrumbs
3 eggs, beaten
300g (¾lb) stoned dates
75g (3oz) walnuts, chopped
450ml (15 fl oz) whipped cream (whipping or double)
Nuts

Mix the sugar, butter and bread-crumbs with the beaten eggs, dates and walnuts. Cook in a shallow pan until cooked (20 minutes). When cold, crumble with a fork. Layer fruit mixture and stiffly whipped cream in tall glasses and top with a rosette of whipped cream. Decorate with a nut.

Facing page: Almond Pear (top), Gateau American (right) and Orange and Lemon Chiffon Flan (bottom).

Summer Desserts

Gooseberry Pie

PREPARATION TIME: 20 minutes
COOKING TIME: 1 hour
OVEN: 220°C (425°F) Gas Mark 7 for 30 minutes, then 180°C (350°F) Gas Mark 4 for 30 minutes

Pastry
275g (10oz) plain flour
Pinch of salt
65g (2½oz) butter (cut into small pieces)
65g (2½oz) lard (cut into small pieces)
2½ tablespoons cold water

Filling
900g (2lb) gooseberries, topped and tailed
225g (8oz) granulated sugar
Milk to glaze or beaten egg
Single cream or custard

Pastry
Sift the flour with the salt. Add the fat and mix until it resembles breadcrumbs. Stir in the water and form into a firm dough. Roll out half the pastry on a lightly floured surface and use it to line a 20cm (8 inch) flan dish or pie dish.

Filling
Mix the gooseberries with the sugar and fill the lined pastry dish. Roll out the remaining pastry and cover the pie. Dampen the edges and seal together. Any excess pastry can be used to make leaves to decorate. Make a small hole in the centre of the pie and brush the pastry with milk or beaten egg. Place on baking tray and cook in a hot oven. Serve with single cream or custard.

Melons and Mangoes on Ice

PREPARATION TIME: 1¼ hours

1 medium size Ogen melon
2 large mangoes

Slice melon in half and scoop out flesh in balls. Peel mangoes and slice. Mix mango slices and melon balls together and arrange in a glass bowl. Chill for 1 hour.

Frozen Gooseberry Fool

PREPARATION TIME: 20 minutes plus freezing
COOKING TIME: 15 minutes

650g (1½lb) gooseberries
450ml (¾ pint) water
Sprig of mint
150g (6 oz) caster sugar
A little green food colouring
450ml (¾ pint) double cream, lightly whipped

Top and tail gooseberries. Place in a pan with the water and mint. Cover and simmer for approximately 15 minutes or until soft. Take off the heat and stir in the sugar until dissolved, then add food colouring. Take out the sprig of mint. Sieve and ensure all pips are removed. Cool and blend with the cream. Place in container and freeze.

Brown Bread Ice Cream

PREPARATION TIME: 20 minutes plus freezing

475ml (17 fl oz) vanilla ice cream
4 small slices brown bread
1 teaspoon ground cinnamon
125ml (4 fl oz) water
75g (3oz) sugar

Put the ice cream into a large mixing bowl and break it up, allowing it to soften. Cut the crusts from the bread and discard. Crumble the slices into a bowl, adding the ground cinnamon, reserve. Put the water and sugar into a small saucepan and stir until the sugar has dissolved. Boil until the mixture caramelises and turns brown. Remove from the heat and stir in the breadcrumbs and cinnamon mixture. Blend the mixture into the ice cream, making sure the breadcrumbs do not form large lumps. Turn the mixture into a rigid container for freezing, (leave 10mm (½ inch) space at the top of the container). Freeze the mixture and serve.

Brown Bread Ice-Cream (top left), Melons and Mangoes on Ice (top right), Frozen Gooseberry Fool (bottom left) and Gooseberry Pie (bottom right).

Cherry 'Spoom'

PREPARATION TIME: 20 minutes plus freezing

250g (9oz) sugar
300ml (½ pint) water
Juice of 2 limes
2 fresh peppermint leaves
600ml (1 pint) Sauternes
3 egg whites
Cherry brandy

Boil 100g (4oz) of the sugar with the water, lime juice and peppermint leaves. Leave to cool and strain into the Sauternes. Freeze the sorbet. Whisk the egg whites and add the remaining sugar until it peaks. Remove the sorbet from the freezer and whisk in the meringue mixture. Serve in glasses and pour over the cherry brandy.

Apple and Sultana and Brandy Ice

PREPARATION TIME: 10 minutes plus soaking and freezing time

600ml (1 pint) apple juice
50g (2oz) caster sugar
42g (1½oz) packet dried apple flakes
100g (4oz) sultanas
A few drops green food colour
1 egg white, stiffly whisked

Put the apple juice in a pan with sugar. Heat gently until the sugar has dissolved. Boil quickly for 5 minutes and remove from heat. Cool. Soak apple flakes and sultanas in brandy and add enough apple syrup to cover mixture. Soak for 4 hours. Then mix apple, sultanas and brandy adding a few drops of food colour mixture with the remaining apple syrup in a shallow container and freeze. Mash with a fork and fold in egg whites. Return to the freezer. Serve frozen in glasses.

This page: Burgundy Granita (top), Apple and Sultana and Brandy Ice (centre) and Champagne Granita (bottom).

Facing page: Cherry 'Spoom' (top), Raspberry Malakoff (centre) and Cherry Cinnamon Sorbet (bottom).

Burgundy Granita

PREPARATION TIME: 15 minutes plus freezing

75g (3oz) sugar, plus 2 tablespoons
Juice of ½ lime and ½ orange
1 tablespoon water
Small bunch lemon balm leaves
½ bottle good Burgundy
125ml (4 fl oz) double or whipping cream
Blackberries to decorate

Boil half the sugar with the lime and orange juice and water, and the balm leaves. Cool, strain and add to Burgundy. Freeze in a shallow container. To serve: whip the cream with the remaining sugar. Scrape the granita with a spoon to produce ice shavings and serve shavings into glasses, decorate with cream and blackberries.

Champagne Granita

PREPARATION TIME: 5 minutes plus freezing time

⅔ bottle champagne
Fresh blackcurrants and raspberries
Caster sugar to dust

Freeze the champagne in a shallow container. When frozen, scrape off and serve into glasses. Decorate with blackcurrants and raspberries. Dust with caster sugar.

Raspberry Malakoff

PREPARATION TIME: 35 minutes plus chilling

175g (6oz) caster sugar
175g (6oz) butter
300ml (½ pint) double cream
175g (6oz) ground almonds
3 tablespoons kirsch
225g (8oz) fresh raspberries
1 packet boudoir biscuits
Whipped cream

Beat the sugar and butter until fluffy. Whip the cream until it peaks and fold in the ground almonds. Add the kirsch and raspberries. Mix the sugar and butter with the cream fruit mixture. Line an 18cm (7 inch) cake tin with non-stick silicone paper. Stand the boudoir biscuits round the sides of the cake tin with the sugary side outermost. Spoon the malakoff mixture into the middle and press it down. Make sure the top is smooth. Refrigerate until the malakoff feels firm. With a sharp knife, trim the biscuits to the same level as the malakoff mixture. Turn the malakoff out upside down. Decorate with whipped cream if desired. Serve chilled.

Cherry Cinnamon Sorbet

PREPARATION TIME: 25 minutes plus freezing

175g (10oz) sugar, plus 1 tablespoon
300ml (½ pint) water
1 piece cinnamon stick
500g (18oz) fresh sour cherries
Juice of ½ lemon
200ml (7 fl oz) whipping cream
Seeds of ¼ vanilla pod
Fresh cherries

Boil 175g (10oz) of the sugar for 3 minutes in water and cinnamon and leave to cool. Remove the cinnamon sticks and stone the cherries. Purée the cherries and stir in the lemon juice. Mix with the sugar syrup and freeze. Flavour the cream with the tablespoon of sugar and vanilla. Whip until thick. Put the sorbet into individual glasses and decorate with cream and cherries.

Strawberry Alaska

PREPARATION TIME: 10 minutes
COOKING TIME: 2-3 minutes
OVEN: 140°C (275°F) Gas Mark 1

1 shop-bought strawberry jam swiss roll
Soft-scoop strawberry ice cream to cover

Meringue
2 egg whites
100g (4oz) caster sugar

Cover swiss roll with ice cream. Return to freezer. Whisk egg whites until they form stiff peaks. Whisk in half the sugar. Then fold in the rest. Remove ice cream covered swiss roll from freezer and cover with meringue mixture. Place in oven and cook meringue until just turning golden. (Approximately 2-3 minutes.) Serve immediately.

Strawberry Yogurt Ice

PREPARATION TIME: 20 minutes plus freezing

225g (8oz) fresh or thawed, frozen strawberries
300ml (½ pint) plain low fat yogurt
2 teaspoons gelatine
2 tablespoons water
1 egg white
65g (2½oz) caster sugar
A few strawberries

Blend strawberries and yogurt until smooth. Sprinkle gelatine over the water in a small bowl. Place bowl in a pan of hot water until the gelatine is dissolved. Cool slightly and add to the strawberry mixture. Pour into the container and freeze until icy round the edges. Put mixture into bowl and beat until smooth. In another bowl whisk the egg white stiffly, carefully adding the sugar and fold into strawberry mixture. Pour back into container and freeze. To serve – scoop into glasses and decorate with strawberries.

Peach Melba

PREPARATION TIME: 10 minutes

1 large can peaches (2 halves per person)
2 scoops ice cream per person
Chocolate sauce or raspberry purée
Flaked almonds

Place 2 scoops of ice cream per serving in individual bowls. Place 2 peach halves on top. Serve with chocolate sauce or raspberry purée. Decorate with flaked almonds.

Lemon Sorbet

PREPARATION TIME: 15 minutes plus freezing

Grated rinds and juice of 2 lemons
Cold water
75g (3oz) caster sugar
1 teaspoon gelatine
2 egg whites

Mix the lemon juice and rind with cold water to make 1 litre (1¾ pints) of fluid. Put the liquid in a saucepan with the sugar and boil. Remove from the heat and whisk in the gelatine. Pour into a mixing bowl and place in the freezer until it begins to harden. Whisk the egg whites until stiff and beat them into the lemon mixture. Return to the freezer, leaving a 10mm (½ inch) head space in the container.

Pastel Coupé

PREPARATION TIME: 35 minutes plus freezing

Yellow
600ml (1 pint) water
2 level teaspoons gelatine
250g (10oz) caster sugar
3 lemons
2 egg whites

Green
600ml (1 pint) water
2 level teaspoons gelatine
200g (8oz) caster sugar
2 lemons
2 egg whites
2 tablespoons crème de menthe

Yellow
Measure out two tablespoons of water and sprinkle with gelatine. Place the remaining water and sugar in a saucepan. Add pared lemon rinds and stir over the heat until the sugar has dissolved. Bring to the boil and simmer for 5 minutes. Remove from heat and add gelatine mixture. Dissolve completely and stir in the lemon juice. Leave to cool. Strain the mixture into a container and freeze until partially frozen. Place in chilled mixing bowl and whisk with beaten egg whites until thick and snowy. Return to container and freeze.

Green
For the green pastel coupé use basic method and ingredients as listed. Add the crème de menthe with lemon juice. To serve: use an ice-cream scoop, take half the green and half the yellow into one scoop. Serve in meringue cases or glasses.

Facing page: Strawberry Yogurt Ice (top), Peach Melba (centre) and Strawberry Alaska (bottom).

Curaçao Granita with Champagne

PREPARATION TIME: 10 minutes plus freezing

75g (3oz) sugar
150ml (¼ pint) water
Juice of 1 lime
Juice of 1 orange
3 tablespoons blue Curaçao
⅔ bottle champagne

Boil half the sugar with the water, lime and orange juice for two to three minutes. Cool, strain, add to the Curaçao and the champagne. Pour into a flat freezer-proof container and freeze. To serve: scrape with a spoon and serve in glasses.

Blackcurrant Sorbet

PREPARATION TIME: 20 minutes plus freezing

1kg (2lb) fresh or thawed, frozen blackcurrants
225g (9oz) sugar
300ml (½ pint) water
2 egg whites

Put all the ingredients except the egg whites into a saucepan. Heat slowly and cook for 15 minutes. Rub the fruit mixture through a sieve and pour into a freezer-proof container with a lid. Freeze until mushy. Whisk the egg whites until firm and fold into the mixture. Return to the freezer.

Inset illustration: (from top to bottom) Curaçao Granita with Champagne, Lemon Sorbet, Pastel Coupé and Blackcurrant Sorbet.

Ginger Syllabub

PREPARATION TIME: 15 minutes

1 100g (4oz) jar preserved ginger
600ml (1 pint) double cream, lightly whipped

Chop 2 pieces of the ginger and mix into the cream along with 2 tablespoons of the syrup. Serve in glasses or bowls and decorate with sliced ginger. Chill until ready to serve.

Apricot Ice Roll

PREPARATION TIME: 35 minutes plus freezing

COOKING TIME: 12 minutes

OVEN: 220°C (425°F) Gas Mark 7

Sponge mixture
2 eggs
50g (2oz) caster sugar
50g (2oz) plain flour

Filling and decorating
4 tablespoons apricot jam
600ml (1 pint) soft-scoop ice cream (vanilla)
Cream to decorate
Dried apricots, thinly sliced

Whisk eggs and sugar until light and fluffy. Carefully fold in flour. Turn into a greased and floured swiss roll tin and bake. Turn out onto a tea towel and leave to cool. Spread sponge with apricot jam and softened ice cream. Roll up using tea towel. Place in freezer until ice cream is hardened. Decorate with cream and sliced apricots.

Mango Sorbet

PREPARATION TIME: 15 minutes plus freezing

250ml (8 fl oz) mango purée
Juice of ½ lime
Scant 150ml (5 fl oz) dry white wine
Scant 150ml (5 fl oz) mineral water
1 egg white
50g (2oz) sugar

Mix the mango purée with the lime juice, white wine and mineral water. Whisk the egg white until it peaks and slowly add the sugar. Fold the egg white into the mango mixture and freeze.

Apricot Ice Roll (far left), Ginger Syllabub (centre) and Mango Sorbet (left).

Banana Ice Crêpes

PREPARATION TIME: 30 minutes

12 cooked crêpes
2 large bananas
12 scoops soft-scoop vanilla ice cream
Chocolate sauce

Mash one banana, and combine with ice cream. Fold the crêpes in half and place on individual plates. Fill crêpes with the mixture of banana and ice cream. Decorate with other sliced banana. Serve with chocolate sauce.

Mousse Glacée au Chocolat

PREPARATION TIME: 20 minutes plus freezing

4 egg yolks
2 tablespoons caster sugar
2 teaspoons vanilla essence
300ml (½ pint) double cream
2 egg whites, stiffly whipped
Chocolate sauce

Whisk egg yolks and sugar until light and creamy. Add vanilla essence. Add the cream and egg whites. Freeze the mixture. Serve with chocolate sauce.

Chocolate Banana Ice

PREPARATION TIME: 35 minutes plus freezing

150ml (¼ pint) milk
40g (1½oz) caster sugar
40g (1½oz) plain chocolate (broken into bits)
1 egg, beaten
½ teaspoon vanilla essence
150ml (¼ pint) double cream, whipped until soft peaking

Banana Cream
4 medium bananas
1 tablespoon lemon juice
25g (1oz) icing sugar, sieved
150ml (¼ pint) whipped double cream

Place the milk, sugar and chocolate in a saucepan and heat gently. Pour onto the beaten egg and stir constantly until mixed. Return the mixture to the saucepan and cook until the custard thickens. Strain the mixture, add the vanilla essence and allow to cool. Fold the cream into the custard mixture. Whisk rapidly and turn into a metal freezing container.

Banana Cream
Peel and chop the bananas and sprinkle with lemon juice. Dust the fruit with icing sugar and fold the whipped cream in with the bananas. Stir the chocolate mixture with banana cream and freeze. Remove from freezer to fridge 20 minutes before serving.

Refreshing Sorbet

PREPARATION TIME: 15 minutes plus freezing

75g (3oz) caster sugar
425ml (¾ pint) water
3 ripe mangoes, peeled, stoned and mashed
Juice of 3 lemons
3 tablespoons white rum
3 egg whites, whisked

Over low heat, dissolve sugar in the water, boil for 10 minutes. Leave to cool. Blend mangoes with lemon juice and rum. Add the syrup. Pour into a container and freeze until just frozen. Turn into a bowl. Fold in the egg whites. Freeze.

Minted Lime Ice

PREPARATION TIME: 15 minutes plus freezing

175g (6oz) caster sugar
375ml (12 fl oz) water
Grated rind and juice of 6 limes
4 tablespoons fresh mint, finely chopped
150ml (5 fl oz) double cream
3 tablespoons single cream

Place the sugar and water in a saucepan. Stir gently over a low heat. When the sugar has dissolved bring the mixture to the boil. Remove the pan from the heat. Stir in the grated rind of the limes. Add the juice and stir in the mint. Let the mixture cool and pour into ice trays. Freeze the mixture, covered with foil. When the mixture is frozen, crush it. Lightly whip the creams together. Stir the lime ice into the cream and re-freeze. Slightly thaw and spoon into small glasses to serve.

Lemon Ice Cream Sponge

PREPARATION TIME: 20 minutes plus freezing

COOKING TIME: 15 minutes

OVEN: 220°C (425°F) Gas Mark 7

Sponge
3 large eggs
75g (3oz) caster sugar
75g (3oz) self raising flour, sieved

Filling
4 level teaspoons lemon curd
1 grated rind of lemon
6 scoops soft-scoop vanilla ice cream

To decorate
3 tablespoons double cream
Icing sugar
Sugared lemon slices

Sponge
Whisk eggs and sugar until light and fluffy. Sieve in flour and mix in carefully. Bake in a large 13cm (5 inch) baking tin. Turn out and cool.

Filling
Slice the cake into three horizontally. On bottom and middle slices spread lemon curd. Mix together the lemon rind and vanilla ice cream. Spread on top of the lemon curd. Sandwich together and freeze.

To decorate
Whip cream until stiff; place in piping bag with a star nozzle; pipe rosettes on top of the sponge. Dust with icing sugar and add lemon slices.

Custard Ice Cream

PREPARATION TIME: 20 minutes

5 egg yolks
150ml (¼ pint) single cream
150g (6oz) caster sugar
300ml (½ pint) double cream

Combine egg yolks, single cream and 100g (4oz) of the sugar in a basin. Place over a pan of simmering water and stir until mixture coats the back of a spoon. Strain mixture into a bowl and leave to cool. Whip double cream lightly. Mix with custard carefully. Fold in remaining 50g (2oz) of sugar. Pour into a freezer-proof container. Cover and freeze.

Coconut Sorbet

PREPARATION TIME: 20 minutes plus freezing

250ml (8 fl oz) tinned coconut juice
Scant 150ml (5 fl oz) mineral water
2 tablespoons dark rum
2 egg whites
100g (4oz) sugar

To decorate
2 bananas, sliced
Chocolate sauce

Mix the coconut juice with the mineral water and rum. Whisk the egg whites until stiff, gradually adding the sugar. Stir the egg whites into the coconut mixture with a balloon whisk and freeze until creamy. Serve with banana slices and chocolate sauce.

Honey Ice Cream

PREPARATION TIME: 15 minutes plus freezing

450g (1lb) raspberries
150ml (5 fl oz) clear honey
150ml (5 fl oz) double cream
2 tablespoons lemon juice
3 egg whites
120ml (4 fl oz) water
150ml (5 fl oz) single cream
4 x 15ml tablespoons granulated sugar

Cook the raspberries in a saucepan with the honey and water. Add the sugar and cook for 5 minutes until dissolved. Leave to cool. Rub the mixture through a sieve and chill. Beat the double cream until thick and stir in the single cream. Fold the creams into the fruit mixture. Freeze until almost solid. Whisk and re-freeze.

Facing page: Mocha Soufflé (top), Chocolate Banana Ice (centre left), Banana Ice Crêpes (centre right) and Mousse Glacée au Chocolat (bottom).

Fancy Ice

PREPARATION TIME: 15 minutes
COOKING TIME: 10 minutes
OVEN: 220°C (425°F) Gas Mark 7

Sponge
2 eggs
50g (2oz) caster sugar
50g (2oz) flour

Topping
200g (8oz) fondant icing
1 tablespoon lemon juice
A few drops yellow food colour

Filling and decoration
Blackberry sorbet
Apricot purée
Blackberries

Sponge
Whisk eggs and caster sugar until light and fluffy. Sieve in the flour, fold gently into mixture. Lightly grease and flour a bun tin. Spoon into 12 portions and bake until golden brown. Turn out and cool on a wire rack.

Topping
Melt the fondant icing. Add the lemon juice and food colouring. Spoon over the cakes, leave to harden and set.

Filling and decoration
Fit a star nozzle on a piping bag and fill with blackberry sorbet. Cut the sponges in half and pipe onto top of base of cake; top with another. Serve with a spoonful of apricot purée on the side and decorate with blackberries.

Mocha Soufflé

PREPARATION TIME: 30 minutes plus chilling

15g (½oz) gelatine
4 tablespoons warm water
25g (1oz) cocoa
1 teaspoon instant coffee
450ml (¾ pint) milk
4 eggs, separated
75g (3oz) caster sugar
2 tablespoons rum
150ml (5 fl oz) fresh double cream, whipped
Chocolate curls

Dissolve the gelatine in a small basin with the warm water. Mix the cocoa and coffee with the milk and bring to the boil in a saucepan. In a mixing bowl beat the egg yolks and sugar together until pale and fluffy. Gradually beat in the milk mixture. Place the bowl over a saucepan of hot water for 15 minutes. Stir gently. Remove from heat and stir in the rum and dissolved gelatine. Allow to cool. Whisk the egg whites until they peak and fold into the mixture. Mix in half of the double cream. Pour into a prepared ½ litre (1 pint) soufflé dish. Chill until set. Decorate with the remaining whipped cream and chocolate curls.

This page: Fancy Ice (top), Custard Ice Cream (centre) and Coconut Sorbet (bottom). Facing page: Refreshing Sorbet (top), Minted Lime Ice (centre left), Honey Ice Cream (centre right) and Lemon Ice Cream Sponge (bottom).

Desserts for Autumn

Illustrations below: Charlotte (left), Steamed Chocolate Pudding with Rum Sauce (centre) and Viennoise Pudding with German Sauce (right).

Charlotte

PREPARATION TIME: 30 minutes
COOKING TIME: 40 minutes
OVEN: 180°C (350°F) Gas Mark 4

450g (1lb) cooking apples
100g (4oz) white breadcrumbs
50g (2oz) shredded suet
75g (3oz) brown sugar
1 lemon
Caster sugar for topping
Custard or cream

Wash, peel, core and slice the apples. Mix together the breadcrumbs, suet, sugar and grated lemon rind. Sprinkle a little of this mixture in the bottom of a greased pie dish. Then add a layer of apple slices (sprinkled with juice from the lemon) and fill the dish with alternate layers of the breadcrumb mixture and sliced apples – finishing with a layer of breadcrumbs. Bake in the oven for 40 minutes. Turn out onto a hot dish and sprinkle lightly with caster sugar. Serve with custard or cream.

Steamed Chocolate Pudding with Rum Sauce

PREPARATION TIME: 25 minutes

COOKING TIME: 1½ hours or until firm to touch

75g (3oz) plain cooking chocolate
Few drops of vanilla essence
75g (3oz) butter
150g (6oz) caster sugar
3 eggs
250g (9oz) self-raising flour
7½ tablespoons milk

Sauce

3 tablespoons cornflour
¾ pint milk
3 tablespoons sugar
3 tablespoons dark rum

Put the chocolate, vanilla and butter in a heatproof bowl placed over a pan of hot water. Heat gently, stirring to melt the chocolate and butter. When melted remove from the heat and cool. Stir the sugar into the chocolate mixture and beat in the eggs. Sift the flour and mix in well. Stir in the milk. Grease a 1.2 litre (2 pint) pudding basin. Pour the mixture into the pudding basin. Cover with a foil lid tied on securely with string. Steam pudding for 1½ hours.

Sauce

In a saucepan dissolve the cornflour in the milk. Stir in the sugar and heat gently, stirring constantly. Bring the mixture to the boil and then reduce heat and simmer until it thickens and is smooth. Stir in the rum. Turn out the pudding and serve hot with sauce.

Viennoise Pudding with German Sauce

PREPARATION TIME: 60 minutes

COOKING TIME: 90 minutes

25g (1oz) sugar cubes
1 tablespoon water
300ml (½ pint) milk
150g (6oz) bread
Grated rind of 1 lemon
75g (3oz) sultanas
40g (1½oz) chopped candied peel
3 eggs
½ wineglass of sherry
75g (3oz) caster sugar

Sauce

2 egg yolks
¼ pint sherry
12g (½oz) caster sugar
Strips of lemon rind

Using a thick pan, dissolve the sugar in a tablespoonful of water. Heat gently until dissolved, then bring to the boil and boil rapidly until the syrup turns brown. Heat the milk and pour over the syrup. Remove the crusts from the bread, then cut the bread into small cubes. Add the lemon rind, sultanas and candied peel. Beat the eggs and add the milk/syrup mixture to the eggs. Then add the sherry and caster sugar. Pour the whole mixture over the bread and leave to soak for 30 minutes. Transfer to a greased basin, cover with greased foil and steam for 60-90 minutes until firm.

Sauce
Beat the egg yolks, warm the sherry and then mix together with the sugar and lemon rind. Sit the basin in a pan of hot water and whisk thoroughly for 10 minutes. Do not over-heat the sauce or it will curdle. Serve immediately.

Crêpes

100g (4oz) plain flour
Pinch of salt or sugar (for extra sweetness)
1 egg, lightly beaten
300ml (½ pint) milk
1 teaspoon vegetable oil

Before doing any of the following pancake recipes, follow these instructions for making the crêpes. This mixture makes 12 crêpes. You can also buy them ready made.

Sieve the flour and salt into a bowl. Make a well in the centre and break an egg into it with half the milk. Beat well, then when smooth add the remaining milk. Leave the mixture to stand for 40 minutes. Grease the frying pan (or skillet) and heat it a little. Pour the batter into the pan. Quickly tilt and rotate the pan so the batter coats the bottom of the frying pan and pour off the excess batter. Cook over a moderate heat until the underside of the crêpe is gently brown. Turn crêpe over and brown the other side. Turn onto greaseproof paper and keep warm.

"Sissi" Crêpes

PREPARATION TIME: 25 minutes
COOKING TIME: 20 minutes
OVEN: 200°C (400°F) Gas Mark 6

150g (6oz) almond paste
3 tablespoons sugar syrup
3 tablespoons lemon juice
1½ tablespoons kirsch
25g (1oz) softened butter
6 tablespoons strawberry sauce
6 tablespoons Advocaat
6 scoops vanilla ice cream
Whipped cream

Mix the almond paste with the sugar syrup, lemon juice and kirsch and beat until fluffy. Divide the mixture between the crêpes and roll or fold them. Spread with butter, put in ovenproof dish and heat through at oven temperature 200°C (400°F) Gas Mark 6 for five minutes. Put them on small plates and pour over strawberry sauce and liqueur. Serve with whipped cream and vanilla ice cream.

Chocolate Crêpes

OVEN: 200°C (400°F) Gas Mark 6

150g (6oz) cherry jam
125g (5oz) softened butter
150ml (¼ pint) water
125g (5oz) sugar
40g (1½oz) cocoa powder
3 tablespoons rum
150g (6oz) plain chocolate, chopped
6 tablespoons whipped cream

Fill the crêpes with the jam and roll or fold them. Spread them on top with half of the butter. Heat the crêpes for 5 minutes.

Sauce
In a saucepan boil up the water, sugar and the rest of the butter. Remove the pan from the heat and stir in the rum and chocolate. If the sauce is too thick, thin with single cream. Pour the hot sauce over the crêpes. Decorate with whipped cream.

Crêpes Suzette

PREPARATION TIME: 40 minutes
COOKING TIME: 35 minutes

Rind of 1 orange
6 lumps sugar
60g (2¼ oz) butter
100g (4oz) more sugar
150ml (6 fl oz) fresh orange juice
5 tablespoons orange liqueur
3 tablespoons brandy

Cream the 100g (4oz) sugar and the butter till fluffy. Beat in the orange juice and rub the sugar cubes onto the rind so they look orange, reserve. Add the orange liqueur gradually. Spoon a little of the mixture into each pancake and roll or fold. Put the remaining mixture into a large frying pan and place the crêpes on top. Scatter the sugar cubes on the top. Gently heat the pan and melt the butter. In another saucepan warm the brandy and pour over the pancakes. Ignite the brandy and serve.

Pear and Nut Crêpes

PREPARATION TIME: 25 minutes
COOKING TIME: 15 minutes
OVEN: 180°C (350°F) Gas Mark 4

12 cooked crêpes
150g (6oz) butter
75g (3oz) icing sugar
75g (3oz) ground almonds
Few drops of almond essence
Grated rind of 1 lemon
650g (26oz) of tinned pears, drained and sliced

Cream the butter and sugar together till the mixture is fluffy. Beat the ground almonds, almond essence and lemon rind into the mixture. Fold the pears carefully into the mixture. Divide the mixture between the crêpes and roll or fold each one. Arrange the crêpes in an ovenproof dish and reheat gently in a moderate oven. Serve hot.

Apple and Nut Tart

PREPARATION TIME: 20 minutes
COOKING TIME: 40 minutes
OVEN: 220°C (425°F) Gas Mark 7

250g (9oz) flour
150g (5oz) sugar
Salt
1 egg
125g (4½oz) butter, cut into pieces

Filling
450g (1lb) dessert apples, peeled, cored and sliced
50g (2oz) ground hazelnuts
1 teaspoon ground cinnamon
Juice of 1 lemon
3 tablespoons apricot brandy (optional)
100g (4oz) apricot jam
50g (2oz) chopped nuts

Pastry
Sift the flour and sugar (reserving 25g (1oz) of sugar for filling) and a pinch of salt into a mixing bowl. Make a well in the centre and add the egg. Mix in the butter pieces, rub the ingredients to make a soft smooth dough. Rest the dough by leaving it in the fridge for 30 minutes. Grease a 20cm (8 inch) pie dish. Roll out the pastry, line the dish.

Filling
Layer the apple and hazelnuts. Sprinkle with cinnamon and sugar, lemon juice and apricot brandy. Put the apricot jam in a saucepan and heat until melted. Pour over filling. Sprinkle with the chopped nuts. Bake until golden and fruit is soft. Take tart out of oven and cool.

Treacle Tart

PREPARATION TIME: 25 minutes
COOKING TIME: 30 minutes
OVEN: 180°C (350°F) Gas Mark 4

Pastry
150g (6oz) plain flour
Pinch of salt
30g (1½oz) butter or margarine
30g (1½oz) lard
Cold water to mix

Filling
225g (8oz) golden syrup
50g (2oz) breadcrumbs
Lemon juice

Sieve the flour into a bowl. Add the salt and the lard to the flour. Chop the lard into small pieces with a knife and then rub into the flour with the fingertips. Add the water and mix to a stiff dough. Turn on to a lightly floured board and knead the dough until free from cracks. Roll out a little larger than a 23cm (9 inch) tin. Line the edge of the tin with a strip of pastry (cut from the edge). Damp it well and then line the whole tin with the rolled out pastry. Seal the edges, trim off any excess pastry and decorate the edges.

Filling
Sprinkle the breadcrumbs into the lined tin and cover with golden syrup. Add a little lemon juice. Cut the remaining pastry trimmings into thin strips, twist, and lay across the tart. Bake for 30 minutes.

Facing page: Pear and Nut Crêpes (top left), Crêpes Suzette (top right), Chocolate Crêpes (centre) and "Sissi" Crêpes (bottom).

Cherry Clafoutis

PREPARATION TIME: 15 minutes
COOKING TIME: 15 minutes
OVEN: 180°C (350°F) Gas Mark 4

350ml (12 fl oz) milk
1 tablespoon dark rum
4 eggs
100g (4oz) caster sugar
100g (4oz) flour
Generous pinch of salt
400g (14oz) stoned cherries
Icing sugar

Grease a shallow medium-sized baking dish. Place the milk, rum and eggs in a large mixing bowl and beat with a wire whisk until smooth and frothy. Add the caster sugar a little at a time and beat till the sugar is dissolved. Add the flour, sift it a little at a time, mixing in the salt with the last spoonful. Pour half of the batter into the prepared dish and spread the cherries over the top, then pour the remaining batter over all the cherries. Bake until the pudding is firm in the centre and sprinkle with a little icing sugar. Serve hot.

Red Fruit Crumble

PREPARATION TIME: 15 minutes
COOKING TIME: 25 minutes with a further 15 minutes
OVEN: 190°C (375°F) Gas Mark 5 reduced to 180°C (350°F) Gas Mark 4 after 25 minutes

2 level teaspoons cornflour
75g (3oz) granulated sugar
300g (12oz) raspberries, hulled
3 medium-sized ripe pears, peeled, quartered, cored and sliced.
100g (4oz) plain flour
50g (2oz) margarine
50g (2oz) soft brown sugar
25g (1oz) cornflakes or bran, crushed
Custard or cream

In a large mixing bowl, mix the cornflour and granulated sugar with the raspberries. Grease a 1.1 litre (2 pint) ovenproof dish. Arrange the mixture alternately with the pears. Sieve into another bowl the flour and rub in the margarine. Crush the cornflakes or bran flakes and stir in with the soft brown sugar. Put all the mixture over the fruit and flatten, using the back of the spoon. Cook in a moderate oven, temperature 190°C (375°F) Gas Mark 5 for 25 minutes, then reduce the temperature to 180°C (350°F) Gas mark 4 and cook for 15 minutes until crumble is golden. Serve hot with custard or cream.

Honey Plum Cobbler

PREPARATION TIME: 30 minutes
COOKING TIME: 15 minutes plus a further 30 minutes
OVEN: 200°C (400°F) Gas Mark 6

1 kg (2lb) ripe plums, halved and stoned
4-6 tablespoons clear honey
225g (8oz) self-raising flour
2 tablespoons sugar
50g (2oz) butter or margarine
5-6 tablespoons milk
1 egg, beaten
Cream

Place the plums in an ovenproof dish with the honey, cover with a sheet of foil. Cook in a preheated oven for 15 minutes, temperature 200°C (400°F) Gas Mark 6. While the plums are cooking mix the flour and sugar and rub in the butter or margarine. Using a knife stir in the milk and egg so the mixture forms a soft dough. Lightly flour the work surface and roll out the dough. Cut with 5cm (2 inch) cutter to form cobblers. Remove the plums from the oven and cool. Arrange the cobblers round the top of the dish overlapping slightly. Brush the top of each one with a little milk and sprinkle with sugar. Cook until golden. Serve hot with cream.

Les Bourdaines
(Apples Baked in Pastry)

PREPARATION TIME: 30 minutes
COOKING TIME: 20-25 minutes
OVEN: 160°C (325°F) Gas Mark 3

370g (12oz) plain flour
Pinch of salt
150g (6oz) butter
1½ tablespoons caster sugar
5-7 tablespoons iced water
6 large dessert apples, peeled and cored
6 tablespoons plum jam
1 egg, beaten, to glaze
Cream

Sift the flour and salt into a bowl. Rub in the butter until the mixture is like fine breadcrumbs. Stir in the sugar. Mix in enough water to give a smooth pliable dough. Divide the dough into 6 pieces and roll out each square. Fill the centres of the apples with jam and place an apple on each pastry square. Brush the edges of the squares with water and wrap up the apples, sealing them well. Cut out some pastry leaves and decorate. Place on a baking sheet. Brush the pastry with beaten egg, bake in a moderate preheated oven. Bake until golden brown. Serve hot with cream.

Alma Pudding with Wine Sauce

125g (4oz) butter
2 tablespoons sugar
2 eggs
4 tablespoons plain flour
2 tablespoons orange marmalade
½ teaspoon bicarbonate of soda
75ml (2½ fl oz) milk

Wine Sauce
1 egg
150ml (¼ pint) sherry
1 tablespoon sugar

Beat butter and sugar until light. Add eggs and flour. Add the marmalade, bicarbonate of soda and milk. Place mixture in a pudding basin and cover with foil, tied in place with string. Place in a large pan, pour in hot water until it comes ¾ of the way up the basin. Bring water to the boil and steam for 1 hour. Remove and turn out into a serving plate and serve with wine sauce.

Wine Sauce
Combine ingredients. Place over a pan of boiling water. Whisk until light and frothy. Serve.

This page: Red Fruit Crumble (top left), Cherry Clafoutis (top right) and Honey Plum Cobbler (bottom).

Facing page: Treacle Tart (top left), Les Bourdaines (top right), Apple and Nut Tart (centre) and Alma Pudding (bottom).

Winter Desserts

Yorkshire Apple Tart

PREPARATION TIME: 30 minutes plus chilling

COOKING TIME: 25 minutes plus 15 minutes

OVEN: 190°C (375°F) Gas Mark 5

275g (10oz) shortcrust pastry
350g (12oz) cooking apples, peeled, cored and sliced
2 tablespoons sugar
1 tablespoon water
Little milk and sugar to glaze
100g (4oz) strong cheese, sliced
Whipped cream

Roll out the pastry and use two-thirds to line a 20cm (8 inch) flan ring. Fill the centre with the sliced apples, sprinkle with sugar and water. Seal the edges, cover the tart with the remaining pastry, and brush the top with a little milk and sprinkle with sugar. Place in a preheated moderately hot oven and bake for 20 to 25 minutes until the crust is firm and lightly browned. Leave to cool, then with care remove the crust with a sharp knife. Place the cheese on top of the apples. Replace the crust. Return to the oven and bake for 15 minutes until the cheese has melted. Serve hot with whipped cream. Serves 4 to 6.

Fruit Cobbler

PREPARATION TIME: 20 minutes

COOKING TIME: 20 minutes

OVEN: 220°C (450°F) Gas Mark 7

250g (9oz) self raising flour
125g (4oz) butter
175ml (¼ pint) milk
3 large cooking apples
370g (12oz) can raspberries, drained
50g (2oz) granulated sugar
Cream
50g (2oz) demerara sugar

Sieve flour into a mixing bowl. Rub in butter excluding 10g (½oz), and work into a soft dough by adding milk. Knead the dough and roll out onto a floured board. Cut out the scones. Place the scones on a baking sheet and bake at 220°C (450°F) Gas Mark 7, for 10-15 minutes. Peel the apples and slice them. Put the apples in a saucepan, and cook in a little water with granulated sugar until soft. Drain the apples and add the raspberries. Cut the scones and sandwich together with butter. Put a circle of scones round the edge of the apple and raspberry mixture. Put some cream in the circle left by the scones. Sprinkle with a little demerara sugar and grill until the sugar begins to caramelise. Serve at

Snowballs

PREPARATION TIME: 20 minutes

COOKING TIME: 30 minutes then 3 minutes

OVEN: 190°C (375°F) Gas Mark 5

6 medium cooking apples
75g (3oz) soft brown sugar
¾ teaspoon mixed spice
2 eggs
75g (3oz) caster sugar
Glacé cherries and angelica (optional)

Wash and core the apples. Mix together soft brown sugar and all the spices and fill the centre of the apples. Put the apples on a baking tray and bake. Whisk the egg white until it peaks and fold in the caster sugar. Coat the apples with meringue and then return to the oven for a few minutes. Decorate with glacé cherries and angelica if desired.

Apple Betty

PREPARATION TIME: 30 minutes

COOKING TIME: 30 minutes

OVEN: 180°C (350°F) Gas Mark 4

100g (4oz) butter
100g (4oz) fresh white breadcrumbs
100g (4oz) soft brown sugar
½ level teaspoon ground cinnamon
Grated rind and juice of 1 lemon
800g (2lb) cooking apples, peeled, cored and sliced
3 tablespoons water
Ice cream or cream

Melt the butter in a saucepan. Take the pan off the heat and mix in the breadcrumbs. In a bowl mix the sugar, cinnamon and grated lemon rind. Add the apple slices. Butter the pie dish 1.2 litre (2 pint) size. Sprinkle some of the crumbs in the dish, layer the apple slices with the crumb mixture, ending with the crumb mixture on top. Squeeze the lemon juice and spoon the water over the pudding. Cover the pudding with buttered foil and bake until apples are cooked. The topping should be crisp and golden. Serve with ice cream or cream.

Rainbow Tart

PREPARATION TIME: 15 minutes

COOKING TIME: 35 minutes

OVEN: 109°C (375°F) Gas Mark 5

Pastry
225g (8oz) plain flour
Pinch of salt
50g (2oz) butter or margarine
50g (2oz) lard
About 3 tablespoons water

Filling
1½ tablespoons strawberry jam
1½ tablespoons blackberry jam
1½ tablespoons bilberry jam
1½ tablespoons lemon curd
1½ tablespoons orange marmalade
1½ tablespoons gooseberry purée
1½ tablespoons mincemeat
Custard

Pastry
Sift flour and salt into a bowl. Cut the butter/margarine and lard into pieces and work into the flour with fingers until it looks like breadcrumbs. Stir the water into mixture and mix into a dough. Roll out the pastry on a lightly floured surface. Line a 23cm (9 inch) pie plate, trim the edges and reserve for twists.

Filling
Mark the dough and fill in the sections with the jams, curd and mincemeat. Twist the excess dough into spirals and use it to separate the jam sections. Brush the ends with water and press onto the edge to seal. Flute the edge of pastry case and bake. Remove from the oven and leave to cool for 10 minutes. Serve with pouring custard.

Apple Dumplings with Walnut Sauce

PREPARATION TIME: 30 minutes

COOKING TIME: 35 minutes

OVEN: 200°C (400°F) Gas Mark 6

Dumplings
525g (18oz) shortcrust pastry
6 large cooking apples, cored
9 tablespoons mincemeat
1 egg, lightly beaten

Walnut Sauce
75g (3oz) butter
75g (3oz) light brown sugar
2½ tablespoons double cream
75g (3oz) chopped walnuts

Divide the dough into 6 portions. Roll out each portion into a round large enough to wrap up one apple. Place the apple in the centre of the dough round and fill the cavity (left by removing the core) with mincemeat. Wrap the dough round the apple and moisten the edges with beaten egg. Press together to seal. Place the dumplings on a baking sheet and brush all over with beaten egg. Bake in preheated moderately hot oven for 35 minutes or until golden brown. Meanwhile make the sauce.

Walnut Sauce
Melt the butter in a saucepan and stir in all the sugar. When the sugar has dissolved, stir in the cream and walnuts. Heat gently. Serve the dumplings with the sauce; both should be hot.

Facing page: Fruit Cobbler (top), Apple Betty (centre) and Yorkshire Apple Tart (bottom).

Winter Fruits

PREPARATION TIME: 15 minutes plus 1 hour soaking

COOKING TIME: 40 minutes

OVEN: 190°C (375°F) Gas Mark 5

100g (4oz) seedless raisins
100g (4oz) currants
100g (4oz) sultanas
100g (4oz) chopped mixed peel
Finely grated rind and juice of an orange
6 thick slices of toast, crusts removed
About 50g (2oz) butter or margarine
100g (4oz) soft brown sugar
300ml (½ pint) milk
2 eggs, lightly beaten
¼ teaspoon ground cinnamon
Custard

Put all the dried fruit, peel, orange rind and juice into a bowl and mix well. Put half the fruit mixture in the bottom of a buttered baking dish. Spread the toast with the butter or margarine, then cut it into small squares. Cover the fruit with half the toast and sprinkle with 50g (2oz) of the soft brown sugar. Repeat the layers again. Mix together the milk, eggs and cinnamon and pour over the layered pudding. Leave the pudding to soak for one hour. Bake in a preheated oven until crisp on top. Serve with thin pouring custard.

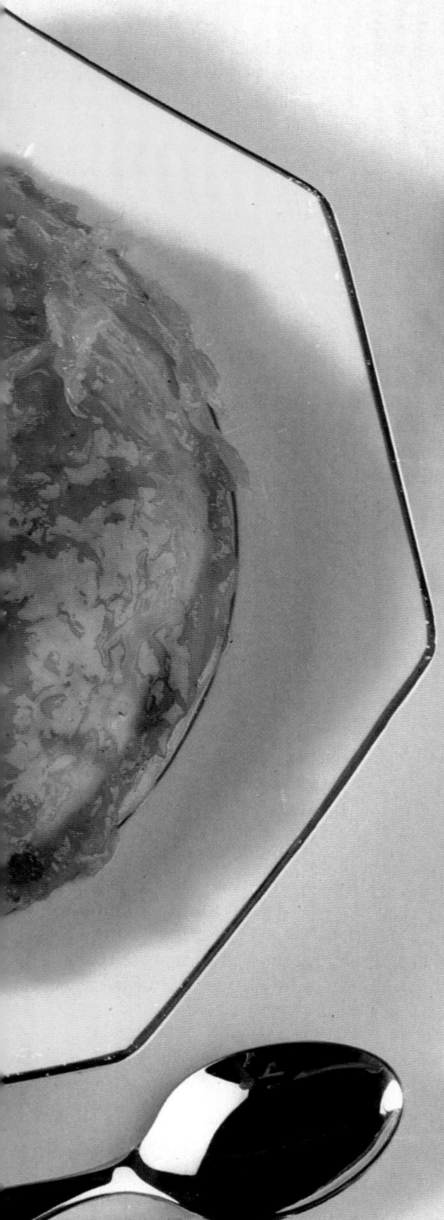

Apricot Pudding

PREPARATION TIME: 25 minutes

COOKING TIME: 2 hours

Pastry
175g (6oz) flour
Pinch of salt
50g (2oz) caster sugar
75g (3oz) shredded suet
5 tablespoons milk

Filling
1 cooking apple
175g (6oz) dried apricots, soaked overnight in cold water
50g (2oz) seedless raisins
½ teaspoon ground mixed spice
3 tablespoons golden syrup
2-3 tablespoons demerara sugar, to finish
Custard or cream

Pastry
Sift the flour and salt into a bowl. Stir in the sugar and suet, add the milk gradually and knead lightly to form a firm dough. Wrap the dough in foil and chill in the fridge.

Filling
Peel and core the apples, then grate into a bowl. Drain the apricots and chop them very finely, then mix in with all the other ingredients for the filling. Roll out the dough on a lightly floured surface. Cut out a small circle large enough to fit the base of a well buttered 900ml (1½ pint) pudding basin. Put the dough in the basin. Layer with fruit and a circle of dough (4 layers of dough, 3 layers of filling). Cover the top of the pudding with a circle of buttered greaseproof paper. Cover the basin with foil tied with string. Put the pudding basin in a steamer or in a pan half-filled with boiling water. Cover with a lid and steam. Keep the water level up. Remove the foil and greaseproof disc and let the pudding stand for a few minutes. Turn out carefully on a warmed serving plate and sprinkle with demerara sugar. Serve hot with pouring custard or cream.

Rhubarb Tart

PREPARATION TIME: 30 minutes

COOKING TIME: 40 minutes, then another 25 minutes

OVEN: 180°C (350°F) Gas Mark 4

Filling
1kg (2lb) rhubarb, cut into 2.5cm (1 inch) pieces.
525g (1lb 3oz) sugar
100g (4oz) butter
3 eggs
2 tablespoons white wine
250g (9oz) flour
2 teaspoons baking powder

Topping
150ml (¼ pint) soured cream
1 teaspoon ground cinnamon
50g (2oz) ground almonds
Icing sugar

Put the rhubarb pieces into a bowl, sprinkle with sugar (reserve 125g [5oz]). Cover and allow the rhubarb to draw. Cream the butter and 75g (3oz) of the granulated sugar. Mix together until light and fluffy. Stir in one egg and the wine. Sift in the flour and baking powder. Stir into the other ingredients. Knead the ingredients together to make a smooth dough. Form into a ball, wrap with greaseproof paper and allow to rest for 30 minutes in the fridge. Grease a 25cm (10 inch) loose-based or spring-clip tin. Roll out pastry on a well floured surface. Line tin with pastry. Strain the rhubarb, arrange in pastry case and bake.

Topping
Beat the cream and remaining eggs together and stir in the remaining sugar, the cinnamon and ground almonds. Mix thoroughly until smooth. Take the tart out of the oven and pour the topping over the rhubarb. Return to the oven and bake for another 25 minutes. Remove from the oven, turn out and dust with icing sugar, cool before serving.

Facing page: Rhubarb Tart (top), Winter Fruits (bottom left) and Apricot Pudding (bottom right).

Carrot Pudding

PREPARATION TIME: 15 minutes
COOKING TIME: 45 minutes
OVEN: 180°C (350°F) Gas Mark 4

50g (2oz) butter or margarine
50g (2oz) sugar
2 eggs, separated
50g (2oz) plain flour
1 teaspoon ground cinnamon
225g (8oz) carrots, peeled and grated
1 tablespoon chopped walnuts
4 tablespoons dry red wine
Grated rind, and juice of 1 lemon
Pinch of salt

Cream the butter or margarine with the sugar until the mixture is light and fluffy. Beat in the egg yolks. Sift in the flour and cinnamon, carrots, walnuts, wine, lemon rind, juice and salt. Beat the egg whites until stiff and fold into carrot mixture. Pour into a greased baking dish. Bake in a preheated moderate oven. Serve hot from the dish.

Orange Round

PREPARATION TIME: 30 minutes
COOKING TIME: 15 minutes for pastry 20 minutes for filled flan
OVEN: 180°C (350°F) Gas Mark 4

318g (10oz) shortcrust pastry
3 oranges, thinly sliced
2 eggs, beaten
75g (3oz) ground almonds
3 tablespoons sugar
3 tablespoons clear honey

Roll out the pastry and line a 20cm (8 inch) flan dish. Prick the base of the flan. Cut a piece of greaseproof paper, line the pastry and sprinkle with baking beans (or any dried beans, to bake blind). Bake for 10 minutes at 190°C (375°F) Gas Mark 5. While the case is baking, prepare the orange filling. Put the oranges in a saucepan. Add enough water to cover the oranges and simmer for 20 minutes. Cook until the orange peel is soft and drain the water. Beat the egg, almonds and sugar until smooth. Spread the mixture in the flan case. Arrange the poached orange slices on top of the mixture. Spoon the clear honey over all the slices. Cook the flan for 20 minutes.

Yuletide Pudding (Round)

PREPARATION TIME: 30 minutes
COOKING TIME: 5 hours plus 3 hours before serving

350g (12oz) mixed dried fruit
150g (6oz) stoned raisins
75g (3oz) chopped mixed peel
350g (12oz) soft dark brown sugar
40g (1½oz) almonds, blanched and chopped
150g (6oz) fresh white breadcrumbs
150g (6oz) shredded suet
150g (6oz) plain flour
½ level teaspoon ground nutmeg
½ level teaspoon ground cinnamon
¼ level teaspoon salt
1 carrot, grated
1 cooking apple, peeled, cored and grated
Grated rind and juice of 1 lemon
3 tablespoons brandy
1 large egg

Put all ingredients in a large mixing bowl and blend together well. Grease 2 1.2 litre (2 pint) pudding basins. Put the mixture into the pudding basins, dividing the mixture evenly between both. Fill the basins, but leave a gap of about 2.5cm (1 inch) at the top. Cover both puddings with buttered round of greaseproof paper. Make a foil pudding lid with a pleat and tie securely onto basin. Stand the puddings in pans and add enough water to keep the pans two-thirds full. Cover the pans and boil for 5 hours. Keep the pans topped up with hot water. Remove the basins from water and gently loosen one pudding from its basin, turn it out onto the other pudding. Press the puddings together to make one pudding. Press down on the top pudding. Leave to cool completely, then cover together with greaseproof paper and foil. Before serving boil for three hours. Again make sure the water is topped up. Unwrap carefully and turn out of the bowl.

Pacific Pudding

225g (8oz) can pineapple rings
100g (4oz) caster sugar
100g (4oz) soft margarine
Grated rind of 1 orange
2 eggs, beaten
75g (3oz) self raising flour, sifted
50g (2oz) white breadcrumbs
50g (2oz) glacé cherries, quartered
50g (2oz) stoned raisins
25g (1oz) angelica
2 tablespoons golden syrup

Drain the pineapple and keep the juice. Cut 3 rings in half and reserve. Chop the remainder coarsely. Cream together the margarine and sugar, add the orange rind and beat in the eggs. Fold in the flour and breadcrumbs. Add the chopped pineapple, cherries, raisins and angelica, and mix well. Butter a 900ml (1½ pint) pudding basin. Put the syrup in the bottom and arrange the pineapple rings in a circle. Spoon in the sponge mixture on top and level it. Cover with buttered paper and foil. Put the pudding basin in a saucepan of boiling water two-thirds full. Boil for 1¾ hours. Serve with tangy butter.

This page: Rainbow Tart (top), Carrot Pudding (centre) and Apple Dumplings with Walnut Sauce (bottom).

Facing page: Yuletide Pudding (top), Pacific Pudding (centre left), Orange Round (centre right) and Snowball (bottom).

Zabaglione

PREPARATION TIME: 5 minutes
COOKING TIME: 10 minutes

4 egg yolks
4 tablespoons caster sugar
4 tablespoons Marsala wine

Put all the ingredients into a large heatproof bowl. Beat with a balloon whisk until light and frothy. Stand the bowl in a pan of water over a low heat and continue to whisk. The mixture will froth and is now ready to serve. Pour into heatproof glasses and serve immediately with the sponge fingers. An instant Italian dessert. Note: Do not overheat or the mixture will curdle and not become frothy.

Raspberry Brioches

PREPARATION TIME: 15 minutes

12 small brioches (use either fresh or frozen brioches, or choux buns as illustrated).
50g (2oz) sugar
1 tablespoon lemon juice
2 tablespoons honey
Scant 150ml (¼ pint) water
1 teaspoon raspberry liqueur
400g (1lb) fresh raspberries
2 tablespoons toasted, flaked almonds

Let the sugar, lemon juice, honey and water boil for three minutes. Add the raspberry liqueur. Using some of the syrup, soak the brioches. Fill with the raspberries. Sprinkle over the rest of the syrup and add the flaked almonds. Serve.

This page: Poor Knights of Windsor (top left), Zabaglione (top right) and Coffee Liqueur Crêpes (bottom).

Facing page: Lemon Syllabub (top), Hot Fruit Brioches (centre) and Raspberry Brioches (bottom).

Hot Fruit Brioches

PREPARATION TIME: 20 minutes

12 small brioches
75g (3oz) sugar
Scant 150ml (¼pint) water
300g (10oz) apricots, peeled and halved
150g (6oz) fresh blackberries
3 tablespoons brandy

Sabayon Sauce
6 egg yolks
200g (7oz) sugar
250ml (8 fl oz) very dry white wine

Heat the sugar and water in a saucepan. Add the apricots and poach until glossy. Meanwhile make up the sabayon sauce and reserve. Add the blackberries and brandy, leave for 4 minutes and reserve them. Cut the tops off the brioches and hollow them. Fill the hollowed brioches with the poached apricots and saturate the top with remaining syrup. Pour over sabayon sauce and put the lid on.

Sabayon Sauce
Cream the egg yolks and sugar together. Place the bowl over warm water and add the wine. Stir continuously. A last minute alternative. They are delicious with hot stewed fruit, and the sabayon sauce adds a dash of extravagance.

Poor Knights of Windsor

PREPARATION TIME and COOKING TIME: 15 minutes inclusive

1 egg
1 tablespoon of milk
2 tablespoons caster sugar
6 small slices of fruit or plain bread, crusts removed
50g (2oz) butter
1 teaspoon ground cinnamon

To decorate
350g (15oz) can apricot halves in juice (drained)
Whipped cream
1 tablespoon toasted almonds

Beat the egg and mix with sugar and milk. Dip the bread into the custard mixture and fry. Sprinkle bread with ground cinnamon and decorate with apricot halves, whipped cream and toasted almonds. Serve hot.

Coffee Liqueur Crêpes

PREPARATION TIME: 35 minutes

Crêpes
100g (4oz) plain flour
Pinch of salt
1 teaspoon caster sugar
250ml (8 fl oz) cold milk
1 egg
4 tablespoons cold strong black coffee
1 teaspoon vegetable oil
Oil for frying

Sauce
15g (½oz) butter
Grated rind and juice of ½ a lemon
2 tablespoons coffee liqueur

Crêpes
Sift the flour, salt and sugar into a bowl. Add the milk, egg, coffee and oil and whisk until smooth. Lightly oil a frying pan and fry the crêpes until golden brown. Toss and cook on the other side. Keep the crêpes warm.

Sauce
Melt the butter in a large frying pan. Arrange the crêpes folded in the pan. Add the lemon rind and juice and coffee liqueur. Heat gently until hot. Serve immediately.

Syllabub

PREPARATION TIME: 10 minutes plus overnight soaking

Thinly pared rind of 1 lemon
6 tablespoons of lemon juice
9 tablespoons sweet white wine or sherry
15ml (3 tablespoons) brandy
75g (3oz) caster sugar
450ml (¾ pint) double cream
Grated nutmeg

Put the lemon rind and juice, brandy and wine or sherry in a bowl. Leave overnight. Remove the lemon rind and stir in the sugar. Gradually stir in the cream until it peaks. This will require beating. Spoon into glasses and sprinkle with grated nutmeg.

Caramel Oranges

PREPARATION TIME: 15 minutes

6 oranges (large and juicy)
150g (6oz) caster sugar
450ml (¾ pint) water

Peel the oranges. Put the sugar and water in a heavy saucepan. Boil the mixture until it begins to caramelise. Place the oranges in a presentation dish and pour over the liquid caramel. Serve immediately.

Blackberry Fluff

PREPARATION TIME: 10 minutes

450g (1lb) blackberries, drained
300ml (10 fl oz) double cream
1 egg white
50g (2oz) caster sugar
Pieces of angelica to decorate
Sponge finger biscuits

Sieve the blackberries. Whip the cream until thick and stir into the blackberry purée. Beat the egg white, adding the sugar slowly until the mixture is stiff. Fold the egg white into the blackberry cream. Spoon into individual serving glasses and serve with sponge finger biscuits. A quick and luscious dessert. Make it in advance but in individual glasses. Store in the refrigerator and serve chilled.

Spiced Pears

PREPARATION TIME: 20 minutes

750g (1½lb) can of pear halves
450ml (¾pint) red wine
3 teaspoons ground cinnamon
75g (3oz) stem ginger, chopped

Drain the pears, saving 150ml (¼ pint) of the juice. Put the pears in the wine, with the juice and cinnamon. Boil for 10 minutes and reduce the heat. Simmer for ten minutes. Add the chopped ginger and leave to cool. Serve chilled.

Cherries Jubilee

PREPARATION TIME: 10 minutes

375g (1½lb) tinned black cherries
1½ tablespoons grated lemon rind
75g (3 tablespoons) cornflour
6 tablespoons brandy
Vanilla ice cream

Drain the cherries, reserving the tinned juice. Put all except one tablespoon of juice into a saucepan, add the lemon rind and bring to the boil. Simmer for 2 minutes and strain the juice. Return the juice to the saucepan and add the cherries. In the reserved tablespoon of juice, dissolve the cornflour. Add this to the saucepan and stir constantly until thick. Warm the brandy and set it alight. Pour it as it flames into the cherry mixture and stir until the flames die down. Serve immediately with ice cream.

Redcurrant and Blackcurrant Compote

PREPARATION TIME: 10 minutes plus chilling

750g (1½lb) redcurrants (or 350g (12oz) each of redcurrants and blackcurrants)
275g (10oz) sugar
1 tablespoon water
2 tablespoons gin or brandy
Whipped cream
Sponge finger biscuits

Put the fruit, sugar and water into a saucepan. Shake gently over the heat until sugar has dissolved. Remove from heat and stir in the gin or brandy. Cool. Spoon the compote into serving dishes. Chill for three hours before serving. Serve in the cream and sponge finger biscuits.

Tarte Aux Fruits

PREPARATION TIME: 15 minutes

1 pastry or sponge flan case
450g (1lb) grapes, black and green (or 450g (1lb) fresh fruit tinned or bottled)
575ml (1 pint) of custard (optional)

Glaze
½ pint juice from the fruit after poaching
OR
drained syrup from tin
OR
1 heaped tablespoon apricot jam
OR
sugar syrup

Facing page: Caramel Oranges (top), Blackberry Fluff (centre left) and Cherries in Wine (bottom).

Halve and stone the grapes. Place them cut side down in alternate rings around a flan case. Glaze with one heaped tablespoon of warmed apricot jam, poured and brushed over the fruit. Alternatively, spread the base of the flan with 575ml (1 pint) of made custard before covering with fruit. Glaze with either apricot jam or sugar syrup.

Cherries in Wine

PREPARATION TIME: 5 minutes
COOKING TIME: 10 minutes

250g (1lb) cherries, stoned
½ teaspoon ground cinnamon
4 tablespoons sugar
300ml (½ pint) light red wine
4 tablespoons redcurrant jelly
2 teaspoons cornflour

Put the cherries, cinnamon, sugar and most of the wine into a heavy saucepan. Boil slowly. Mix the redcurrant jelly and cornflour with the rest of the wine and form into a paste before stirring into the saucepan. Simmer for three minutes, then remove from heat. Leave covered for five minutes. Serve cold.

Brandy Bananas

PREPARATION TIME: 10 minutes

75g (3oz) butter
3 tablespoons soft brown sugar
3 tablespoons lemon juice
6 bananas
3 tablespoons brandy
Single cream

Put the butter, sugar and lemon juice in a frying pan. Add the bananas and fry gently, making sure they are coated with the mixture. Add the brandy and cook for a second to warm the brandy through. Ignite, and let the flames die naturally. Serve at once. Serve hot with single cream.

Raspberry Jelly Mould

PREPARATION TIME: 8-10 minutes plus setting

1 packet raspberry jelly
300ml (½ pint) milk
150ml (¼ pint) water
200g (8oz) fresh or thawed, frozen raspberries
150ml (¼ pint) water to melt jelly
Cream

Put the jelly into a saucepan with 150ml (¼ pint) water and melt slowly. Stand until the jelly is tepid, then slowly stir in 300ml (½ pint) of milk and 150ml (¼ pint) of water. Wet the jelly mould and fill with the fruit. Pour in the jelly and leave until set. To serve, decorate with any fruit, and cream.

Simple Trifles

PREPARATION TIME: 15 minutes

6 trifle sponges
3 tablespoons Cointreau or orange liqueur
3 oranges
4 tablespoons lemon curd
3 egg whites
6 lemon twists

Break trifle sponges into pieces and place in 6 individual dishes. Sprinkle each one with half a tablespoon of Cointreau. Peel the oranges. Chop them and remove all pith. Divide equally between the portions. Place the lemon curd in a bowl. Whisk the egg whites until stiff and fold them into the lemon curd. Spoon this mixture over each serving and decorate with twists of lemon. Chill and serve.

This page: Brandy Bananas (top left), Cherries Jubilee (centre right) and Spiced Pears (bottom).

Facing page: Simple Trifle (top left), Tarte Aux Fruits (top right), Redcurrant and Blackcurrant Compote (far right) and Raspberry Jelly Mould (bottom).

Stuffed Baked Peaches

PREPARATION TIME: 15 minutes
COOKING TIME: 30 minutes
OVEN: 180°C (350°F) Gas Mark 4

6 large peaches, peeled, halved and stoned
75g (3oz) macaroons, crushed
40g (1½oz) ground almonds
1 teaspoon finely grated orange rind
2 egg yolks
40g (1½oz) butter, cut into small pieces
225ml (7½ fl oz) sweet white wine

Put the peaches on a baking dish, cut side up. In a small mixing bowl put the macaroons, almonds, orange rind and egg yolks. Mix together and use to fill the peaches. Put a knob of butter on top of each peach. Pour the wine into the baking dish and bake. Serve warm.

Fruit Salad with Cottage Cheese

PREPARATION TIME: 20 minutes

75g (3oz) cranberries
75g (3oz) raspberries
4 tablespoons orange juice
60g (2½oz) granulated sugar
2 tablespoons brandy
1 ogen melon
3 kiwi fruit
25g (1oz) icing sugar
200g (7oz) cottage cheese

Raspberry Sauce
200g (7oz) raspberries
75g (3oz) sugar
75ml (2½ fl oz) red wine
Small piece of lemon rind
Walnut pieces to decorate

Boil the cranberries, raspberries and orange juice with the granulated sugar for five minutes. Strain the mixture through a sieve. Stir in the brandy and cool. Peel and slice the melon and kiwi fruit. Arrange the fruit on individual plates. Stir the icing sugar into the cottage cheese and place a little on top of each plateful of fruit. Chill. Decorate using any of the fruit contained in the sauce.

Raspberry Sauce
Purée the raspberries. Boil for 5 minutes adding the sugar and wine and lemon rind. Continue to boil for three minutes. Serve hot or cold.

Baked Orange Rhubarb

PREPARATION TIME: 10 minutes
COOKING TIME: 45 minutes
OVEN: 160°C (325°F) Gas Mark 3

1kg (2lb) rhubarb, cut into 2.5cm (1 inch) pieces
1 finely grated rind of, and juice of one orange
6 tablespoons clear honey

Place the rhubarb in a baking dish and sprinkle over the orange rind, juice and honey. Cover and bake in a moderate oven. Serve.

Plums Baked in Port

PREPARATION TIME: 5 minutes
COOKING TIME: 45 minutes
OVEN: 150°C (300°F) Gas Mark 2

1kg (2lb) plums, halved and stoned
100g (4oz) brown sugar
150ml (¼ pint) port

Place the plums in a baking dish. Sprinkle over the sugar and port. Cover them and bake in a cool oven until the plums are tender. Serve warm or lightly chilled.

Pêches Carmen

PREPARATION TIME: 10 minutes

8 ripe peaches
675g (1½lb) raspberries
2 tablespoons kirsch
75g (3oz) icing sugar

Slice the peaches into a serving dish. Add the raspberries and kirsch. Leave to stand for an hour in a cool place. Spoon into individual dishes and sprinkle with icing sugar. Chill and serve with cream.

Facing page: Highland Cream and Ginger Snaps (top), Stuffed Baked Peaches (centre) and Fruit Salad with Cottage Cheese (bottom).

This page: (left picture) Pèches Carmen (top), Stuffed Oranges (centre) and Plums in Port (bottom). (Right picture) Sour Cream Peaches (top), Ginger Roll (centre) and Baked Orange Rhubarb (bottom).

Sour Cream Peaches

PREPARATION TIME: 10 minutes

COOKING TIME: 10 minutes

6 large peaches, peeled, sliced and stoned
3 tablespoons brown sugar
½ teaspoon ground cinnamon
300ml (½ pint) sour cream
6 tablespoons granulated sugar

Divide the peach slices between 6 flameproof serving dishes. Mix together the brown sugar and cinnamon. Sprinkle this over the peaches. Spoon the sour cream over the top. Sprinkle a tablespoon of sugar over each portion. Grill quickly until the sugar melts and caramelises.

Ginger Roll

PREPARATION TIME: This dish should be started the night before required, to allow the ginger biscuits to absorb the rum.

36 ginger snap biscuits
6 tablespoons rum
600ml (1 pint) double cream
2 teaspoons ground ginger
2 teaspoons soft brown sugar
2 tablespoons ginger syrup (from stem ginger)
Stem ginger slices

Put the biscuits in a flat dish and sprinkle with rum. When the rum has been completely absorbed, whip the cream with the ground ginger and sugar and add the ginger syrup. Use some of the cream to sandwich together the biscuits. Cover with the remaining cream and decorate with stem ginger slices. Serve.

Stuffed Oranges

PREPARATION TIME: 15 minutes

3 large oranges
2 dessert apples, peeled, cored and chopped
1½ tablespoons raisins
1½ tablespoons dates, chopped
1½ tablespoons nuts, toasted and chopped
1½ tablespoons soft brown sugar
180ml (6 fl oz) double cream
2 teaspoons icing sugar
Orange twists

Halve the oranges and scoop out the flesh, keeping the shells intact. Chop the flesh, discarding all the pith, and put it in a bowl. Add to the orange flesh the brown sugar, apple, raisins, dates and nuts. Mix well. Scoop the mixture back into the orange halves. Whip the cream with the icing sugar until it forms soft peaks. Spoon this cream on top of the orange mixture. Chill and serve. Decorate with twists of orange.

Highland Cream Served with Ginger Snaps

PREPARATION TIME: 15 minutes

4 tablespoons ginger marmalade
375ml (12 fl oz) double cream
4 tablespoons caster sugar
3 tablespoons whisky
3 tablespoons lemon juice
3 egg whites
Soft brown sugar
1 packet ginger snap biscuits

Divide the marmalade between serving dishes. Whip the cream, adding the caster sugar gradually. Fold in the whisky and lemon juice. Whisk the egg whites and fold into the cream. With a spoon, put a little of the cream mixture over the marmalade. Decorate with brown sugar and ginger snaps.

Orange Tart

PREPARATION TIME: 30 minutes
COOKING TIME: 25 minutes
OVEN: 190°C (375°F) Gas Mark 5

1 cooked pastry case
2 navel oranges, boiled
2 egg yolks, beaten
150g (6oz) sugar

To decorate
3 navel oranges
Apricot jam, melted

Purée the boiled oranges. Stir in the egg yolks and sugar. Slice the remaining three oranges. Fill the pastry case with the orange purée and decorate with slices of orange. Bake in a moderate oven until bubbling. Remove from oven and brush on melted apricot jam. Return to oven and bake for a further 10 minutes.

Fraises Escoffier

PREPARATION TIME: 15 minutes plus chilling

1kg (2lb) strawberries
2 oranges
50g (2oz) sugar cubes
75ml (2½ fl oz) Grand Marnier

Hull and slice the strawberries; peel and slice the oranges. Mash half the strawberries with sugar cubes and Grand Marnier. Stir in the remaining fruit and chill for one hour. Serve in individual dishes.

Lemon Mousse

PREPARATION TIME: 6-10 minutes

150g (6oz) caster sugar
3 eggs, separated
5 lemons
12g (½oz) gelatine
2 tablespoons warm water

Put the grated rind of the lemons in a basin with the egg yolks and sugar. Beat until stiff. Beat the egg whites until they peak. Dissolve the gelatine in the water and mix with the egg yolk mixture. Beat until the mixture begins to set. Fold in the egg whites. Fill the glasses with mousse. Serve chilled.

Fraises Escoffier (right), Orange Tart (centre right) and Lemon Mousse (far right).

Strawberry Sauce

50g (2oz) sugar
1½ tablespoons lemon juice
1½ tablespoons brandy
250g (9oz) strawberries

Place sugar, lemon juice and brandy in a pan. Place over a low heat until sugar dissolves. Sieve strawberries to remove seeds and combine with syrup. Cool.

Caramel Chips

50g (2oz) caster sugar

Put the sugar in a heavy saucepan and heat gently until the sugar liquifies and turns golden. Pour quickly onto foil and leave until cold. Break the chips with a rolling pin and use for decoration.

Apricot Purée

3 tablespoons sugar
1 tablespoon water
1 teaspoon lime juice
2 tablespoons apricot brandy
250g (9oz) well-ripened apricots

Combine sugar, water, lime juice and apricot brandy in pan. Dissolve sugar over low heat. Cool. Sieve or purée apricots in blender. Combine with syrup.

Chocolate Sauce

100g (4oz) plain dark chocolate
2 tablespoons milk
2 rounded tablespoons golden syrup

Melt the chocolate in a bowl over a pan of simmering water. Beat in the milk and golden syrup until glossy.

Sugar Syrup (medium syrup)

75g (3oz) sugar (granulated)
150ml (5 fl oz) water

Boiling sugar for dessert making can be easily done without a thermometer. Mix together water and sugar in a small saucepan and boil until the mixture begins to thicken.

Rock Cakes

PREPARATION TIME: 10 minutes
COOKING TIME: 10-15 minutes
MAKES: 16-18 cakes

8oz (225g) self-raising flour
¼ tsp (1.25ml) salt
¼ tsp (1.25ml) mixed spice
3oz (85g) butter or margarine
3oz (85g) caster sugar
1 egg
2 tblsp (30ml) milk
A little demerara sugar

Sift flour, salt and mixed spice into a bowl; add fat and rub into flour mixture. Add sugar and mix. This can be done in the electric mixer if you have one.
Lightly beat egg and milk and mix in with other ingredients with a fork. Grease a baking sheet and divide mixture into heaps, about a dessertspoonful each, spaced well apart on the baking sheet. Sprinkle a little demerara sugar on each. Bake at 200°C, 400°F, Gas Mark 6 for 10-15 minutes. Remove from baking sheet and cool on a wire rack, placing a quarter glace cherry on each before cooling. Makes 16-18 cakes.

Apple Cake

PREPARATION TIME: 20 minutes
COOKING TIME: 45 minutes

6oz (175g) butter or margarine
6oz (175g) caster sugar
6oz (175g) self-raising flour
1 level tsp (5ml) cinnamon
3 eggs
2 tblsp (30ml) milk
2-3 eating apples

Add the cinnamon to the flour and sift into a bowl. Cream butter and sugar until light and soft. Beat in one egg then add a tblsp (15ml) of the flour and beat in another egg. Repeat this once more then fold in two thirds of the remaining flour. Stir in the milk then fold in the last of the flour. This can all be done in an electric mixer if you have one. Quarter, peel and core the apples. Slice them very thinly. The slicing attachment of a food processor does this in seconds. Grease either a lasagne dish or a roasting tin approx 11x8½ inches (28x21.5cm). Spread half the mixture in the bottom, distribute the apple slices over it and cover with the rest of the mixture. Bake in the oven at 180°C, 250°F, Gas Mark 4 for 15 minutes then at 170°C, 325°F, Gas Mark 3 for 30 minutes until golden brown and firm to the touch.

Raspberry Souffle

PREPARATION TIME: 1 hour
SERVES: 6 persons

Irish gardens produce bumper crops of raspberries because of the mild climate. Of course, the best way to eat them is just as they come, or served with cream and a sprinkling of sugaar. However, when there is a glut of them a raspberry souffle makes an excellent dessert.

1lb (450g) raspberries (frozen raspberries, thawed, may also be used)
2oz (60g) icing sugar
½oz (15g) gelatine dissolved in ¼ pint (150ml) hot water
4 eggs, separated
4oz (115g) caster sugar
½ pint (300ml) double cream, lightly whipped

Tie a greased sheet of greaseproof paper round a 6 inch (15cm) souffle dish to form a collar above the rim of the dish. Reserve a few of the raspberries and sieve the rest. Fold the icing sugar into the purée. Heat the gelatine in the water over a pan of hot water until it has dissolved completely and allow it to cool a little. Whisk the egg yolks and sugar together over the hot water. Fold in the raspberry purée and the gelatine and cool. Fold in half the cream. Whisk the egg whites until stiff, and fold into the mixture with a metal spoon. Turn into the prepared souffle dish and leave to set. When set, remove the collar carefully and decorate the souffle with the remaining whipped cream and raspberries.

Irish Coffee Cake

PREPARATION TIME: 3-4 hours
COOKING TIME: 35-40 minutes

4oz (115g) butter or margarine
4oz (115g) caster sugar
4oz (115g) self-raising flour
2 tsp (10ml) instant coffee powder dissolved in 2 tblsp (30ml) hot water
2 size 4 eggs

Syrup
¼ pint (150ml) strong coffee
4oz (115g) sugar
3 tblsp (45ml) Irish whiskey

Topping
¼ pint (150ml) whipped cream
1 heaped tblsp (20ml) icing sugar
1 tblsp (15ml) Irish whiskey
Chopped hazelnuts

Grease an 8 inch (20cm) ring tin and coat well with flour. In a bowl, cream together the butter and sugar, then add the eggs one at a time. Sift the flour and fold in ⅔ of it then add the 2 tblsp (30ml) strong coffee. Fold in the remainder of the flour. Place in the prepared cake tin and bake in a pre-heated oven for 35-40 minutes at 180°C, 350°F, Gas Mark 4. Test with a skewer and when done turn out onto a wire rack to cool.
To make the syrup: heat sugar in coffee until it has all dissolved, then boil rapidly for 1 minute. Remove from heat and beat in the whiskey. Return the cooled cake to well-washed tin and pour the syrup over it. Leave it to soak for several hours. Beat up whipped cream with icing sugar and whiskey. Turn the cake out onto a serving plate and decorate with cream and chopped hazelnuts. Chill before serving.

Tipsy Cake

PREPARATION TIME: 45 minutes
SERVES: 8 persons

Generally known as trifle, Tipsy Cake provided a way of using up left over sponge cakes. My old Irish cooking book says 'take five or six penny sponge cakes' which proves just how old it is! Some recipes are well laced with Irish whiskey as well as with sherry.
My version is a great standby for unexpected guests as all the ingredients can be kept in the store cupboard, apart from the cream, which can be kept in the freezer.

6 trifle sponges
Raspberry jam
14oz (400g) tin fruit cocktail
2oz (60g) ratafia biscuits
2oz (60g) flaked almonds
2 fl oz (50ml) sherry

Custard
½ pint (300ml) milk
1oz (30g) vanilla sugar (or caster sugar and ½ tsp (2.5ml) vanilla essence)
2 level tblsp (30ml) cornflour
1 egg
1 tblsp (15ml) sherry
½ pint (300ml) whipped cream, not too stiff
Few glace cherries

Drain fruit into a bowl. Measure out 2 fl oz (50ml) of the juice and add the sherry. Crumble the rataffias, saving some for decoration. Slice the trifle sponges in half and spread them with raspberry jam. Cut each diagonally

Irish Coffee Cake (left) and Tipsy Cake (below).

Carrigeen Moss

PREPARATION TIME: 30 minutes
SERVES: 6 persons

It seems to be spelt 'Carrigeen' in County Cork and 'Carrageen' in the West of Ireland, but whichever way you spell it, it is a seaweed which grows on the rocks on the Atlantic coastline. It is picked at low tide in early summer and laid out to dry in the sun. It is washed once or twice in fresh water and spread out to dry again, after which it will keep for several years. It contains a rich jelly which is used as a thickening agent in cooking and also contains iron and other minerals.

Carrigeen Moss Pudding

Approx ¼oz (8g) Carrigeen moss
1 pint (600ml) milk
Grated rind of ½ lemon
2 tblsp (30ml) sugar

Take as much Carrigeen as will fit in your fist when almost clenched. Wash it in warm water for a few minutes, removing any grasses or other foreign bodies. Place the moss in a saucepan with the milk, grated lemon rind and sugar. Bring slowly to the boil and simmer gently for 15-20 minutes. Strain through a sieve, being sure to scrape all the jelly into the bowl. Stir well and transfer the mixture into a wet mould or serving bowl. Leave to set in a cool place overnight or for several hours before turning out onto a serving dish. Serve with cream and strawberry or raspberry jam.

Bananas with Irish Mist

COOKING TIME: 10 minutes
SERVES: 4 persons

4 bananas
2oz (60g) butter
2 dsp (20ml) caster sugar
2 dsp (20ml) Irish Mist

Melt the butter in a heavy frying pan. Peel the bananas and put them

and line the bottom of a glass serving bowl with the wedges. Place half the fruit on top and sprinkle with some ratafias and flaked almonds and ⅓ of the juice and sherry. Repeat this once, then cover with the final layer of sponge and add the rest of the juice.
I keep a vanilla pod in a screw-top jar of caster sugar and just top up with sugar as I use it. Put cornflour and sugar in a small mixing bowl, mix with 2 tblsp (30ml) of the milk and bring the rest of the milk to the boil. Pour it over the cornflour mixture, stirring all the time. Return the pan to the heat and bring the custard back to the boil and simmer for 1 minute. Remove from heat and beat in the tablespoonful (15ml) of sherry and the lightly beaten egg. Cool and, while luke-warm, pour over the trifle, allowing some to trickle down between the trifle and the bowl. When quite cold top with whipped cream and sprinkle on the remainder of the ratafias and almonds and a few pieces of chopped glace cherry.

This page: Bananas with Irish Mist (top), Dulse (centre right) and Yellow Man (bottom). Facing page: Scrap Bread Pudding (top) and Carrigeen Moss Pudding (bottom).

in the pan, turning them carefully in the melted butter. Cook them over a low heat for about 3 minutes either side until they are heated through. Put them on individual plates and keep them warm while you make the sauce. Add the caster sugar to the remaining butter in the pan. Stir over a low heat until the granules have dissolved. Add the Irish Mist, stir well and bring the mixture to the boil. Spoon the sauce along the top of the hot bananas and serve.

Almond Tartlets

PREPARATION TIME: 10 minutes
COOKING TIME: 10 minutes
SERVES: 12 persons

Mrs Myrtle Allen of Ballymaloe Hotel, County Cork, where the best of Irish food may be tasted, gave me the recipe for these little almond tartlets, which are one of the specialities of her sweet trolley.

3oz (85g) butter
3oz (85g) sugar
3oz (85g) ground almonds

Beat the butter, sugar and almonds together to a cream. Put 1 tsp (5ml) of the mixture into sixteen small patty tins. Bake at 180°C, 350°F, Gas Mark 4 for about ten minutes or until golden brown. Cool in tins but do not allow to set hard before removing to a wire rack. Fresh fruits such as raspberries, peaches or blackberries should be placed on these just before decorating with whipped cream and serving.

Barm Brack

PREPARATION TIME: 2-3 hours
COOKING TIME: 1 hour 10 minutes

1lb (450g) flour
½ tsp (2.5ml) cinnamon
½ tsp (2.5ml) salt
Pinch grated nutmeg
2oz (60g) softened butter
3oz (85g) caster sugar
½ pint (300ml) tepid milk
¾oz (20g) fresh yeast
1 egg (size 2)
½lb (225g) sultanas
6oz (175g) currants
2oz (60g) cut mixed peel

Add salt and spice to flour and sift into a large mixing bowl. Rub in the butter, this can be done in the electric mixer at low speed. Add a tsp (5ml) of the sugar and a tsp (5ml) of the milk to the yeast and mix well. Add the remainder of the sugar to the flour mixture and mix in. Lightly beat the egg, add the milk and pour this onto the yeast mixture. Add this to the flour and beat very well by hand, or in a mixer fitted with a dough hook, until the batter becomes stiff and elastic. Fold in the mixed fruit at this stage and cover the bowl with a lightly greased polythene bag. Leave bowl in a warm place for 1-2 hours, to allow the dough to rise. Divide the mixture between two greased loaf tins 8½x4½ (21x11cm), or two 7 inch (19cm) cake tins. Cover again and allow to rise for half an hour. Bake for one hour in centre of oven at 200°C, 400°F, Gas Mark 6. Dissolve a tblsp (15ml) of sugar in a quarter cup of hot water and brush over brack, return it to the oven for five minutes with the heat turned off. Turn out onto a rack to cool. Slice and butter.

Barm brack is a delicious fruit loaf eaten all the year round in Ireland, but especially popular at Hallowe'en when, by tradition, a ring is hidden in the loaf and the one who finds it will be the next to wed.

Almond Tart

PREPARATION TIME: 25 minutes
COOKING TIME: 35 minutes
SERVES: 8-10 persons

6oz (175g) frozen puff pastry
2oz (60g) grated almond paste (left uncovered in the refrigerator before grating to harden)
Damson jam
4oz (115g) butter or margarine
4oz (115g) caster sugar
2 eggs
4oz (115g) self-raising flour (sifted)
1 egg-cup of milk
½ tsp almond essence

Take ⅔ of the puff pastry, roll it out thinly and line a greased 10 inch (25cm) tart plate with it, allowing a 1 inch (2.5cm) overlap all round. Roll out the remainder of the pastry slightly thicker, cut into strips ½ inch (1.5cm) wide and set aside.
Cream slightly softened butter or margarine and sugar together, add eggs one at a time, beating well and beating in 1 tblsp of the sifted flour before adding the second egg. Mix the almond essence with the egg cup of milk, add to the mixture then fold in the remainder of the flour. This can be done in the food processor if you have one.
Spread the jam on the pastry case to within 1 inch (2.5cm) of the rim. Sprinkle the grated almond paste on top. Cover with the sponge mixture using a spatula and taking care not to disturb the filling. Make a lattice with the pastry strips over the top and crimp the edges, turning in the overlap of pastry to form a rim.
Bake in the oven at 200°C, 400°F, Gas Mark 6 for 20 minutes, then 180°C, 350°F, Gas Mark 4 for a further 15 minutes.

Guinness Cake

PREPARATION TIME: 1 hour 30 minutes-2 hours
COOKING TIME: 2 hours

8oz (225g) butter or margarine
8oz (225g) brown sugar
½ pint (300ml) Guinness
½lb (225g) raisins
½lb (225g) currants
½lb (225g) sultanas
4oz (115g) mixed peel
1¼lb (560g) plain flour
½ tsp (2.5ml) bicarbonate of soda
1 tsp (5ml) mixed spice
1 tsp (5ml) nutmeg
3 eggs

Grease and line a 9 inch (23cm) cake tin with greased greaseproof paper. Place the butter, sugar and

This page: Barm Brack (top) and Guinness Cake (bottom). Facing page: Almond Tart (top) and Almond Tartlets (bottom).

the Guinness in a saucepan and bring slowly to the boil, stirring all the time until the sugar and butter have melted. Mix in the dried fruit and peel and bring mixture back to the boil. Simmer for 5 minutes. Remove from heat and leave until cold. Sift flour, spices and bicarbonate of soda into a large mixing bowl, stir in cooled fruit mixture and beaten eggs, turn into cake tin and bake in centre of pre-heated oven, 160°C, 325°F, Gas Mark 3 for 2 hours. Test with a skewer. When done, cool in tin before turning out.

Baked Custard

PREPARATION TIME: 15 minutes

COOKING TIME: 45 minutes

SERVES: 4 persons

This used to be regarded as a nursery pudding but, if it is properly made and generously sprinkled with nutmeg, it can be delicious with stewed fruit or even tinned fruit such as apricots or plums. Garden fruits like damsons or plums can be cooked in the oven with sugar and a little water at the same time as the custard.

1 pint (600ml) milk
1oz (30g) caster sugar
2 eggs
Grated nutmeg

Beat the eggs with the sugar in a mixing bowl. Heat the milk but do not let it boil. Pour it slowly onto the egg and sugar mixture, stirring all the time. Pour the mixture into a greased ovenproof dish or casserole and grate nutmeg over the top. Place the dish in a meat tin containing about 1 inch (2.5cm) of warm water and bake in the oven for 45 minutes at 170°C, 325°F, Gas Mark 3.

Yellow Man

An Ulsterman recently described this to me as 'a frothy, yellow sugar confectionary'. It has been associated for centuries with 'The Ould Lammas Fair' which takes place every year at Ballycastle, Co. Antrim.

1lb (450g) golden syrup
½lb (225g) brown sugar
1 heaped tblsp (20ml) butter
1 tsp (5ml) baking powder
2 tblsp (30ml) vinegar

Melt the butter and coat the inside of the pan with it. Add the sugar and syrup and finally the vinegar. Stir over a low heat until the sugar and syrup have melted. Bring it to the boil and simmer without stirring. Test by dropping a little into a cup of cold water to see if it sets. Add the baking powder, which will make the mixture foam up. Stir well again, pour into a greased tin and cut into squares. It may also be turned out onto a slab after the boiling process, then pulled until it becomes pale yellow in colour. When it hardens it is broken into pieces with a little hammer like toffee used to be.

Dulse

The Ulsterman sang me a song about 'The Ould Lammas Fair' which goes:

Did you treat your Mary Anne
to dulse and Yellowman
at the Ould Lammas Fair, at
Ballycastle, O?

Dulse is a reddish-brown seaweed which grows on the rocks all around the Irish coast. It is dried like Carrigeen Moss, but is usually eaten raw. Sometimes it is cooked, in which case it must first be soaked for several hours. It is sometimes used, instead of scallions, to make Dulse Champ. It has a much stronger smell and flavour than Carrigeen Moss.

Hydropathic (Summer) Pudding

PREPARATION TIME: 30 minutes

SERVES: 8 persons

I have in my possession an Irish cookery book which must be almost 100 years old. It has lost its original cover but I know it was used as a text book by the young ladies who did a domestic economy course at the Munster Institute in Cork at the end of the last century. In my family it is always referred to as 'Aunt Anna's cookbook', and it contains some very quaint recipes and household tips.
The recipe for trifle begins: 'take 4 or 5 penny sponge cakes'. Then there is a recipe for Hydropathic Pudding. On reading it through I realised that it was Summer Pudding and would love to know why it was called Hydropathic Pudding.

Here is the original recipe, but since no measurements are given I would suggest 1½lbs (675g) fruit (raspberries, redcurrants and blackberries are the best to produce the lovely ruby-red colour, but other stewing fruits may be included), and ¼lb (115g) sugar. The pudding bowl should be 1½ pint (900ml) size.

Bread
Fruit
Sugar to taste

Line a pudding with bread as follows. Cut some slices of bread about half an inch in thickness. From one of these cut a round to fit easily in the bottom of the bowl. For the sides cut the bread in finger pieces, the height of the bowl in length, and, in breadth, about one and a half inches at one end and one inch at the other. Pack these tightly around the sides of the bowl.
Stew the fruit, adding sugar to taste, and if not very juicy add a little water. Pour while hot into the lined bowl and cover the top with bread. Set it on a plate so as to catch any juice that may flow over. Place a small plate on top and over this a weight. When cold turn out and pour round it any juice that may have run into the plate. Serve with custard, cream or milk.

Scrap Bread Pudding

PREPARATION TIME: 40 minutes

COOKING TIME: 2 hours 30 minutes steaming or 1 hour 15 minutes baking

SERVES: 6-8 persons

8oz (225g) bread scraps, crusts removed
2oz (60g) sugar
1 tsp (5ml) mixed spice
1 tsp (5ml) grated lemon rind
1oz (30g) flour
2oz (60g) suet (chopped)
2oz (60g) each of currants, raisins, sultanas
1oz (30g) mixed cut peel
1 egg, beaten
1 tsp (5ml) baking powder
½ pint (300ml) milk

Break up the bread and leave to soak in the milk for half an hour. Sift the flour, mixed spice and baking powder into a bowl. Add the chopped suet and lemon rind. Squeeze as much milk as possible out of the bread into a bowl. Beat all lumps out of the bread with a fork. Mix in the flour and suet and

Hydropathic (Summer) Pudding (above right) and Baked Custard (right).

the dried fruit. Add the beaten egg and the milk the bread was soaked in. This can either be turned out into a greased pudding bowl, covered with greaseproof paper and steamed for 2½ hours, or spread into a greased ovenproof baking dish or tin and baked for 1¼ hours in the oven, 180°C, 350°F, Gas Mark 4. Serve hot with custard or the baked version can be allowed to cool before cutting into squares and serving like cake.

Italian Sweets

Vanilla Cream Melba

PREPARATION TIME: 15 minutes
COOKING TIME: 10 minutes
SERVES: 4 people

90g (3oz) soup pasta
450ml (¾ pint) milk
45g (1½oz) brown sugar
150ml (¼ pint) cream, lightly whipped
Few drops vanilla essence
1 can peach halves
1 tsp cinnamon

Melba sauce:
225g (8oz) raspberries
30g (1oz) icing sugar

Cook pasta in milk and sugar until soft. Stir regularly, being careful not to allow it to boil over. Draw off heat and stir in vanilla essence. Pour pasta into a bowl to cool. When cool, fold in cream. Chill. Meanwhile, make Melba sauce. Push raspberries through a sieve. Mix in icing sugar to desired thickness and taste. Serve pasta with peach halves and Melba sauce. Dust with cinnamon if desired.

Black Cherry Ravioli with Soured Cream Sauce

PREPARATION TIME: 30 minutes
COOKING TIME: 15 minutes
SERVES: 4 people

Dough:
275g (9oz) strong plain flour
1 tbsp sugar
3 eggs

Large can black cherries, pips removed
60g (2oz) granulated sugar
1 tsp arrowroot
115ml (4 fl oz) soured cream
115ml (4 fl oz) double cream

Put cherries in a sieve. Strain off juice and reserve. Make dough by sifting flour and sugar in a bowl. Make a well in the centre and add lightly-beaten eggs. Work flour and eggs together with a spoon, and then by hand, until a smooth dough is formed. Knead gently. Lightly flour board, and roll dough out thinly into a rectangle. Cut dough in half. Put well-drained cherries about 4cm (1½″) apart on the dough. Place the other half on top, and cut with a small glass or pastry cutter. Seal well around edges with the back of a fork. Boil plenty of water in a large saucepan, and drop in cherry pasta. Cook for about 10 minutes, or until they rise to the surface. Remove with a draining spoon and keep warm.

This page: Black Cherry Ravioli with Soured Cream Sauce.

Facing page: Vanilla Cream Melba (top) and Chocolate Cream Helène (bottom).

Keep 2 tablespoons cherry juice aside. Mix 1 tablespoon cherry juice with arrowroot; mix remaining juice with sugar and set over heat. Add arrowroot mixture, and heat until it thickens. Meanwhile mix soured cream and double cream together, and marble 1 tablespoon of cherry juice through it. Pour hot, thickened cherry juice over cherry ravioli. Serve hot with cream sauce.

Chocolate Cream Helène

PREPARATION TIME: 15 minutes

COOKING TIME: 10 minutes

SERVES: 4 people

90g (3oz) soup pasta
450ml (¾ pint) milk
45g (1½oz) caster sugar
150ml (¼ pint) cream, lightly whipped
1 tsp cocoa
1 tbsp hot water
1 large can pear halves

Garnish:
Chocolate, grated

Cook pasta in milk and sugar until soft. Stir regularly, being careful not to allow it to boil over. Meanwhile, dissolve cocoa in hot water, and stir into pasta. Pour pasta into a bowl to cool. When cool, fold in lightly-whipped cream. Chill. Serve with pear halves, and a sprinkling of grated chocolate.

Honey Vermicelli

PREPARATION TIME: 1 hour

COOKING TIME: 15 minutes

SERVES: 4 people

225g (8oz) vermicelli
60g (2oz) butter
3 tbsps clear honey
2 tsps sesame seeds
¼ tsp cinnamon

Sauce:
75ml (5 tbsps) double cream
75ml (5 tbsps) soured cream

Cook vermicelli in boiling salted water for 5 minutes or until tender, stirring regularly with a fork to separate noodles. Drain, and spread out to dry on a wire tray covered with absorbent paper or a tea-towel. Leave for about an hour. Make sauce by mixing soured cream and double cream together. Melt butter in frying pan. Add sesame seeds, and fry until lightly golden. Stir in honey, cinnamon and vermicelli, and heat through. Serve hot, topped with cream sauce.

Cream Cheese Margherita

PREPARATION TIME: 1 hour

COOKING TIME: 10 minutes

SERVES: 4 people

115g (4oz) soup pasta
150ml (¼ pint) single cream
225g (8oz) packet cream cheese
½ tsp ground cinnamon
60g (2oz) caster sugar
60g (2oz) sultanas
Juice and grated rind of ½ a lemon

Garnish:
1 tbsp flaked almonds
Lemon peel, cut into slivers

Soak sultanas in lemon juice for about 1 hour. Meanwhile, cook the pasta in plenty of boiling, lightly-salted water until tender, stirring occasionally. Work the cream cheese, sugar and cream together until smooth. Beat in grated lemon rind and cinnamon. Fold in pasta and sultanas. Divide between individual dessert glasses or small sweet dishes, and cover top with flaked almond and slivers of lemon peel. Chill.

Honey Vermicelli (top right) and Cream Cheese Margherita (right).

Oriental Desserts

Bananas Cooked in Coconut Milk

PREPARATION TIME: 20 minutes
COOKING TIME: 20 minutes
SERVES: 4 people

4-6 large, ripe bananas, peeled and sliced diagonally into 3 or 4 pieces
1 tbsp brown sugar
115g (4oz) desiccated coconut
450ml (¾ pint) milk

Garnish
Desiccated coconut

Put sugar, coconut and milk into wok, and bring to simmering point. Turn off heat and allow to cool for 15 minutes. Push through sieve or a piece of muslin to squeeze out juices. Return to wok, and simmer for 10 minutes, or until creamy. Add bananas, and cook slowly until bananas are soft. Serve immediately sprinkled with desiccated coconut.

Steamed Custard

PREPARATION TIME: 10 minutes
COOKING TIME: 20 minutes

450ml (¾ pint) milk
30g (1oz) sugar
2 eggs, beaten
3 drops vanilla essence
Sprinkling of ground nutmeg or cinnamon

Place sugar and milk in wok. Heat gently until the milk reaches a low simmer and the sugar has dissolved. Remove from wok and leave to cool for 5 minutes. Meanwhile, wash wok and place steaming rack inside, with 4-5cm (1½"-2") of hot water. Return to heat and bring water to simmering point. Pour milk and sugar mixture over beaten eggs. Beat again, and add the vanilla essence, stirring well. Pour mixture into a heat-proof dish or metal moulds and sprinkle lightly with nutmeg or cinnamon. Place on rack and cover with greaseproof paper, so condensation does not drop into custard. Cover wok and steam for 10-15 minutes. To test if cooked, a knife inserted in centre will come out clean, and custard will be set and gelatinous. Cover and cool for 1 hour, then place in refrigerator until needed.

Bananas Flambés

PREPARATION TIME: 5 minutes
COOKING TIME: 10 minutes
SERVES: 4 people

4 firm, ripe bananas, peeled and cut in half lengthways
60g (2oz) unsalted butter
60g (2oz) brown sugar
45ml (3 tbsps) brandy
Juice of 2 oranges

Heat wok, and add half the butter. When hot, add bananas, rounded edge down, and fry until golden on underside. Add remaining butter, and carefully turn the bananas over, so their flat sides are in contact with the wok surface. Sprinkle with sugar, 15ml (1 tbsp) of brandy, and orange juice, and allow to simmer for 3 minutes. Heat remaining brandy, set alight, and pour over bananas. When flame is extinguished, serve immediately. (Flaming can be done in serving dish).

Sesame Toffee Apples

PREPARATION TIME: 45 minutes
COOKING TIME: 30 minutes
SERVES: 4 people

2 large, firm Granny Smith or Golden Delicious apples
1 tbsp flour

Batter
30g (1oz) plain flour
30g (1oz) cornflour
1 large egg
30ml (2 tbsps) water
1 tsp sesame oil

Oil for deep frying
90ml (6 tbsps) peanut oil
10ml (2 tsps) sesame oil
9 tbsps sugar
2 tbsps white sesame seeds

Peel, core and cut apples into 2.5cm (1") chunks. Toss in 1 tbsp of flour. Combine flour, cornflour, egg and sesame oil in a small bowl. Mix to a batter with water and leave for ½ hour. Place oil for deep frying in wok, and heat to a moderate temperature (180°C; 350°F). Put fruit in batter and coat well. Deep fry several pieces at a time until they are golden. Remove with slotted spoon and drain on kitchen paper. Repeat until all fruit is fried. Repeat process to fry fruit a second time for a couple of minutes. Remove with slotted spoon and drain. When fat has cooled, carefully drain and clean wok. Fill a bowl with cold water and ice cubes, and put on side. Put peanut and sesame oil and sugar into wok, and heat until sugar melts. When it begins to caramelise stir and add sesame seeds and then add all of fruit. Toss around gently to coat in caramel. Take out quickly, and drop into iced water a few at a time, to prevent sticking together. Serve at once. (This can also be made with sliced bananas).

Facing page: Bananas Flambés (top) and Sesame Toffee Apples (bottom). Steamed Custard (right) and Bananas Cooked in Coconut Milk (below).

Cake Making and Icing

Lining Cake Tins

All tins must be greased and lined unless you are using a non-stick cake tin, in which case follow the manufacturer's instructions.
If using a shallow tin, only the base needs to be lined for whisked sponges and the quick cake mixture.
If you are making a fruit cake, which will take longer to bake, then the sides as well as the base need lining using a double thickness of greaseproof paper.

To Grease the Tin

Brush with melted lard, margarine or oil. Grease the greaseproof paper with melted fat or oil; if you are using non-stick silicone paper do not grease it. In the preparation of tins, it is necessary to grease and dust them with flour if you are not lining them.

Round Tins

To line a deep, round tin, draw with a pencil round the edge of the cake tin on double thickness greaseproof paper and cut the resulting shape out.
Using a piece of string, measure round the tin. Use another piece of string to measure the height plus 2.5cm (1 inch). Cut out one long strip or two shorter lengths of greaseproof paper to the equivalent of these measurements. If making two lengths, add on a little extra for them to overlap. Make a fold 5mm (¼ inch) deep along one edge and cut into the fold at regular intervals at a slight angle. Place one of the circles of paper in the bottom of the tin, followed by the side pieces and, finally, the second paper circle which will cover the slashed edges.

Square Tins

To line a deep, square tin follow the instructions above for a round tin, but fold the long strips so they fit into the corners of the tin.

Rich Fruit Cake

CAKE SIZES	12cm (5in) round 10cm (4in) square	15cm (6in) round 12cm (5in) square	18cm (7in) round 15cm (6in) square	20cm (8in) round 18cm (7in) square	23cm (9in) round 20cm (8in) square	25cm (10in) roun 23cm (9in) squar
APPROX COOKING TIME:	2½ hours	2¾ hours	3¼ hours	3¼ hours	4 hours	4¼-4½ hours
OVEN:	140°C/275°F Gas Mark 1	140°C/275°F Gas Mark 1	140°C/275°F Gas Mark 1	140°C/275°F Gas Mark 1	140°C/275°F Gas Mark 1	140°C/275°F Gas Mark 1
	Note for all recipes: First ⅔ of cooking time at 150°C/300°F Gas Mark 2					
Butter	65g/2½oz	75g/3oz	125g/4oz	150g/5oz	200g/7oz	250g/9oz
Eggs	2	2	3	4	5	6
Plain flour	75g/3oz	125g/4oz	175g/6oz	200g/7oz	250g/9oz	300g/11oz
Dark soft brown sugar	75g/3oz	90g/3½oz	150g/5oz	175g/6oz	225g/8oz	275g/10oz
Black treacle	½ tblsp	½ tblsp	1 tblsp	1 tblsp	1 tblsp	1 tblsp
Ground almonds	25g/1oz	25g/1oz	40g/1½oz	50g/2oz	65g/2½oz	75g/3oz
Ground mixed spice	½ tsp	½ tsp	¾ tsp	1 tsp	1¼ tsp	1½ tsp
Grated lemon rind	½ lemon	½ lemon	1 lemon	1 lemon	1 lemon	2 lemons
Grated orange rind	½ orange	½ orange	1 orange	1 orange	1 orange	2 oranges
Grated nutmeg	¼ tsp	¼ tsp	¼ tsp	½ tsp	½ tsp	¾ tsp
Chopped almonds	25g/1oz	40g/1½oz	50g/2oz	65g/2½ oz	90g/3½oz	125g/4oz
Currants	150g/5oz	175g/6oz	225g/8oz	275g/10oz	375g/13oz	450g/1lb
Raisins	25g/1oz	50g/2oz	75g/3oz	125g/4oz	150g/5oz	175g/6oz
Sultanas	75g/3oz	125g/4oz	150g/5oz	200g/7oz	250g/9oz	300g/11oz
Chopped mixed peel	25g/1oz	40g/1½oz	50g/2oz	65g/2½oz	90g/3½oz	125g/4oz
Glacé cherries	25g/1oz	40g/1½oz	50g/2oz	65g/2½oz	90g/3½oz	125g/4oz
Orange juice	1 tblsp	1 tblsp	1 tblsp	1 tblsp	2 tblsp	2 tblsp
Brandy	1 tblsp	1 tblsp	1 tblsp	2 tblsp	2 tblsp	3 tblsp

Swiss Roll Tins (Long, Shallow Tins)
Grease and line a shallow tin so that the cake may be easily removed. Line the sides of the tin with paper at least 4cm (1½ inches) longer than the tin, cutting into each corner.

Loaf Tins
When lining a loaf tin the method is again the same, but the paper should be 15cm (6 inches) larger than the top of the tin.

8cm (11in) round 5cm (10in) square	30cm (12in) round 28cm (11in) square
-5¼ hours	6 hours
40°C/275°F Gas Mark 1	140°C/275°F Gas Mark 1
ee note opposite	
00g/11oz	375g/13oz
	8
00g/14oz	450g/1lb
50g/12oz	400g/14oz
½ tblsp	2 tblsp
0g/3½oz	125g/4oz
½ tsp	2 tsp
lemons	2 lemons
oranges	2 oranges
¼ tsp	1 tsp
50g/5oz	175g/6oz
75g/1¼lb	675g/1½lb
00g/7oz	225g/8oz
75g/13oz	450g/1lb
50g/5oz	175g/6oz
50g/5oz	175g/6oz
tblsp	3 tblsp
tblsp	4 tblsp

Oiling and lining cake tins.

Rich Fruit Cake

This is a traditional recipe which cuts well and is rich, dark and moist. Traditional fruit cake improves with keeping and is used for celebration cakes – weddings, birthdays and Christmas – marzipanned and royal iced.
Prepacked dried fruit is ready washed, but if you are buying your fruit loose, rinse it through with cold water and dry it well with kitchen paper or clean cloths. Then spread it out on a tea towel placed on a baking sheet in a warm (not hot) place for 24 hours. Do not use wet fruit in a cake as the fruit will sink.
Mix the sultanas, currants and raisins together. Cut the glacé cherries into quarters, rinse in warm water and dry with kitchen paper. Add the cherries to the fruit together with mixed peel, almonds, and grated orange and lemon rind.

Sift the flour with a pinch of salt, ground cinnamon and mixed spice. Cream the butter until soft, then add the sugar and cream until light and fluffy (do not overbeat). Add the eggs one at a time, beat well and after each egg add a spoonful of flour. Add the black treacle, orange juice and brandy, if desired. Add the remaining flour, then the fruit, and mix well.
Spread the mixture evenly into a greased and double-lined tin. Use the back of a spoon to make a slight hollow in the centre of the cake so it will be flat when cooked. Tie two thicknesses of brown paper round the tin then bake in the centre of the oven at 150°C, 300°F, Gas Mark 2 (see chart for the suggested time). With large cakes turn the oven down to 140°C, 275°F, Gas Mark 1, after two-thirds of the cooking time. To test the cake, push a skewer into the centre. It should come out clean if the cake is cooked. When the cake is cooked, remove the tin from the oven and leave the cake in the tin to cool. Turn the cake onto a wire rack and remove the lining paper. Spike the top of the cake with a skewer and spoon a few tablespoons of brandy or other spirit over the top. To store the cake, wrap it in greaseproof paper and foil. If possible, repeat the spooning over of brandy or spirit every few weeks. The cake can be allowed to mature for 2-3 months.

Quick Mix Cake

This is a quick cake, which is ideal for novelty cakes, and the mixture is firm enough to cut into any shape; it is moist and crumbly and can be filled with cream, butter or jam.
Put the margarine, sugar, eggs, sifted flour and baking powder in a bowl. Mix together all the ingredients with either a wooden spoon or electric mixer. Beat for 1-2 minutes until the mixture is smooth and glossy. In a food processor this will take 30 seconds-1 minute. Put the mixture in a prepared tin. Level the top with the back of a spoon and bake in the centre of the oven at 160°C, 325°F, Gas Mark 3 (see chart for the suggested time). When baked, the cake will be firm to the touch and shrink away from the sides of the tin. Loosen the sides of the cake from the tin and leave it to cool on a wire rack. Turn the cake right way up onto another wire rack.

Whisked Sponge Cake

This cake mixture is ideal for afternoon tea and the cake may be filled with cream, butter icing or fruit. It does not keep well and is best eaten the same day it is made, although it can be kept in the freezer for up to 2 months.
Put the eggs and sugar in a

heatproof bowl over a saucepan of hot, not boiling, water. The bowl must not touch the water. Whisk the mixture until it becomes thick enough to leave a trail when lifted. Sift the flour and baking powder together and fold into the egg mixture with a metal spoon, taking care not to knock the air out. Pour the mixture into a prepared tin and gently shake the mixture level. Bake in the centre of the oven (see chart for oven temperature and suggested time). Remove from the tin and cool on a wire rack. When making a Swiss roll, turn out the cake onto a sheet of greaseproof paper sprinkled with caster sugar. Quickly peel off the lining paper and trim the cake edges. Fold and roll the cake up without cracking it. Let it cool a little, then unroll and remove the greaseproof paper. Fill and re-roll the cake.

Madeira Cake

Madeira cake is a moist cake that can be covered with marzipan and then iced with royal icing or any other icing.

PREPARATION TIME: 15 minutes

COOKING TIME: 1 hour 15 minutes to 1 hour 30 minutes

OVEN TEMPERATURE: 160°C, 325°F, Gas Mark 3

175g (6oz) butter
175g (6oz) caster sugar
Grated rind of 1 lemon
3 eggs
225g (8oz) plain flour
7.5ml (1½ tsp) baking powder
30ml (2 tblsp) warm water

Cream the butter and sugar until they are light and fluffy. Beat the eggs in one at a time, then after each egg add a spoonful of flour. Sift in the remaining flour and fold it into the flour with lemon rind and juice. Turn into a prepared cake tin and bake in the oven for 1¼-1½ hours. When cooked, the cake should be firm to the touch. Leave it in the tin to cool for 5-10 minutes, then turn onto a wire rack and remove the lining paper.

Whisked Sponge Cake

CAKE SIZES	2 x 18cm (7in) sandwich tins	20cm (8in) sandwich tin 18cm (7in) square tin	28 x 18cm (11 x 7in) Swiss roll tin	18 sponge drops	20cm (8in) round cake tin	2 x 20cm (8in) sandwich tins
APPROX COOKING TIME:	20-25 minutes	25-30 minutes	10-12 minutes	5-10 minutes	35-40 minutes	20-25 minutes
OVEN:	180°C/350°F Gas Mark 4	180°C/350°F Gas Mark 4	190°C/375°F Gas Mark 5	190°C/375°F Gas Mark 5	180°C/350°F Gas Mark 4	180°C/350°F Gas Mark 4
Eggs (sizes 1-2)	2	2	2	2	3	3
Caster sugar	50g/2oz	50g/2oz	50g/2oz	50g/2oz	75g/3oz	75g/3oz
Plain flour	50g/2oz	50g/2oz	50g/2oz	50g/2oz	75g/3oz	75g/3oz
Baking powder	½ tsp	½ tsp	½ tsp	½ tsp	½ tsp	½ tsp

Quick Mix Cake

CAKE SIZES	2 x 18cm (7in) sandwich tins	18 paper cake cases or patty tins	20cm (8in) sandwich tin 20cm (8in) ring mould 18cm (7in) deep square tin	*900ml (1½ pint) pudding basin **add 25g/1oz cornflour sifted with the flour*	About 26 paper cake cases or patty tins	2 x 20cm (8in) sandwich tins
APPROX COOKING TIME:	25-30 minutes	15-20 minutes	35-40 minutes	about 50 minutes	15-20 minutes	30-35 minutes
OVEN:	160°C/325°F Gas Mark 3	160°C/325°F Gas Mark 3	160°C/325°F Gas Mark 3	160°C/325°F Gas Mark 3	160°C/325°F Gas Mark 3	160°C/325°F Gas Mark 3
Soft tub margarine, chilled	100g/4oz	100g/4oz	100g/4oz	100g/4oz	175g/6oz	175g/6oz
Caster sugar	100g/4oz	100g/4oz	100g/4oz	100g/4oz	175g/6oz	175g/6oz
Eggs (sizes 1-2)	2	2	2	2	3	3
Self-raising flour	100g/4oz	100g/4oz	100g/4oz	100g/4oz	175g/6oz	175g/6oz
Baking powder	1 tsp	1 tsp	1 tsp	1 tsp	1½ tsp	1½ tsp
Vanilla essence	4 drops	4 drops	4 drops	4 drops	6 drops	6 drops

For Victoria Sponge see 'Tea Time Treats'.

Variations

Chocolate Victoria Sponge
Replace 25g (1oz) flour with 25g (1oz) sifted cocoa powder. Add this to the other flour.

Coffee Victoria Sponge
Replace the water with coffee essence, or dissolve 10ml (2 tsp) instant coffee powder in 15ml (1 tblsp) boiling water.

Lemon Victoria Sponge
Add the very finely grated rind of 1 lemon.

28 x 18 x 4cm (11 x 7 x 1½in) slab cake	30 x 23cm (12 x 9in) Swiss roll tin
30-35 minutes	12-15 minutes
180°C/350°F Gas Mark 4	200°C/400°F Gas Mark 6
3	3
75g/3oz	75g/3oz
75g/3oz	75g/3oz
½ tsp	½ tsp

Basic Icing Recipes and Their Uses

Quick Frosting

This is an easy white frosting which is a quick version of the traditional American frosting. A sugar thermometer is not required for this recipe, but the icing must be used very quickly before it sets.

PREPARATION TIME: 7-10 minutes

1 egg white
150g (6oz) caster sugar
Pinch of salt
30ml (2 tblsp) water
Pinch of cream of tartar

Put all the ingredients into a heatproof bowl and mix. Put the bowl over a pan of simmering hot water and beat the mixture. If possible, use an electric mixer until the icing peaks. Remove the icing from the heat and pour it over the cake, spreading it quickly. This will cover an 18cm (7 inch) cake.

Chocolate Fudge Icing

PREPARATION TIME: 10 minutes

This is a delicious chocolate icing which is quick and easy to make.

50g (2oz) butter
45ml (3 tblsp) milk
250g (8oz) icing sugar, well sifted
30ml (2 tblsp) cocoa powder, sifted

Melt the butter in a small saucepan with the milk. Add the icing sugar and cocoa and beat well until smooth and very glossy. Cool until lukewarm and pour over cake. This is enough to fill and ice the top of a 20cm (8 inch) cake.
NB: if the icing is too thick to pour, reheat gently to thin. This icing can also be made in a small bowl over a pan of gently simmering water.

23cm (9in) sandwich tin	28 x 18 x 4cm (11 x 7 x 1½in) slab cake 20cm (8in) round tin 20cm (8in) square tin	1 litre (2 pint) pudding basin	29 x 21 x 4cm (11½ x 8½ x 1½in) slab cake	23cm (9in) round tin 23cm (9in) square tin	30 x 25 x 5cm (12 x 10 x 2in) slab cake
about 25 minutes	35-40 minutes	about 1 hour	about 40 minutes	about 1 hour	50-60 minutes
160°C/325°F Gas Mark 3	160°C/325°F Gas Mark 3	160°C/325°F Gas Mark 3	160°C/325°F Gas Mark 3	160°C/325°F Gas Mark 3	160°C/325°F Gas Mark 3
175g/6oz	175g/6oz	175g/6oz	200g/8oz	200g/8oz	275g/10oz
175g/6oz	175g/6oz	175g/6oz	200g/8oz	200g/8oz	275g/10oz
3	3	3	4	4	5
175g/6oz	175g/6oz	175g/6oz	200g/8oz	200g/8oz	275g/10oz
1½ tsp	1½ tsp	1½ tsp	2 tsp	2 tsp	2½ tsp
6 drops	6 drops	6 drops	8 drops	8 drops	10 drops

Sponges: Whisked Sponge, Madeira Cake.

Marzipan or Almond Paste

This is a paste which is made firm and rollable, and is traditionally used as a base cover for fruit cakes before coating with royal icing or any other decorative icing.
Prepare the cake by levelling the top, if necessary. Dust a work surface with icing sugar and roll out half the almond paste 2.5cm (1 inch) larger than the top of the cake. Brush the top of the cake with the apricot glaze, or the egg white and brandy. Invert the cake onto the almond paste and, using a palette knife, draw up the top of the almond paste around the cake. Put the top of the cake down on a board and brush the sides of the cake with apricot glaze. Cut two pieces of string or thread, one the height of the cake and the other equal in length to the circumference. Roll out the remaining almond paste into a strip, equal in height and length of circumference of the cake, using the strings as a guide, or cut two short strips of paste instead. Carefully wrap the almond paste round the cake, pressing firmly round the sides and joins. For a square cake, cut the string into four lengths, equal to the sides of the cake and cut the paste to match. Press lightly on the paste when it is placed round the cake in order to produce sharp corners. When covered, leave the cake for 24 hours to dry. Wedding cakes should be left for up to 1 week before icing, otherwise almond oil will stain the icing if the cake is kept after the wedding.

Guide to Almond Paste Quantities Required for Cakes

Square	Round	Paste / marzipan
12.5cm (5 inch)	15cm (6 inch)	350g (12oz)
15cm (6 inch)	18cm (7 inch)	550g (1lb 4oz)
18cm (7 inch)	20cm (8 inch)	675g (1½lb)
20cm (8 inch)	23cm (9 inch)	675g (1½lb)
23cm (9 inch)	25cm (10 inch)	900g (2lb)
25cm (10 inch)	28cm (11 inch)	1kg (2¼lb)
28cm (11 inch)	30cm (12 inch)	1.25kg (2½lb)
30cm (12 inch)		1.5kg (3lb)

Marzipan or Almond Paste

PREPARATION TIME: 15 minutes

100g (4oz) caster sugar
100g (4oz) icing sugar
200g (8oz) ground almonds
5ml (1 tsp) lemon juice
A few drops almond essence
1 or 2 egg yolks, beaten

Mix the sugars and the ground almonds in a bowl. Make a well in the centre and add the lemon juice, almond essence and egg yolk or yolks to the mixture and form into a pliable dough. Lightly dust the work surface with icing sugar and turn out the dough. Knead until smooth. The marzipan can be stored in a polythene bag or wrapped in foil for 2-3 days before use. Makes 450g (1lb).

Apricot Glaze

PREPARATION TIME: 10 minutes

This glaze can be stored in an airtight container for up to 1 week, if kept in the refrigerator. Re-boil the glaze and cool before applying to the cake.

175-225g (6-8oz) apricot jam
30ml (2 tblsp) water

Put the jam and water in a saucepan and heat until the jam has melted, stirring occasionally. Pour the jam through a sieve and return it to a clean saucepan. Re-boil and simmer until you have a slightly thickened consistency. Cool before applying to the cake.

How to Royal Ice

It does not matter whether you ice the top or the sides first. The important point to remember is that the icing should be applied in several thin coats. Try icing a section first, rather than doing all of it in one go. Your aim is to achieve a smooth surface and you must let each coat dry before applying another. Most cakes require 2 coats on the top and sides, with maybe 3 on the top for a very smooth finish. Wedding cakes require three coats all over and the bottom tiers need 4 coats. For a 2 or 3-tier cake apply 4 coats to the bottom tier; for a 4-tier cake apply 4 coats to the bottom 2 tiers.

Method for Icing a Cake – Icing the Sides of a Round Cake

A flat-sided scraper is essential for producing smooth sides. Put plenty of icing on the side of the cake and, using a small palette knife, move it back and forth to get a relatively smooth surface and to remove little air pockets. For round cakes, put your arm round the back of the cake and move the scraper forwards on the cake as you can try to get a smooth, sweeping movement without stopping. The scraper should be upright against the side of the cake. Move the scraper off the cake at an angle so the join is not noticeable. If you use a turntable, it will make icing larger cakes easier. Hold the scraper to the side of the cake and use the other hand round the cake so the turntable moves round quickly and smoothly in one revolution. Scrape off any extra icing with a small palette knife. Wipe the cake board and allow each coat to dry for 2-3 hours or overnight before icing the top.

Icing the Top

When icing the base tier of a wedding cake, remember not to add glycerine. Spread the icing on the cake and, using a metal, or firm, plastic, ruler held at a 30° angle, draw it gently across the cake with a positive movement. Try not to press down too hard or the icing will be too thin. Remove any surplus icing from the sides of the cake with a clean palette knife. Leave the icing for at least a day to dry. Remove any rough edges round the joins with clean, fine-graded sandpaper. If the coating is not enough, repeat this 2-3 times. Wait 24 hours before piping decoration onto the cake.

Icing a Square Cake

Ice 2 opposite sides first, then the other 2 sides to produce sharp corners. Hold the palette knife parallel with the side of the cake when icing.

Royal Icing

The consistency of royal icing depends upon its use. For rosettes and flat icing it should be quite firm, whereas for piping latticework and writing it should be a little thinner. When icing is required for any flooding and runouts, it should be thin and smooth. Royal icing can be made in any quantity in the proportion of 1 egg per 225g (8oz) of sieved icing sugar. Keep the icing bowl covered with a damp cloth to keep it moist. As an egg substitute, egg albumen (white) can be bought in specialist cake decoration shops and the instructions for use are given on the packet. The addition of glycerine will aid the softening of the icing when it is dry. This makes it easier to cut.

Wedding Cakes

When icing wedding cakes, do not add glycerine to the two top layers of icing on the bottom tier, so the cake can support the other tiers. Made icing can be stored in an airtight container in a cool atmosphere for 2 days. Before use the stored icing should be stirred well.
Beat the egg whites until frothy with a wire whisk, making sure that the bowl is clean and dry first. Gradually beat in half the icing sugar using a wooden spoon. Beat in the remaining half of the icing sugar with the glycerine and, if using lemon juice, add it now. Beat the mixture thoroughly until smooth and white. Beat in enough icing sugar to give the mixture a consistency which is stiff and stands in peaks. Add the colour, if required. Cover the bowl with a damp cloth and leave the icing to stand for several hours. This allows any air bubbles to rise to the surface of the icing and burst. Before using, stir well with a wooden spoon. Do not overbeat. Note: if you are using an electric mixer, use the slowest speed and leave the icing for 24 hours. It will incorporate more air and will need longer to stand.

Facing page: covering with marzipan, and using apricot glaze.

Guide to Royal Icing Quantities Required to Flat Ice in Two Thin Coats

Square	Round	Icing Sugar
12.5cm (5 inch)	15cm (6 inch)	675g (1½lb)
15cm (6 inch)	18cm (7 inch)	900g (2lb)
18cm (7 inch)	20cm (8 inch)	1.25kg (2½lb)
20cm (8 inch)	23cm (9 inch)	1.5kg (3lb)
23cm (9 inch)	25cm (10 inch)	1.6kg (3½lb)
25cm (10 inch)	28cm (11 inch)	1.6kg (3½lb)
28cm (11 inch)	30cm (12 inch)	2kg (4½lb)
30cm (12 inch)	2kg (4½lb)	

Moulding Icing

PREPARATION TIME: 20 minutes

This is also known as kneaded fondant. It is very easy to use and can be rolled out like pastry. It is ideal for covering novelty cakes and even rich fruit cake. The icing sets and becomes firm. Moulding icing can be used to cover a cake directly or over almond paste or marzipan. If using marzipan first, allow the paste to dry before covering with the icing, which can also be used to make flowers and other decorations.

450g (1lb) icing sugar
1 egg white
50g (2oz) liquid glucose
Food colouring or flavouring, if desired

Sift the icing sugar into a mixing bowl and add the egg white and the liquid glucose to the centre of the sugar. Beat the ingredients with a wooden spoon, gradually incorporating the icing sugar to result in a stiff mixture. Knead the icing until you have a pliable paste. This icing can be stored by placing it into a bag, or wrapping it in cling film, or sealing it in a plastic container and storing it in a cool place for up to 3 days. If adding a colour, sprinkle with a little more sifted icing sugar to keep the icing the same consistency.

To Apply Moulding or Gelatine Icing
Attach the icing by first brushing either the cake with apricot glaze or the marzipan with egg white. Roll out the icing on a surface dusted with icing sugar or cornflour, or between two sheets of dusted polythene. Roll out the icing at least 7.5cm (3 inches) larger than the top of the cake. Support the icing on a rolling pin and drape it over the cake. Dust your hands with cornflour or icing sugar and rub the surface of the cake, working in circular movements with the palms of your hands to make the icing thinner and ease down the sides of the cake. Smooth out any folds in the icing and cut off the excess. If icing a square cake, mould the corners so that the square keeps it shape. Leave to dry.
NB: liquid glucose is available from chemists.

Gelatine Icing

PREPARATION TIME: 20 minutes

This icing can be used in the same way as moulding icing, but when it dries it becomes quite brittle. The icing can be used to make decorations such as flowers and leaves.

10ml (2 tsp) gelatine powder
30ml (2 tblsp) water to dissolve the gelatine
450g (1lb) icing sugar
1 egg white

Put the gelatine powder into the water, which is contained in a small heatproof basin held over a saucepan of hot water. Stir until the gelatine has dissolved. Sift the icing sugar into another bowl and add the dissolved gelatine and egg white. Stir well until firm, then knead with the fingers until smooth. Dust with extra icing sugar, if necessary. If adding food colouring, sprinkle with more icing sugar to keep the icing to the same consistency. This icing can be stored for 2 to 3 days before use. To do so, wrap it in cling film or a polythene bag and keep it in a sealed container. If it begins to dry, place or keep the icing in its sealed polythene bag and dip briefly in hot water. Leave for 1 hour and knead well before use.

Glacé Icing

PREPARATION TIME: 10 minutes

Probably the quickest icing to make, it is used on sponges, small cakes and biscuits. To keep the icing liquid, place the bowl over a pan of hot water.

250g (8oz) icing sugar
30ml (2 tblsp) warm water
Various flavourings and colourings

Sift the icing sugar into a mixing bowl and gradually add the water. The icing should be thick enough to coat the back of a spoon when it is withdrawn from the mixture. Add the flavouring and the colouring, if desired. This quantity will ice 18 small cakes and half the amount will ice the top of a 20cm (8 inch) cake.

Variations

Coffee
Replace 15ml (1 tblsp) warm water with 15ml (1 tblsp) coffee essence.

Orange or Lemon
Replace 15ml (1 tblsp) warm water with 15ml (1 tblsp) orange or lemon juice. Add the grated rind of one orange or lemon and a few drops of food colouring.

Chocolate
Sift 45ml (3 tblsp) cocoa powder with the icing sugar.
NB: you must be careful not to keep the icing in too hot a bowl of water, otherwise it will lose its gloss. Also, if a newly-iced cake is moved around without being given a chance to set, the glacé icing could crack and spoil the smooth surface.

Buttercream Icing

This icing is good for covering sponge and quick cake mixture cakes. Butter icing is ideal for covering novelty cakes, as it can be flavoured and coloured easily and is no problem to pipe.

PREPARATION TIME: 10 minutes

125g (4oz) butter
225g (8oz) sifted icing sugar
30ml (2 tblsp) milk
Flavourings (see 'Variations')

Beat the butter and some of the icing sugar until smooth. Add the remaining icing sugar with the milk and flavouring. Beat until creamy. This icing will cover and fill a 20cm (8 inch) sandwich cake. Store in an airtight container in the refrigerator, for several weeks if necessary.

Variations

Lemon or Orange
Add the grated rind of 1 lemon or orange to the butter. Replace the milk with lemon or orange juice. Add a few drops of orange or lemon colouring.

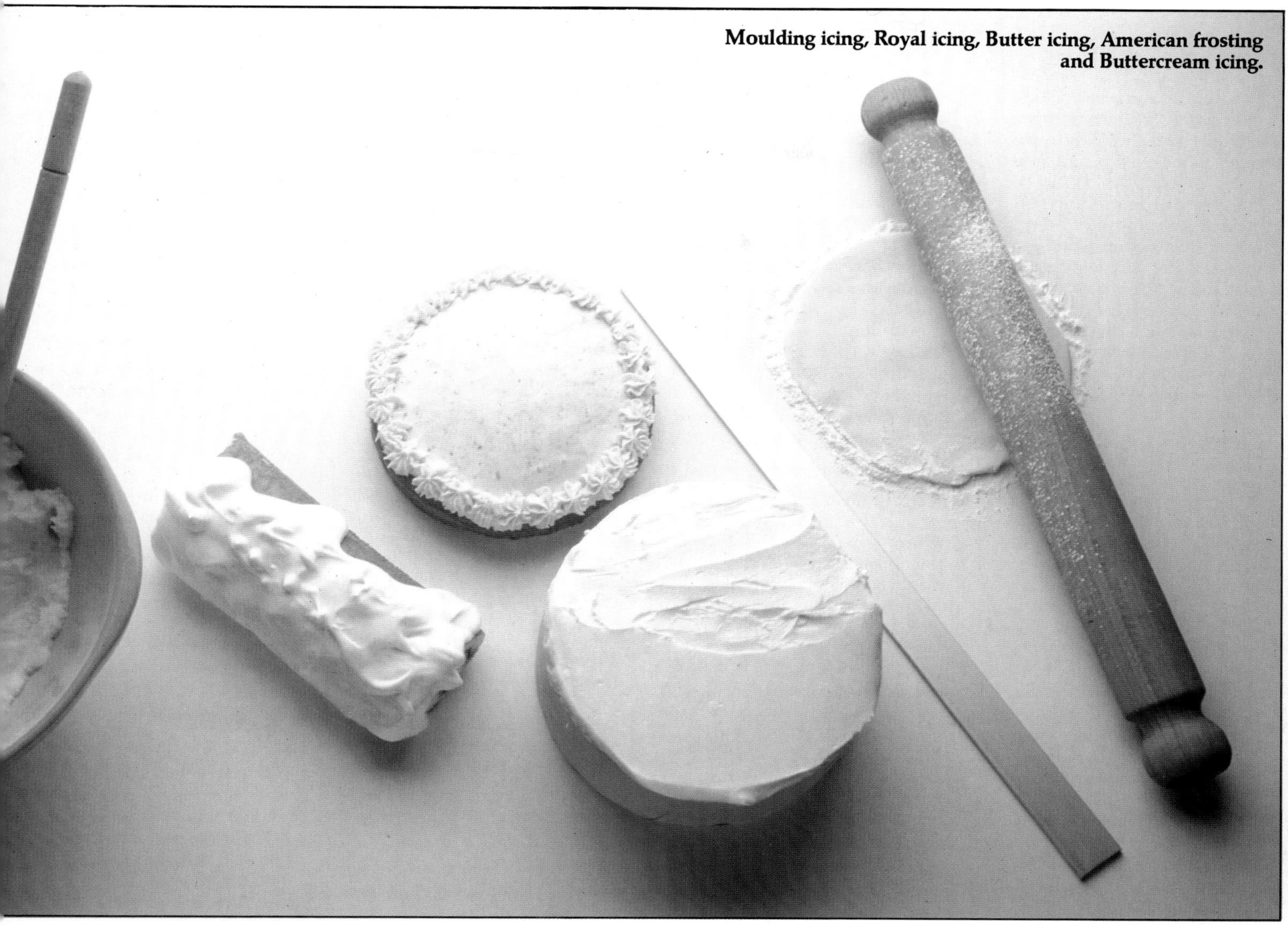

Moulding icing, Royal icing, Butter icing, American frosting and Buttercream icing.

Chocolate
Blend 30ml (2 tblsp) cocoa powder with 30ml (2 tblsp) boiling water. Cool, then add to the mixture with 15ml (1 tblsp) milk.

Coffee
Replace 15ml (1 tblsp) milk with 15ml (1 tblsp) coffee essence.

Crème au Beurre

PREPARATION TIME: 15 minutes

2 egg whites
125g (4oz) icing sugar, sifted
125g (4oz) unsalted butter
Flavourings (see 'Variations')

Place the egg whites and icing sugar in a bowl over a pan of simmering water. Whisk until the mixture holds its shape. Cool. Cream the butter until soft then beat into the egg white mixture, a little at a time. Flavour or colour as required.

Variations

Chocolate
Melt 50g (2oz) plain chocolate in a bowl over a pan of hot water. Cool and beat into the egg white mixture.

Coffee
Add 15ml (1 tblsp) coffee essence to the egg white mixture.

Praline
Gently heat 50g (2oz) of both caster sugar and blanched almonds in a small pan until the sugar turns brown round the nuts. Turn the mixture onto an oiled baking sheet, cool and crush with a rolling pin. Add the 45ml (3 tblsp) of this crushed praline to the egg white mixture.

NB: this icing can be stored in an airtight container in the refrigerator for several weeks.

Confectioner's Custard

PREPARATION TIME: 10-15 minutes

3 egg yolks
50g (2oz) caster sugar
25g (1oz) plain flour
300ml (½ pint) milk
25g (1oz) butter
10ml (1 dsp) sherry

Put the egg yolks and sugar in a bowl and beat until smooth and creamy. Stir in flour and mix well. Heat the milk until hot, but not boiling, and stir into the egg mixture. Return the mixture to the pan and stir, bringing it gently to the boil. Remove from the heat and beat in the butter and the sherry. Pour into a bowl, stirring occasionally to prevent a skin forming. Makes 450ml (¾ pint) of custard.
NB: the custard can be stored in the refrigerator for up to 48 hours.

Basic Equipment and Practising Skills
You will probably have most of the basic pieces of equipment needed for decorating simple cakes: various-sized bowls and basins, measuring jugs, measuring spoons, wooden spoons, spatula, pastry brush, rolling pin, kitchen scales, airtight containers, cocktail sticks, artist's brush and a skewer, to name but a few. However, special icing equipment is often required, so it is wise to invest in a good, basic selection. You can extend your

range as the need arises. Palette knives are ideal for smoothing and spreading icing. They come in various sizes and one would prove most useful. An icing ruler is essential for flat icing the tops of cakes. Choose a firm, not flexible, ruler – at least 30cm (12 inches long, but preferably 36cm (14 inches). An icing rule is even better. An icing turntable is invaluable for icing and decorating large cakes. There are several types of icing scrapers and these are used for pulling round the sides of the cake until it is smooth. Icing cones come into the same category and have serrated teeth of various sizes.

Piping Nozzles
Piping nozzles come in various forms, the metal types giving the best definition. Try to start with a few basic nozzles. The range available starts from size 00. A basic icing-nozzle kit should consist of a fine, a medium and a thick writing nozzle; a shell nozzle; a leaf and a scroll nozzle; a ribbon nozzle (which is also used for basketwork); a forget-me-not and an 8-point and 10-point star nozzle.
Nozzles are available in two styles: plain or screw-on types. Screw-on nozzles are used in conjunction with nylon piping bags and a screw connector. Plain nozzles can be used with paper or nylon icing bags. With this type of nozzle remember that the icing has to be removed in order to change a nozzle. You can either make your own, or use a nylon piping bag or icing pump.
To make a paper icing bag, cut a piece of good quality greaseproof paper or non-stick silicone paper into a 25cm (10 inch) square. Fold in half to form a triangle. Fold the triangle in half to make a yet smaller triangle. Open out the smaller triangle and re-shape into a cone. Turn over the points of the cone so that it stays conical. Secure the join with a little sticky tape. Cut about 1cm (½ inch) off the tip of the bag and push in a nozzle.

Nylon Piping Bags
Nylon bags are sold in various sizes and can be easily filled. These bags are used with a screw connector. The connector is pushed into the bag and protrudes through the hole at the tip of the bag. This allows the nozzle to be placed at the end and secured with a screw-on attachment, allowing the nozzle to be changed without emptying the piping bag.
Nylon piping bags are most useful for gâteaux as they can be filled with cream, and a meringue nozzle (a large decorative nozzle) can be attached to pipe rosettes.

Icing Pumps
These are bought as part of an icing set; some are made of metal and others of plastic. They consist of a tube with a screw attachment for the screw-on type of nozzle. The icing is controlled with a plunger and is unscrewed to refill the tube. Unfortunately, they are difficult to use for delicate work and you cannot feel the movement of the icing to help control it.

Piping Decorations

Stars
Stars, for example, can be piped with various-shaped nozzles ranging from 5 to 8, or more, points. With the 5-point star, use a nozzle number 13 or 8. These are the most useful sizes. Place the star nozzle in the bag and fill with icing. Hold the bag upright and pipe out enough icing to form a star. Remove the nozzle from the surface of the piped star swiftly. Stars should be fairly flat without a point in the centre.

Rosettes
These are piped with a star nozzle, but using a circular movement. Start at one side of the circle and finish slightly higher than the surface of the icing in the middle of the circle.

Shell
Use either a star nozzle or a special shell nozzle No. 12. Shell nozzles give fatter shells. Hold the icing bag at an angle to the surface on which the shell is required and start piping towards the centre of where the shell will rest. First move the nozzle away from you and then towards you. Push out more icing for the thicker parts of the shell. Link the shells together by starting the second shell over the tail of the first.

Leaves
Use a leaf nozzle, which is No. 10 and has a pointed tip, or sometimes an indentation in the centre of the point. Leaves can be piped straight onto the cake, or on non-stick silicone paper, left to dry and then placed onto the cake for decoration. When piping you can make two or three overlapping movements to give the leaf some form.

Basket Weaving
See 'Tracy Rose Wedding Cake'.

Templates
These are patterns made of paper or card which are used to transfer the pattern onto the top of a cake. It is easy to create your own or, for simple decorations, i.e. circles and squares, draw round a saucepan lid or plastic storage container. On the 21st birthday cake we use a round template. Draw a circle the size required onto a piece of greaseproof paper and cut it out with a pair of scissors.
Fold the circle in half, into quarters and into eighths, ending with a flattened cone shape. Draw a line in a concave shape from one point to another and cut it out. When the circle is opened, the edge of it will be scallop shaped.

Piped Flowers
Use a large, medium or fine petal nozzle, depending on the size of flower required, and an icing nail, or a piece of waxed paper cut into squares and attached to a cork. Once piped, leave the flowers to dry for at least 1 day before transferring them to a cake.

Rose
Hold the piping bag with the thin part of the nozzle upright. Pipe a cone of icing, twisting the nail quickly through the fingers and thumb. Pipe three, four or five petals round the centre of the rose by curving them outwards.

Forget-me-nots
Pipe these straight onto the cake, using a No. 2 writing nozzle for the petals, by joining five or six dots together round the edge of the piping nail and piping a curved petal in the centre. Alternatively use a forget-me-not nozzle.

Holly Leaves
Colour some marzipan green and roll out onto waxed paper and cut into rectangles. Using an icing nozzle, cut each holly leaf into shape by cutting first two corners of the rectangle and working your way down the sides until you have a holly leaf shape. Mark the 'veins' with a knife point. Roll out a little more marzipan and colour it red for the holly berries.

Christmas Roses
Cover the top of an essence bottle with a little foil and take a piece of moulding icing the size of a pea and dip it into cornflour and roll it into a ball. Shape another piece into a petal (see 'Moulded Roses'). Repeat until you have five petals. Place the small ball in the foil and surround it with the petals, overlapping them. Leave to dry. Remove from the foil and paint the centre yellow with a little food colouring.

Mistletoe
Roll out a little moulding icing, or marzipan, coloured green. Cut into tongue shapes and round the ends. Mark a definite vein down the middle of the leaf with a knife and leave it to dry. Make small, pea-sized balls out of either natural marzipan or white moulding icing.

Moulded Roses
Make a cone with a little coloured, moulded icing and press it out at the base so that it stands. Place a piece of icing the size of a pea in a little cornflour and roll it into a ball. Using a hard-boiled egg, flatten the icing in your hand with quick strokes. Use more cornflour if it gets too sticky. Gently try to get the icing very thin. Carefully wrap the petals round the cone and turn the edges outwards. Repeat the process until a fully shaped rose is achieved. Leave the rose to dry and cut off the base. It may be necessary to use a cocktail stick to curl the petals.

Chocolate Leaves
Break the chocolate into small pieces and place in a bowl over a pan of hot water. Gently heat until the chocolate melts. Do not overheat the chocolate or let any water dilute it. With an artist's small paintbrush, making sure that the chocolate spreads evenly over the surface of the leaf, paint the underside of the freshly-picked, undamaged and washed rose leaf. Allow the chocolate to set and, when hard, carefully peel the leaf away from the chocolate, starting from the tip.

Facing page: a variety of cake decorations.

Gâteau

Minted Lime Gâteau

PREPARATION TIME: 35 minutes

COOKING TIME: 20 minutes

OVEN TEMPERATURE: 190°C, 375°F, Gas Mark 5

125g (4oz) caster sugar
3 eggs
75g (3oz) plain flour
40g (1½oz) melted butter
Grated rind of 1 lime
Flesh of 1 lime, de-pipped

Decoration
300ml (½ pint) double cream
1 fresh lime
Grated chocolate (optional)

Whisk the sugar and eggs together in a basin, over a saucepan of hot water, until the mixture is thick. Sieve the flour twice and fold into the whisked mixture. Mix in the lime flesh and grated rind. Grease and flour a 20cm (8 inch) cake tin and fill with the mixture. Bake in the oven for 20 minutes. Cool on a wire rack.

To Decorate
Whip the cream and spread over the gâteau, reserving a little for piping. Fill a nylon piping bag with the remaining cream and, using a star nozzle, pipe rosettes to decorate the gâteau. Sprinkle the sides with chocolate, if desired, and decorate with slices of lime.

Gâteau St Honoré

PREPARATION TIME: 1 hour 30 minutes

COOKING TIME: 30 minutes

OVEN TEMPERATURE: 160°C, 325°F, Gas Mark 3

This is a fantasy choux pastry dessert. Also known as a croquembouche, it can be built directly onto a serving stand or onto a meringue or shortcrust pastry base, and is a French favourite for weddings. If making the choux pastry a day in advance, the buns can be crisped by heating in a preheated oven at 180°C, 350°F, Gas Mark 4, for 5 minutes. Cool before filling and assembling.

Choux Pastry
75g (3oz) butter
175ml (6 fl oz) water
100g (4oz) plain flour
Pinch of salt
3 beaten eggs

Filling
600ml (1 pint) double cream
30ml (2 tblsp) milk
30ml (2 tblsp) sifted icing sugar
30ml (2 tblsp) raspberry liqueur

Caramel
225g (8oz) granulated sugar
150ml (¼ pint) water

Sift the flour and salt together. Melt the butter in a heavy saucepan, with the water, and bring to the boil. Remove from heat. Add flour and salt mixture to the pan as soon as liquid has boiled. This should be carried out rapidly. Beat with a wooden spoon until glossy. The mixture should be the right consistency to form small balls at this stage. Turn out onto a plate and spread out to cool. Return it to the pan and gradually beat in the eggs. Fill a piping bag with the choux paste. Attach a 2cm (¾ inch) plain nozzle. Pipe the choux paste in small balls onto a greased baking sheet. Make sure they are well apart. Bake in the oven for 25 minutes until well risen and golden brown. They should be firm to touch. Pierce each bun to allow the steam to escape and return them to the oven for 2 minutes. Cool on a wire rack.

Filling
Whip half the cream with the milk, fold in the icing sugar and the raspberry liqueur. Whip the remaining cream and use half to form a mound in the centre of the serving plate or stand. With the other half, fill a piping bag fitted with a star nozzle and reserve. Use the raspberry cream to fill another piping bag fitted with a plain nozzle and fill each of the choux buns. Stick the choux buns round the cream mound so that it is completely covered and pipe rosettes between each bun using the plain cream.

For the Caramel
Melt the sugar gently in a saucepan with the water and boil until it turns brown and caramelizes. Cool until the caramel begins to thicken but not set and pour quickly, but gently, over the gâteau. Leave to set and chill for ½ hour before serving.

Loganberry Gâteau

PREPARATION TIME: 40 minutes

COOKING TIME: 35 minutes

OVEN TEMPERATURE: 190°C, 375°F, Gas Mark 5

4 eggs
125g (4oz) caster sugar
75g (3oz) plain flour
25g (1oz) melted butter
25g (1oz) cornflour
Grated rind of ½ lemon

Filling
450g (1lb) loganberries, fresh (or drained, if tinned)
90ml (6 tblsp) sherry
450ml (¾ pint) double cream, whipped
Finely-grated chocolate or chocolate vermicelli

Put the sugar, eggs and lemon rind in a basin over a pan of hot water and whisk until pale and thick. Remove from the heat and continue to whisk until cool. Sieve the flour and cornflour together. Fold the flour and melted butter into the mixture using a metal spoon. Bottom line and grease a 20cm (8 inch) square cake tin, fill with mixture and bake in the oven for 35 minutes. When cooked, turn out and cool on a wire rack. Cut the cake in half horizontally and sprinkle with sherry. Spread the bottom layer with whipped cream and reserve a little cream for decoration. Cover the cream with half the loganberries. Put the top layer of the sponge onto the loganberry filling and cover the sides of the cake with a thin layer of cream using a palette knife. Press the chocolate over the sides of the cake. Cover the top of the cake with a thin layer of cream and fill a nylon piping bag fitted with a large nozzle with the remaining cream. Pipe a cream border round the top of the cake. Fill the top with the remaining loganberries.

Apricot Meringue

PREPARATION TIME: 30 minutes

COOKING TIME: 1 hour to 1 hour 15 minutes

OVEN TEMPERATURE: 140°C, 275°F, Gas Mark 1

6 egg whites
350g (12oz) caster sugar
450ml (15 fl oz) whipping cream, whipped
6 apricot halves, sliced

Line a baking sheet with non-stick paper. Whisk the egg whites in a clean, dry bowl until stiff. Continue to whisk and add the sugar, 15ml (1 tblsp) at a time, until the mixture is very stiff and glossy. Fit a large star nozzle to a piping bag and pipe 8 swirls onto the baking sheet. Bake in the oven for 1-1¼ hours until crisp and dry. Leave to cool and peel from the paper. Lay half the meringue swirls onto a presentation plate and fill a piping bag, fitted with a star nozzle, with the whipped cream. Pipe a line of cream onto each swirl and layer with slices of apricot. Pipe with cream again. Sandwich with another meringue swirl and pipe with cream around the edge of the top meringue and decorate the cream with further slices of apricot.

Facing page: Gateau St Honoré (top left), Minted Lime Gateau (top right) and Loganberry Gateau (bottom).

Black Forest Gâteau

PREPARATION TIME: 35 minutes
COOKING TIME: 40 minutes
OVEN TEMPERATURE: 190°C, 375°F, Gas Mark 5

3 eggs
125g (4oz) caster sugar
75g (3oz) plain flour
15g (½oz) cocoa powder

Filling
425g (15oz) tin black cherries, pitted
15ml (1 tblsp) arrowroot
30ml (2 tblsp) Kirsch
300ml (½ pint) double cream
Grated chocolate or chocolate flakes to decorate

Place the eggs and sugar in a basin and whisk over a saucepan of hot water until thick. Remove from the heat and continue to whisk until cool. Sieve the cocoa powder and flour together and gently fold into the mixture using a metal spoon. Grease and line the bottom of a 20cm (8 inch) cake tin. Pour the mixture into the tin and bake in the oven for 40 minutes. Turn out and cool on a wire rack.

Filling and Decoration
Drain the juice from the cherries into a pan and blend with a little arrowroot. Bring to boil and stir until it thickens. Add the cherries to the syrup and allow to cool. Cut the cake in half and sprinkle the base with a little Kirsch. Whip the cream and use it to fill a nylon piping bag fitted with a large star nozzle. Pipe a circle of cream into the border edge of the base cake. Fill with half the cherry mixture. Sprinkle the top of the cake with a little Kirsch and place on top of the filling. Spread a little cream on the sides of the gâteau and press the grated chocolate onto it, using a palette knife. Pipe swirls of cream on top of the gâteau and fill the centre with the remaining cherries. Sprinkle with a little chocolate.

Walnut and Banana Galette

PREPARATION TIME: 45 minutes
COOKING TIME: 25 minutes
OVEN TEMPERATURE: 180°C, 350°F, Gas Mark 4

175g (4oz) butter
175g (6oz) plain flour
125g (4oz) caster sugar
100g (4oz) chopped walnuts
Grated rind of ½ lemon

Filling and Decoration
300ml (½ pint) double cream
30ml (2 tblsp) icing sugar
4 bananas

Cream the butter, sugar and lemon rind until fluffy. Fold the flour in and knead it until you have a soft dough. Put the dough in a polythene bag and chill for ½ hour in the refrigerator. Grease and flour 3 baking sheets and mark an 18cm (7 inch) circle on each. To make the circles, use a saucepan lid as a guide. Divide the dough into 3 and place a piece of dough on each circle. Press it out until it fills the circle. Sprinkle the top of each circle with chopped walnuts and bake in the oven for 25 minutes. When cooked, allow to cool before turning onto a wire rack.

Filling and Decoration
Whip the cream and fold in the icing sugar. Slice the bananas and sprinkle them with a little lemon juice, which prevents them from discolouring. Sandwich the layers with some cream sprinkled with banana slices. Using a nylon piping bag filled with the remaining cream and fitted with a large star nozzle, pipe the decoration around the top of the galette and decorate with slices of banana. Allow the galette to stand for 30 minutes before serving.

Brandied Chestnut Roll

PREPARATION TIME: 35 minutes
COOKING TIME: 12 minutes for the base, 10 minutes for the filling
OVEN TEMPERATURE: 220°C, 425°F, Gas Mark 7

3 eggs
100g (4oz) caster sugar
30ml (2 tblsp) brandy
100g (4oz) plain flour

Filling
15ml (1 tblsp) caster sugar
300ml (½ pint) double cream
250g (8¾oz) tin chestnut purée (crème de marrons)
175g (6oz) plain chocolate
15g (½oz) butter
30ml (2 tblsp) brandy

Whisk the eggs and sugar until thick. Gently fold in the sieved flour and the brandy with a metal spoon. Line and grease (bottom only) a 23x33cm (9x13 inch) Swiss roll tin. Pour the mixture into the tin and bake in the oven for 12 minutes. Cover a clean, damp tea towel with a sheet of greaseproof paper. Sprinkle the paper with 15ml (1 tblsp) caster sugar. Turn the cake out onto the paper and remove the greaseproof paper used to line the tin. The edges of the cake will be crisp, so trim with a sharp knife. Roll up the cake by putting a clean sheet of greaseproof paper over the cake. Cool on a wire tray.

Filling
Whip the cream and sugar until stiff and stir half the cream into the chestnut purée. The chestnut purée mixture must be smooth before use. Gently unroll the cake and remove the greaseproof paper rolled with it. Spread the chestnut cream on the inner side of the cake and re-roll. Melt the chocolate in a bowl over a pan of hot water, adding the butter and brandy. Cover the cake completely with the chocolate mixture. Mark the chocolate-coated cake with a fork when half set. Pipe the whipped cream with a large nozzle into whirls on top of the cake.

Ginger Ice Cream Gâteau

PREPARATION TIME: 1 hour
COOKING TIME: 25 minutes
OVEN TEMPERATURE: 160°C, 325°F, Gas Mark 3

Ice Cream
150ml (5 fl oz) milk
1 egg
75g (3oz) caster sugar
50ml (2 fl oz) green ginger wine
300ml (½ pint) double cream

Almond Base
3 egg whites
150g (5oz) caster sugar
50g (2oz) cornflour
100g (4oz) ground almonds

Topping
150ml (5 fl oz) double cream
60ml (4 tblsp) apricot jam, sieved
3 pieces stem ginger, chopped
50g (2oz) toasted whole or flaked almonds

Ice Cream
Put the milk, egg and sugar into a basin over a pan of hot water. Stir continuously until the custard mixture begins to thicken. When it will coat the back of the spoon, remove it and let it cool. Stir in the ginger wine and cream. Pour into a rigid, shallow freezer container and partially freeze. When the ice cream is partially frozen, remove from the freezer and pour into a bowl. Whisk until smooth and creamy. Line a 20cm (8 inch) sandwich tin with cling film and pour in the ice cream. Return to the freezer until frozen.

Almond Base
Whisk the egg whites in a clean bowl until they are stiff. Add the sugar and whisk again. Gently fold in the cornflour and ground almonds. Line the bottom of a baking tray. Fill a nylon piping bag fitted with a 1cm (½ inch) nozzle with some of the almond mixture. Spread the mixture in a 20cm (8 inch) circle and smooth evenly. Bake in the oven for 25 minutes. Place the almond base on a flat plate. Carefully lift the ice cream out of the tin and peel off the cling film. Place the ice cream on the almond base.

For the Topping
Whip the cream, fold in the jam, stem ginger and almonds and spread over the ice cream.

Brandied Chestnut Roll (left), Walnut and Banana Galette (below) and Black Forest Gâteau (bottom).

Peach and Almond Gâteau

PREPARATION TIME: 60 minutes

COOKING TIME: 60 minutes for cake, 20 minutes for confectioner's custard

OVEN TEMPERATURE: 180°C, 350°F, Gas Mark 4

4 eggs, separated
100g (4oz) caster sugar
100g (4oz) self-raising flour
30ml (2 tblsp) corn oil
45ml (3 tblsp) boiling water
5ml (1 tsp) almond essence

Filling
30ml (2 tblsp) apricot jam, warmed

Confectioner's Custard
3 egg yolks
50g (2oz) caster sugar
25g (1oz) plain flour
300ml (½ pint) milk
25g (1oz) butter
10ml (1 dsp) sherry

To Decorate
300ml (½ pint) double cream
50g (2oz) flaked almonds, toasted
410g (14½oz) tin sliced peaches, drained

Grease and line a 20cm (8 inch) loose-bottomed, deep cake tin. Place the egg yolks, sugar, flour, oil, water and almond essence in a bowl and beat for 2 minutes with a wooden spoon. Stiffly whisk the egg whites and fold into the cake mixture using a metal spoon. Pour the mixture into a prepared tin and cook in the oven for about 60 minutes until well risen. Remove cake from tin and cool on a wire rack. Remove paper when cake is cold.

For the Confectioner's Custard
Put egg yolks and sugar in a bowl and beat until smooth and creamy. Stir in the flour and mix well. Heat the milk until hot, but not boiling, and stir into the egg mixture. Return the mixture to the pan and stir, bringing it gently to the boil. Remove from the heat and beat in the butter and the sherry. Pour into a bowl, stirring occasionally to prevent a skin forming.

Assembling the Gâteau
Cut the cake into 3 layers, placing the bottom layer on a serving plate. Spread the cake with 15ml (1 tblsp) of jam and half the confectioner's custard. Place the second layer on top and spread with the remaining jam and custard. Put the top of the cake onto the filling. Spread the cake with half the cream and arrange the peaches on the top. Fit a piping bag with a medium star nozzle and pipe the remaining cream to decorate the gâteau. Sprinkle on the toasted almonds.

Chocolate Torte

PREPARATION TIME: 35 minutes

COOKING TIME: 1 hour 30 minutes

OVEN TEMPERATURE: 150°C, 300°F, Gas Mark 2

175g (6oz) plain chocolate
15ml (1 tblsp) strong black coffee
175g (6oz) butter
175g (6oz) caster sugar
4 eggs, separated
150g (5oz) self-raising flour

Filling and Icing
Cherry jam
175g (6oz) plain chocolate
30ml (2 tblsp) strong black coffee
175g (6oz) icing sugar
150ml (5 fl oz) double cream or 100g (4oz) chocolate shavings
410g (14½oz) tinned black cherries, pitted

Melt the chocolate and coffee over a basin of hot water. Allow it to cool. Cream the butter and sugar together until light and fluffy. Slowly beat in the egg yolks and the cooled chocolate mixture. Fold in the flour using a metal spoon. Whisk the egg whites in a clean, dry bowl until stiff, then fold into the mixture. Line and grease the base of a 20cm (8 inch) cake tin and bake in the oven for 1½ hours. Allow the cake to cool in the tin for 10 minutes before turning onto a wire rack. Cut the cake horizontally and sandwich together with the cherry jam. Melt the chocolate and coffee for the icing in a basin over a saucepan of hot water and remove from the heat. Beat in the icing sugar. Pour the chocolate icing over the cake, working it over the sides of the cake with a palette knife. When set, decorate with either the whipped cream or chocolate shavings and drained cherries.

Avocado Cheesecake

PREPARATION TIME: 30 minutes plus chilling

Biscuit Base
225g (8oz) chocolate digestive biscuits
75g (3oz) butter, melted

Filling
2 ripe avocado pears
100g (4oz) cream cheese
75g (3oz) caster sugar
Juice of ½ a lemon
Grated rind of 1 lemon
10ml (2 tsp) gelatine powder
2 egg whites
150ml (5 fl oz) double cream, whipped

Decoration
150ml (5 fl oz) double cream, whipped

Crush the biscuits into fine crumbs and stir in the melted butter. Use the mixture to line a 19cm (7½ inch) springform tin. Press it down to line the base and the sides. Chill well.

For the Filling
Peel and stone the avocados and save a few slices for decoration. Put the remainder into a basin and mash well. Mix in the lemon juice and grated rind, cream cheese and sugar. Beat until smooth. Dissolve the gelatine in 30ml (2 tblsp) of hot water and stir into the mixture. Whisk the egg whites in a clean, dry bowl and fold into the mixture with the whipped cream. Pour onto a prepared biscuit base and chill thoroughly until set.

To Decorate
Carefully remove the cheesecake from the tin. Fill a nylon piping bag, fitted with a star nozzle, with the cream reserved for decoration. Pipe a border of cream round the edge of the cake. Decorate with the avocado slices.
NB: sprinkle the avocado with lemon juice to prevent it from discolouring. This is useful when reserving the slices for decoration.

This page: Chocolate Torte (top) and Apricot Meringue (bottom).

Facing page: Avocado Cheesecake (top), Ginger Ice Cream Gâteau (centre left) and Peach and Almond Gâteau (bottom).

Teatime Treats

Baking at home is not as difficult as some might expect and in very little time one can create some appetising treats for the tea table. Here are lots of recipes which may tempt you to try them for yourself at picnics, birthdays and tea parties.

Scones

PREPARATION TIME: 15 minutes

COOKING TIME: 10-15 minutes

OVEN TEMPERATURE: 200°C, 400°F, Gas Mark 6

225g (8oz) plain flour
5ml (1 tsp) cream of tartar
2.5ml (½ tsp) bicarbonate of soda
Good pinch of salt
40g (1½oz) butter or margarine
75g (3oz) caster sugar
40g (1½oz) sultanas
15g (½oz) sugared ginger pieces
15g (½oz) sunflower seeds
2 eggs, plus a little milk if required
1 egg, beaten or a little milk for glazing

Sieve the dry ingredients twice. Rub in the fat, add sugar, sultanas, ginger pieces and sunflower seeds and mix to a soft dough with eggs. Knead lightly on floured surface. Roll out to approximately 1cm (½ inch) thickness. Place on floured baking sheet and brush the top with beaten egg or milk. Bake in the oven for 10-15 minutes.

Walnut Cake

PREPARATION TIME: 15 minutes

COOKING TIME: 35 minutes

OVEN TEMPERATURE: 180°C, 350°F, Gas Mark 4

4 eggs
175g (6oz) caster sugar
125g (4oz) plain sifted flour
15ml (1 tblsp) oil
125g (4oz) walnuts, finely chopped
Recipe butter cream
Walnut halves to decorate

Grease and line two 20cm (8 inch) sandwich tins. Place the eggs and sugar in a heatproof bowl and whisk over a pan of hot, but not boiling, water until thick (see whisked sponge method). Partially fold in the flour, add the oil and chopped walnuts and fold in gently. Divide the mixture between the prepared tins and bake in the oven for 35 minutes. When the cake is cooked, it will spring back when touched. Turn onto a wire rack to cool. Split each cake in half and fill with butter cream. Swirl the remaining butter cream on top of the cake and decorate with walnut halves.

Welsh Cakes (above), Walnut Cake (right) and Scones (far right).

Welsh Cakes

PREPARATION TIME: 15 minutes

COOKING TIME: 8 minutes (4 minutes per side)

OVEN TEMPERATURE: 140°C, 275°F, Gas Mark 1

100g (4oz) self-raising flour
Pinch of salt
40g (1½oz) butter or margarine
40g (1½oz) sugar
1 egg, plus a little milk if required
40g (1½oz) currants
2.5ml (½ tsp) ground nutmeg

Sieve the flour and salt. Rub in the fat and stir in sugar, nutmeg and currants. Mix to a pastry consistency with egg. Roll out to 6mm (¼ inch) thickness and cut with a 6mm small pastry cutter. Cook on baking stone or large greased pan. Switch oven off for 15 minutes then grease and reheat for second batch. Dredge with caster sugar and serve. Makes 10.

Flapjacks

PREPARATION TIME: 15 minutes
COOKING TIME: 30 minutes
OVEN TEMPERATURE: 180°C, 350°F, Gas Mark 4

125g (4oz) margarine
125g (4oz) soft brown sugar
75g (3oz) golden syrup
250g (8oz) rolled oats

Melt the margarine, sugar and syrup in a bowl over a pan of hot water. Stir in the rolled oats and mix thoroughly. Grease a shallow 20cm (8 inch) square tin. Turn the mixture into the tin and smooth down the top. Bake in the oven for 30 minutes until golden. Cool in the tin for 3 minutes before cutting into fingers. Remove from tin when cool. Makes 16.

Coconut Specials

PREPARATION TIME: 20 minutes
COOKING TIME: 30 minutes
OVEN TEMPERATURE: 160°C, 325°F, Gas Mark 3

225g (8oz) puff pastry
A little jam, melted
50g (2oz) melted butter
100g (4oz) desiccated coconut
100g (4oz) sugar
2 eggs

Roll out the puff pastry. Using a round pastry cutter, cut rounds and use to line a patty tin. Using a pastry brush, coat the pastry with a little jam. Beat together the butter, coconut, sugar and eggs. Divide the coconut mixture between the patty tins. Bake in the oven for 30 minutes until golden brown. When cooked, remove from tin and cool on a wire rack. Makes 14.

Victoria Sponge

PREPARATION TIME: 30 minutes
COOKING TIME: 20-25 minutes
OVEN TEMPERATURE: 190°C, 375°F, Gas Mark 5

125g (4oz) butter or margarine
125g (4oz) caster sugar
2 eggs
125g (4oz) self-raising flour, sifted with a pinch of salt
15ml (1 tblsp) hot water
45ml (3 tblsp) jam
150ml (1/4 pint) double cream, whipped
Caster sugar

Grease and line 2x18cm (7 inch) sandwich tins. Cream the fat and sugar until light and fluffy. Beat in the eggs singly and fold in 15ml (1 tblsp) of flour with each egg. Fold in the remaining flour, then add the hot water. Divide the mixture between the tins and bake in the oven for 20-25 minutes until the cakes are golden. When the cakes are cooked, they spring back when lightly pressed. Turn the cakes onto a wire rack to cool. Sandwich the cakes together with jam and cream. Sprinkle the top with caster sugar.

Chocolate Fudge Triangles

PREPARATION TIME: 25 minutes
COOKING TIME: 30 minutes for base, 10 minutes for topping
OVEN TEMPERATURE: 180°C, 350°F, Gas Mark 4

125g (4oz) butter
50g (2oz) caster sugar
175g (6oz) plain flour

Fudge Topping
125g (4oz) butter
50g (2oz) caster sugar
30ml (2 tblsp) golden syrup
150ml (5 fl oz) condensed milk
125g (4oz) plain chocolate

Cream the butter and sugar together until fluffy. Add the flour and stir until the mixture binds. Knead until smooth. Roll out and press into a shallow 20cm (8 inch) square tin. Prick with a fork and bake in the oven for 30 minutes. Cool in the tin. Put the ingredients for the topping in a heavy saucepan and stir until dissolved. Slowly boil and stir for 7 minutes. Cool the topping a little and spread over the biscuit base. Leave it to set. When set, cut into squares, then cut diagonally to make triangles.

Lemon July Cake

PREPARATION TIME: 30 minutes
COOKING TIME: 25 minutes
OVEN TEMPERATURE: 190°C, 375°F, Gas Mark 5

Base
100g (4oz) butter or margarine
100g (4oz) sugar
1 egg, beaten
175g (6oz) self-raising flour

1st Topping
150ml (1/4 pint) water
45ml (3 tblsp) sugar
15ml (1 tblsp) cornflour
Juice of two lemons

2nd Topping
150ml (1/4 pint) milk
5ml (1 tsp) cornflour
25g (1oz) butter
75g (3oz) sugar
Desiccated coconut to sprinkle

Base
Cream the butter and sugar, add the egg and flour and pour into a tin and press down. Bake in the oven for 20 minutes.

1st Topping
Mix the water with the cornflour to make a paste. Boil with the other ingredients until the mixture begins to thicken, stirring constantly. Spread on the cooked cake base while the mixture is still warm.

2nd Topping
Boil milk and cornflour until it thickens. Add the the butter and sugar, creamed. Mix well and spread on top of the July. Sprinkle with the desiccated coconut, cut into fingers and serve.

This page: Chocolate Brownies (top), Chocolate Fudge Triangles (centre) and Flapjacks (bottom).

Facing page: Victoria Sponge (top right), Lemon July Cake (centre left) and Coconut Specials (bottom).

Chocolate Brownies

PREPARATION TIME: 25 minutes
COOKING TIME: 35 minutes
OVEN TEMPERATURE: 180°C, 350°F, Gas Mark 4

125g (4oz) self-raising flour
1.25ml (¼ tsp) baking powder
125g (4oz) plain chocolate
50g (2oz) butter
125g (4oz) soft brown sugar
2 eggs
75g (3oz) walnuts
75g (3oz) mixed fruit

Icing
125g (4oz) plain chocolate
15g (½oz) butter

Sift the flour and baking powder together in a bowl. Melt the chocolate in a bowl over a small saucepan of hot water. Cream the butter for the brownies with the sugar until light and fluffy. Beat in the eggs separately, adding the flour with the second egg. Beat the melted chocolate into the mixture, then fold in the walnuts and fruit. Grease and line a shallow 20cm (8 inch) square tin and bake in the oven for 35 minutes. Cut into squares while still warm and cool in the tin.

Spiced Biscuits

PREPARATION TIME: 20 minutes
COOKING TIME: 15 minutes
OVEN TEMPERATURE: 180°C, 350°F, Gas Mark 4

125g (4oz) wholewheat flour
2.5ml (½ tsp) bicarbonate of soda
5ml (1 tsp) ground cinnamon
5ml (1 tsp) mixed spice
50g (2oz) rolled oats
75g (3oz) sugar
75g (3oz) butter or margarine
5ml (1 tblsp) golden syrup
5ml (1 tblsp) milk

Put the flour, bicarbonate of soda, cinnamon, mixed spice, oats and sugar into a bowl. Melt the butter in a small saucepan with the syrup and milk. Pour the liquid into the dry ingredients and beat until smooth. Make the mixture into little balls and place them a little apart on a lightly-greased baking sheet. Flatten each one. Bake in the oven for 15 minutes until golden and cool on the baking sheet.

Macaroons

PREPARATION TIME: 20 minutes
COOKING TIME: 20 minutes
OVEN TEMERATURE: 180°C, 350°F, Gas Mark 4

250g (8oz) caster sugar
150g (5oz) ground almonds
15ml (1 tblsp) rice flour
2 egg whites
Rice paper
20 split almonds

Mix the sugar, almonds and rice flour together. In a separate bowl, beat the egg whites lightly and add the ready-mixed dry ingredients. Let the mixture stand for 5 minutes. Line a baking sheet with rice paper. Mould the mixture into little balls and place them on the lined baking sheet slightly apart. Gently flatten the macaroons and put an almond on each one. Bake in the oven for 20 minutes, then cool on baking sheet. Makes 20.

Almond Slices

PREPARATION TIME: 20 minutes
COOKING TIME: 20 minutes
OVEN TEMPERATURE: 200°C, 400°F, Gas Mark 6

Pastry Base
200g (8oz) plain flour
100g (4oz) butter
1.25ml (¼ tsp) salt
Cold water to mix

Topping
60ml (4 tblsp) jam
100g (4oz) caster sugar
100g (4oz) icing sugar
175g (6oz) ground almonds
1 egg, plus 1 egg white
A few drops almond essence
25g (1oz) flaked almonds to decorate

Sift the flour and salt into a bowl and rub in the butter until it resembles fine breadcrumbs. Add enough water to mix into a pliable dough. Roll out the dough onto a floured surface and use to line a greased or dampened shallow 25x15cm (10x6 inch) baking tin. Pinch the long edges to form a border. Cover the base with jam. In a clean bowl, mix together the sugars and almonds. Beat well and then add the whole egg, egg white and almond essence. Use the almond mixture to cover the jam, spreading evenly with a knife. Sprinkle with almonds. Bake in the oven for 20 minutes until well risen and golden. When cooked, cut in the tin and leave to cool for 10 minutes. Then remove from tin and leave to finish cooling on a wire rack.

Viennese Fingers

PREPARATION TIME: 20 minutes

COOKING TIME: 15 minutes

OVEN TEMPERATURE: 180°C, 350°F, Gas Mark 4

175g (6oz) butter or margarine
50g (2oz) icing sugar
Grated rind of 1 orange
125g (4oz) plain flour
50g (2oz) cornflour

Cream together the butter, sugar and orange rind until fluffy. Sieve the flour and cornflour together and beat well into the mixture. Fill a piping bag fitted with a 2.5cm (1 inch) fluted nozzle and pipe 7.5cm (3 inch) fingers, well separated, on a sheet of non-stick silicone paper. Bake in the oven for 15 minutes and, when cooked, transfer to a wire rack to cool. If required, two fingers can be sandwiched together with a little apricot jam. Makes 12.

Chocolate Fudge Cake

PREPARATION TIME: 15 minutes

COOKING TIME: 45-50 minutes

OVEN TEMPERATURE: 160°C, 325°F, Gas Mark 3

200g (7oz) plain flour
5ml (1 tsp) bicarbonate of soda
5ml (1 tsp) baking powder
30ml (2 tblsp) cocoa powder
150g (5oz) soft brown sugar
30ml (2 tblsp) golden syrup
2 eggs
150ml (¼ pint) oil
300ml (½ pint) milk

Chocolate Icing
175g (6oz) plain chocolate
30ml (2 tblsp) single cream

To Decorate
1 packet chocolate buttons
75g (3oz) chocolate sugar strands or
Whole nuts

Sift together the dry ingredients into a bowl and make a well in the centre. Add the sugar, syrup, eggs, oil and milk and beat until smooth. Grease and line a 23cm (9 inch) cake tin and pour in the cake mixture. Cook in the oven for 45-50 minutes; leave in the tin for a few minutes before turning out the cake onto a wire rack.

To Make the Chocolate Icing
Put the chocolate and cream into a small, heavy pan and heat gently until melted. Cool the mixture slightly and pour over the cake. Decorate with chocolate buttons, chocolate strands, or nuts.

Harvest Crunchies

PREPARATION TIME: 20 minutes

COOKING TIME: 15 minutes

OVEN TEMPERTURE: 190°C, 375°F, Gas Mark 5

75g (3oz) self-raising flour
2.5ml (½ tsp) mixed spice
75g (3oz) wholewheat flour
25g (1oz) oatmeal
125g (4oz) butter or margarine
50g (2oz) soft brown sugar
25g (1oz) sultanas
30ml (2 tblsp) milk

Sift the flour and spice into a bowl. Stir in the wholemeal flour and oatmeal. Rub the fat into the mixture until it resembles breadcrumbs. Add the brown sugar and the sultanas, then add the milk, a little at a time, and mix until the consistency is that of stiff dough. Flour a work surface and turn the dough out onto it. Lightly knead the dough and roll it out until very thin. With a 7.5cm (3 inch) fluted biscuit cutter, cut out rounds and place them on a lightly-greased baking sheet. Bake in the oven, then cool on a wire rack. Makes 20.

Facing page: Macaroons (top), Spiced Biscuits (right) and Harvest Crunchies (bottom left).

This page: Chocolate Fudge Cake (top), Viennese Fingers (left) and Almond Slices (bottom).

Festive Cakes

Special cakes are traditionally used for the celebration of religious festivals; the most popular being the traditional Christmas cake and the simnel cake at Easter. Not everybody enjoys rich cake, so there are sponge variations in this book for both Easter and Christmas.

Simnel Cake

PREPARATION TIME: 40 minutes

COOKING TIME: 3 hours

OVEN TEMPERATURE: 160°C, 325°F, Gas Mark 3 reduced to 150°C, 300°F, Gas Mark 2

20cm (8 inch) round, rich fruit cake mixture
800g (1¾lb) marzipan
30ml (2 tblsp) apricot glaze
1 egg white, beaten
Ribbon to decorate

Place half the mixture in a prepared, deep cake tin. Roll out a quarter of the marzipan into a 20cm (8 inch) circle and lay it on top of the mixture. Spread the remaining mixture on the top of the marzipan. Bake in the oven for 1 hour, lower the temperature and bake for a further 2½ hours. Leave in the tin for 5 minutes and turn onto a wire rack to cool. Roll out a third of the remaining marzipan into a 20cm (8 inch) circle. Brush the top of the cake with apricot glaze. Press the marzipan circle on top of the cake and brush with beaten egg white. Shape the remaining marzipan into balls and place round the edge. Brown under a hot grill and allow to cool. Decorate with ribbon.

This page: Daffodil Cake (top) and Simnel Cake (bottom).

Facing page: Easter Cake with Chicks (top) and Easter Nest (bottom).

Daffodil Cake

23cm (9 inch) round Madeira cake
Recipe vanilla-flavoured butter icing
Moulding icing daffodil
45ml (3 tblsp) apricot jam
15ml (1 tblsp) cocoa powder

Slice the cake and spread with the jam. Use half of the butter icing and sandwich the cake together. Spread the top of the cake with a ¼ of the remaining butter icing. Smooth it with a palette knife. Fill a piping bag with the remaining butter icing and fit it with a 5-point star nozzle. Pipe shells round the edge of the cake. Put the daffodil on the cake. Mix a little butter icing with cocoa powder. With a piping bag fitted with a writing nozzle, pipe 'Easter' on the cake, below the daffodil.

Easter Nest

20cm (8 inch) round lemon sponge (whisked or Victoria)
1 box orange-flavoured chocolate sticks
100g (4oz) candy-coated chocolate speckled eggs
Recipe lemon-flavoured butter icing

Put the cake on a plate or cake board. Cover the cake with lemon-

flavoured butter icing. Put a ribbon round the side of the cake and make a bow. Lay the orange-flavoured chocolate sticks at angles round the sides of the cake, leaving an uncovered area in the centre of the cake. Fill the centre with eggs.

Fruit Easter Cake with Chicks

PREPARATION TIME: 45 minutes

COOKING TIME: 1 hour 30 minutes to 1 hour 45 minutes

OVEN TEMPERATURE: 160°C, 325°F, Gas Mark 3

175g (6oz) butter
175g (6oz) caster sugar
3 eggs
125g (4oz) plain flour
175g (6oz) mixed dried fruit
150g (5oz) self-raising flour
50g (2oz) chopped mixed peel
50g (2oz) glacé cherries, halved
Grated rind of 1 orange
75ml (5 tblsp) orange juice
1 crushed sugar cube

To Decorate
Fluffy chicks
Yellow ribbon

Cream the butter and sugar together until light and fluffy. Beat in the eggs singly, adding a little flour after each. Toss the fruit in the remaining flour with the orange rind and juice. Grease and line a 18cm (7 inch) cake tin. Fill with the mixture and smooth with the back of a spoon. Sprinkle with some of the crushed sugar cube. Bake in the oven for 1½- 1¾ hours. Turn out and cool on a wire rack. Decorate with yellow ribbon, chicks and fresh or artificial flowers. Sprinkle top of cake with remaining sugar cube.

Festive Garland

If you prefer you can make edible decorations for this cake.

20cm (8 inch) quick mix cake, baked in a ring mould
Recipe apricot glaze
Recipe butter icing
1 round cake board
Holly leaves, berries, Christmas roses, mistletoe, candle and ribbon (colour of your choice)

Split the cake and sandwich together with the glaze. Put the cake on the plate or cake board and cover with the icing, peaking it as you go around. Press the roses, holly leaves, berries and mistletoe into the cake, leaving a gap for the bow. When the icing is dry and hard, place a candle in the centre of the ring and attach the bow in the space reserved.

Christmas Bells

18cm (7 inch) or 20cm (8 inch) square Christmas cake
Royal icing, made with 1.25kg (2½lb) sugar
½ recipe white moulding icing
100g (4oz) granulated sugar
4 sprigs of holly, real or artificial
1 metre (1 yard) narrow, white satin ribbon
Food colouring – pink

Put the cake on a silver cake board. Royal ice the cake and leave to dry between coats. Roll out the moulding icing and, using a bell shape cutter, cut 10 bells and leave them to dry on non-stick silicone paper. Mix the granulated sugar and pink food colour well until the sugar becomes pink. Sprinkle over the bells and leave to dry. Fill a piping bag, fitted with a medium-sized star nozzle, with the royal icing. Pipe a row of shells round the bottom of the cake. Pipe a border of shells round the top of the cake and a line of shells up each of the 4 corners of the cake and allow the icing to dry. Make 5 bows with the narrow, white ribbon. With a little icing sugar secure two icing bells on each side panel of the cake. The tops of the bells should be nearest to each of the 4 corners. Two of the bells should be placed in the centre of the top of the cake, with the tops of the bells together. Put a ribbon bow above each of the bells. Position the sprigs of holly in each of the four corners on top of the cake.

Christmas Tree

20cm (8 inch) square quick mix cake or rich fruit cake mix
Recipe apricot glaze
Recipe marzipan, if using fruit cake
Recipe butter icing, if using quick mix cake
450g (1lb) moulding icing

To Decorate
1 cake board
Silver balls
Desiccated coconut to sprinkle
Recipe royal icing
225g (8oz) moulding icing, white
Chocolate sticks
Gold or silver non-toxic food colouring
Food colouring – red, blue, green, yellow

Cut the cake diagonally and place the outer edges of the square next to one another, i.e. back-to-back to produce a triangular shape. If using a fruit cake, brush with apricot glaze and cover with marzipan. If using a butter icing on a quick cake mixture, cover the cake with the butter icing and leave on the cake board. Roll out the moulding icing and, using a fluted pastry cutter, cut circles and then cut each one in half and use to stick onto the butter icing. Start at the bottom edge of the cake and overlap slightly until you reach the top. With the remaining icing, make some small presents and a square tub for the tree. Cover the tree trunk with a little of the remaining butter icing and lay the cocolate sticks vertically on the tree trunk. Use any remaining icing to frost the leaves of the tree, or pipe if desired. Decorate with the silver balls and sprinkle with desiccated coconut. With the white icing to decorate, colour small pinches in various colours and, with the white royal icing, pipe strings around the various coloured shapes to make more little parcels. Roll out the remaining white icing and cut it into a star. Colour with a little non-toxic gold or silver food colouring.

Traditional Christmas Cake with Holly and Roses

18cm (7 inch) round Christmas cake
Recipe apricot glaze
675g (1½lb) marzipan
Royal icing, made with 900g (2lb) icing sugar

To Decorate
Silver balls
Christmas roses
Marzipan holly leaves and berries, small snowman or Santa, if available
Ribbon

Brush the cake with apricot glaze. Cover with the marzipan and leave to dry. Flat ice the top and sides of the cake with royal icing and leave to dry again. Use a piping bag fitted with a 5-star nozzle to pipe shells around the top edge of the cake and then on the top, round the sides of the cake and, finally, around the bottom edge of the cake. When dry, pipe a further row between the top 2 rows using the 5-star nozzle upright to pipe stars. Decorate the top of the cake with marzipan holly and piped or moulded Christmas roses and a small snowman or Father Christmas, if desired. Tie the ribbon round the cake and make a bow. Push a silver ball into the centre of each of the stars.

Christmas Tree (right) and Festive Garland (below).

Frosted Mistletoe Cake

This is a quick and easy Christmas cake, which can be made either round or square. Any bought decorations can be used to complement the design.

18cm (7 inch) or 20cm (8 inch) square or round Christmas cake
Recipe apricot glaze
675g (1½lb) marzipan
900g (2lb) green moulding icing
12 mistletoe leaves and berries made from marzipan
60cm (2ft) x 5cm (2 inch) length of green ribbon
Food colouring – green

Put the cake on a silver cake board. To decorate, roll out the green moulding icing. With a small, sharp knife cut out several mistletoe leaves. Make them long and narrow with rounded ends and mark them with a knife to indicate the veins. With the uncoloured moulding icing roll small, pea-sized balls of icing to represent the berries. Use the mistletoe to decorate the top of the cake. With the ribbon, tie a large bow and attach it to the top of the cake with a little royal icing. Fill a shaker with a little icing sugar, or put it through a small sieve and shake it gently round the edge of the cake, dusting some of the mistletoe.

Christmas Candles

2 jam-filled Swiss rolls
450g (1lb) green moulding icing
100g (4oz) white moulding icing
Recipe apricot glaze
Rectangular silver cake board
Food colourings – red, yellow, blue
Red ribbon
3 cocktail sticks

Cut one Swiss roll ¾ of the way down. Brush the Swiss rolls with apricot glaze. Roll out the green moulding icing and cover the Swiss rolls. Stand them upright with something for support. In a small, heavy saucepan stir to dissolve half to three-quarters of the white

This page: Christmas Bells Cake (top) and Traditional Christmas Cake with Holly and Roses (bottom).

Facing page: Frosted Mistletoe Cake.

moulding icing. Roll out the remaining white icing on a surface dusted with icing sugar or cornflour and cut out 3 flame shapes. Leave on non-stick silicone paper to dry. When dry, paint a blue dot near the bottom; surround by yellow and edge with red. Reserve to dry. Pour the liquid moulding icing over the candles in a drizzle so that it dries like wax. Stick a flame into the top of each candle, using a cocktail stick to support them. Decorate with ribbons.

Postbox

This makes a quick and easy festive cake for those who do not like traditional Christmas cake.

1 chocolate Swiss roll
225g (8oz) red moulding icing
Recipe royal icing
Recipe apricot glaze

Roll out the moulding icing and cut out two circles to cover the ends of the Swiss roll. Roll out the remaining icing to cover the rest of the Swiss roll. Brush the Swiss roll with the apricot glaze and cover with moulding icing. Fit a piping bag with a writing nozzle and fill with some royal icing. Pipe the detail onto the postbox and leave to dry. With the remaining icing, spoon half on top of the postbox and the remainder at the bottom. Dust with a little icing sugar.

Icicles with Holly

18cm (7 inch) or 20cm (8 inch) square or round, rich fruit cake
Recipe apricot glaze
675g (1½lb) marzipan
Royal icing, made with 900g (2lb) icing sugar
Blue ribbon
Marzipan holly leaves and berries

Brush the top and sides of the cake with apricot glaze and cover with marzipan; leave to dry. With a little icing, attach the cake to the cake board and flat ice the top and sides. Leave it to dry between and after coats. Using a piping bag fitted with a shell nozzle, pipe a circle of shells on the top edge of the cake and again round the bottom of the cake. Fit the piping bag with a plain or fine-band nozzle. Place the ribbon round the sides of the cake. Pipe the icicles down and over the ribbon, varying them in length and width. Fit the piping bag with a writing nozzle and overpipe to make smaller icicles, which should hang free of the cake. Use the remaining icing to secure the holly in a pattern on top of the cake.

This page: Postbox and Christmas Candles. Facing page: Icicles with Holly.

BRUT
REIMS
CHAMPAGNE

INDEX